clara

the rhinoceros

gijs van der ham

RIJKS MUSEUM

contents

foreword

Everywhere the rhinoceros Clara appeared she caused a sensation among the general public, while scientists regarded her as a wonder beast and artists adopted her as their muse. She became the most famous rhinoceros in European history. The story of her life demonstrates how the exhibition of this then-unknown animal brought about a profound change in the understanding and image of the rhinoceros all over Europe. Artists played a key role in the process by frequently depicting Clara in their paintings, drawings and sculptures. Without them she would very likely have been as good as forgotten. Clara's tale is about the power of images and of the sometimes fine dividing line between myth and reality. At the same time her story touches on themes of great relevance today, such as humans' treatment of animals, the damage to biodiversity and the threatened future of a balanced world where there is room for all living creatures. Clara's story holds a mirror up to us all.

In this publication Gijs van der Ham, Senior Curator of History at the Rijkmuseum between 2001 and 2021, shares his longstanding fascination with Clara. Based on new research, he offers an extensive reconstruction of her travels and life among humans. In addition, he unravels her impact on the knowledge and image of the rhinoceros.

The exhibition *Clara the Rhinoceros* reflects the ambition of the Rijkmuseum to showcase the interplay between art and history. With Clara's story the exhibition illustrates how new knowledge altered a global image and the central role that art played in this shift. For this we were able to draw on the Rijksmuseum collection, which contains several pieces relating specifically to Clara. But it is the works from other domestic and foreign collections that star in the museum's rooms. Without the life-size portrait of Clara by the painter Jean-Baptiste Oudry from the collection of the Staatliches Museum Schwerin the exhibition would not have been complete. We wish to thank the museum for loaning us this spectacular painting. In addition, we are extremely grateful to all our other lenders for their generosity. We are especially indebted to the many institutions and individuals who provided the Rijksmuseum with information, advice and financial support. The exhibition and this publication have been made possible in part thanks to generous contributions from a private donor and Stichting Every Act Matters through the Rijksmuseum Fonds. Finally, we wish to express our thanks to Gijs van der Ham who continued to work on this exhibition and book beyond his retirement.

Clara was a sensation everywhere she was shown. I hope that this special exhibition will generate a similar sense of excitement and wonder, and will inspire further reflection.

Taco Dibbits
General Director, Rijksmuseum

wonder beast

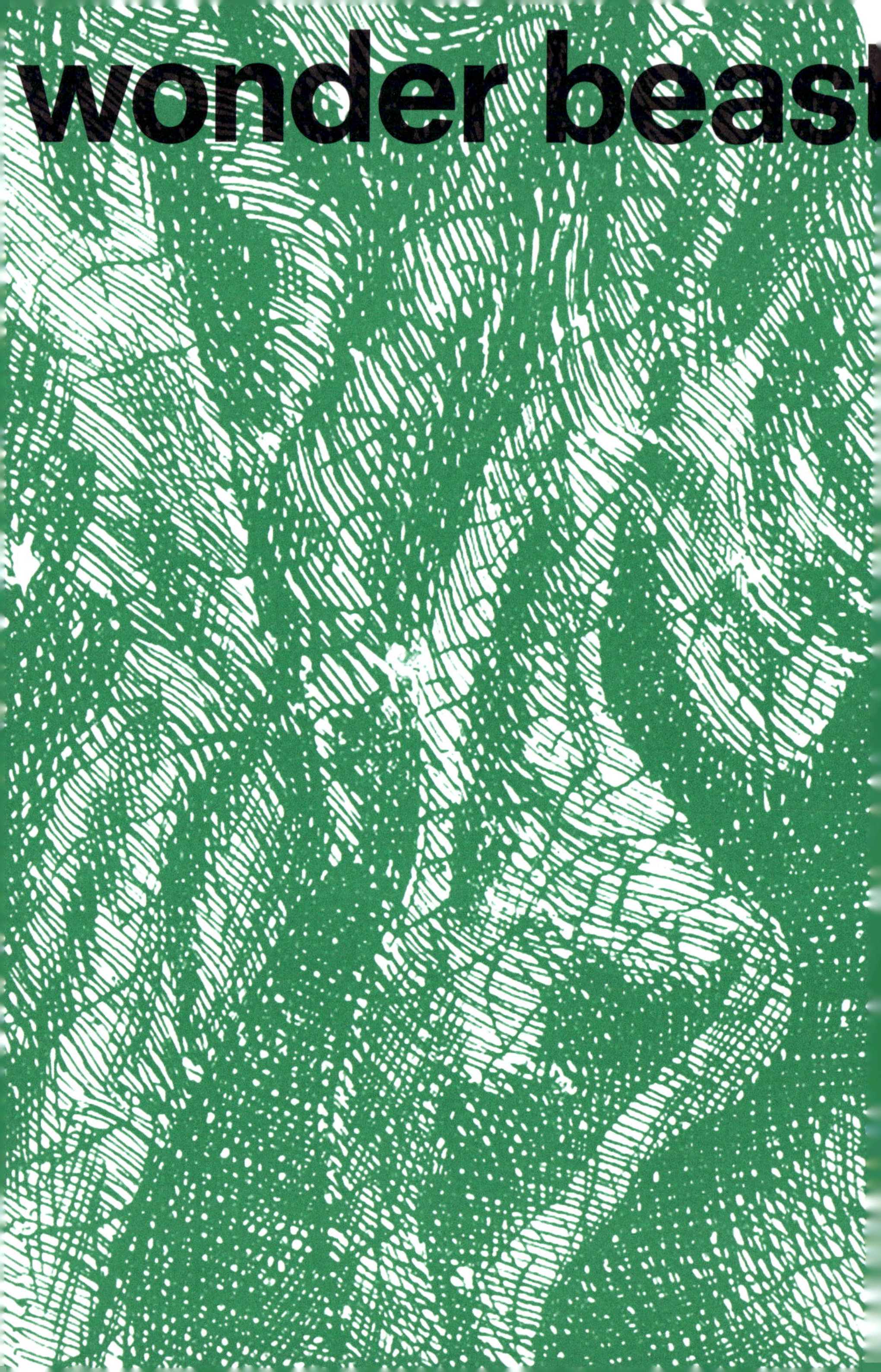

clara

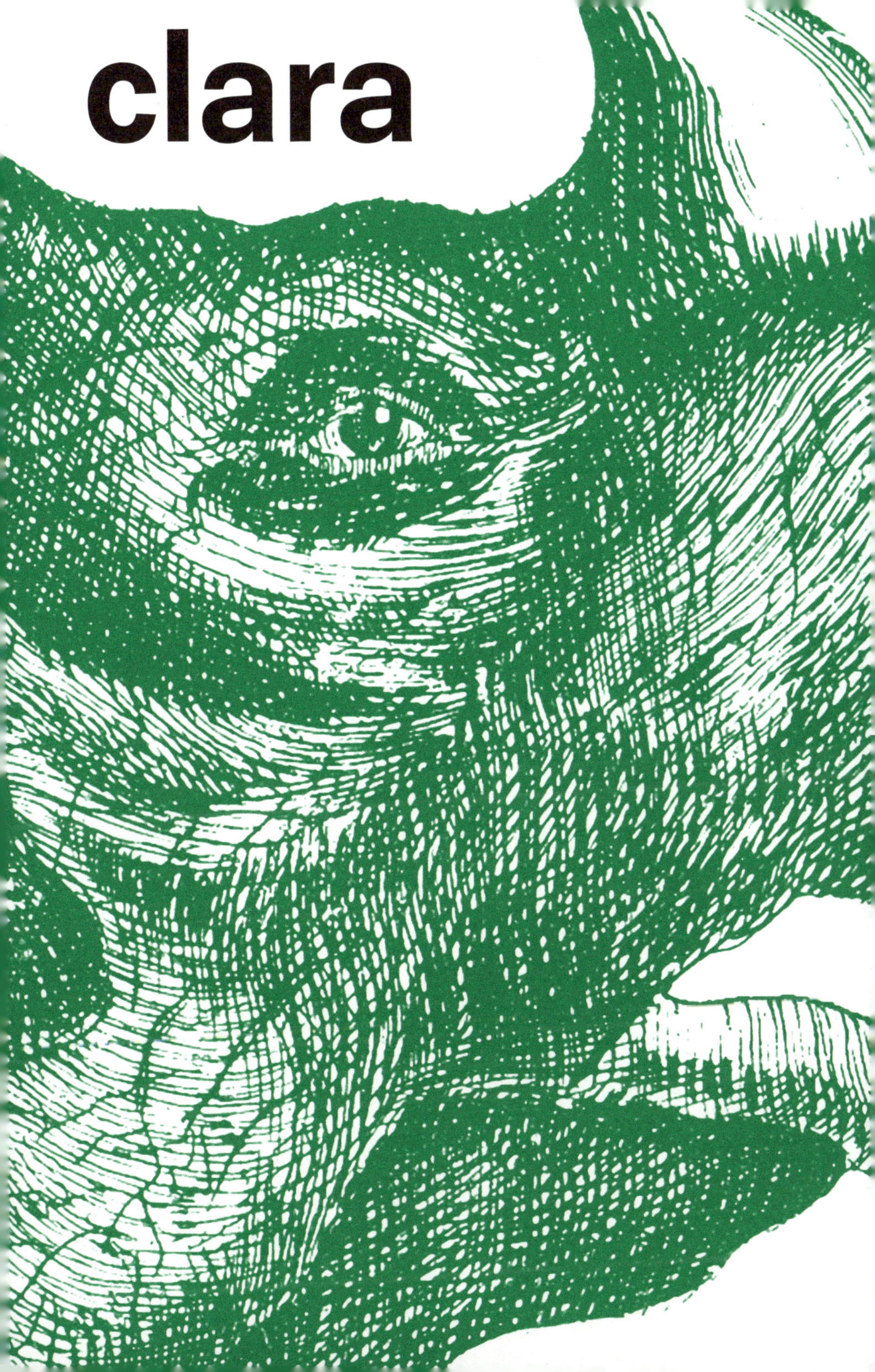

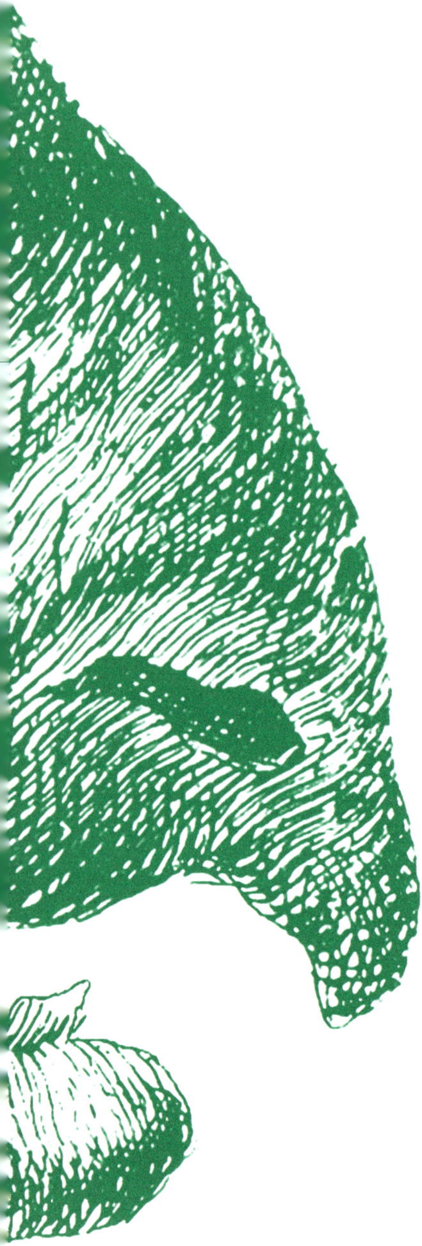

'A rhinoceros is coming to your town, a living rhinoceros! Such a wonder beast from distant parts has never been seen here before. It is exceedingly large and moreover an enormous glutton. You have a chance to see this animal with your own eyes, a rare opportunity not to be missed!' News like this was circulating all over Europe in the years around 1750, announced in newspapers and on posters, and passed on in the streets, at markets and inns. Everywhere the colossus was the talk of the day, a sensation nobody could fail to know about.

In every town or city crowds flocked to see the rhinoceros. They were left speechless, overwhelmed by a feeling of wonder. Some thought she was monstrous or regarded her as a weird attraction and simply gawped at her; others were fascinated and wanted to know everything about her. Some scrutinized her from top to toe, from horn to tail; others took up their drawing pens to examine the strange, exotic creature from every angle. They discussed her and recorded their findings in texts, sketches, paintings and sculptures. As a result, this rhinoceros was also known to the many people who, to their regret, were unable to see the animal themselves, and so they too knew what a rhinoceros really looked like.

For some seventeen years the rhinoceros – a female – was dragged here, there and everywhere. Her owner showed her to anyone who was willing to pay. In the meantime, she developed from a calf into a fully grown animal, thousands of kilometres from her homeland, in a part of the world where rhinoceroses do not belong. All that time she was the only rhinoceros on the European mainland. She was unique and became a celebrity, complete with her own name: Clara. She was even affectionately referred to as Miss Clara. And that is how she is still known today, more than two hundred and fifty years after her death in 1758.

Clara is the main character of this story, even though she spent the whole of her life in captivity. Her lot was determined by people and throughout her life she met far more people than rhinoceroses. At the same time, she has come to symbolize her species. When Clara arrived in Europe, hardly anyone knew anything about rhinoceroses, and what they did know was invariably incorrect. The simple fact that she was here meant that Clara was able to change this. Her presence led to curiosity, knowledge, appreciation and possibly even to a certain understanding, although she – and the rhinoceros in general – remained essentially alien to humans. On this account alone she continues to be a wonder beast.

a true

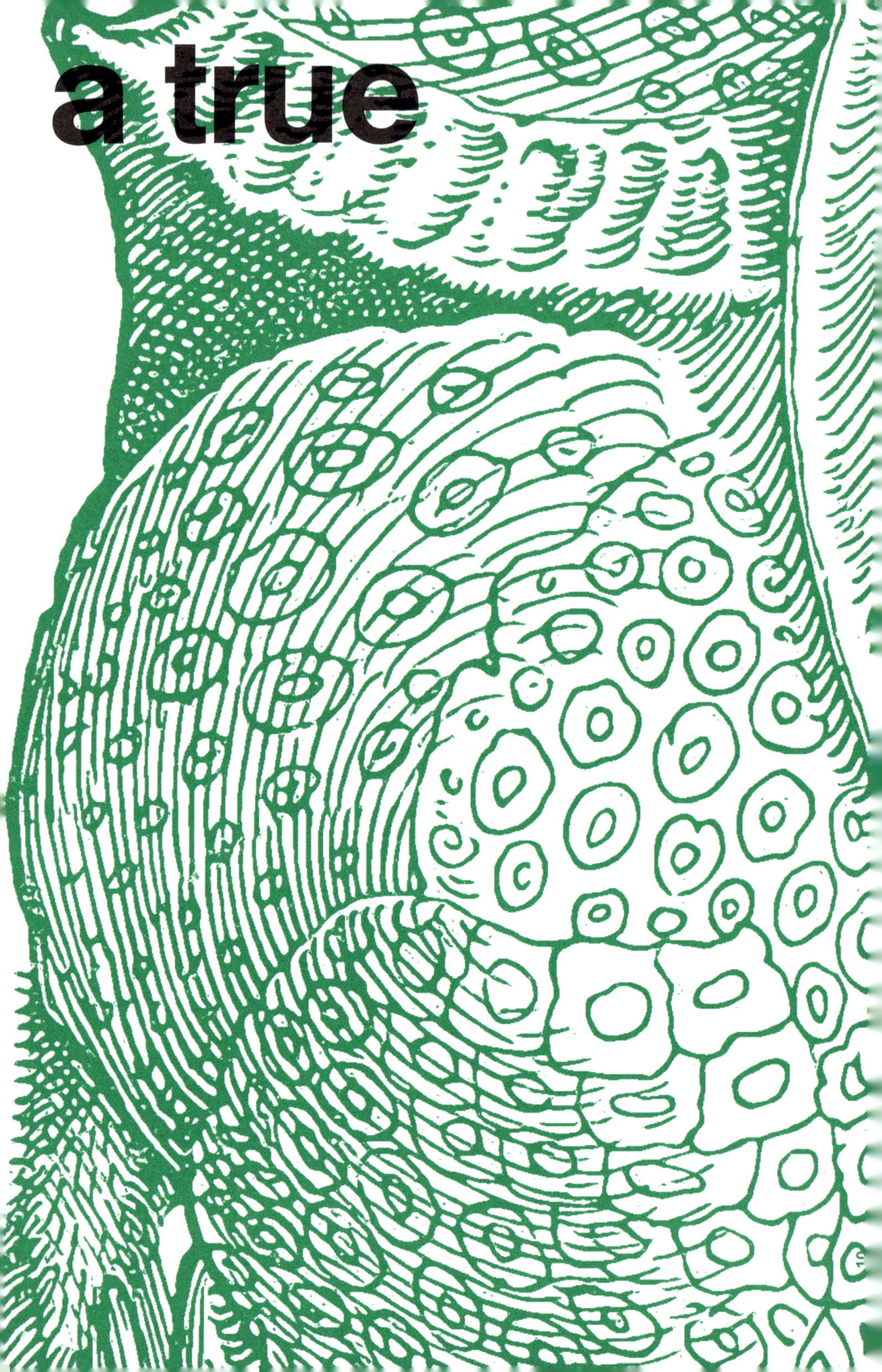

rhinoceros?

In 1741, Clara was the first rhinoceros ever to set foot on Dutch soil, unless we go back tens of thousands of years to the time when woolly rhinoceroses roamed what was then the European Steppe. This species was long extinct, however, and in the mid-eighteenth century no-one had any notion of its earlier existence. In the many European countries that Clara was to visit, people had never set eyes on a rhinoceros. The odd Indian and African rhinoceros had been taken to Rome and perhaps an occasional Italian city, but that was some fifteen-hundred years earlier, at the time of the Roman Empire. The books that have come down to us by writers such as Pliny the Elder, Dio Cassius and Martialis recount how in theatres and arenas these animals were pitted against elephants, lions and bears in life-and-death contests. This led Pliny to conclude in his famous *Naturalis historia*, the first edition of which appeared in AD 77, that rhinoceroses and elephants were natural enemies, a claim that was taken at face value for centuries thereafter. The name 'rhinoceros' (literally 'nosehorn') actually dates from the same time and was coined by the Greek historian Strabo. Thanks to ancient writings such as these, people in Europe knew that rhinoceroses must live in Asia and Africa, but for centuries this was as far as their understanding of rhinoceroses stretched.[1]

Knowledge about these animals did not increase until Europeans began to venture into then-unknown parts of the world. Now and then a rhinoceros crops up in their descriptions, for the first time at the end of the thirteenth century in the writings of Marco Polo. He remarked that while the animal had a single horn, for the rest it bore remarkably little resemblance to the much-described unicorn in age-old European tales: a slim, white, horse-like animal with a long spiralling horn – on its forehead, not its nose – that symbolized the virginity of the Virgin Mary, the mother of Christ. Obviously, no-one had ever seen a unicorn in reality, for it existed purely in myths and fables, but given his description, the Italian explorer was the first European in centuries to see a real rhinoceros.

While some Europeans knew or suspected that rhinoceroses existed, nobody yet had any idea what the animal actually looked like.

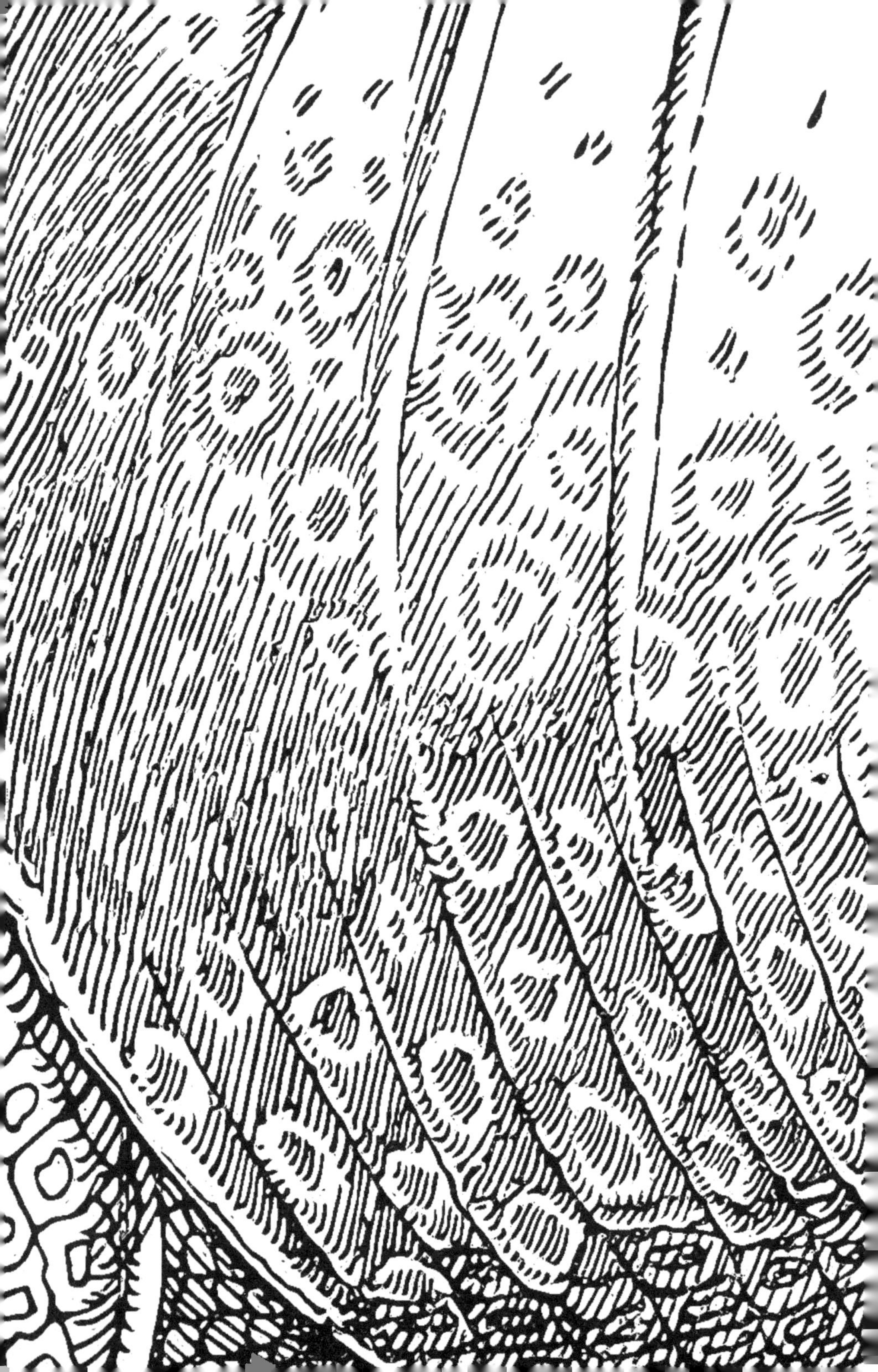

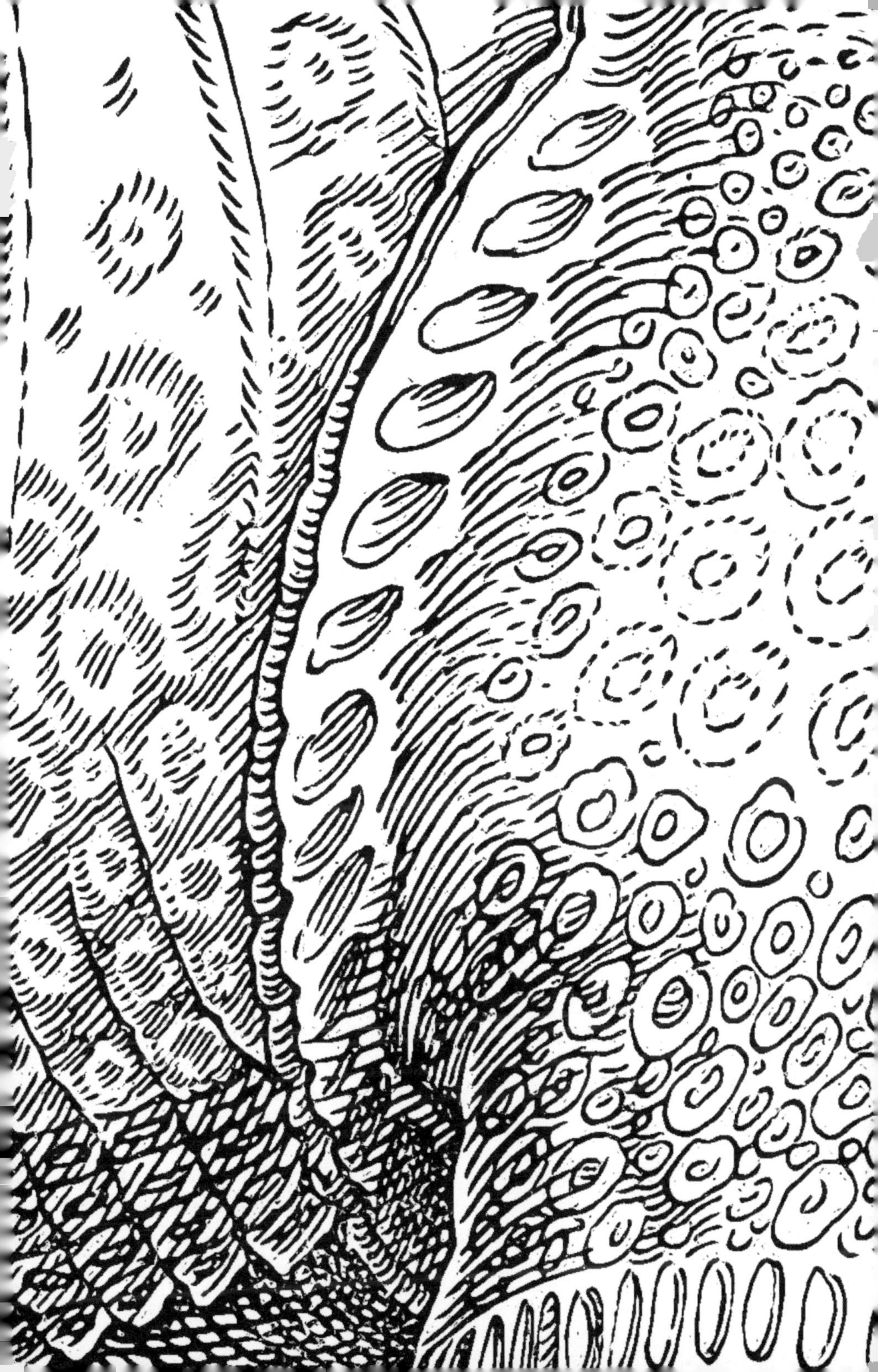

For a long time, all Europeans had to go by were a few Roman coins on which a rhinoceros was very roughly portrayed. Until 1515, that is, when an adult rhinoceros imported from India landed in Lisbon.

A decade before, the Portuguese had sailed round the southern tip of Africa to Asia with the aim of trading there. As the Verenigde Oost-Indische Compagnie (VOC), the Dutch East India Company, was later to discover, this was often only possible by using violence or by building a good relationship with the powerful rulers there. Often a combination of warfare and diplomacy proved the most effective approach. The exchange of gifts helped to lubricate these relations. This was how governer of Portuguese India, Afonso de Albuquerque, had endeavoured to win over Muzaffar Shah II, sultan of the north-western Indian Sultanate of Gujarat. As a return gift, Albuquerque had then been given a rhinoceros. In fact the Portuguese governor was at a loss as to what to do with the enormous beast, but he obviously could not refuse it. After giving the matter some thought, he decided to send the rhinoceros on to his own ruler, King Manuel I. And so it happened in May 1515 that the rhinoceros arrived in Lisbon along with its Indian keeper, alive and well after five months at sea. King Manuel was extremely flattered by the gift, and the strange animal attracted a great deal of attention. A year later, however, the king decided to pass the rhinoceros on to Pope Leo X as an exclusive gift, along with an array of costly presents, in the hope of securing the influential papal prince's support for Portuguese interests. But on its way to Rome early in 1516, the ship sank off the Italian coast. The rhinoceros drowned, chained to the deck.[2]

Although only people in Lisbon had been able to see this live rhinoceros, for over two centuries it was drawings made of this particular animal that defined what Europeans thought a rhinoceros looked like. One of the artists was a dealer who in June 1515 had written to a friend and business partner in the German city of Nuremberg informing him of the arrival of the rhinoceros. With his letter he had enclosed a sketch which subsequently found its way to a local artist, no-one less than the forty-four-year-old Albrecht Dürer. As a painter, illustrator and printmaker Dürer had a huge reputation in large parts of Europe. His engravings and woodcuts, both still relatively new techniques at the time, attest to his unprecedented craftsmanship. These prints became known far and wide, for they could be published in large editions and broadly distributed.

When Dürer saw the sketch from Lisbon he realized how special it was that this virtually unknown animal had now finally been recorded. He first worked the sketch up and then made a woodcut from it [fig. 1]. The word 'Rhinocerus' is clearly written between the date 1515 and

Dürer's monogram. In the upper part of the print he reproduced information from the letter about the animal's origins and appearance. For instance, the colour of the beast was said to resemble that of a speckled tortoise and the skin to be made up of thick scales. Further, the rhinoceros was linked to the elephant, which was far better known in Europe, and the two animals were said to be natural enemies. By combining partly old and partly new information a new image was created.

The print definitely depicts a rhinoceros, but anyone who has actually seen one cannot but admit that it is not a good likeness. Squeezed in between the borders of the woodcut, the animal, which is portrayed from the side, looks oddly compacted. The animal stares to the right motionless, its comparatively large head slightly lowered. The skin seems to consist of a series of plates hanging over its body, the fairly long horn on its nose noticeably pointing backwards. On its back just behind its head is a small, spiral-shaped second horn which a real rhinoceros does not have. Whether consciously or unconsciously, Dürer's rendition of the original, presumably amateurish, sketch proved so convincing and so appealing that a vast number of images were subsequently based on it. His rhinoceros served as the definitive model, not just for his contemporaries but for many generations to come.[3]

Curiously, other depictions of the Lisbon rhinoceros remained virtually unknown, despite being more faithful likenesses. A woodcut by the Augsburg artist Hans Burgkmair, and an illustration in the very first treatise on the rhinoceros, *Forma e natura e costumi de lo Rhinocerothe* by the Italian Giovanni Giacomo Penni, both published in 1515, show no second horn and the skin is more accurately rendered. However, these images were seldom copied.[4]

Only one edition of Dürer's print appeared during his lifetime, but his woodcut was reprinted on at least four occasions, the last around 1620 in The Hague.[5] Soon copies were also produced from this, such as the copper engraving by the Italian Enea Vico, which was issued in 1548, and around the same year a woodcut by the Antwerp printmaker Hans Liefrinck.[6] All these prints merely encouraged artists to follow Dürer's example if they sought to depict a rhinoceros, whether it be a scientific work, a painting, a goblet, a tapestry or a statuette [figs. 2, 3, 4, 5].[7] This continued for over two centuries. The most spectacular version of the Dürer rhinoceros, and one of the last, is undoubtedly the over one-metre-long porcelain figure created in 1731 by Johann Gottlieb Kirchner, modeller at the oldest European porcelain factory in Saxony, Meissen, which was cast in a small edition [fig. 6].[8] It was commissioned by Augustus the Strong, Elector of Saxony and founding father of the factory, for the porcelain menagerie at his palace in Dresden, which

Nach Chriſtus gepurt. 1513. Jar. Adi. j. May. Hat man dem groſmechtigen Kunig von Portugall E
Rhinocerus. Das iſt hye mit aller ſeiner geſtalt Abcondertfet. Es hat ein farb wie ein geſpreckelte Schildtk
Aber nydertrechtiger von paynen/ vnd faſt werhafftig. Es hat ein ſcharff ſtarck Horn vorn auff der naſ
fantz todt feyndt. Der Helffandt furcht es faſt vbel/ dann wo es Jn ankumbt/ ſo laufft Jm das Thier mi
vñ erwürgt Jn/ des mag er ſich nit erwern. Dann das Thier iſt alſo gewapent/ das Jm der Helffandt ni

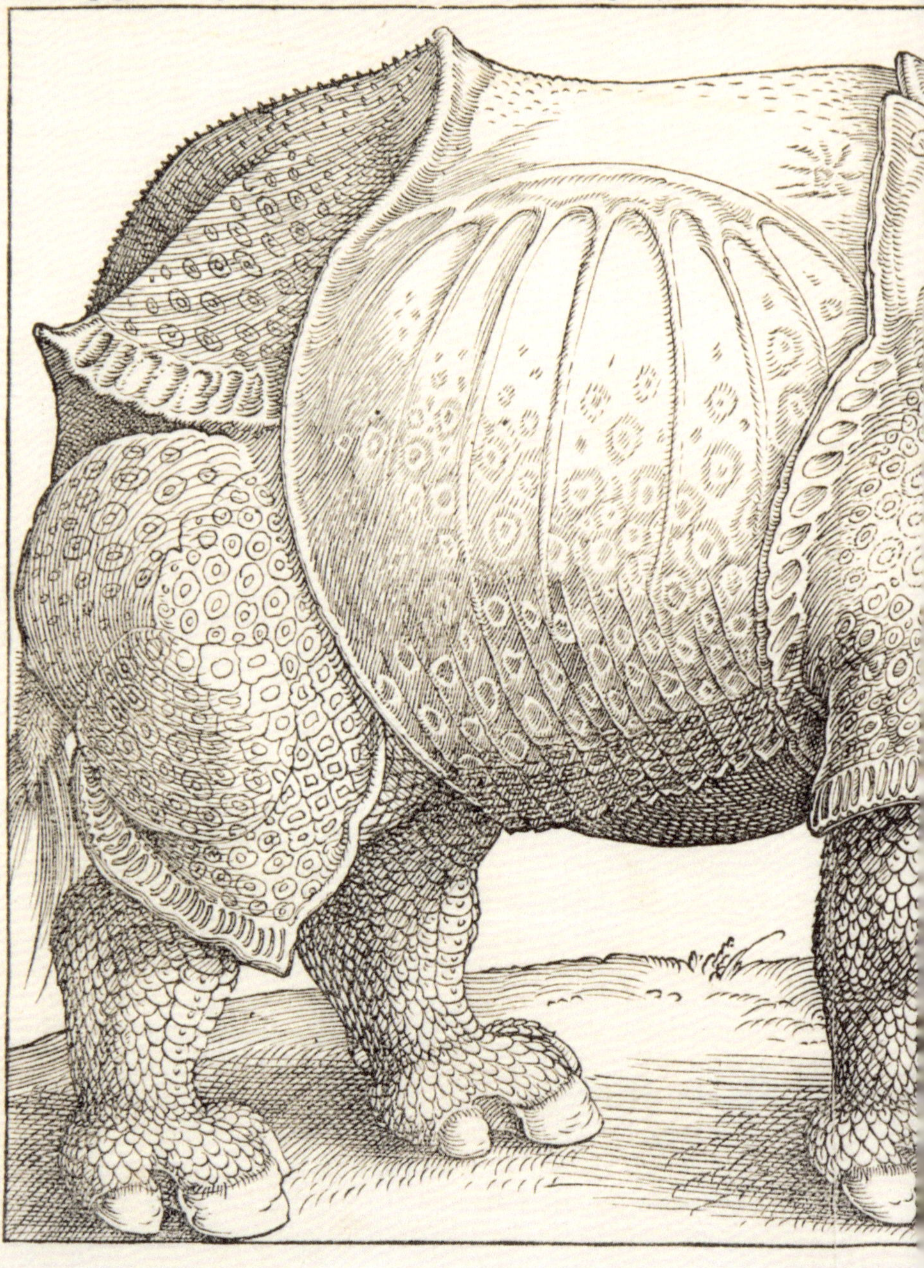

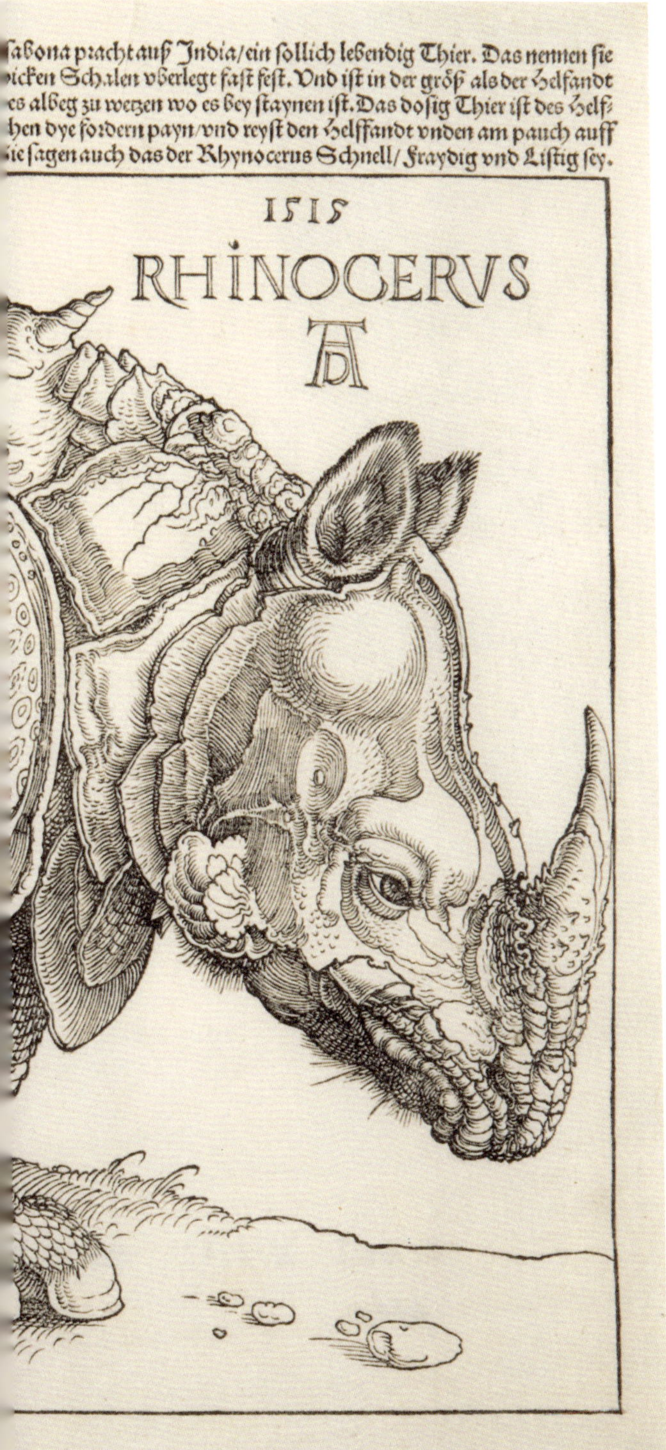

1 Woodcut created by Albrecht Dürer in 1515 which for a long time determined the image people in Europe had of the rhinoceros

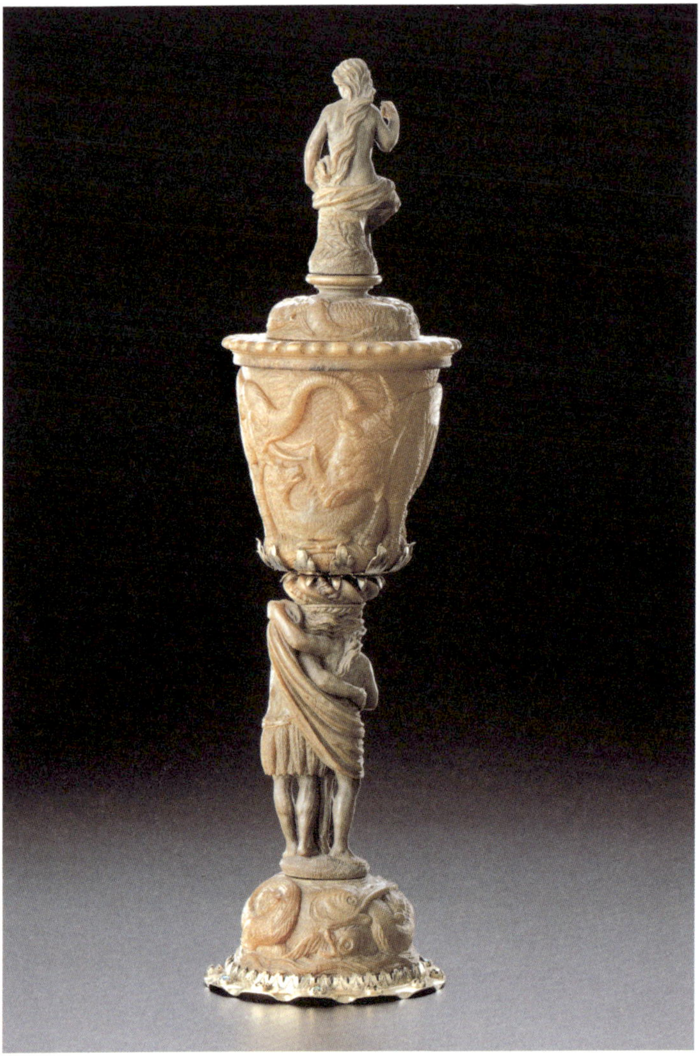

2

Lidded goblet made from rhinoceros horn, with on the beaker a scene of a rhinoceros and an elephant fighting, attributed to Hans Mayer, c. 1650

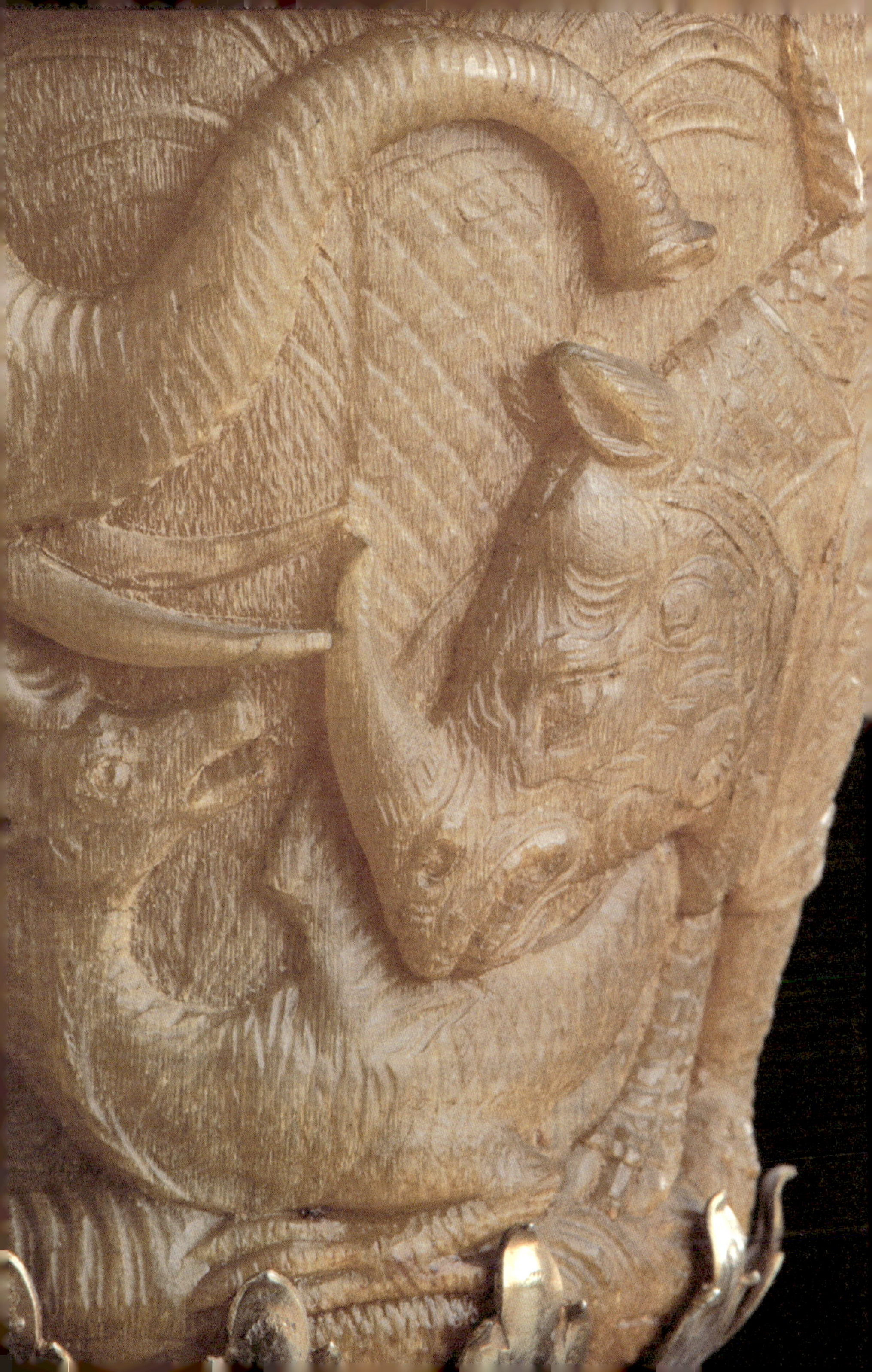

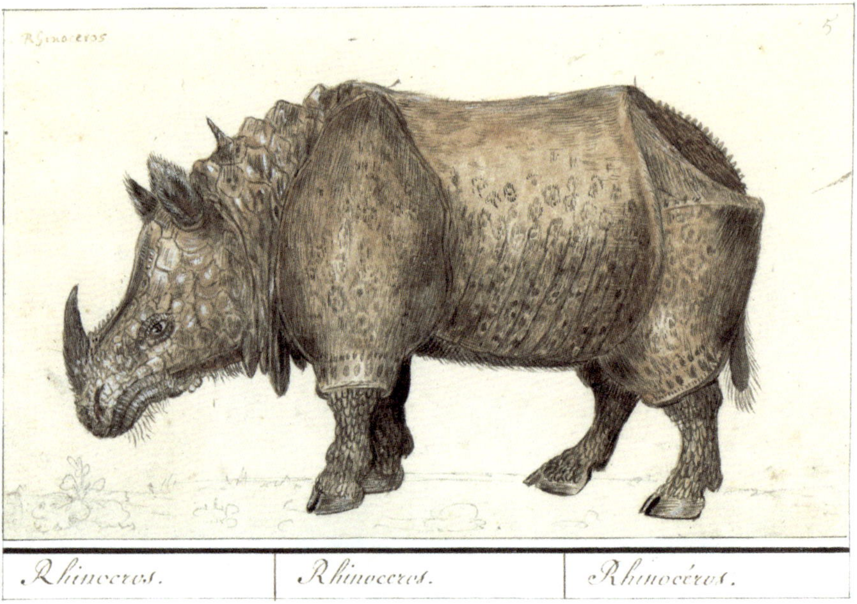

3
Indian rhinoceros by
Anselmus de Boodt after
the example of Albrecht Dürer, 1596–1610

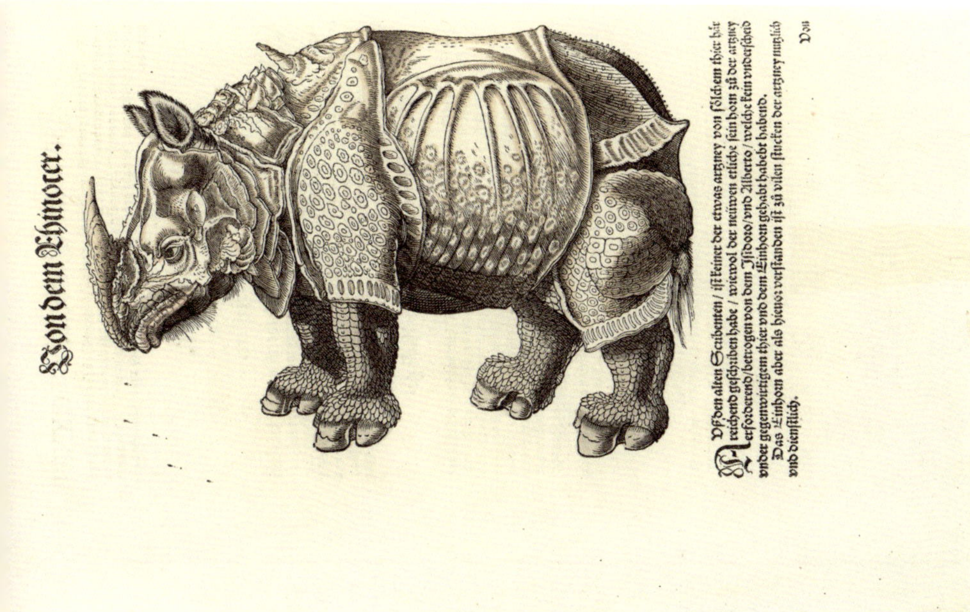

4

Picture of a rhinoceros in Conrad Gessner's *Thierbuch*, 1563

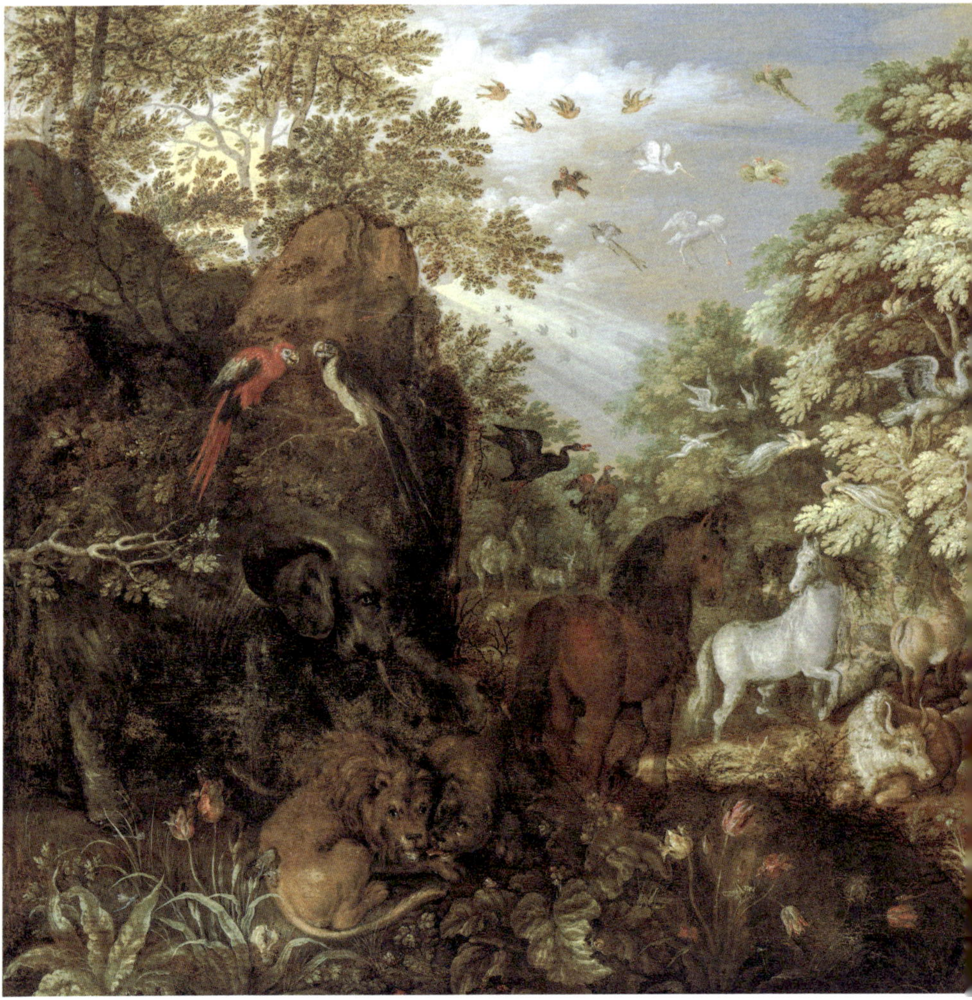

5
Orpheus charms the animals with his music, with a rhinoceros upper right, Roelant Savery, 1627

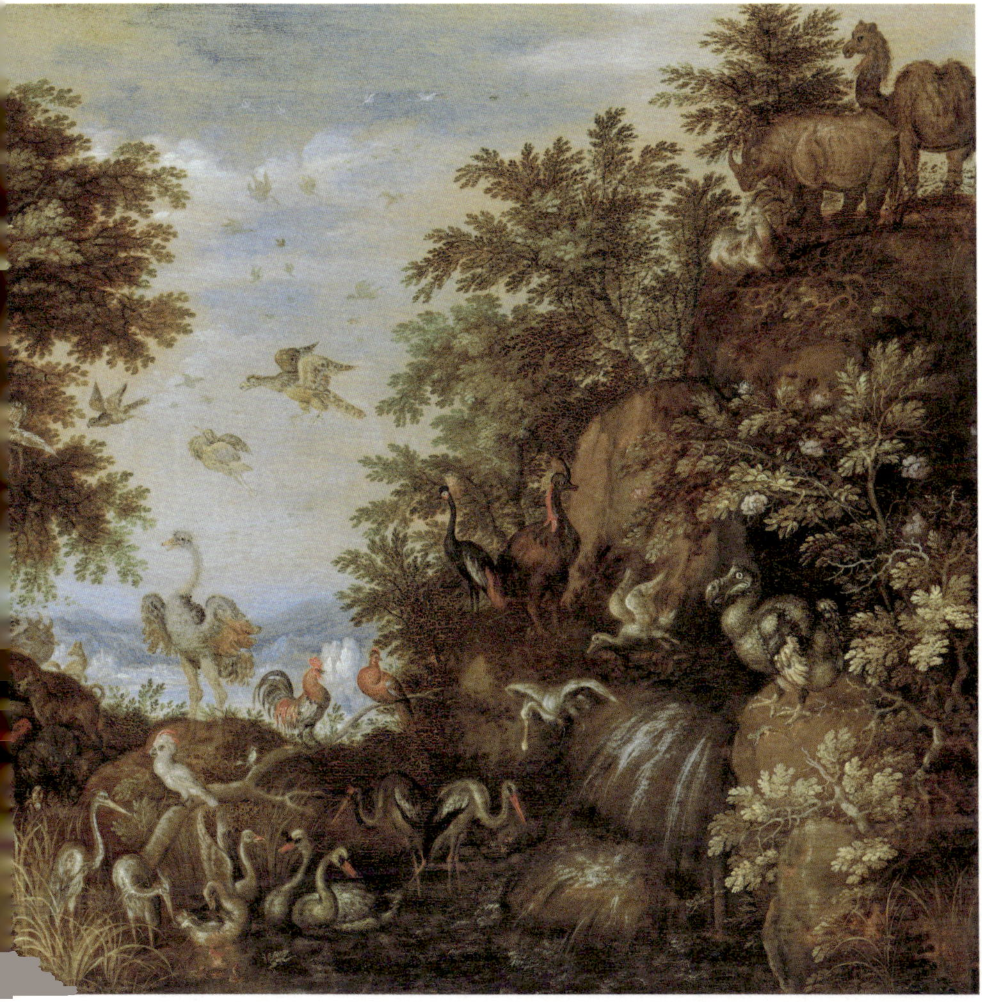

would have been incomplete without a rhinoceros. Kirchner understandably based his figure on Dürer's 1515 archetype, although the head hangs lower, the mouth is half open, the tail thicker and the horn on its back larger, for he too had no other example to go by.

Between 1515 and 1741, the year when Clara arrived in the Netherlands, other rhinoceroses had likewise been brought to Europe, but they had remained largely unknown and hence had failed to correct the prevailing model. The second rhinoceros to appear in Europe, in 1581, again in Lisbon, had been taken to Madrid four years later in the retinue of the Spanish king Philip II. There the animal was housed at the Escorial, the royal palace outside the city, where only a few people had a chance to see it. And even though a print of this animal by the Antwerp engraver Philips Galle was issued in 1586, this portrait was rarely copied and failed to diminish the influence of Dürer's likeness.[9]

Over the next one-and-a-half centuries it proved quite difficult to ship a rhinoceros out of India and deliver it safely to Europe. In 1651, for instance, two animals captured in Thailand and presented by a Javanese ruler to a Dutch governor-general as a parting gift on his return home, had died after months at sea. And they were not the only ones to lose their lives on a voyage. When in 1677 another rhinoceros died at sea, the skin of the dead animal was immediately salted and preserved on board the VOC ship. Upon its arrival in the Netherlands the VOC directors decided to stuff the deceased animal and present it to Leiden University. There the animal was given a place in the gallery of the botanic garden where it was placed on public display amid other 'curiosities and rarities'.[10] Occasionally a stuffed specimen such as this could be seen elsewhere in the Netherlands. For instance, from 1662 the Surgeons' Guild in Delft owned a young rhinoceros that had died during a crossing which, though hardly visible, is depicted in the dark background of the *Anatomy Lesson of Cornelis 's-Gravesande* that Cornelis de Man painted in 1681 [fig. 7]. In 1667 this taxidermy animal had for a while been rented out to two Amsterdammers who planned to exhibit it as a rarity for money, whereupon it had been valued at a thousand guilders.[11] Thus, there was clearly an interest in rhinoceroses, but the public had to make do with a stuffed specimen or a body part of an animal, as in the Leidse Theatrum Anatomicum, where the 'The Skin and Horn from the Head of a Rhinoceros' were on display near the entrance.[12]

Meanwhile, most new images continued to be based on the Dürer version, even after another live specimen had at long last landed in Europe in August 1684, this time in England. The rhinoceros was imported specially for the purpose of exhibition to the public for money, based on a similar successful formula with elephants. But within a mere two years the animal died, putting an end to this commercial venture and to the animal's fame. Before its death, prints had been made, but once again they failed to adjust the image of the rhinoceros that had meanwhile evolved. One print seems to depict the exhibited animal itself, with a ring through its nose to which a chain is attached, but several others are merely variants on Dürer's engraving, even though the horn on the back has disappeared or been reduced to a minimum, as in the engraving by Pieter van den Berge after Francis Barlow depicting a fight between a rhinoceros and an elephant [fig. 8].[13]

It was not until 1737 that another rhinoceros arrived in London from Calcutta, the British headquarters in Bengal, this time a four-year-old female. Immediately upon her arrival she was displayed at various locations in the city. Moreover, in 1739 she was joined by a two-year-old male that had originally been presented to the British trading settlement in Patna on the River Ganges, and from there had been shipped to England along with his Bengali keeper.[14] This meant there were two living rhinoceroses in London at the same time, and at times they could even be seen together! Both were then exhibited by their owners in various English towns and cities. The male was to die within a few years, but the female toured England and Scotland for many years before passing away in 1754. Nonetheless, it was not the female but the male who commanded the most attention, particularly from the scientific community. Shortly after the male's arrival, the physician James Douglas, of the eminent Royal Society, had informed his fellow members at length about the rhinoceros, aided among other things by meticulous drawings that his assistant James Parsons had made. It was a new approach. Never before had a rhinoceros been so accurately studied, described and drawn. What is more, after Douglas's death, in 1743 Parsons published an illustrated report on their findings in the *Philosophical Transactions* of the Royal Society, which commanded a great deal of attention and had a considerable impact.[15] But by the time the report came out, yet another rhinoceros from the same region as the two rhinoceroses already in London had appeared on the mainland. It was this rhinoceros that was to alter the image and general understanding of rhinoceroses for ever. Her name was Clara.

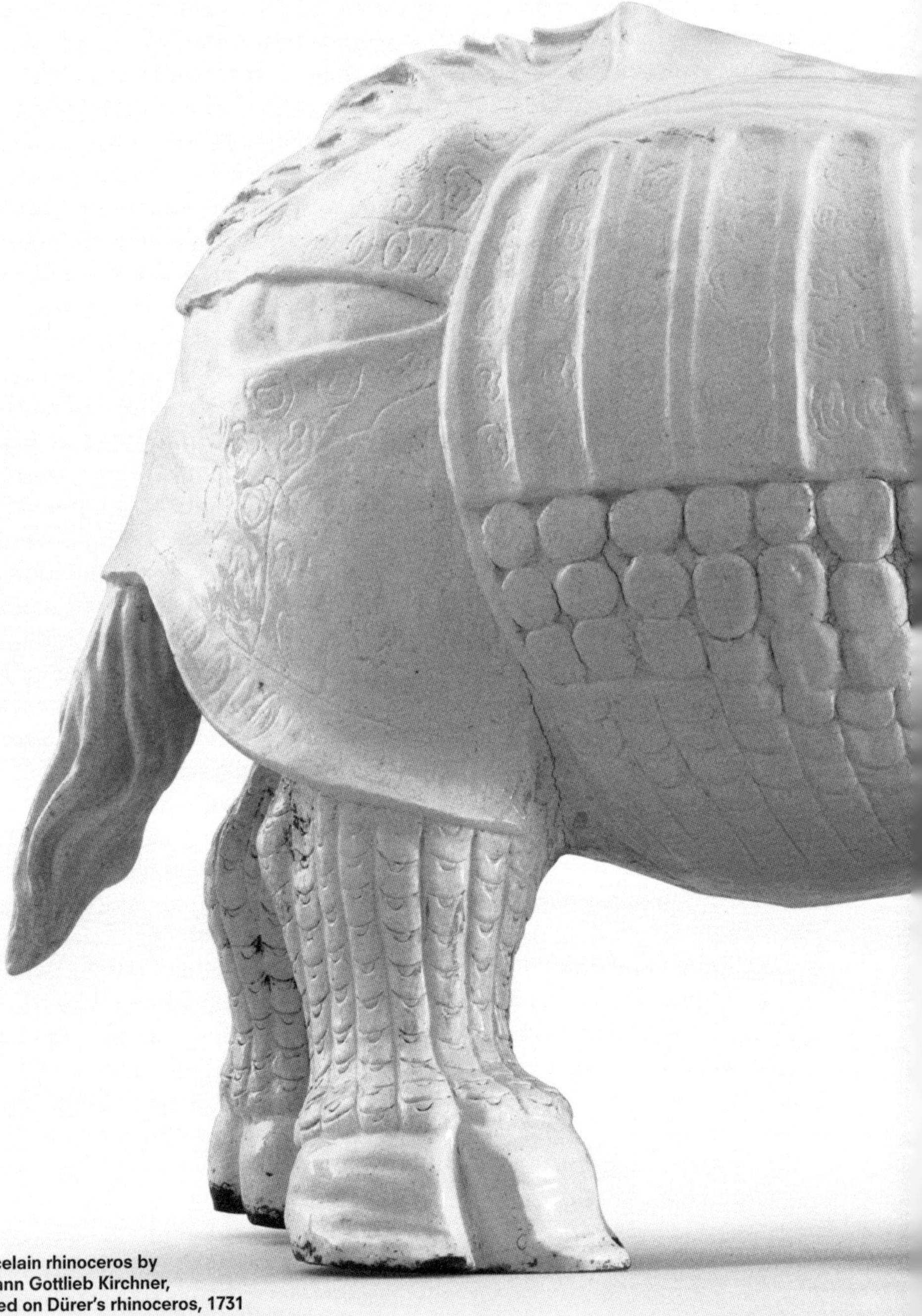

6
Porcelain rhinoceros by Johann Gottlieb Kirchner, based on Dürer's rhinoceros, 1731

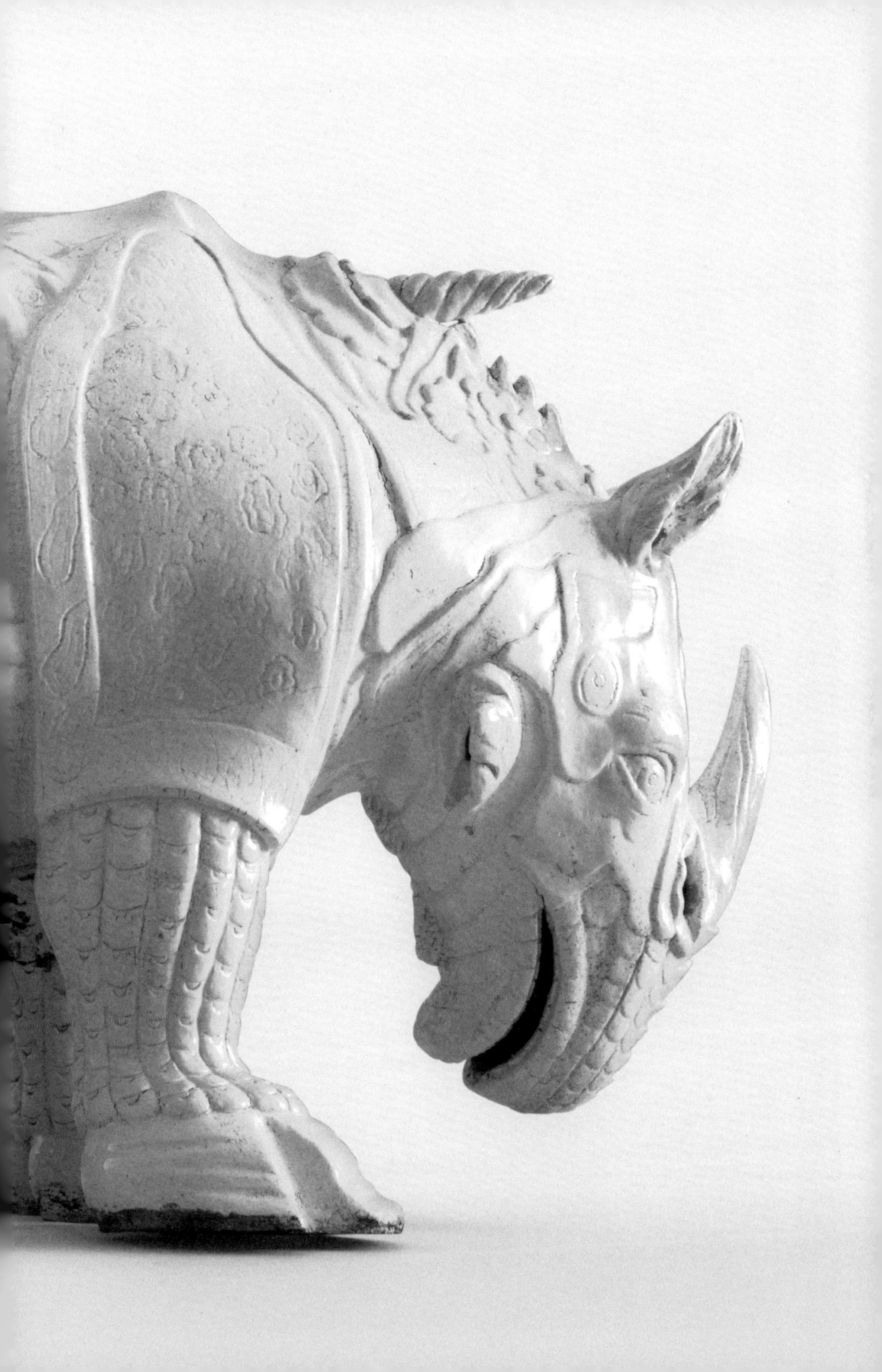

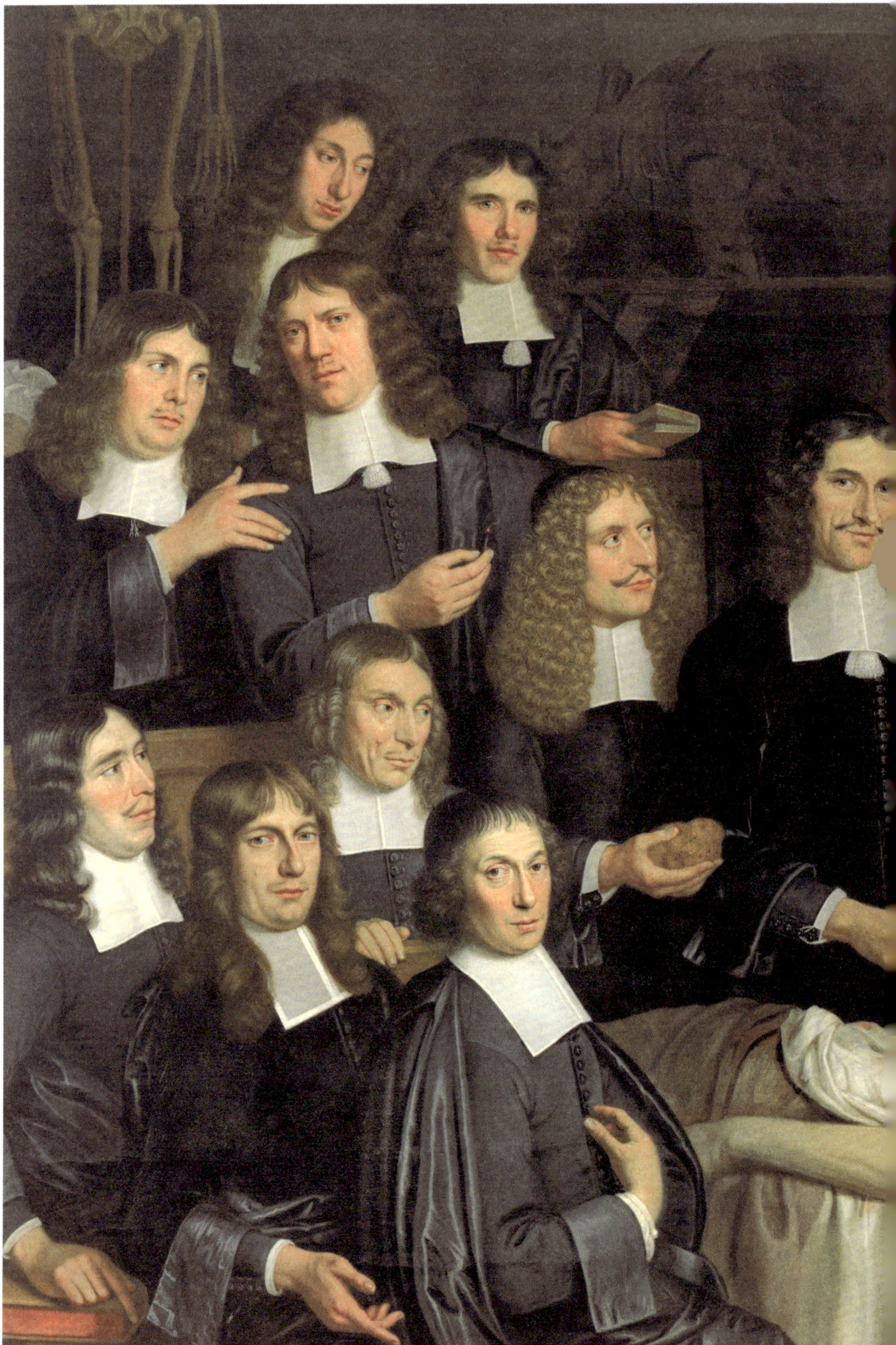

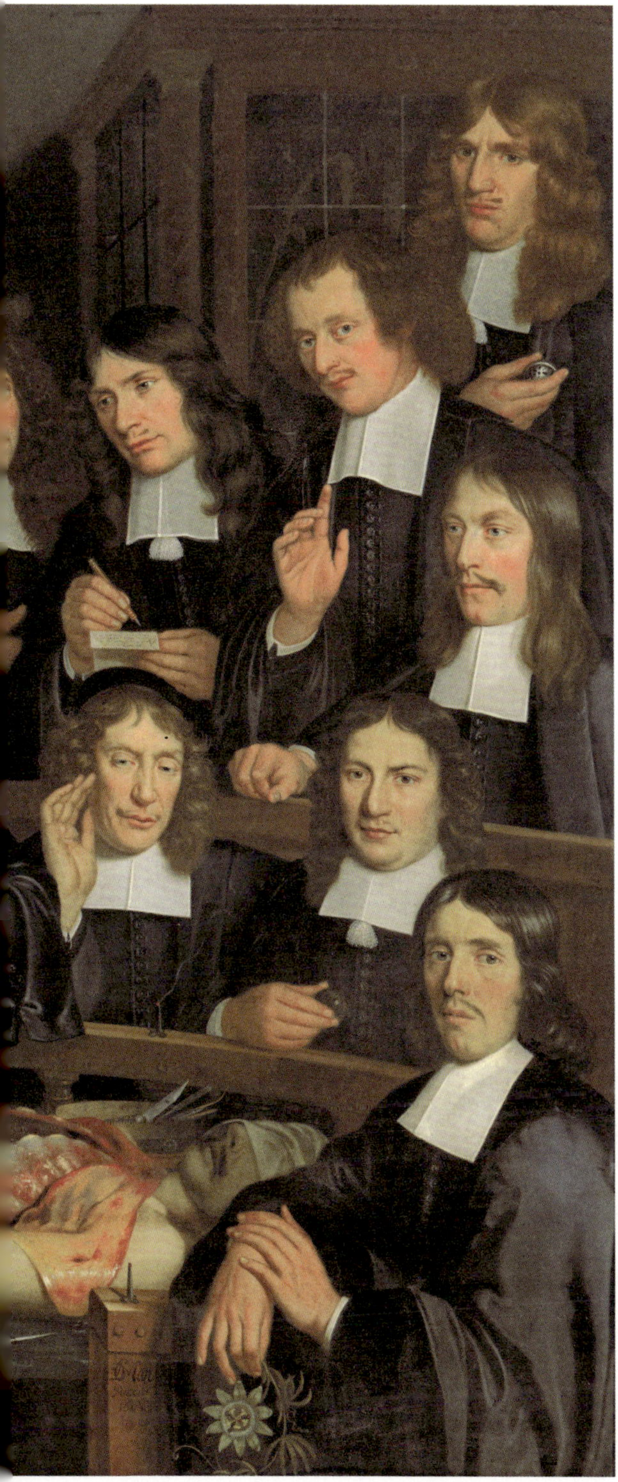

7
Anatomy lesson of Cornelis 's-Gravesande in Delft, with a stuffed young rhinoceros in the background, Cornelis de Man, 1681

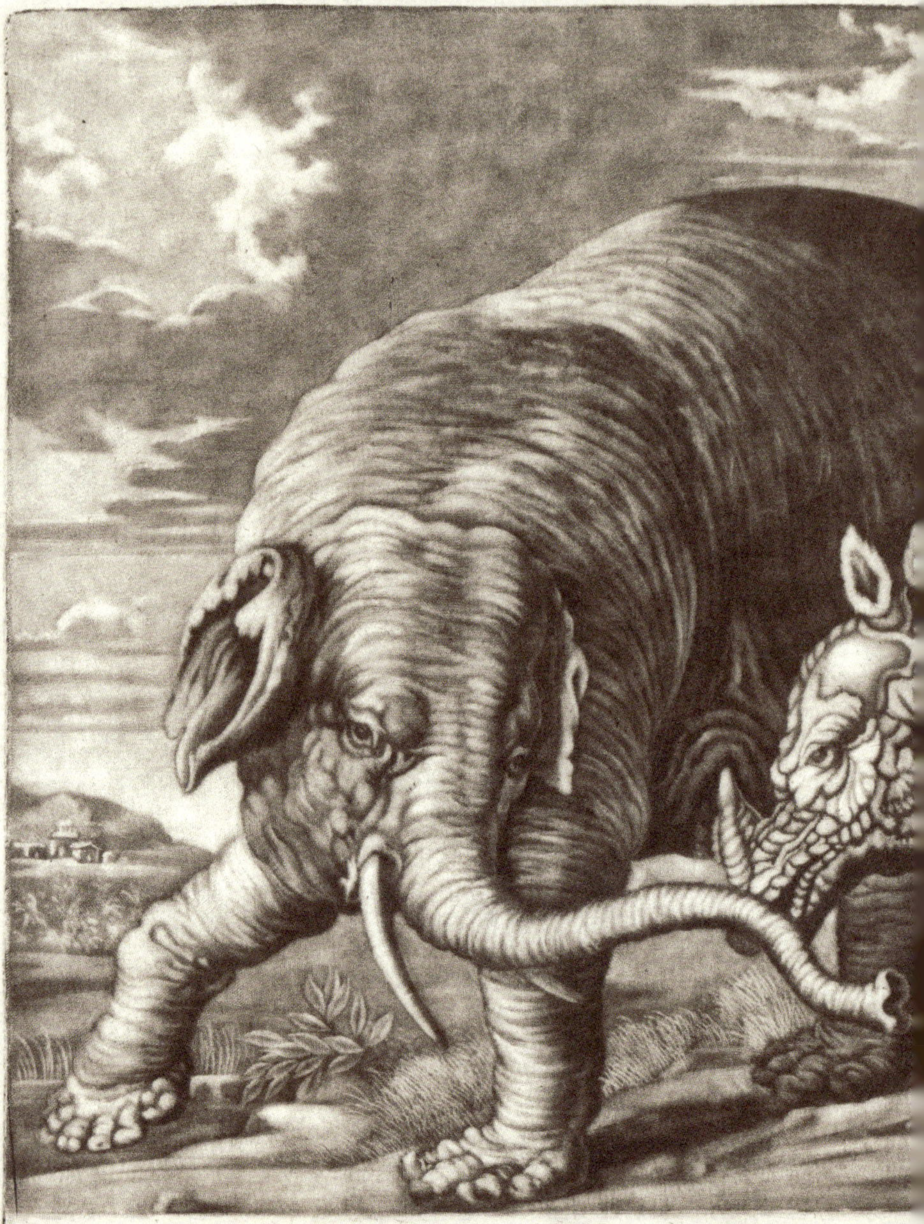

Portrait au Naturel d'vn Elephant et d'vn
Orientalles a

P. Vanden Berge Fecit

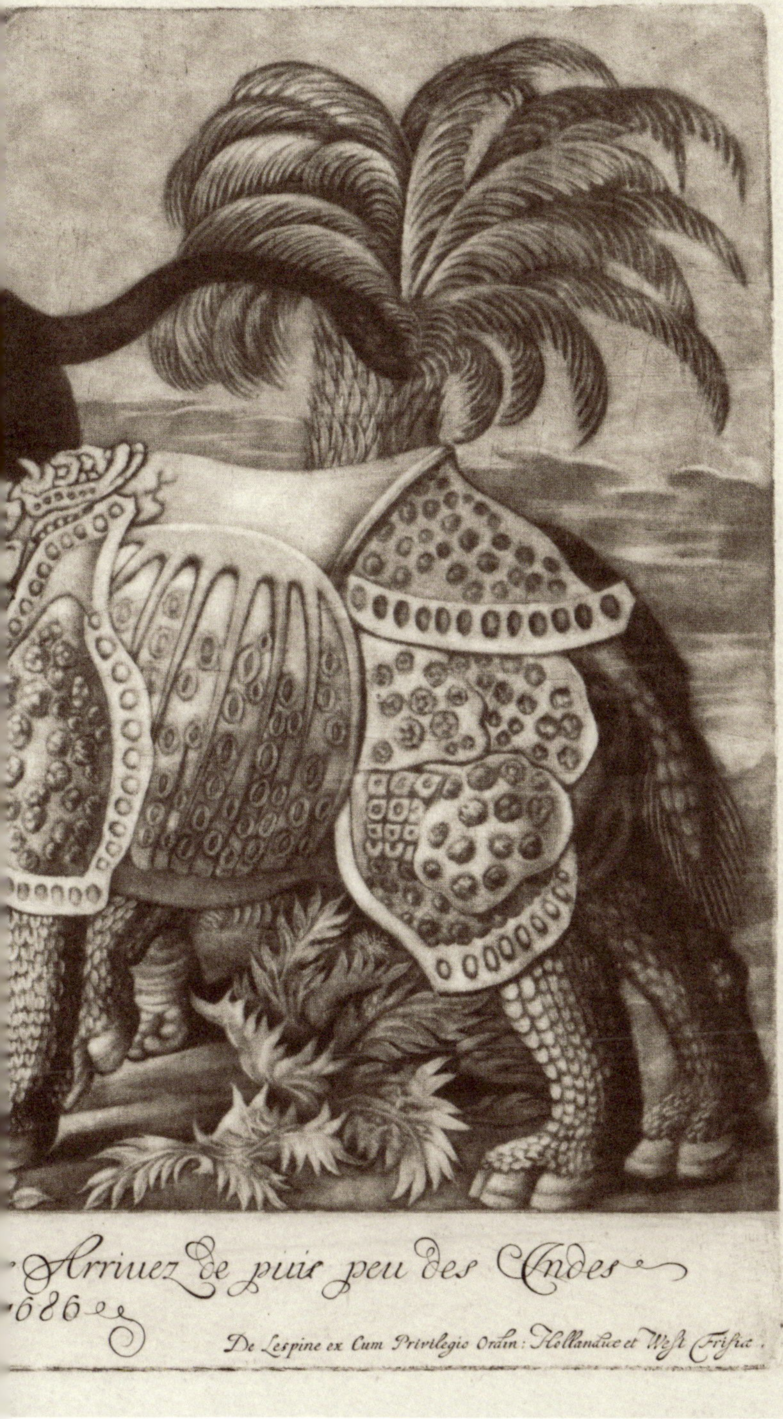

8
Fight between an elephant and a rhinoceros,
Pieter van den Berge after Francis Barlow,
1686–1696

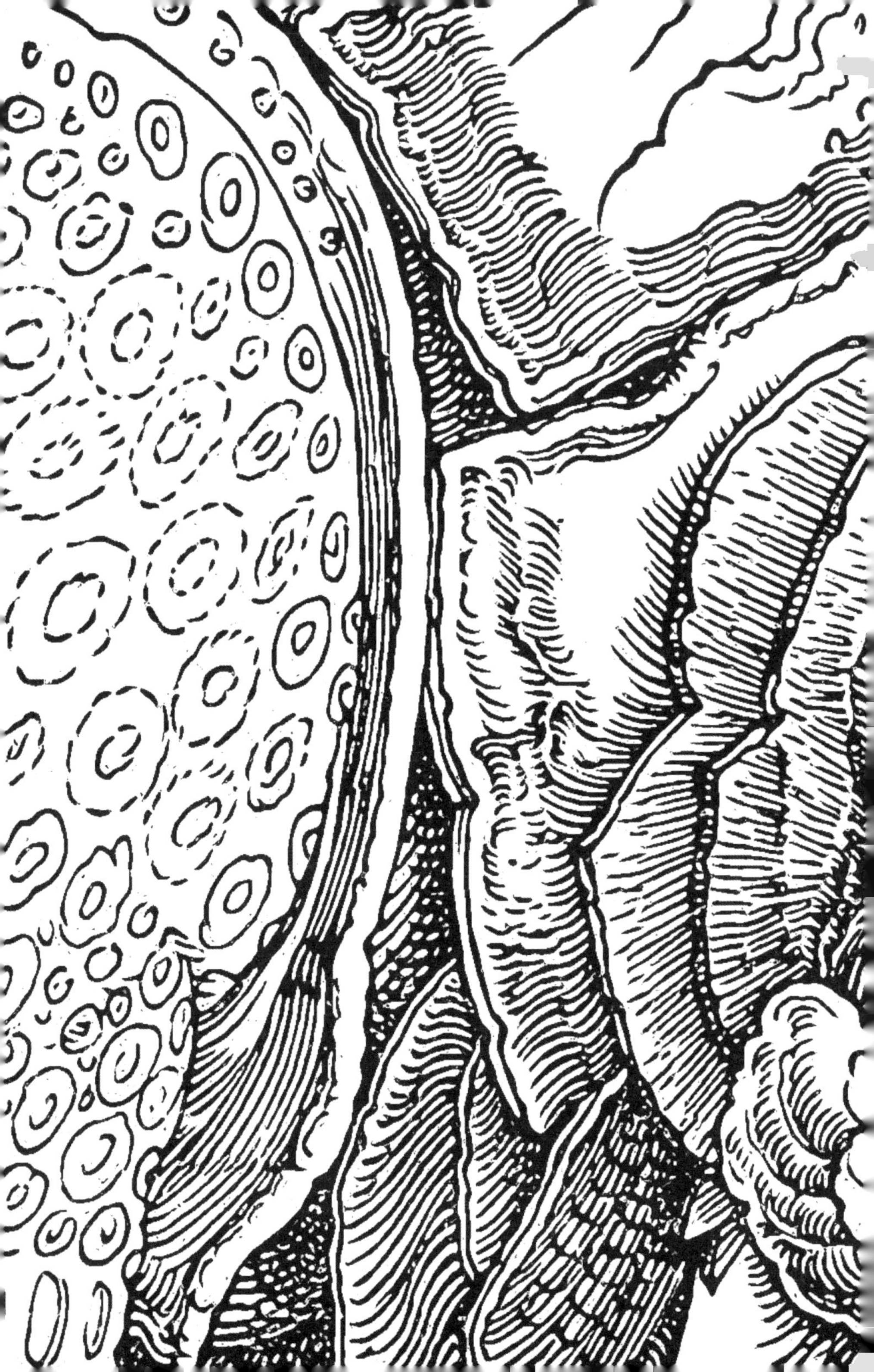

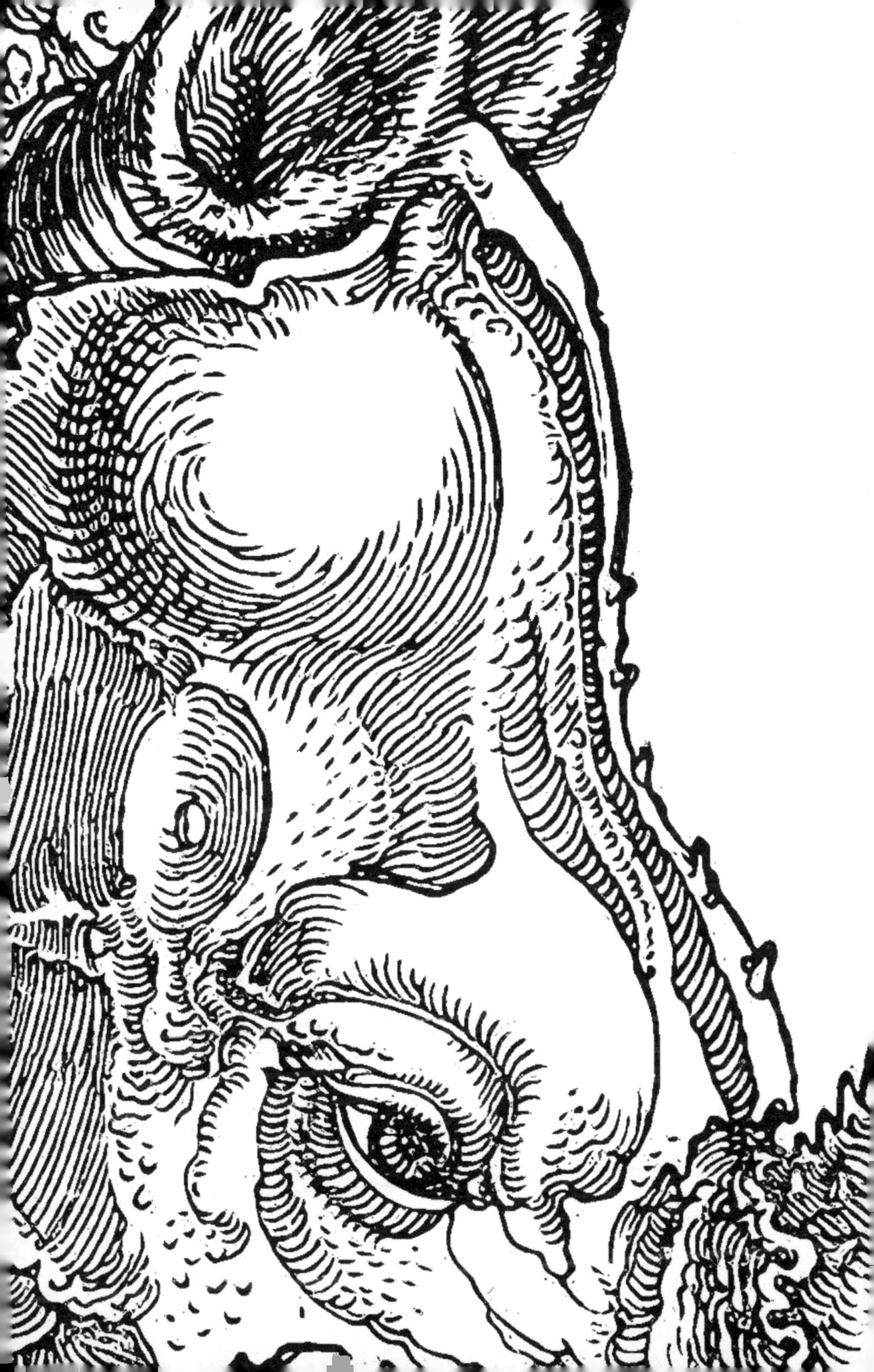

diplomatic

gift

The rhinoceros calf that was later named Clara was still very young when her life drastically changed from one moment to the next. After a pregnancy of some sixteen months, her mother had given birth to her at some point in the summer of 1738. In an ideal situation, a young calf would remain with its mother for three to four years. But Clara awaited a very different fate. Accounts vary somewhat, but most report that the young calf was about a month old when her mother was killed by arrows during a hunting party. A net was flung over her and she was carried off by the hunters.[16]

The region where Clara was captured and her mother killed was later described in prints for her European visitors as the 'Territory of the Great Mughal in the Assam Region'. To emphasize how special it was for this animal to be seen in Europe, it was often added that this lay in Asia, at least four thousand miles away.[17] The territory of the Great Mughal referred to that part of India which from the mid-sixteenth century had been taken from Kabul in Afghanistan by the Mughals, who were of Turkish origin. Assam was not a part of this Mughal territory, though it was connected to it in various ways. This hilly country, which lies along the eastern flanks of the Himalaya mountains and is traversed by the wide River Brahmaputra, had been home to large numbers of rhinoceroses for many centuries. In the valleys lay abundant stretches of open land with tall grass and a scattering of trees and bushes, with damp, marshy areas in between. Ideal for rhinoceroses, which like concealment and have to eat large amounts of grass and leaves in order to keep their stomachs filled. They also need a lot of water, not only to drink, but also to prevent their hairless, leathery skin from drying out in the sun. They swim a lot and like to wallow in the mud. In Clara's days, many rhinoceroses also lived in the basin of the Ganges and the Indus to the west – rivers which likewise flowed to the sea from the Himalayas. Today their habitat is confined to reserves in Nepal and Assam, where some 3,500 animals live, far fewer than when Clara was born.[18]

Clara was an Indian rhinoceros, known by the scientific name of *Rhinoceros unicornis*. Once fully grown, this species has a single horn on its head.[19] Deep folds appear to separate the supple skin into large sections, creating the impression of separate plates, giving rise to the name 'armoured' rhinoceros in German. They are solitary animals which, unlike elephants, for example, do not live in herds. As a result, Clara's mother was alone when she gave birth to her calf and was killed.

Hunting rhinoceroses was a privilege reserved for rulers and powerful nobility whereby the hunt revolved around the 'heroic' combat between man and beast; rulers or noblemen regularly had to fight such battles to demonstrate their power and strength. The swift and powerful lone rhinoceros, which was difficult to spot in the tall grass and thick brushwood, was regarded as a formidable opponent, and hence a prized trophy. The royal hunt of rhinoceroses with all its atrocities is occasionally represented in miniatures that were painted from the end of the sixteenth century to illustrate stories which extolled the glorious feats of the Mughal princes, the new rulers of India. A miniature painted around 1590 for the *Baburnama*, the memoirs of the first Great Mughal Zahiruddin Muhammad Babur, shows the mounted ruler attacking a rhinoceros with a long lance [fig. 9]. In the foreground the rider of an elephant shoots at another rhinoceros with a bow and arrow, while several assistants finish the animals off with lances. One rhinoceros lies slain on its back, its legs in the air and its tongue hanging out of its mouth.[20] Incidentally, in the case of Clara's mother, the hunter is more likely to have been a lower-ranking prince or a governor of an eastern province than the Great Mughal himself, whose hunting grounds were situated closer to his capital Delhi.

Dead rhinoceroses were skinned, not for their meat but for their skin and horn. The strong leathery hide was sometimes used to make shields and armour – when dried it is very hard and therefore extremely effective as a protective covering for the body in combat. The horn was considered particularly valuable, as it still is. Mughal rulers had thumb rings made of it, which they used in archery, while the nobility wore rhino-horn earrings.[21] Intact horns were highly prized, particularly outside India. In China, and from the sixteenth century also in Europe, they were transformed into articles of unprecedented luxury, such as goblets. Sometimes the horn itself was carved, for instance, with a fighting scene between a rhinoceros and an elephant [see fig. 2]. Often showpieces like this would be displayed in the cabinets of curiosities or 'wonder rooms' of the European elite where, besides *objets d'art* and other rarities, unworked horns could also be found as natural phenomena, as a reference to an animal they only knew from hearsay.

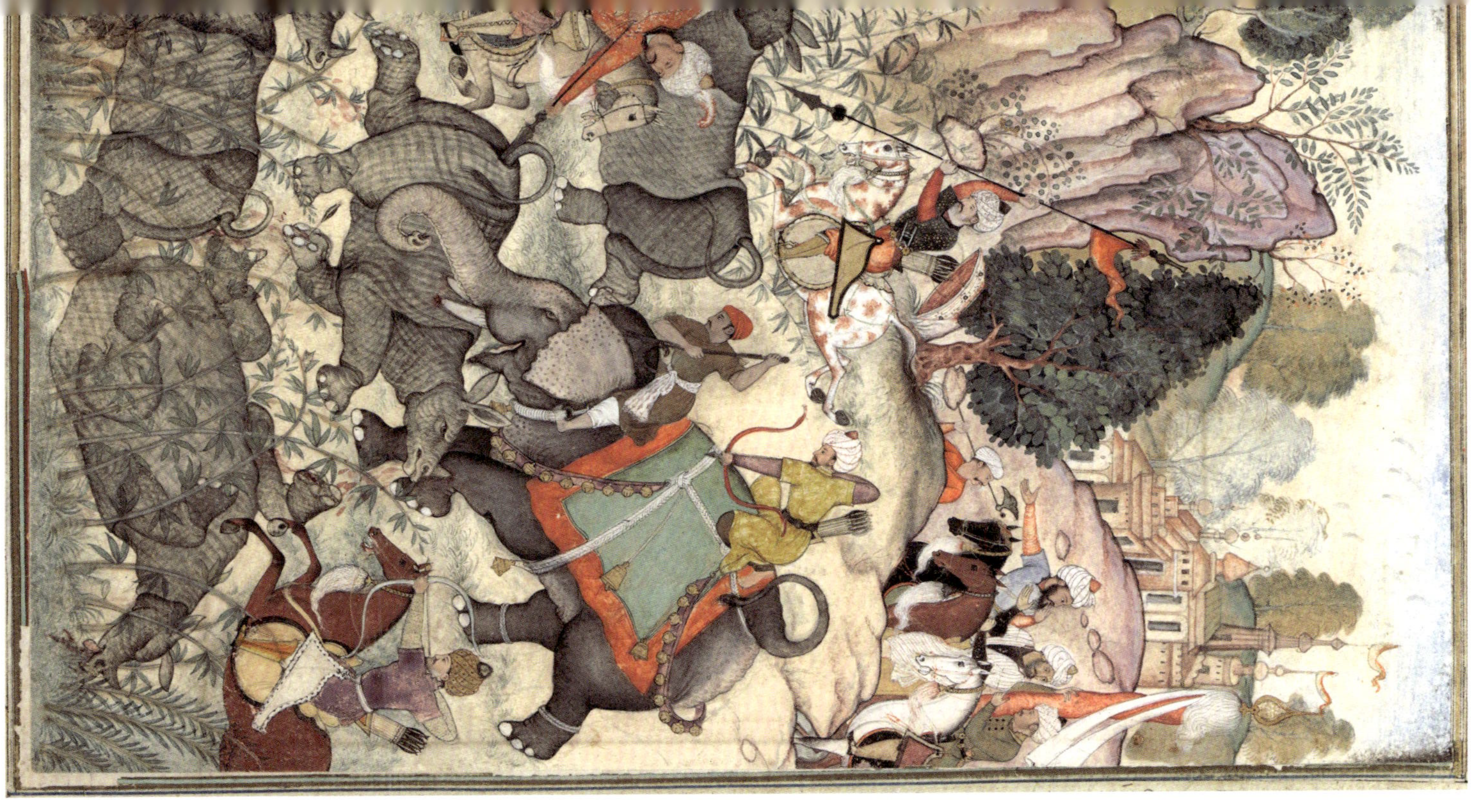

9
Great Mughal Zahiruddin Muhammad Babur on horseback attacks a rhinoceros with a long lance, miniature, attributed to Bishandas, c. 1590

The young calf had no horn as yet and was far too small for her to be of any value if she were skinned. An arrow had slightly injured her ear, but otherwise, although helpless, she was very much alive.[22] The royal hunters realized that it was here that her value lay. She was rare and special. She was spared. And so she found herself in a new and strange world.

A few weeks or months later, but well before the end of 1738, an Indian ruler must have arranged for the young rhinoceros to be handed over officially to the most important Dutchman in Bengal, the Groningen-born Jan Albert Sichterman, director of the trading post of the Dutch East India Company (VOC) [fig. 10]. During the closing years of the sixteenth century, in the wake of the Portuguese, Dutch merchants had sailed to Asia to buy lucrative goods, such as spices. In 1602 the VOC had been founded, a company which took charge of all Dutch trading relations with and within Asia. From its base in Java and the Moluccas, in a fairly short space of time, the company extended its activities to other parts of the continent, started trading in a wide range of commodities, besides spices such as pepper, cloves and nutmeg, and even managed to secure a role in trading within Asia itself.

Dutch merchants had been active since the early seventeenth century in Bengal, a large area in the north-east of India and what is now Bangladesh. In 1635 the VOC had founded a trading post on the right bank of the Hooghly, a tributary of the mighty River Ganges, which connected a large and important part of northern India to the sea. These headquarters, where the director held office and which was likewise known as Hooghly, were situated near the Indian town of Chinsurah some two hundred kilometres from the sea. A bird's-eye-view painted in 1665 reveals that the post consisted of a large, walled, strictly organized complex made up of a variety of buildings housing offices, warehouses, living quarters and workshops as well as stables for the elephants, horses and other animals [fig. 11]. Some two hundred and fifty Europeans worked there on average in addition to numerous people who were enslaved.[23] Some of them can be seen in this painting.

It was here to Hooghly that the rhinoceros calf was sent as a gift, to enhance the status of Sichterman as the most important Dutchman in the region. A stable would have been vacated for her as well as a tract of land where she could graze, and arrangements made for her to be looked after. Under normal circumstances she would have been nursed by her mother for at least a year, but she now had to be fed in some other way. It is reasonable to suppose that an Indian keeper was sent with her, a person possibly enslaved for the purpose.

Sichterman would have been delighted to accept the gift. He understood the significance of the gesture, for gifts played a vital role in relations between the Dutch traders and the many Indian rulers with whom they did business. The VOC was there to buy valuable local products, but they were certainly not the only ones with an interest in these. They faced fierce competition from other European as well as Asian traders, all of whom vied for the favour of the Indian rulers and merchants. They in turn could pick and choose and could spread their privileges and merchandise over the different parties.

The VOC always drew up formal contracts with the different rulers. These stipulated that the Dutch, like their competitors, had to pay tax and tolls in exchange for concessions to purchase goods. Gift-giving was the lubricant needed to make trade a real and permanent success and to make good money, and this took place at all levels. The Great Mughal had to be satisfied, as did his governor in Bengal (the nawab) and the countless local rulers and nobles the VOC had to deal with. It was above all the purchasing parties who had to dip into their pockets, particularly the European trading companies: the Dutch, the British, the French and the Swedes. Besides cash, gifts included a range of special objects and animals, varying from exquisite fabrics and Japanese lacquer boxes to parrots and other Asiatic birds, telescopes and microscopes from the Netherlands, and a host of other items – the Indians often having submitted very specific wish lists. The young rhinoceros may have been one of the return gifts. Overall, far less is known about these than about the many gifts presented by the Dutch, which had to be meticulously accounted for in the VOC's official records. Animals certainly figured more frequently among the gifts Indians made to Europeans. Rogier Beerenaart, Sichterman's predecessor as the director of Bengal, for instance, was successively given an 'Elephant, fine and well tusked' and a chestnut-brown horse with a white right back leg by the nawab in 1731 and 1732.[24]

All these gifts served the Dutch to good purpose. In the second half of the seventeenth century, the Bengali trading post accounted for an ever-growing share of the VOC's Asian trade, and in the first half of the eighteenth century it had become vital to the overall commercial success of the company. The most important products it bought in were cotton and silk weaves in a variety of colours, patterns and qualities, which enjoyed enormous popularity in Europe from the late seventeenth century. Another important export product was saltpetre, which formed the raw material for gunpowder in Europe where wars were constantly being waged. People were also traded. They were often captured in Bengali villages and enslaved, and subsequently

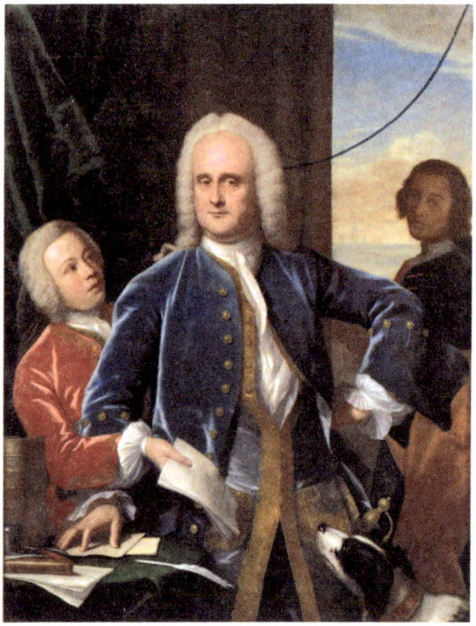

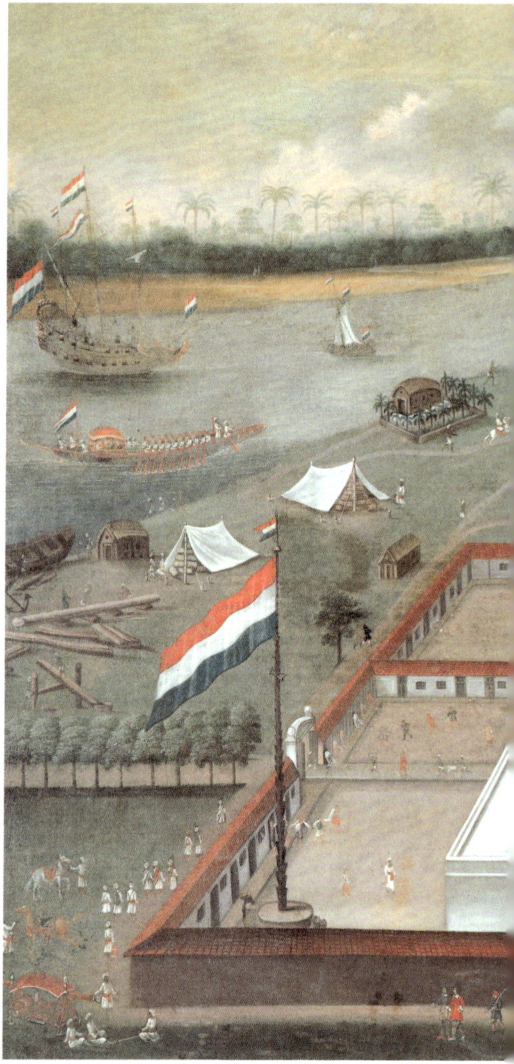

10
Portrait of Jan Albert Sichterman with his sons Jan Albert and Gerrit Jan, painted after his return from Bengal, Philip van Dijk, 1745

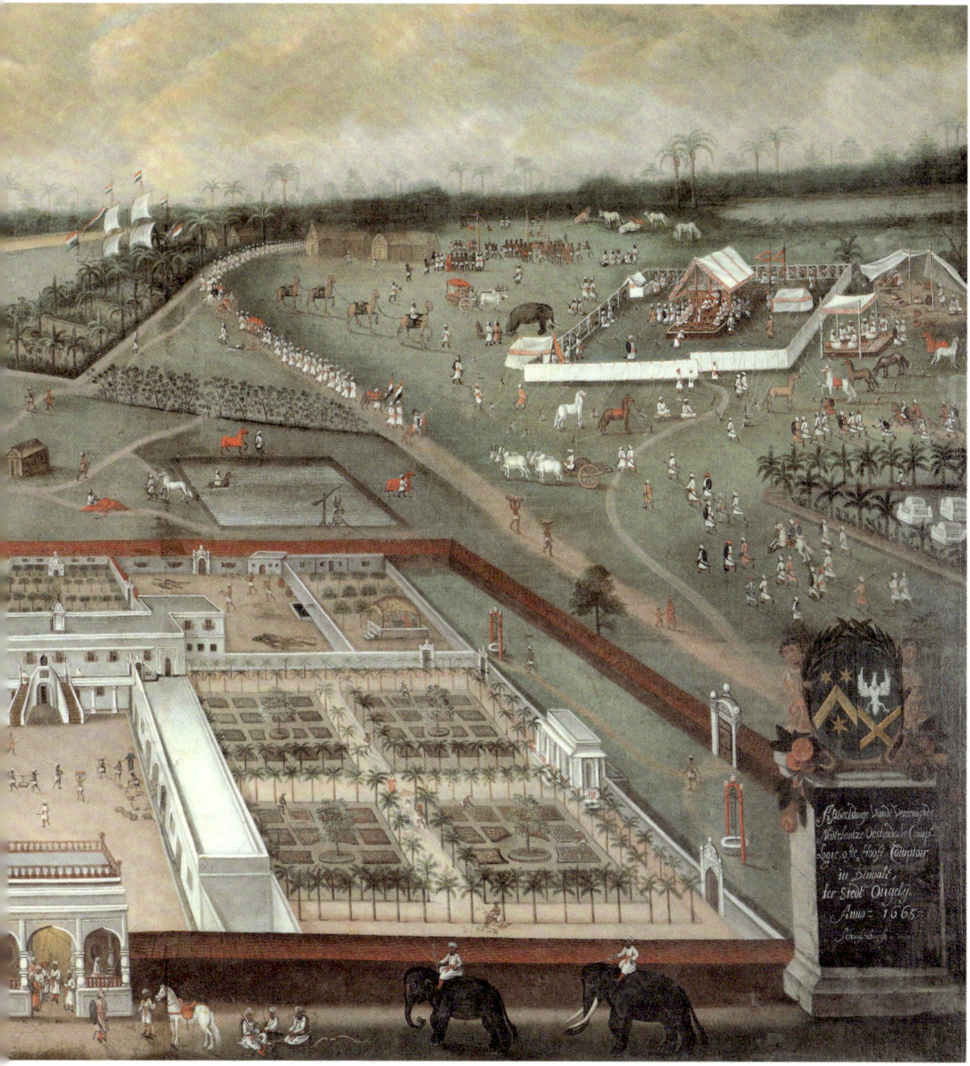

11
The VOC trading post in Hooghly in Bengal, Hendrik van Schuylenburgh, 1665

sent to work as forced labourers in and around Batavia (the Asian headquarters of the VOC on Java), the Banda Islands or in the environs of Cape Town in South Africa. The textiles, the saltpetre and an array of other products, as well as the enslaved people, were paid for in silver that came from South America via the Netherlands, in spices from other parts of Asia, and in copper from Japan. In the end, the whole world was involved in this trade.[25]

Sichterman was second to none when it came to cashing in on the growing demand, particularly for textiles. He had worked in Bengal since 1717, in the service of the VOC. Two years after his arrival at the age of twenty-seven he had married Sybilla Volkera Sadelijn, the daughter of the then deputy director. Together they had eight children. He steadily worked his way up, until in 1734 he was accorded the highest position, that of Director of Bengal. He was to hold this office for almost ten years, until he returned to Groningen in 1745. As a result, Sichterman knew Bengal through and through and like no other knew how to do business there and how best and most effectively to handle the local authorities. He also knew how to profit from his experience for his own personal gain. By making good use of his many valuable Indian contacts and setting up his own business he became exceedingly wealthy. He lived in the lap of luxury and built an imposing collection of Asiatic objects, including an exceptionally large Chinese porcelain dinner service that he had had made to order and which was painted with his own coat of arms [fig. 12]. It is therefore also quite feasible that he came by the young rhinoceros through his private enterprise rather than through the VOC's official channels.[26]

Meanwhile the young rhinoceros had become something of pet in the Sichterman household. Many of the prints that were later made for her exhibition in Europe, mention that she spent the first two years of her life in the house walking round the table, to the delight of the guests dining at the headquarters in Hooghly.[27] Sichterman's children may well have played with her and possibly it is they who named her Clara. Unfortunately, we do not know when she was given the name or how she came by it.

During their early years rhinoceroses grow fast and heavier by the day. There came a time when chasing round a dining room could no longer be tolerated; all the fine chinaware would almost certainly have ended up smashed to smithereens. On top of this, the animal became increasingly costly, whereas she did nothing to earn her keep. She could not be put to any use or set to work, as elephants were made to; rhinoceroses were unsuitable for this. Therefore, after two and half years, Sichterman decided that the only option was to find a new owner for her. In Bengal itself there were no suitable candidates and it was imperative that the generous Indian who had gifted her was not overtly offended. The best solution was to get her out of Bengal. But who would want to take on a rhinoceros? And yet, Sichterman managed to persuade someone to do just that, even though that person had very likely never seen a rhinoceros and, indeed, may never even have heard that such animals existed.

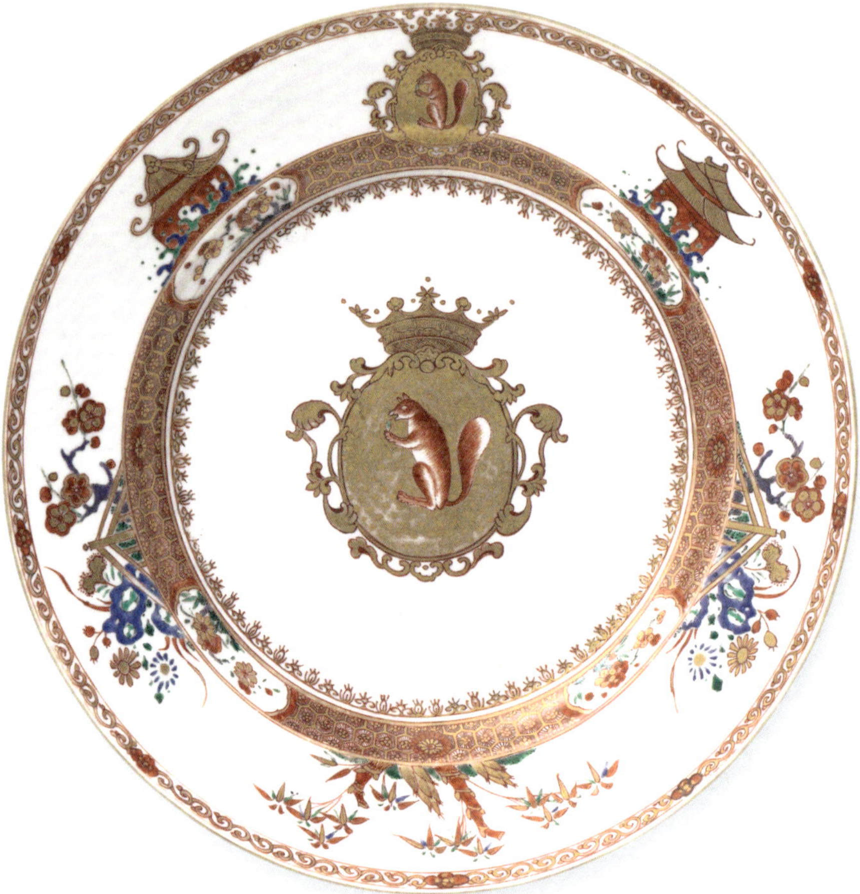

12
Chinese porcelain plate with the coat of arms of the Sichterman family, c. 1730–1735

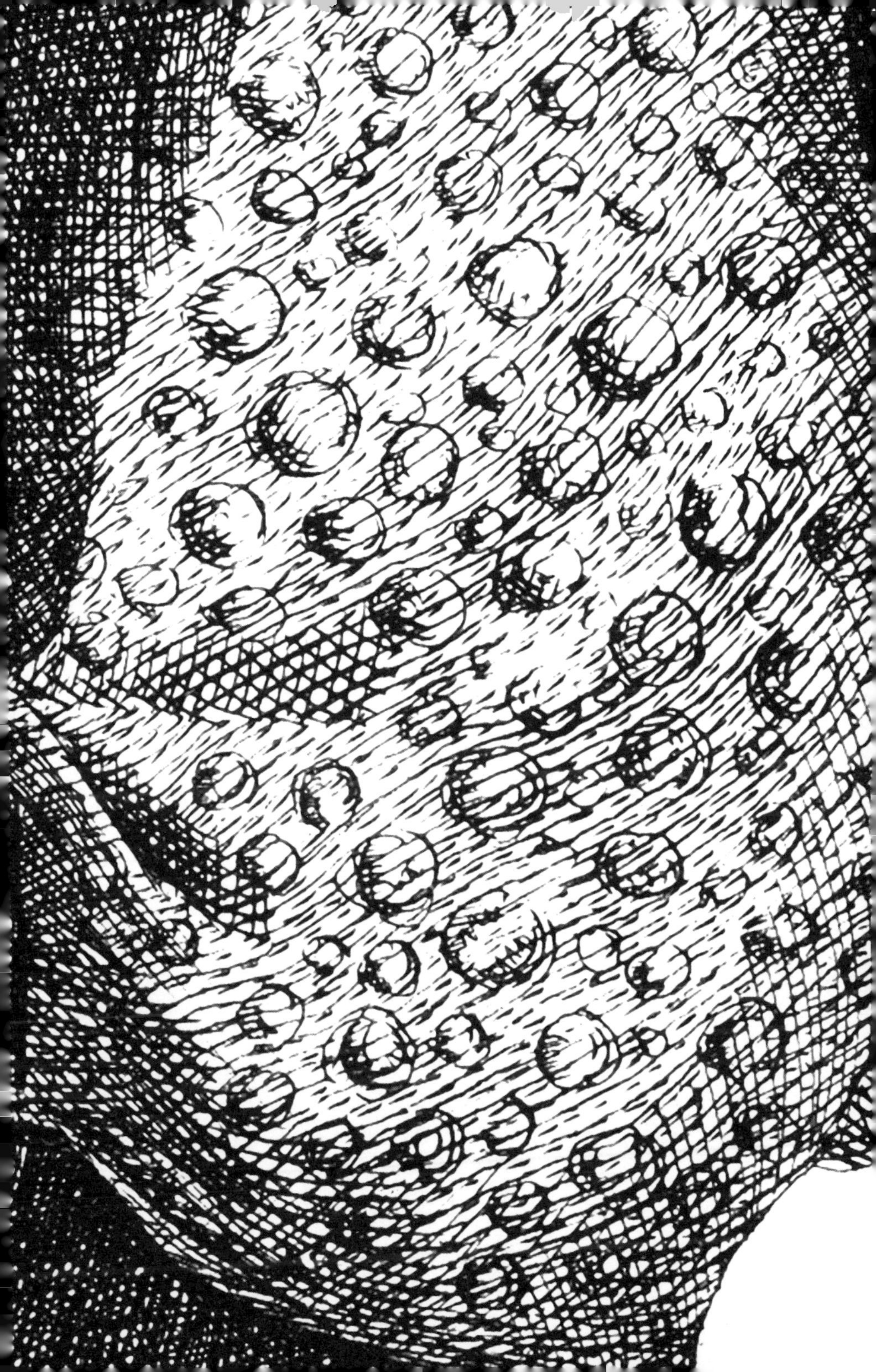

shipped
to the

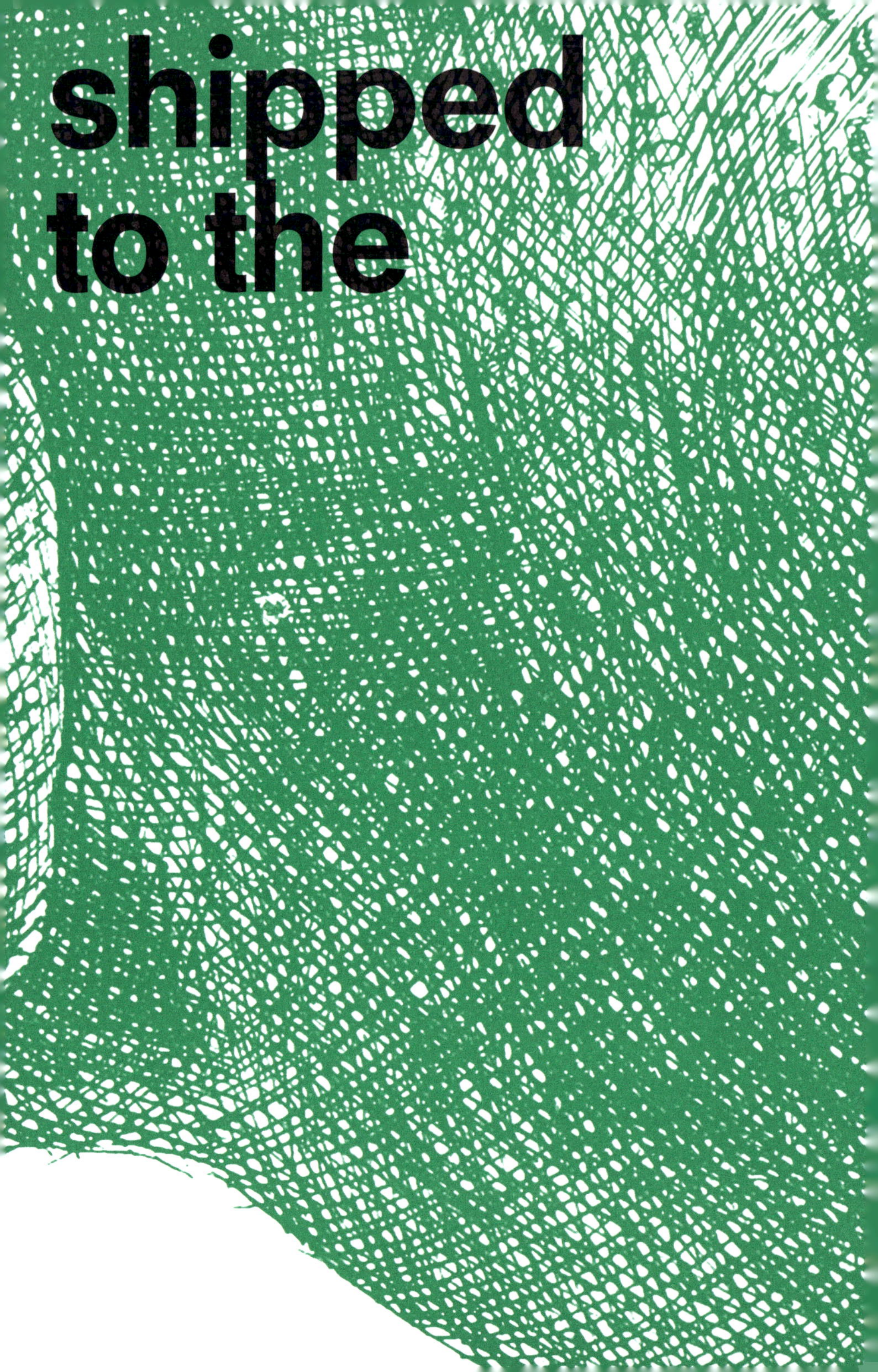

nether-lands

On 11 September 1740 Douwe Jans Mout, captain of the VOC ship *Horssen*, sailed up the Hooghly for the first time in his life. He cast anchor some seventy kilometres from where the river flowed into the Gulf of Bengal. Since it was too dangerous for fully laden and hence low-sitting trading vessels to sail right up to the Bengali headquarters – the current was too unpredictable and the risk of running aground too great for that – part of the cargo was transferred to smaller boats here at this fairly sheltered anchorage just off Phalta, a place the Dutch called Volta. Once off-loaded, the larger ships could also continue their journey up the river. Following his arrival at the headquarters, Mout reported to Sichterman on his voyage. His main point was doubtless that he had suddenly had to take control of the ship following the unexpected death of its captain, Jan Luders. From then on, Mout retained this position, for already on 18 September Sichterman officially installed him in his new function. But when Sichterman heard that the captain of another ship that had just come in was keen to take command of the *Horssen*, Sichterman thereupon appointed Mout commander of the *Knappenhof*, a ship sent out by the Maas Chamber whose home port was Rotterdam.[28]

Douwe Mout came from a real seafaring family. His first experience at sea had most likely been with his father or one of his uncles, who were all captains transporting merchandise within Europe. His father, Jan Pietersz Mout, from the Wadden island of Vlieland who had moved to Amsterdam with his parents in 1692, called on Archangelsk and Marseilles, among other ports. In 1699 he had married Trijntje Douwes whose family came from the Wadden island of Ameland; her father and brothers were also ships' captains. Born in Amsterdam on 12 April 1705, Douwe was their third child and second son.[29]

Mout, now aged thirty-five, was in Asia for the third time. The first time he had made the crossing as third mate at the age of twenty and had not returned to the Netherlands for over five years. In 1736 he was then appointed second mate on the *Duinbeek*. During the return voyage on 21 May 1737 the ship had perished in a storm off the Cape of Good Hope along with seven other returning vessels. Mout survived the shipwreck and returned home safely. He set out on his third voyage on 12 October 1739 as first mate on the *Phoenix*. A few months after arriving in Batavia on 27 April 1740, he sailed to Bengal on the *Horssen*. And now he was officially appointed captain – the pinnacle of his career.[30]

As a result of Mout's new appointment, his contact with Sichterman had been intensive from the start. This may well have led Mout to decide to take Clara over from him. He must have realized how special it was for this still young animal to have become accustomed to people and even dependent on them through its captivity. She was docile and hence manageable. According to a print that appeared after Clara's death, she was a gift from the director,[31] but in this out-and-out commercial environment, it is equally feasible that Sichterman sold her to Mout. Perhaps it had already occurred to Mout that he could make good money out of her in Europe.

In Batavia the *Knappenhof* had taken on board some 200,000 pounds of pepper and 62,000 pounds of sappanwood. To this was added typical Bengali merchandise, including a vast amount of saltpetre (343,500 pounds in 2,400 sacks) and as many as 45 different kinds of fabrics, including 18 chests of plain double armozeen (a thin silk material), 51 bales of tanny silk, 52 bales of '*gerrassen*' (cotton cloths) and 120 bales of Guinean cloth (cotton fabrics destined for the West African coastal region) [fig. 13]. The ship, Sichterman mentions in a letter, was fully laden, as were the other three ships with which it was to sail to the Netherlands. The official cargo of the *Knappenhof* alone had a value of almost 450,000 guilders.[32] In addition, many of the crew had stowed away a whole load of other products with a view to selling them privately for a profit back home.

It was common practice, and to a certain extent permitted, for the crew to take merchandise back to Europe at their own expense. Mout himself must also have bought a lot in. In Hooghly he had taken out loans for at least 27,000 guilders, 18,000 guilders of which from Sichterman and the remainder from two other high officials at the Bengali headquarters: trader and fiscal (public prosecutor) Jan Huyghens and assistant trader Hermanus Blom.[33] He was obliged to repay these loans to their representatives on the spot 'at their first reminder in the fatherland'. This was only possible if he had sold the goods he had purchased with the loans, obviously with the principal object of making a handsome profit and thereby substantially augmenting his official earnings – 1,088 guilders and 9 stivers (5-cent pieces) for the whole voyage of over one year and nine months.[34] An additional reason was a large debt that was still outstanding, which he had presumably run up after his own merchandise had been lost when the *Duinbeek* went down off Cape Town in 1737; in May 1739 he had had to reach a settlement with sixteen creditors for over 19,000 guilders at the Desolate Boedelkamer, the Amsterdam insolvency chamber.[35] He also had to repay this sum and it may well be that he saw the little rhinoceros as a good opportunity to clear his debts.

A promissory note for over 5,500 guilders that Mout handed in on his arrival in Amsterdam offers a glimpse of his own merchandise. The collateral for this consisted of 'twenty-two sea chests of tea (which chests are sealed by him ... with his own stamp), and ten other small chests of green tea'.[36] What the other goods were that he had brought back to sell is unclear, although it would be logical to assume that they included cotton and silk fabrics. Mout would also have run up a bill for his rhinoceros. After all, she was now his personal property – she does not appear on the cargo list – and must have had sufficient food and drink to sustain her during the voyage. That alone cost a tidy amount and he would also have had to borrow money for that. He must have thought the investment worthwhile.

In the course of November 1740 Clara was brought on board the *Knappenhof*, which sailed out from the River Hooghly into the open sea on the thirtieth of that month [map, p. 53]. Along with three other large trading ships, it headed in the direction of the Sunda Strait and then set course via Madagascar for the Cape of Good Hope. From there it continued its journey, with Rotterdam as its final destination.[37] It is not known where the young rhinoceros was kept on board, but it would be reasonable to suppose that she was installed in a pen on the deck. During the long trip someone must have had the task of looking after her and giving her food and drink. He may have been one of the seventy-five crew members on board, all employed by the VOC, but it is more likely that Mout had brought along the man from Bengal who was familiar with rhinoceroses and had already been looking after her in the preceding months. As captain of the ship Mout naturally had his own responsibilities and he could only check up on his rhinoceros now and then.

After sailing the open seas for 221 days and bobbing up and down at anchor for a fortnight in Cape Town, on 20 July 1741 the *Knappenhof* reached anchorage at the Dutch island of Goeree. The ship then sailed on via Hellevoetsluis to Rotterdam, where, as captain, Mout had to report on his voyage to the local VOC directors and account for the cargo he had just delivered. After that he was able to travel on to Amsterdam, where his family was waiting for him: his wife Elisabeth Snel, whom he had married nine years previously in 1732, and his three sons: eight-year-old Jan, six-year-old Jacob, and Nicolaas, his youngest, who was born shortly before his departure.[38] He may even have been back in time to celebrate Nicolaas's second birthday.

Never did anyone imagine that Mout would bring a rhinoceros back as a present; the idea was inconceivable. Obviously, he did not take her to his home near the Herenmarkt, the neighbourhood where he had grown up and had always lived.[39] She was left in Nieuwendam, a village along the northern dyke of the IJ waterway facing Amsterdam, where a temporary stable and pasture would have been found for her. There was no lack of grass, mud and water there, but other than that there was nothing familiar about the place for the rhinoceros.

13 [pp. 51, 52]
The official loading list of the *Knappenhof*, drawn up by the VOC on the ship's departure from Hooghly, November 1740

den Zelven blijkens d' overkomende
Cognos cementen en factura geladen
is, te weten —

lb.	peper		
"	Zappanhout		
"	Zalpeter	in	2400 Zacks
ls.	belaarde Cassas	"	2. packs
"	amirtjes	"	3. "
"	Berriabadijs	"	8. "
"	lacoonijs	"	1. "
lb.	borax	"	12. bladen
"	tanny Zijde eijgen gereede	"	51. balen
60"	tanna banna kleen gestreepte of adarspangij	"	21. "
"	mogta Zijde of flonette garen	"	32. "
ls.	effene dubb: armosijnen	"	18. kisten
"	allegiassen Zijde	"	3. "
"	restassen	"	1. "
"	enkelde armosijnen	"	1. "
"	d°. gerüijte d°.	"	1. "
"	roemaals Zijde	"	2. "
"	datanijs of armozijnen met bloemen	"	1. "
"	bandanoedets of tafta de foelat	"	10. packs
"	Sjassadarrij of gedrukte vrouwe kleedjes	"	5. kisten
"	d°. lens " d°. neusdoeken	"	5. "
"	guinees lijwaat	"	120. packs
"	gerraden	"	52. "
"	Sallempoeris	"	10. "
"	bongrijs gebleekte	"	12. "
"	Zeilkleeden	"	22. "
"	roemaals gaanne	"	33. "
"	Sichtermans roemaals	"	1. "
"	protadsen	"	13. "

Cta

3410.	f.	Taffas	in	41	packen
1900.	//	mallemollen	//	27	packen & stukt:
800.	//	tansjeebs	//	12	//
400.	//	betrilsjes Cangam	//	5	//
510.	//	Douriassen	//	6	//
200.	//	themakaans De Santipour	//	4	//
400.	//	Eamans De Landeraal	//	8	//
300.	//	Sjautaars De Sierpour	//	3	//
300.	//	Sinsicken D° D°	//	3	//
200.	//	gestreepte atlassen	//	2	//
200.	//	Soesjes	//	3	//
300.	//	atsiabanies	//	3	//
200.	//	Krarradlerrijs	//	2	//
100.	//	Chiai Crannijs	//	1	//
200.	//	gingam effene	//	2.	//
500.	//	taffaiketas gingams	//	5	//
200.	//	allegiassen terssende	//	2	//
300.	//	allibanies	//	3	//
100.	//	Sologessjes fijne	//	1	//
300.	//	Zaren gemeene	//	3	//
016.	lb.	kattoene garen	//	6	balen
50.	f.	Zerbettes	//	1	kisten

't afgeladene in dezen bodem bedraagt een montant f 14590[illegible]

Wij wenschen het een en ander uw[illegible]

Achtb: door een Zamprije en voors[illegible]

ge reise van dies brenger wel en t[illegible]

mog gewenden, en dat den almogen[illegible]

Uwe dierbare persoonen met de[illegible]

langen der Maatschappij in Zijn[illegible]

Hoede

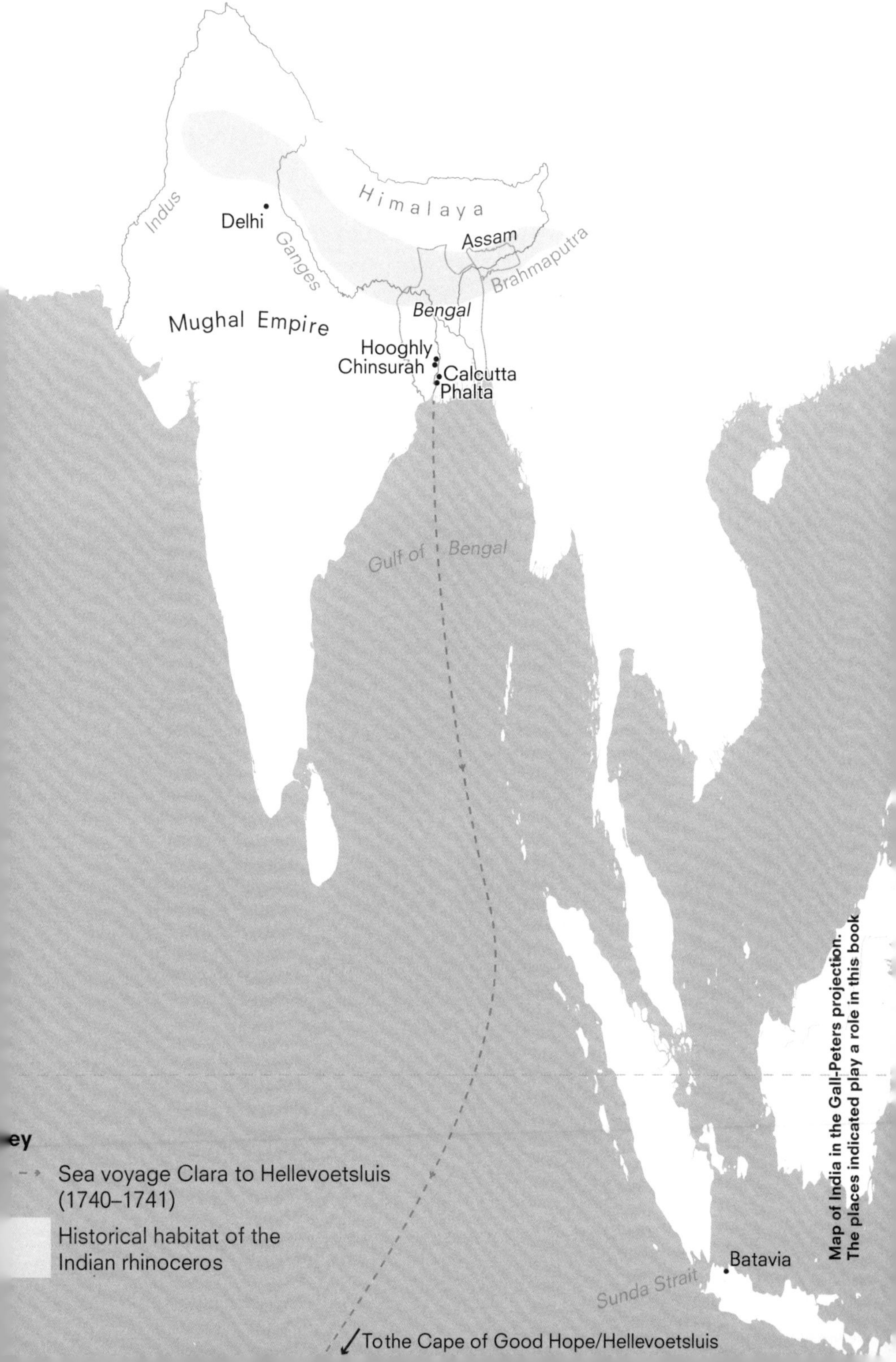

Map of India in the Gall-Peters projection. The places indicated play a role in this book

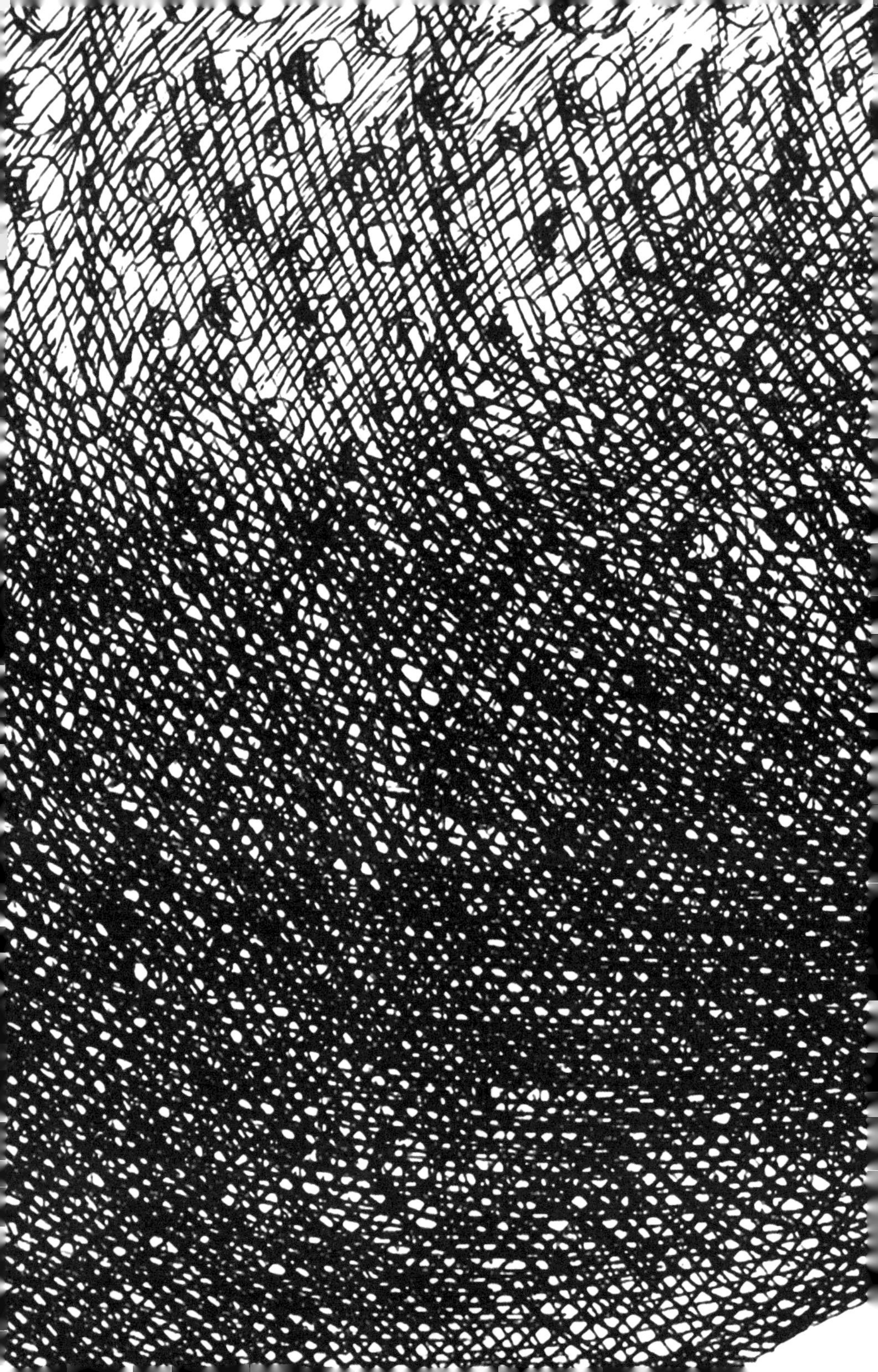

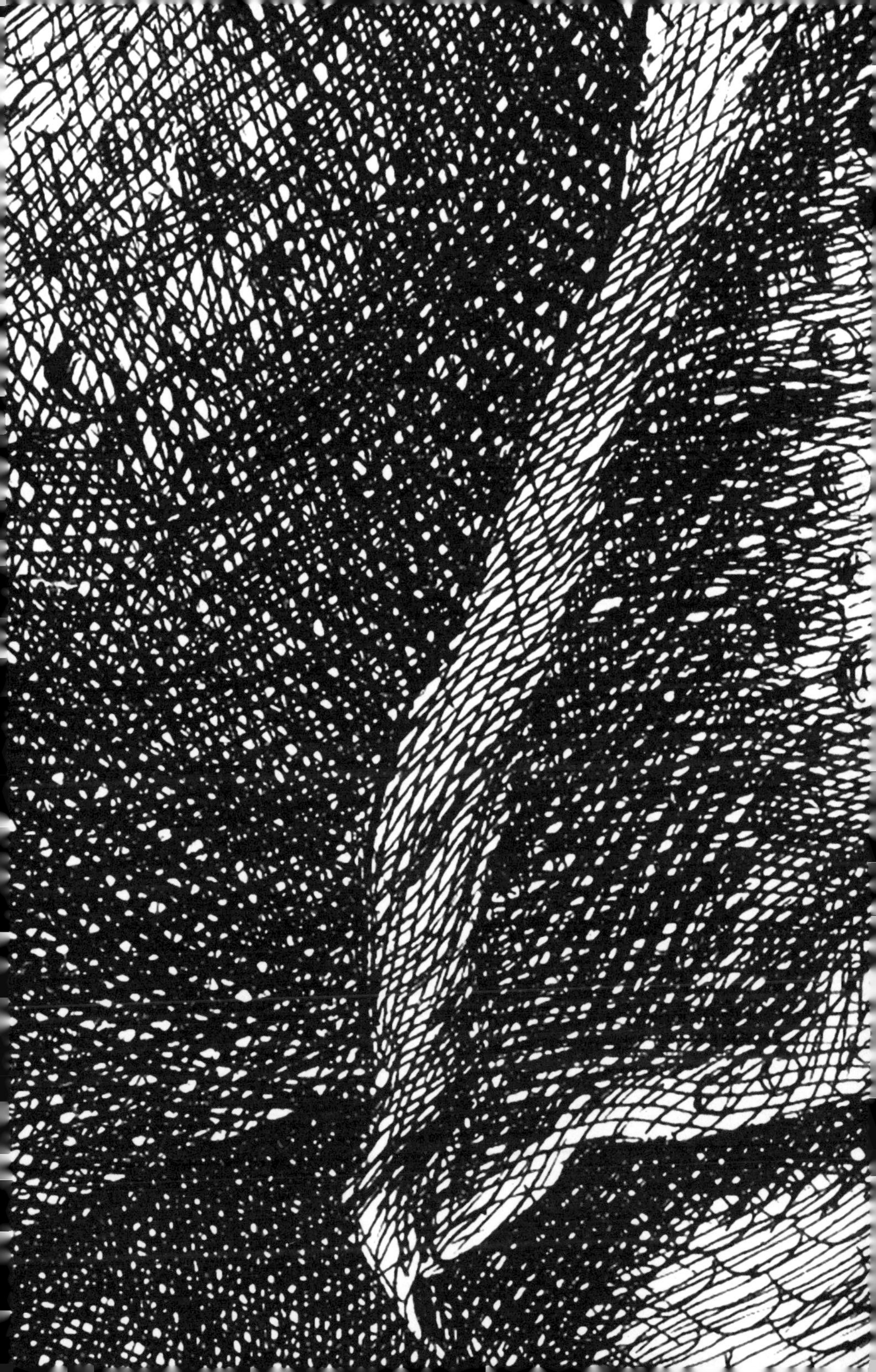

for every person

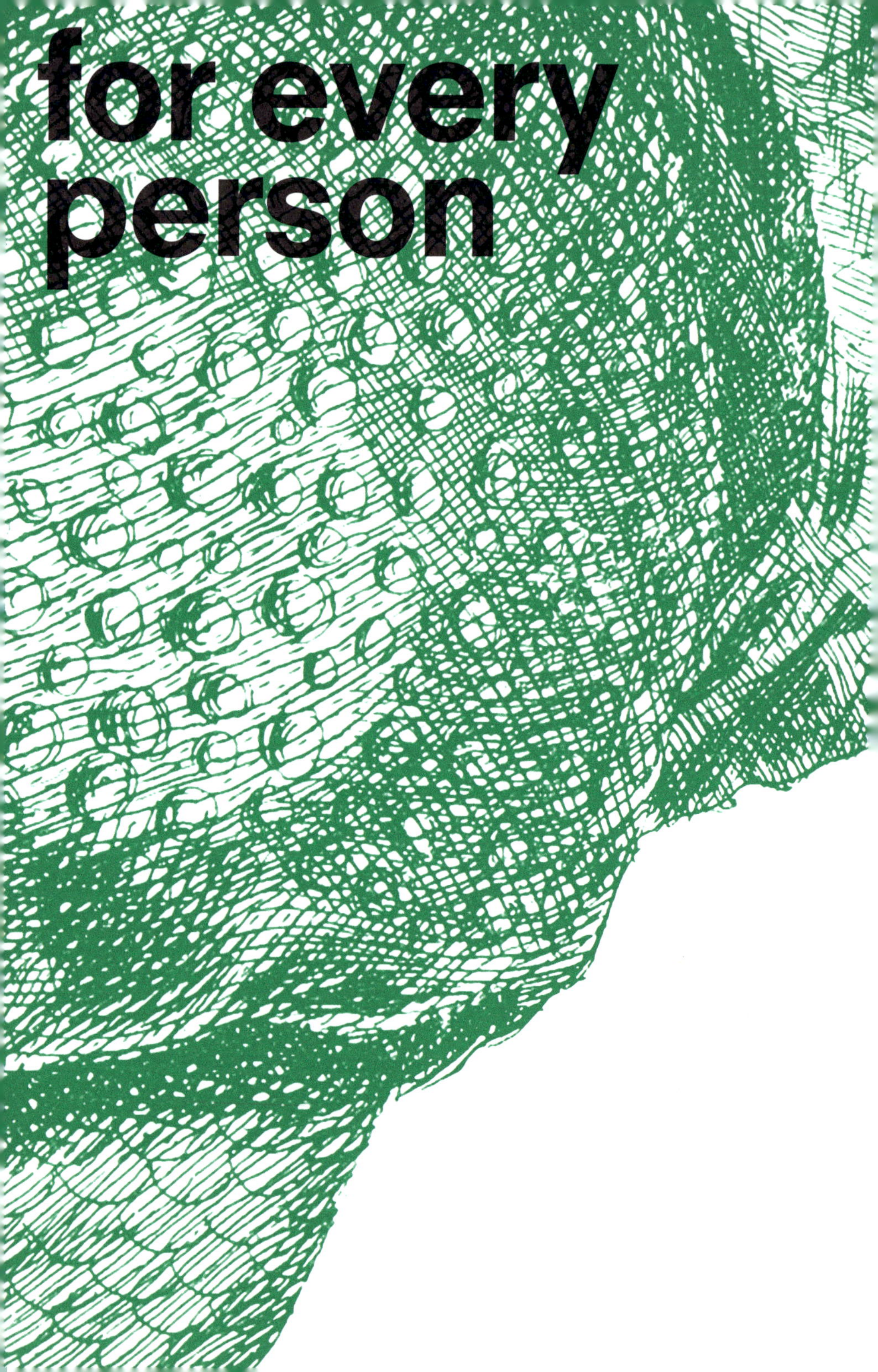

to see

'In Nieuwendam a Living Rhinoceros has arrived, two years old, weighing almost 3,000 pounds ..., the like of which has never been seen here before', the inhabitants of Amsterdam, Leiden and Haarlem read in their newspapers at the end of August 1741. Everyone was invited to come and see the animal on the premises of 'M. Wylacker in Nieuwendam ... for 6 stivers per person'.[40] Douwe Mout had not let the grass grow under his feet. Barely a month after his return, he was exhibiting his young 1,500 kilo rhinoceros, probably outside an inn in this dyke village. He had to, for a regular income was needed in order to keep Clara in good health and make a small profit. He had to capitalize on his new investment as soon as possible and for this he needed a lot of customers.

Nieuwendam could only be the beginning. Clara had to become well known to attract people. The advertisements in the newspapers were a good start. They created a buzz and made the public curious. Meanwhile he was working on a plan to travel around with her. It was, moreover, crucial that he team up with the right person on this risky venture, for on his own he would achieve nothing. What he had in mind exactly, then and in the future, we can only speculate from his actions. Mout left no papers, no personal memoirs. He would have spoken about the future with his wife, probably with his father, with friends and possibly with seamen he had sailed with. And he would have sought advice from people with experience – not with rhinoceroses, for there were none – exhibiting other exotic animals, such as elephants and lions. He consulted people who performed at fairs and markets, who were used to travelling around and going to places that were expected to attract lots of visitors. As for looking after Clara, he would have left that to the Indian who had more than likely travelled with him, as had been the case with other rhinoceroses sent to Europe. Unfortunately, we know nothing about this carer as he is not mentioned in any records.

After just one month, Mout took the plunge and arranged a place for Clara at the *kermis* in Amsterdam, the annual festival that lasted for three weeks. On 21 and 22 September the newspapers announced that, with the city authorities' permission, the rhinoceros would be on display 'for every person to see' next to the weighhouse in Botermarkt (now Rembrandtplein). Admission was six-and-a-half stivers (a little over three euros today), half of which Mout had to hand over to the city to support its poor and needy residents.[41] As everywhere, the *kermis* in Amsterdam was for many city-dwellers an annual highlight which people saved up for, and for countless visitors from outside the city it was a special outing. There were all manner of things on sale and to see: from plays and puppet shows to tightrope walkers, fortune tellers and magicians, as well as exotic animals.[42] It was a setting in which Clara was to regularly find herself in the years to come.

For the first time she now stood before a large crowd who needed to see something really special to stop them from quickly moving on to the next tent. It is impossible to ascertain the number of visitors she received and how much money Mout made, but Clara had clearly been a success. Among those who would have been especially impressed by her size and unfamiliar appearance was the Amsterdammer Jacob Bickers Raye. The thirty-eight-year-old descendant of an affluent regent family wrote in his journal of a 'monstrous body' and was astounded that she was still very young. He expected Clara 'to develop into a terribly large figure of a beast', provided 'she stayed alive'.[43] Others were truly interested in the unknown animal and wanted to know more about her. The Swedish scientist and librarian Magnus Celsius, who had arrived in Amsterdam with his friend Abraham Bäck on 6 September, the first port of call on their European tour, devoted far and away the greater part of his account of his stay in the city to Clara. Although it was his first visit to Amsterdam, he gave far less attention to other attractions at the *kermis* or elsewhere in the city. For instance, he only briefly touched on the equally unfamiliar elephant on display at the *kermis*, whereas he added two simple sketches of the rhinoceros's head [fig. 14]. These are the earliest-known drawings of Clara.[44]

A few months later she generated similar interest in Leiden, where the country's oldest university was located. From the beginning of December she was on display here 'at the Stadsherberg inn at the Witte Poort gate', just outside the city walls on the River Rhine, and in January in Garenmarkt in the city itself.[45] One of those who studied her closely was the nineteen-year-old student Petrus Camper. He paid her frequent visits, as he fondly recalled more than thirty years later. It was an experience that had stood him in good stead throughout his

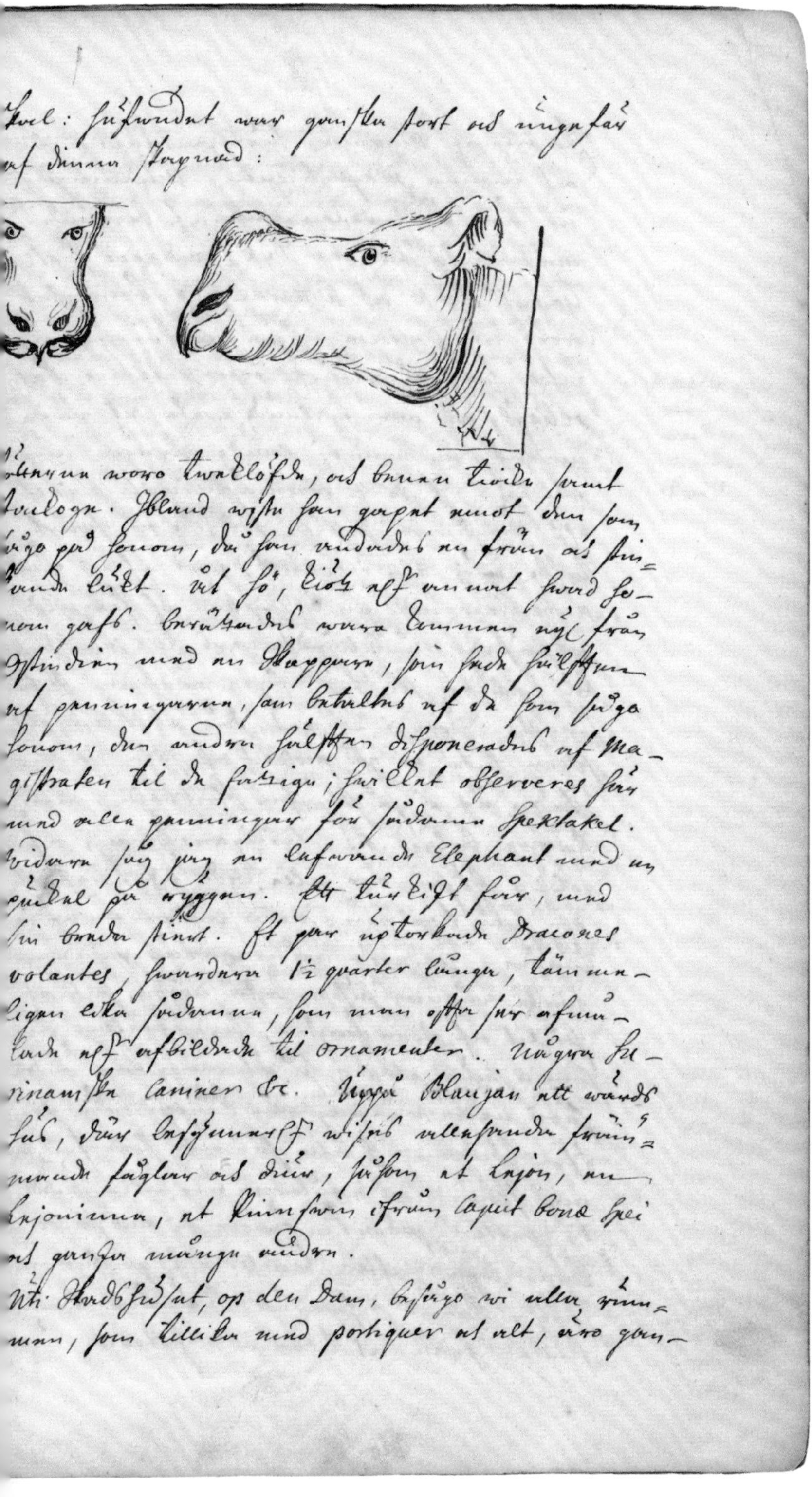

14 **Two sketches of Clara's head drawn at the *kermis* in Amsterdam, in Magnus Celsius's travel journal, 1741**

scientific career. Clara readily allowed herself to be examined. It was this that had led Camper to characterize her unreservedly as 'not malicious'. He saw her eating vegetables, preferably yellow carrots, and also grass and leaves from trees, food that Indian rhinoceroses can easily browse with their characteristic overhanging upper lip. 'I often fed her out of my hand and got her – for she was a female – to open her mouth by holding a carrot out to her.'[46] Whether he realized that the reason for her docility was that she had been used to people from a very early age is highly questionable.

Like Celsius, Camper drew Clara. He sketched her head from the front and the side in black and white chalk on a sheet of blue-grey paper, and on the back he drew her in her entirety, with her head raised and the rest of her body noticeably shortened [figs. 15, 16]. She looks so young that you wonder how Camper could have seen her like that. If she did not have such a lively expression in her eyes, it could have been a picture of the young seventeenth-century stuffed rhinoceros in the botanical garden in Leiden. A third drawing offers a very different impression [fig. 17]. In this Clara is portrayed from the side; a scale indicates her size. She was apparently nine feet long and five feet high with her head raised and her ears pricked. Assuming that Camper used the customary Rhineland foot (12.3557 inches or roughly 31.4 cm) – the length of the foot varied from city to city – this meant she measured 2.8 metres in length and more than 1.5 metres in height. These were not his only portraits of her. In 1772 he mentioned to a Groningen audience that he had also 'painted her in oil paint and modelled her in clay'.[47] Unfortunately, the whereabouts of the painting is unknown but his representation in gilded clay has been preserved [fig. 18].

Later on in life, Camper thought he had made the portraits, which he had not seen for years, in 1748. That is the date on the drawings. But his memory must have been playing tricks on him here, for Clara was never in Leiden that year nor anywhere else in the Netherlands, and what is more she was larger than Camper had depicted her. It seems that Camper was mistaken and that he had added the dates later, possibly when the drawings were back in his possession. The year is much more likely to have been 1742 when Clara and Camper were both in Leiden and Clara was not yet fully grown.

That same year in Leiden, Clara was immortalized in a totally different, highly spectacular manner in a publication where you would hardly expect to find a rhinoceros: an atlas of human anatomy. It was an unprecedented, ambitious project on the part of the Leiden professor of anatomy and surgery Bernard Siegfried Albinus, one of the professors under whom Camper studied, and the artist Jan Wandelaar.

Wandelaar had been making illustrations of the human body for smaller publications by Albinus since 1723. With their new anatomy atlas, entitled *Tabulae sceleti musculorum corporis humani*, they aimed to render all previous atlases redundant. Above all, this meant that the illustrations had to be far more precise and more detailed than any others before. The core of the book consists of ten large prints in which the body is entirely peeled away, as it were, in five stages until the skeleton is all that is left. In each separate print, the human being is accurately depicted from the front and the back in a natural, relaxed pose, as if standing in the open air, in a rocky setting, in a garden, on a hill, or by a ruin. They are amazing illustrations in every respect, and it is no wonder that it took Albinus and Wandelaar some twenty years to produce all the drawings for the atlas and a further seven years to turn them into engravings. As a result, the date on the illustrations varies and the atlas itself did not appear until 1747. Two prints which show only the skeleton and the muscles feature Mout's rhinoceros [figs. 19, 20]. Like the muscle figure, Clara can be seen from the front and the rear. The prints are dated 1742, the year that Clara was in Leiden. When she arrived in their city, the authors must have gone out of their way to incorporate her in their drawings.[48]

Everything indicates that Wandelaar observed the rhinoceros at length with the result that he managed to capture her natural everyday behaviour. This is particularly evident in the frontal view. Here she is quietly grazing without taking any notice of the nearby muscle figure, although her ears are pricked and she is alert. Her skin is meticulously portrayed. And although she is set against an exclusively grey background, which makes the white of the muscle man stand out, she immediately attracts our attention. This is not only due to the unsettling juxtaposition, but also because she is relatively large in comparison with the man, larger than she would have been in reality – this despite Albinus's assurance in his explanatory notes that the relative proportions of man and beast are correct.

Here in Leiden in 1742, for the first time, we have a rhinoceros drawn from life directly recorded in a copper engraving, and moreover in an exceptionally large format. It is unclear whether these prints were circulated right away, however. It may well be that the Leiden publishers of the atlas, Johan and Herman Verbeek, preferred to take advantage of the stir that Clara's appearance was causing to sell loose copies of the prints. On the other hand, it is equally feasible that the publishers waited until the spectacular material was complete in 1747. One thing is certain: if anything shows the enormous impact that Clara had on her viewers, it is these prints.

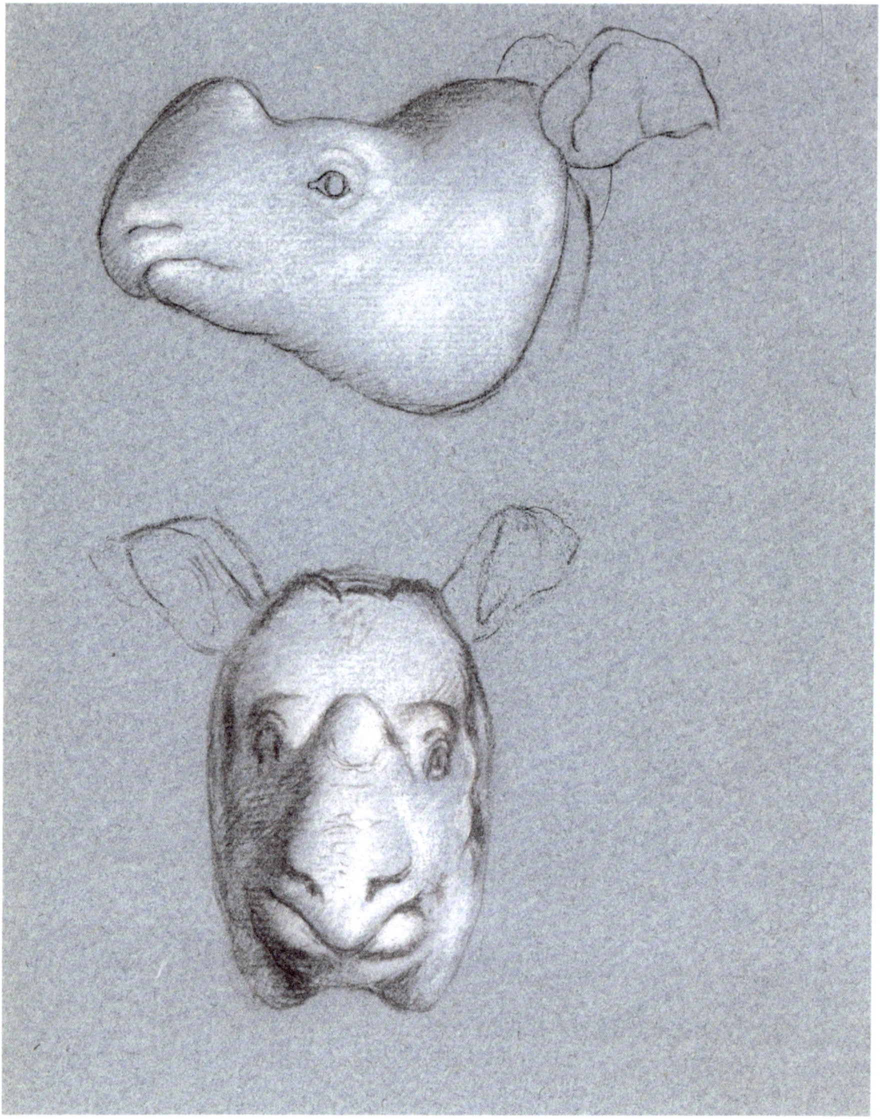

15

Two sketches of Clara's head made in Leiden, Petrus Camper, 1742 (?)

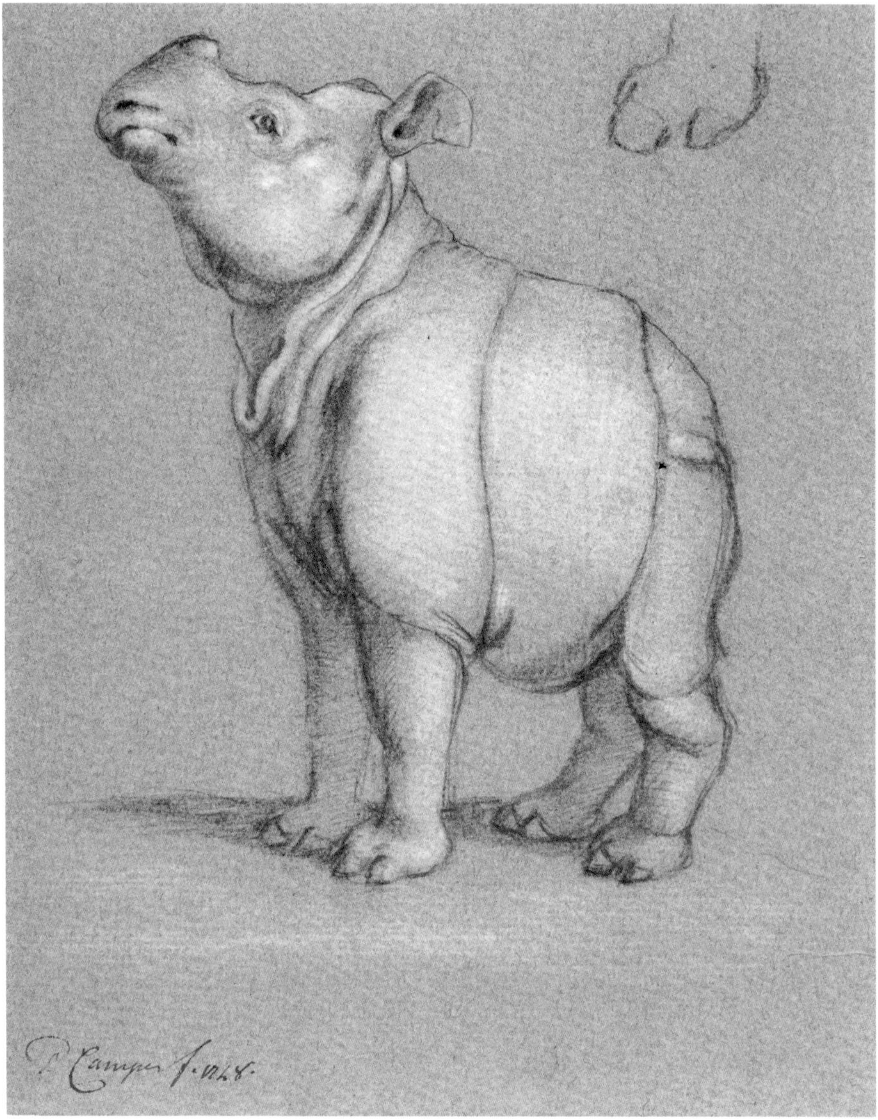

16
Clara as a young rhinoceros,
Petrus Camper, 1742 (?)

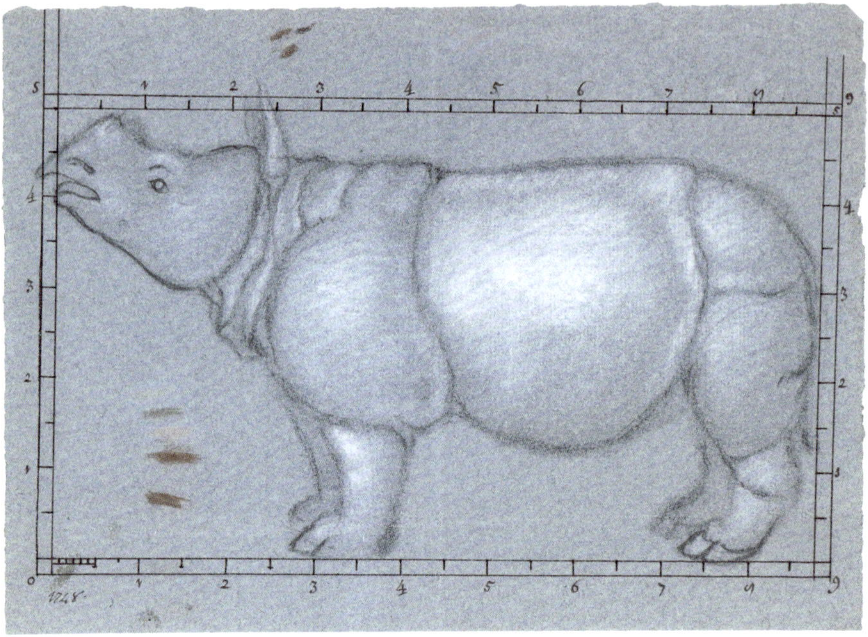

17
Clara measured in Leiden; the scales give her measurements in Rhineland feet, Petrus Camper, 1742 (?)

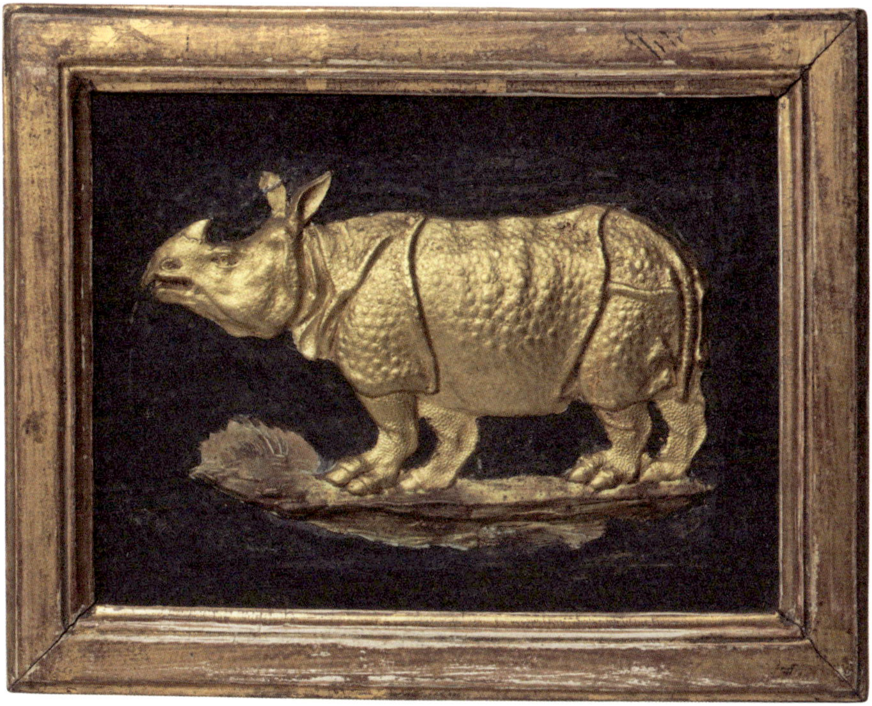

18
A gilded clay relief of Clara, Petrus Camper, 1742 (?)

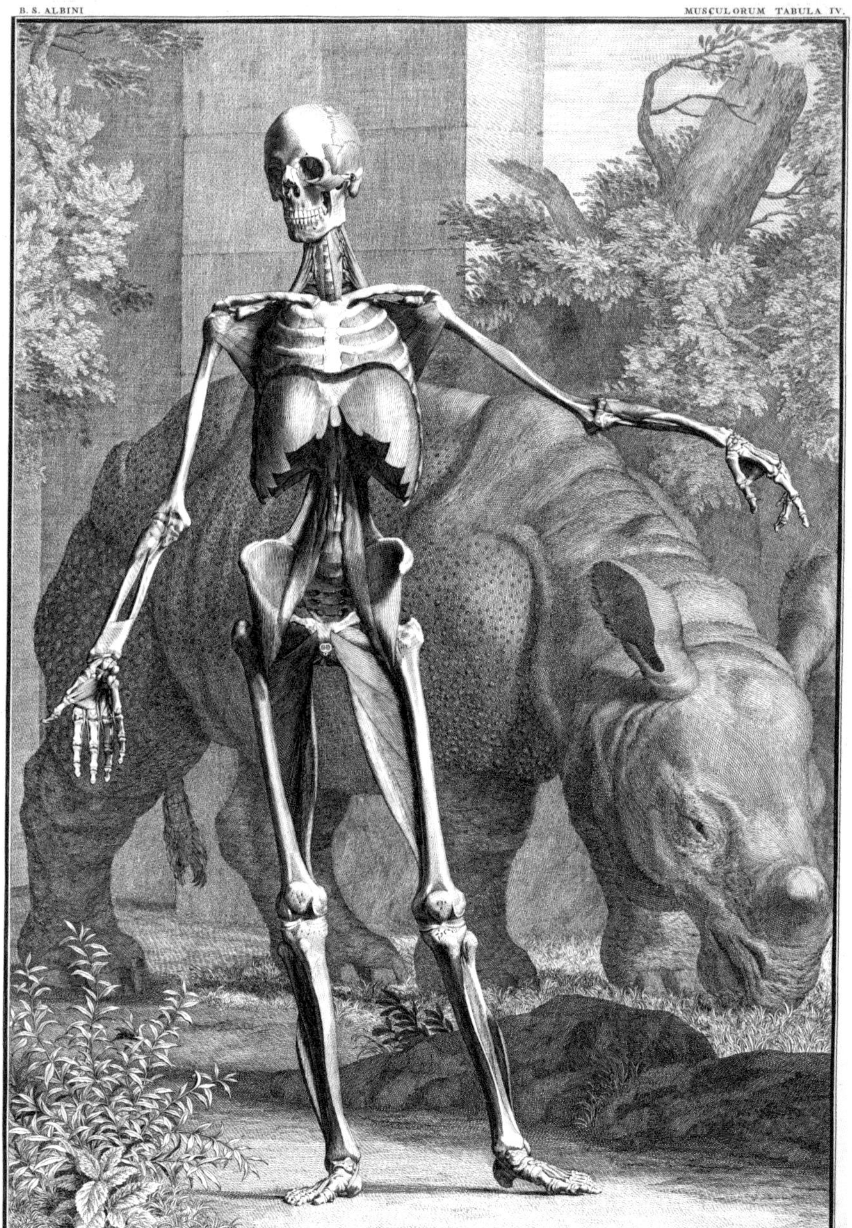

19, 20

Muscle man with rhinoceros, seen from the front and back, illustrations for Bernard Albinus's new anatomy atlas, Jan Wandelaar, 1742

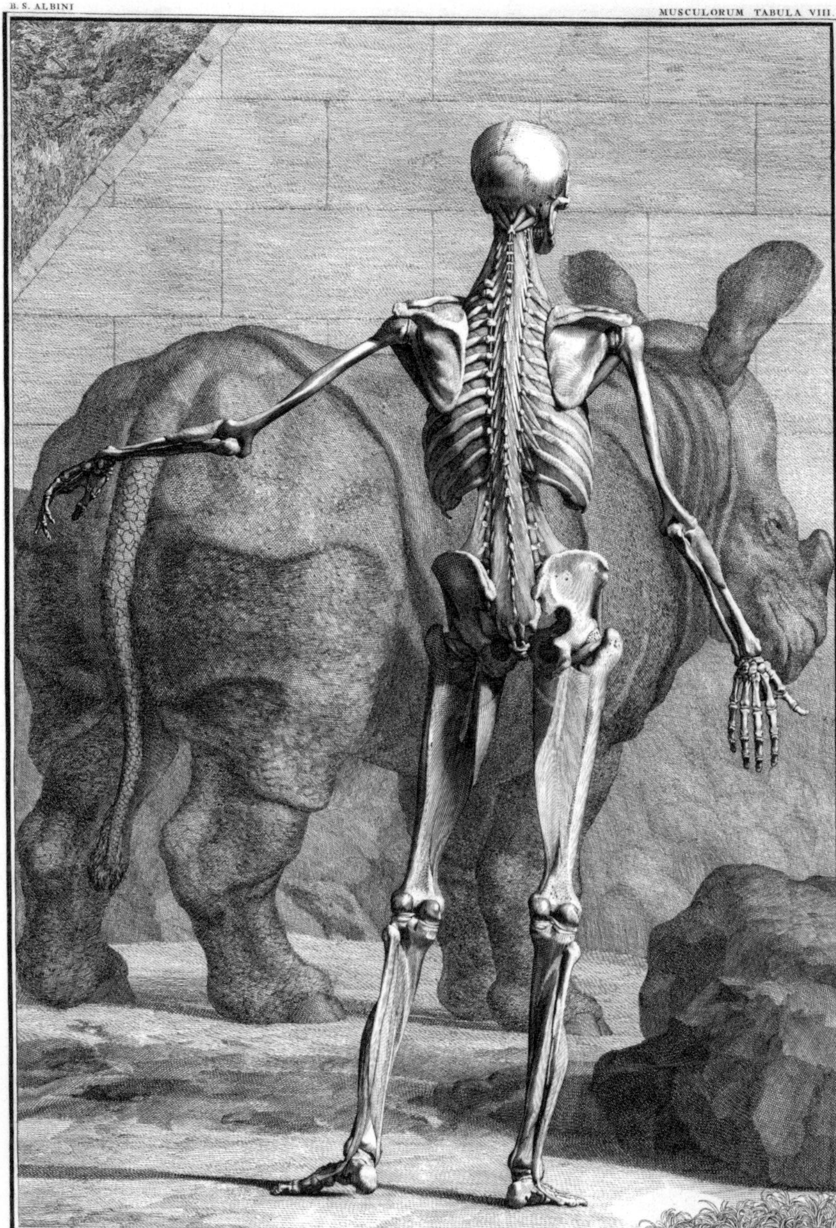

After Clara's success in Amsterdam and Leiden, Mout had every reason to send her to other cities too, and he wasted no time. From 12 June she could be visited on a ship for a while during the annual *kermis* in Delft. In August 1742 she was in Middelburg and in October back at the *kermis* in Amsterdam. The following year in June she travelled successively to Antwerp and Brussels, and then, after a short stay in Amsterdam, sailed on to Hamburg, where she arrived early in November. No doubt she stopped off at other places as well but there is no record of these visits to date.[49]

Clara caused a sensation in all these cities, which were fairly accessible by boat from Amsterdam. Advertising posters announcing her arrival were printed in advance to attract visitors. In Middelburg as well as in Hamburg the rhinoceros was still being portrayed in the style of Albert Dürer, albeit without the second horn. The Middelburg lawyer Pieter Boddaert pasted one of these posters in his notebook [fig. 21] and remarked that the drawing was not quite right: '... the horn on the nose had not yet grown so high, and what is represented as plates here could also be seen in real life, except that these plates were formed by deep folds in the skin, which you could put your whole hand under.'[50]

Clara's fame began to spread around Europe. She was increasingly talked and written about. The Spanish monk Benito Jerónimo Feijóo, who lived in Oviedo, cannot have been the only European scholar to receive a letter about her, in his case from Brussels in the summer of 1743. In this he was told that she had caused a furore in the city and that rumour had it that the French king was even considering acquiring her for his menagerie in Versailles. Feijóo himself was especially moved by the fact that rhinoceroses actually existed and that they were definitely not the same animal as the unicorn that nobody had ever seen. In the essay he wrote about this in 1743, which was published in 1750, he stressed how extraordinary it was that the rhinoceros had unravelled a myth. At the same time, he confessed: 'I cannot conceal from the reader my fear that the news I have received of the Brussels rhinoceros is a fabrication'. He hoped that this would prompt someone to confirm her existence. Again, his appeal shows how much disbelief the arrival of the animal aroused in many people.[51]

Of course, there were scholars who were able to examine the rhinoceros first-hand. In Hamburg this led to the first printed report devoted to Clara. In this article, which appeared in the *Hamburgische Berichte von gelehrten Sachen* in 1744, garrison physician Georg Hannäus and editor-publisher Johann Peter Kohl described the animal's body parts in the greatest possible detail. They began by looking for

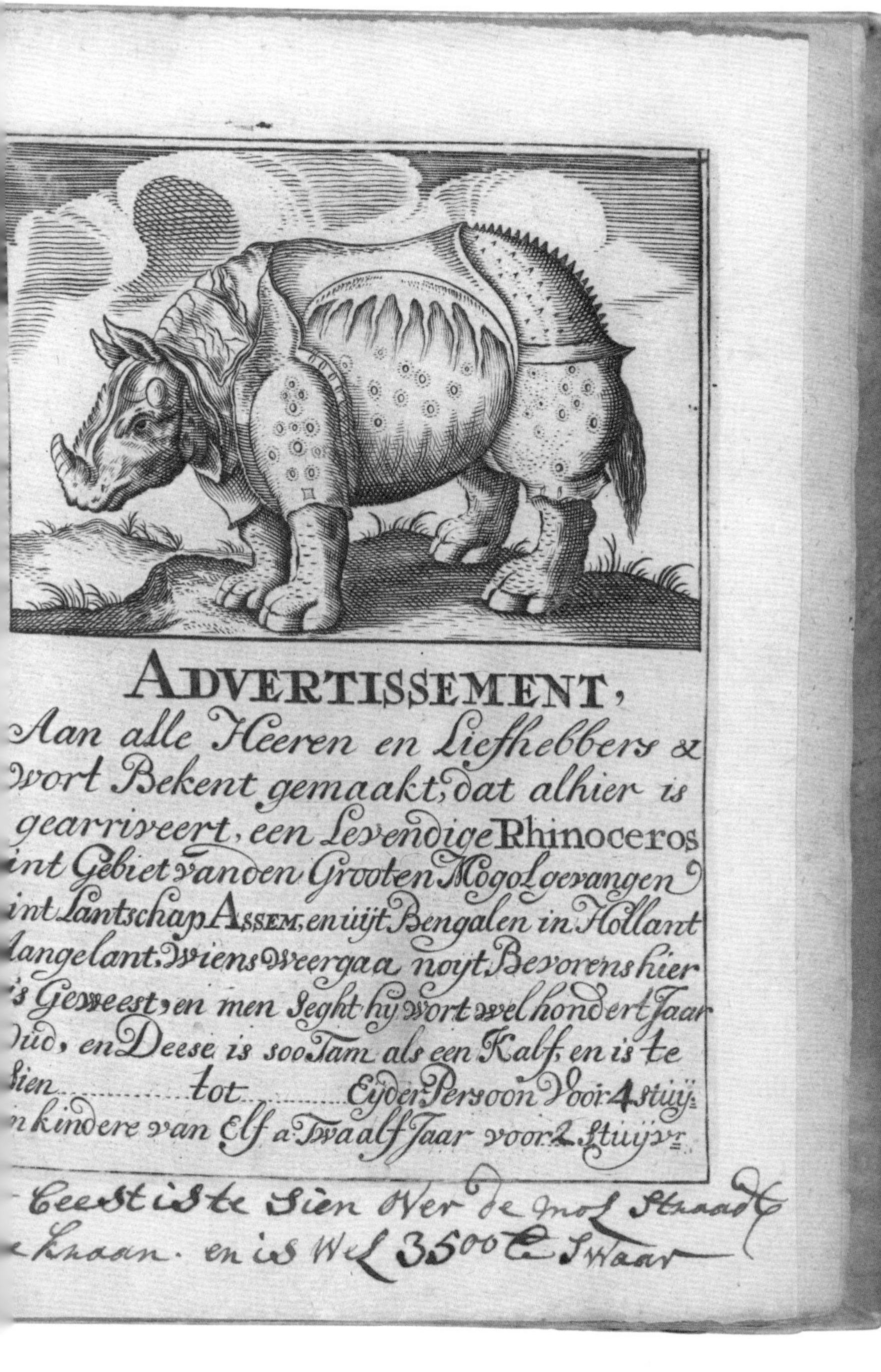

21 'Advertissement' for Clara's exhibition in Middelburg, pasted by Pieter Boddaert into his private album, 1742

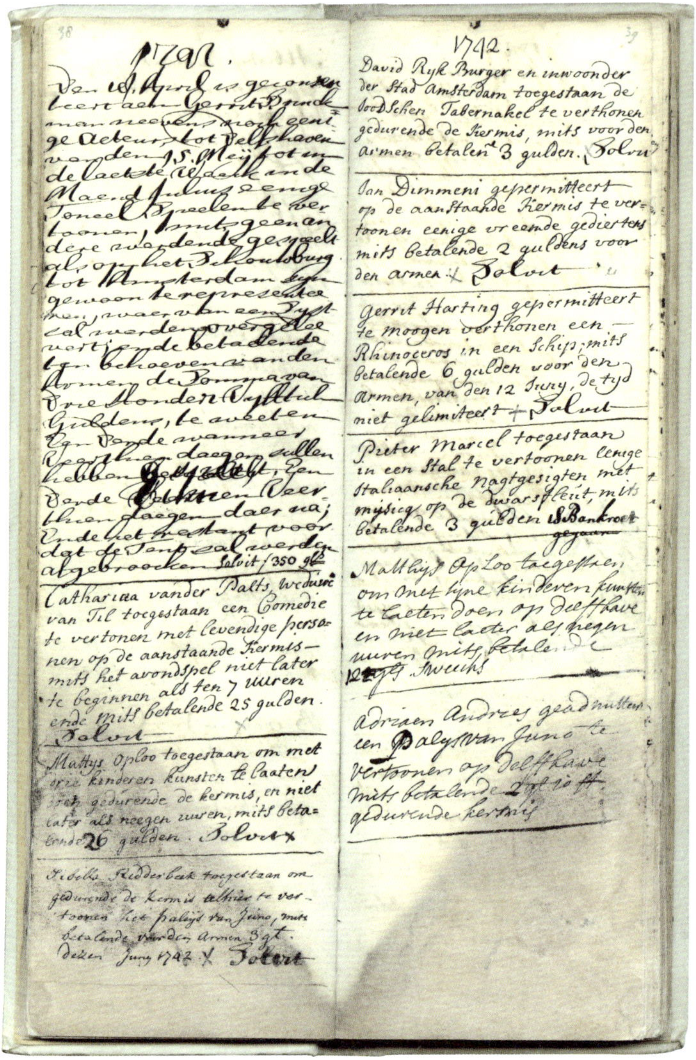

22
Register of licences for activities at the *kermis* in Delft in which Gerrit Harting was given permission to exhibit Clara on a ship

geduurende de Kermis, mits voor den
armen betalende 3 gulden. Solvit

Jan Dimmeni gepermitteert
op de aanstaande Kermis te ver=
toonen eenige vreemde gediertens
mits betalende 2 guldens voor
den armen + Solvit

Gerrit Harting gepermitteert
te moogen verthonen een —
Rhinoceros in een Schip; mits
betalende 6 gulden voor den
armen, van den 12 Juny, de tijd
niet gelimiteert + Solvit

Pieter Marcel toegestaan
in een Stal te vertoonen eenige
Italiaansche Nagtgesigten met
musicq op de dwarsfleuit, mits
betalende 3 gulden 18 Bankroet
gegaan

Matthijs Op Loo toegestaen
om met sijne kinderen konsten
te laeten doen op deesthave
en niet laeter als negen
ueren mits betalende
12 gls. Sweechs

resemblances with animals they knew. They noticed that the rhinoceros had a large head, hooves, tail, sound and rumination (cud-chewing) in common with cattle – particularly oxen – and a fat, sagging body, short legs and lowering of the head in common with pigs. Incidentally, rhinoceroses are not ruminators, they were mistaken there, but the rest of their description confirms that they had studied her closely. An interesting observation was that the keepers rubbed the rhinoceros with cod-liver oil to keep her skin supple, and that for the same reason the animal liked to wallow in mud. Further, they listed the different foodstuffs she ate: hay, apples, bread and especially carrots. But they found it hard to believe that she got through as much as fifty pounds of hay, twenty-five pounds of bread and fourteen buckets of water every day.[52]

It was not Mout who had given the two scientists this information; he was not there, nor in the other cities. In the spring of 1742, after her stay in Leiden, he had given Clara to someone else to look after temporarily. Among those who took over the task would have been Gerrit Harting who in June 1742 had been given permission by the Delft authorities to show her during the kermis [fig. 22]. Mout himself had set off on his fourth trip to Asia on 3 May, this time as captain of the VOC ship the *Goidschalxoord*. He arrived in Batavia (now Jakarta) at the beginning of January 1743, and from there sailed on to Ceylon (now Sri Lanka). It was not until 15 January 1744 that he set sail for the Netherlands again. By the time he returned to Amsterdam at the beginning of August he had been away from home for over two years.[53]

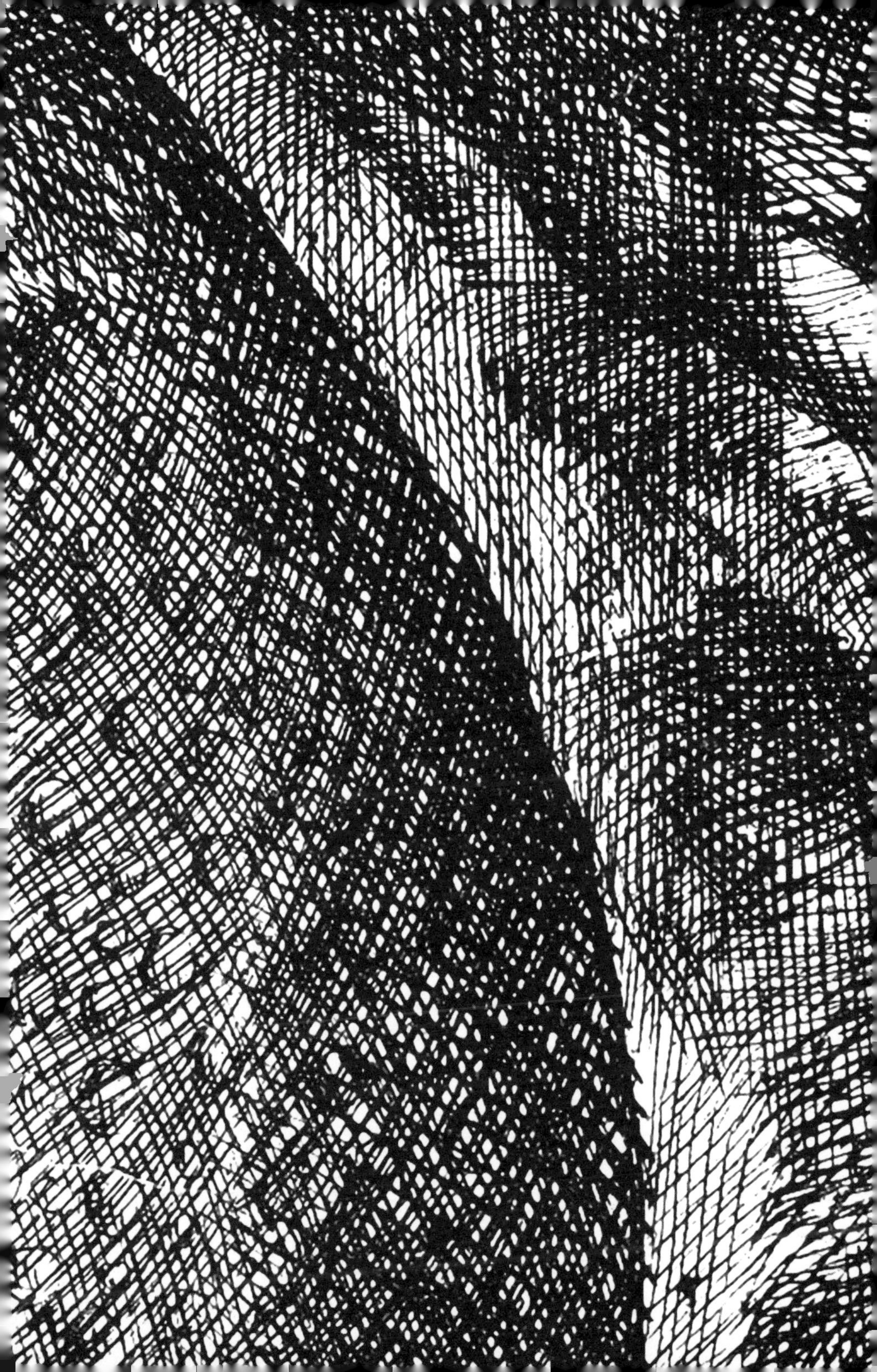

carted from

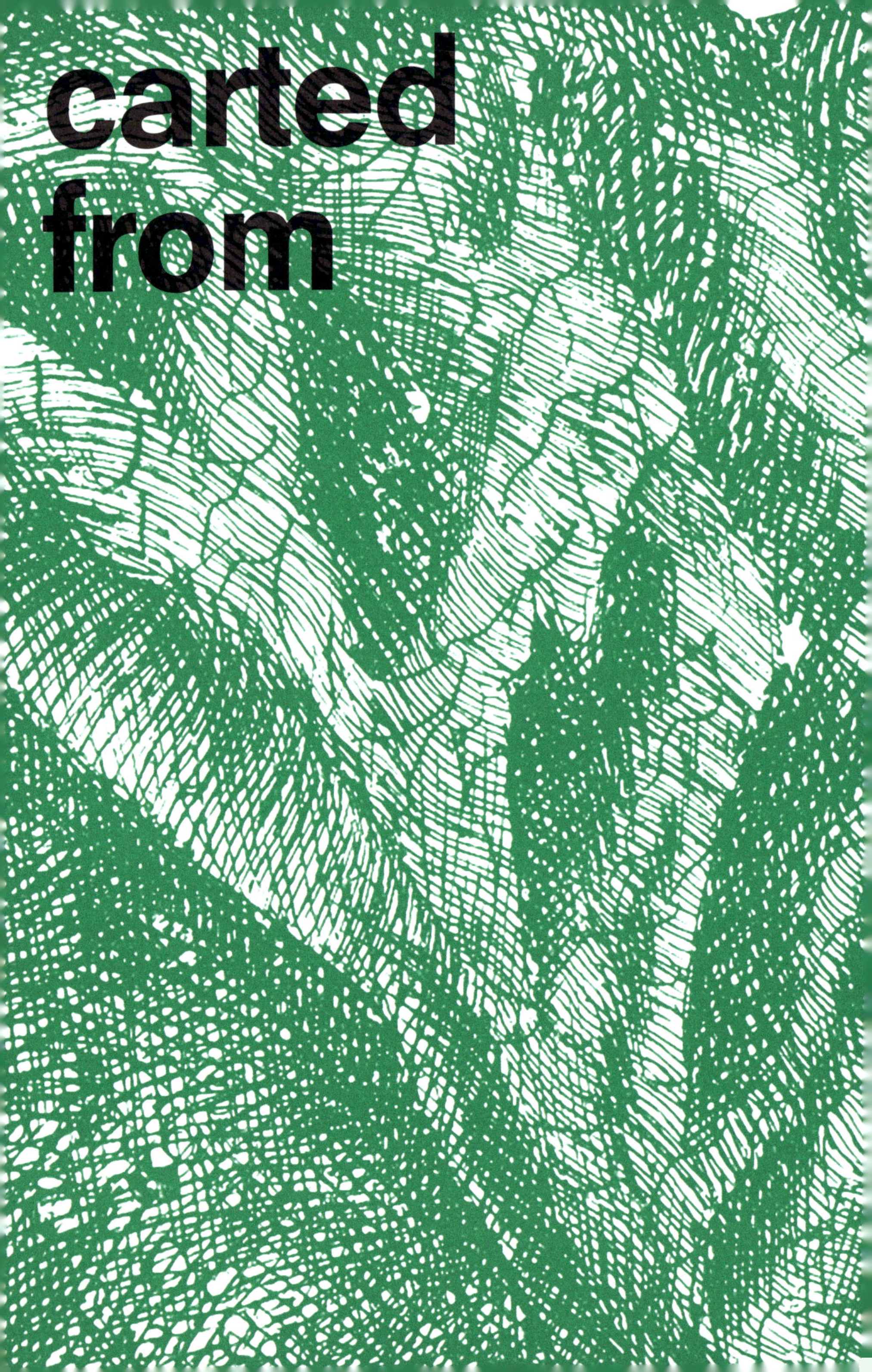

town to town

Mout had used the long voyage to think about his future. Provided Clara was still alive, he would bid the sea farewell. From then on, the rhinoceros would define the course of his life. No doubt he had again stocked up on merchandise to sell at a profit in Amsterdam, money he could now invest in his rhinoceros. Shortly after his return, on 1 October 1744, he took his first major step by buying a large plot of land for 4,500 guilders on the other side of the IJ: the Wilmkebreek [fig. 23]. This deep polder bordered the IJdijk and was known as 'Het Meertje' (the lake). Today it still lies there unspoiled in the middle of Amsterdam Noord.[54] Mout moved there with his family but the most important reason for purchasing this pastureland must have been his rhinoceros. Here Clara had a permanent place where she could graze and roll in the mud, amid the cows which also grazed there. She could even swim in the ditch that surrounded the land. Given these conditions, she could feel reasonably at home here.

The purchase of this tract of land reveals Mout's ambitions, but in order to make any money out of Clara he naturally had to travel again. Mout wanted to show her to the public in as many places in Europe as possible. It would be a long and costly journey, full of risks. For that reason alone the trip had to be well prepared for. His main concern was how to keep Clara alive. How would she get enough to eat and how could she be transported overland without getting hurt? How could she be safely exhibited to inquisitive people? And in which regions and cities could Clara best be shown? To come up with good answers to all these and other questions, Mout was able to draw on his experience over the past three years. In addition, he would have tried to get the people who had helped him with Clara before to join him again. But it remained an exciting undertaking.

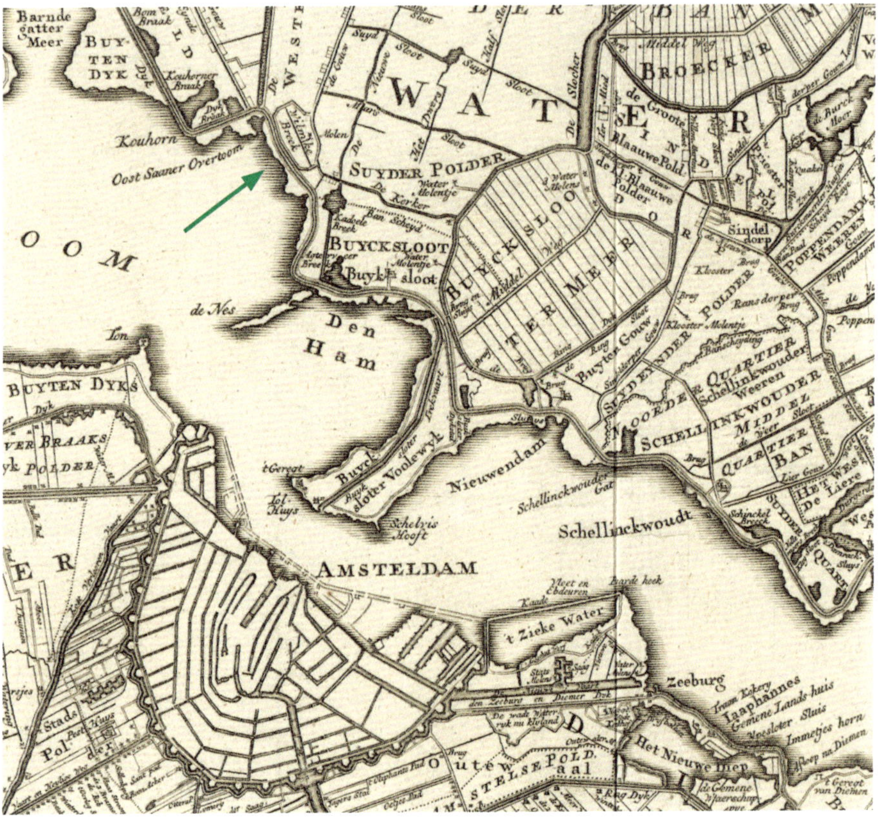

23
Detail from a map of Amsterdam and its environs, with the oval-shaped Wilmkebreek polder to the left on the northern shore of the IJ and to the right the village of Nieuwendam, in or after 1749

The idea was to travel from city to city and show Clara wherever possible. By then Mout realized that he needed a wagon to be able to do this. The elephants that had previously been exhibited in Europe had walked the whole way, but that was out of the question with a rhinoceros. What would happen, Mout himself had warned, if the animal 'tame as it is, noticed it were free and, following its instinct, went wild?' A hundred or even two hundred men would not be able to hold the powerful animal. Also, he was convinced that it was not in the character of these animals to allow themselves to be tethered.[55]

For this reason, Mout had a vehicle built that was strong and robust enough to sustain the weight of this heavy, ever-growing animal that now weighed almost 2,500 kilos while travelling over innumerable bumpy and poorly surfaced roads. He decided on a completely covered wagon – in effect a wooden box on large wheels – so that Clara would be spared curious looks on the way and the journey would not needlessly be held up. Several small hatches ensured that it was not completely dark inside and that fresh air could enter. During the journey Clara stood facing forward, although the wagon was probably wide enough for her to lie down in. Often eight to ten horses or oxen, and occasionally even more, were needed to pull it, especially when they were driving across hilly or mountainous terrain. Given the number of days it took to get from Dresden to Leipzig in April 1747, they would be able to cover some twenty-five to thirty kilometres a day.[56] In the end, the whole tour was to last so long, and the distances they had to cover were so great, that one or more replacement wagons were made [figs. 32, 40].[57]

Mout was not the only person who travelled with Clara. At least two or three men were required to restrain and tend to her, to drive the horses and oxen pulling the wagon, and to arrange her shows. A promotional poster from 1746 states that Mout had as many as ten assistants. It is not known who they were; they are generally referred to as 'those who show the rhinoceros', but Gerrit Harting, who had previously stood in for Mout in 1742, may well have been one. Now and then, one of the assistants is mentioned in passing, though without being named. For instance, a Parisian described how Clara licked the face of one of the assistants guarding her with her thin and sensitive tongue, and in 1753 the bon-viveur Giacomo Casanova encountered a large, tanned man, clad in what he described as 'African dress', guarding the entrance to Clara's tent. In several images one or two are visible: someone pouring water into a tub, a boy with a whip in his hand keeping Clara in check, and a fairly short, elegantly dressed man in a red jacket, a three-cornered hat on his head – no doubt Mout himself [see fig. 40].[58]

It is quite possible that his family, or in any case one or two of his sons, accompanied him for all or part of the tour. His eldest, Jan, was twelve years old in 1745, an age when he would have made a good assistant.

Like many travelling artists and other owners of exotic animals, Mout endeavoured to arrange his trip so that he could attend important *kermissen* and fairs and other events that attracted big crowds. These became the main stopping points on the tour. Clara was then on show there for several weeks or sometimes months on end, whereas in other places where the attendance was expected to be lower she might be exhibited for only a few days. The weather occasionally upset their plans and Clara had to stay on longer in a place than was intended. Even before setting out on their grand tour, the brutal winter weather in Groningen at the start of 1745 held the group up in the city for as long as two months, instead of a week. And in September 1746 heavy rainfall prevented Clara from leaving Breslau, where she had been on display for weeks, as the roads had become impassable. Improvisation was all part of the game. At times Clara even had to get out of her wagon in order to proceed, as in March 1747 when the ferry over the River Regen could not take her weight as well as that of her vehicle. She then swam to the other side by herself, though not until she had 'happily bathed in the river for a while' – one of the rare descriptions of what happened during the trip.[59]

Besides *kermissen* and fairs, Mout did his utmost to show his rhinoceros at the courts. Royal and aristocratic interest was not only good for Clara's reputation, but also for Mout's wallet. If Clara satisfied their often high expectations, her owner could expect a rich reward. For this reason, whenever a king, elector, duke or other person of nobility resided in a city, Mout ensured that Clara visited the court or the court came to Clara.

When the group arrived somewhere, Mout and his team lowered the wagon slightly with the aid of small gears, and then led Clara out backwards over wooden planks. She was usually allocated a spot in the marketplace among the many stalls or else just outside the city gates near an inn, places where lots of people came. Sometimes she was kept indoors, in a stable or, as in Hanover, in the Ballhof, a theatre where exotic animals were regularly exhibited.[60] She was often accommodated in a wooden hut or in a tent, but wherever she was housed, she was always kept in a strong wooden enclosure, separated from the public that came to look at her. Otherwise, it was far too dangerous.

Mout announced Clara's arrival in advance, for he first had to apply for permission from the local authorities to show her for money.

To arrange this, he sent one of his assistants on ahead or submitted an official request weeks beforehand. Often the city authorities imposed certain conditions before coming to a positive decision. In Graz, for instance, Mout was told he was not allowed to make any music or noise, but in most cases, like other travelling exhibits and theatremakers, he was obliged to donate a percentage of his earnings to organizations supporting the city's poor and needy. This might be a quarter of the money he received, sometimes even more. In addition, Mout was told exactly where he could show the rhinoceros.[61]

Clara was usually on display between eight o'clock in the morning and twelve noon and, after a break in the afternoon, until about six or seven in the evening. Mout sold three different entrance tickets so that not only people who were well off but also those of limited means could come and see her. The upper classes were invariably invited to pay whatever they thought it was worth, but of course that had to be more than the highest amount paid by the other visitors.[62]

There she stood, ready to show herself. An elephant can learn tricks to entertain the audience, a lion can be highly active and startle the audience with its loud roar, but a rhinoceros cannot really do anything. The reality is that a rhinoceros mainly stands or lies down. She is above all herself. Large. Heavy. Different. If there was any action at all, it was when she ate or drank: always water, hay and bread, supplemented by fruit, vegetables, leafy twigs and 'anything you give her except fish and meat'. And then she promptly expelled it all in large quantities. A Frenchman was one of several visitors to remark that she liked beer and wine and enjoyed the tobacco smoke the keepers blew into her nostrils and mouth. Sometimes she made a noise, but according to the same Frenchman it sounded like a cow puffing and was therefore not very impressive.[63]

Even though Clara could *do* very little, she was of course something very special: a totally alien creature, a wonder beast, the like of which 'has never been seen here before.'[64] The very fact that such a creature existed was incredible in itself. Whenever Mout promoted Clara, in newspaper advertisements or in his poster-like prints, which he also sold as souvenirs, he began by explaining what she ate and drank every day, how heavy and enormous she was, that she could run fast and could swim and dive like duck, and that she was still very young but could live to be a hundred or a hundred and fifty. To make it more exciting he often added that the rhinoceros was the natural enemy of the elephant – Pliny's well-known story – and that some even believed that this animal was the behemoth from the biblical Book of Job.

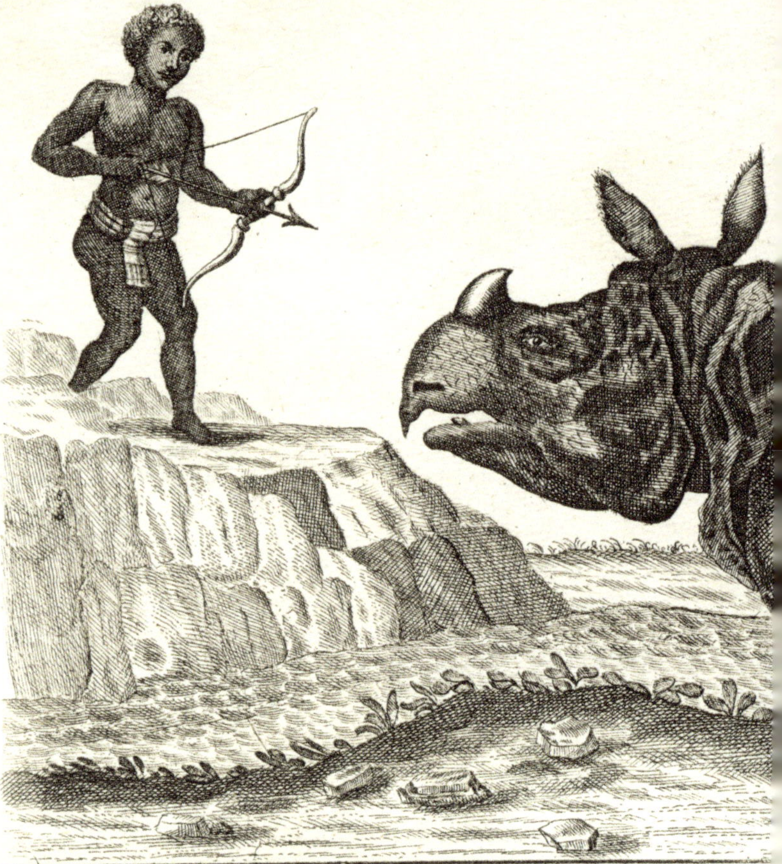

Wahre Abbildung von einem lebendigen Rhinoceros oder Nashorn,
aus Bengalen in Holland übergebracht, und in Asia im Gebiet des Grossen
Meinung der Behemoth, wovon gedacht wird im Buch Hiob am 40. v. 10. dieses
100. Jahre alt werden. Es wieget anjetzo beinahe 5000. Pfund schwer, ist di
Härlein; auf der Nase hat es sein Horn, womit es die Erde sehr geschwinde um
sein Kopf nach und nach forne spitz, die Ohren gleich eines Esels, die Augen na
sie mit Schilden gedeckt sey, dieselben schlagen eine handbreit übereinander hi
grosser Feind von dem Elephanten, so, das wenn es ihn antrift, denselben mit seiner
60 Pfund Heu und 20. Pfund Brod, und trinket 14 Eimer Wasser, und wei
Es hat dieses Thier, wie es gar jung gewesen, 2 Jahr in denen Zimmern um

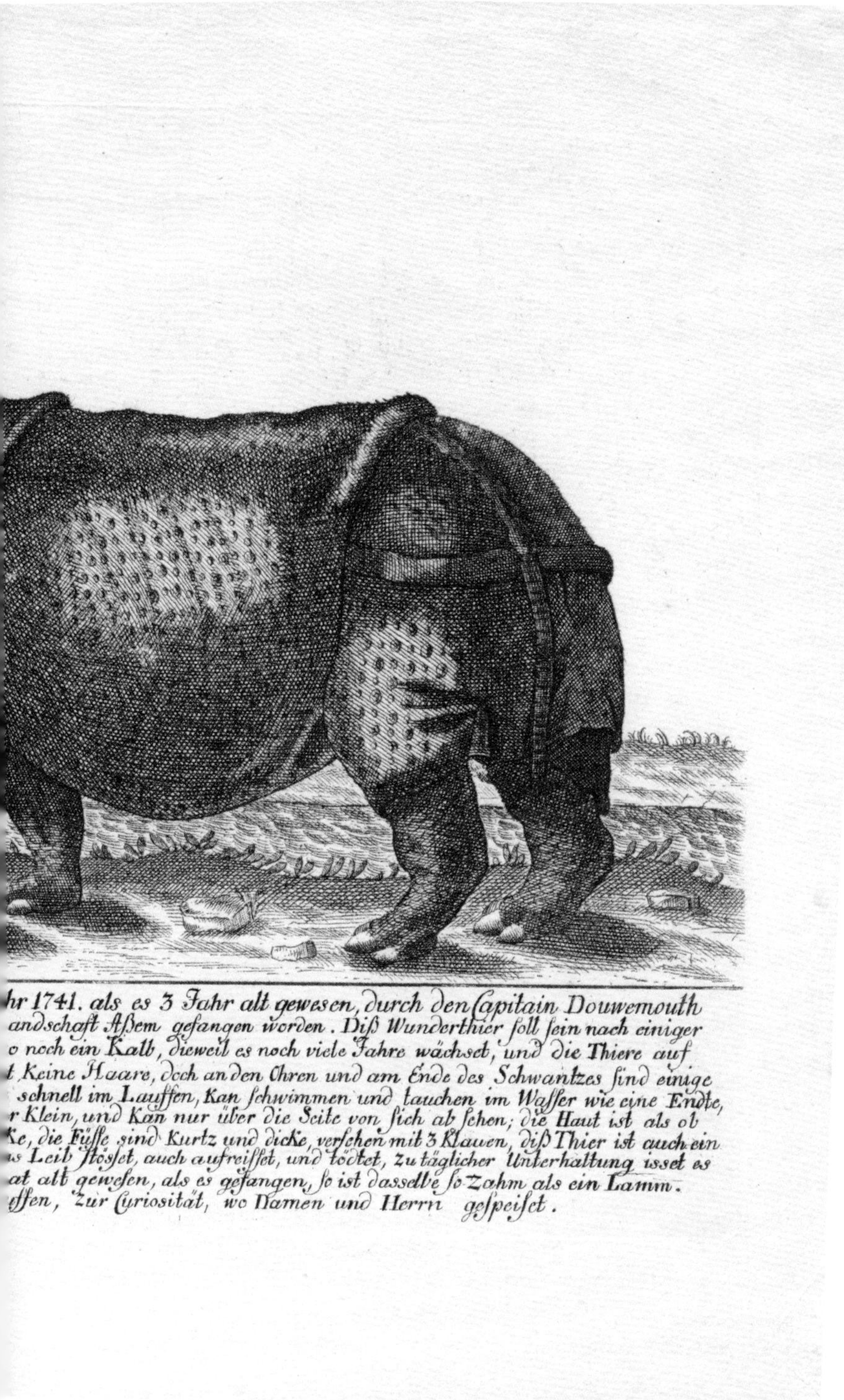

24

Small-format poster advertising the exhibition of Clara, with a Black man holding a bow and arrow in front of her, c. 1745–1746

That mighty animal, which no-one really knows very much about, is described in the Book of Job as ranking 'first among the works of God' which 'only its Maker can approach ... with his sword'. 'Would a man have the hardihood to try to confront it before its eyes and try to pierce its nose with a hook? Who can stand eye in eye with him and put a ring through his nose? ... Lay your hand on it; you will remember the battle and never do it again.'[65] And now everyone had a chance to see such a terrifying creature with their own eyes! At the same time, Mout told them reassuringly that this particular animal was not wild at all but had been tamed and had grown up among people from a very early age and was therefore as docile as a lamb and as gentle as a tender dove 'if it was permitted to use that term'.[66]

Those who were willing to pay more were allowed to come closer and touch her. 'She tolerates people's caresses and seems to see all those who look at her as benefactors, not as enemies,' one of them noted. And yet it struck people that the keeper made sure he himself stayed outside the enclosure until, after reassuring words, the animal lay down on her side and stretched her legs. For there had indeed been occasions when she had become restless and even aggressive, for instance, when it was very busy and when she had been touched too much and too roughly.[67]

Prior to the tour Mout had had a good stock of engravings of Clara printed in various formats.[68] 'True Picture of a living Rhinoceros or "Nosehorn"' one of them reads [fig. 24]. She is always portrayed at full length. She stands firmly on all fours, her ears pricked, her head held up straight, her mouth open, her horn clearly visible, though comparatively small in the initial prints. In most she is set in a hilly landscape with a few palm trees, and alongside her a Black man with a bow and arrow, an 'Indian', allusions to the animal's exotic origins. Some prints have a fairly extensive text in German, others a shorter one in four languages. In all of them Mout is credited as the owner, although his name is often corrupted to Douwemout and even Douwemouth. They were popular and sold so rapidly that Mout regularly had to have new versions printed. Sometimes the demand was so great, as in Braunschweig early in 1746, that local printers had new editions engraved on their own initiative based on an existing print after Clara's departure [fig. 25].[69]

In one of the prints from the early days of the tour the rhinoceros is shown standing on a paved quay with a ship at sea in the background [fig. 26]. To her left a man holds up a large wine glass to her and as in a comic, a speech bubble reproduces what he says: 'Here, Clar, this is for you!'[70] She is addressed by her name, something that rarely

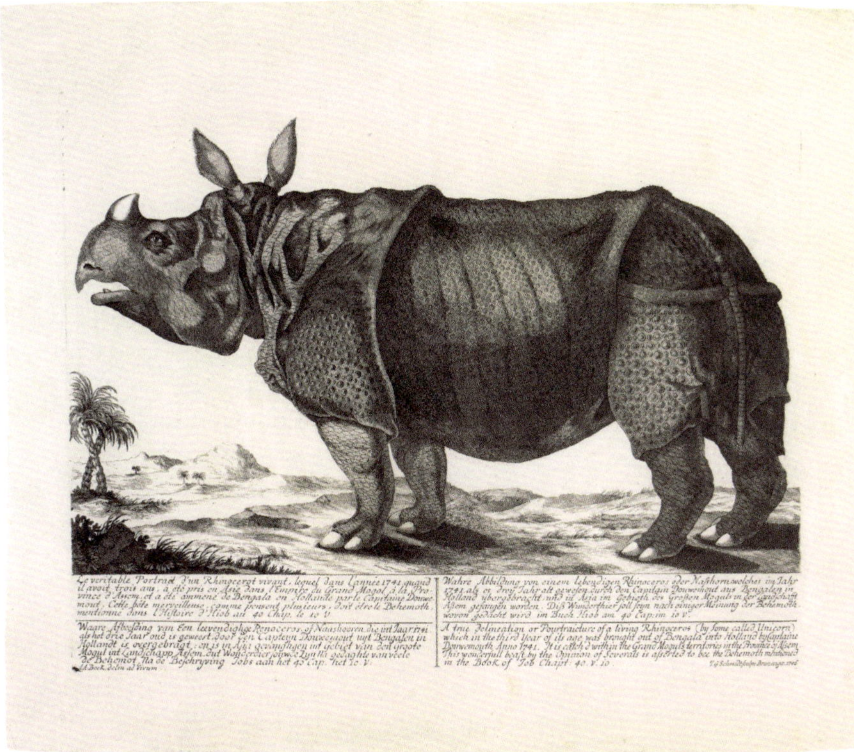

25

Print of Clara with text in four languages, published on the occasion of Clara's stay in Braunschweig, A.A. Beck and J.G. Schmidt, 1746

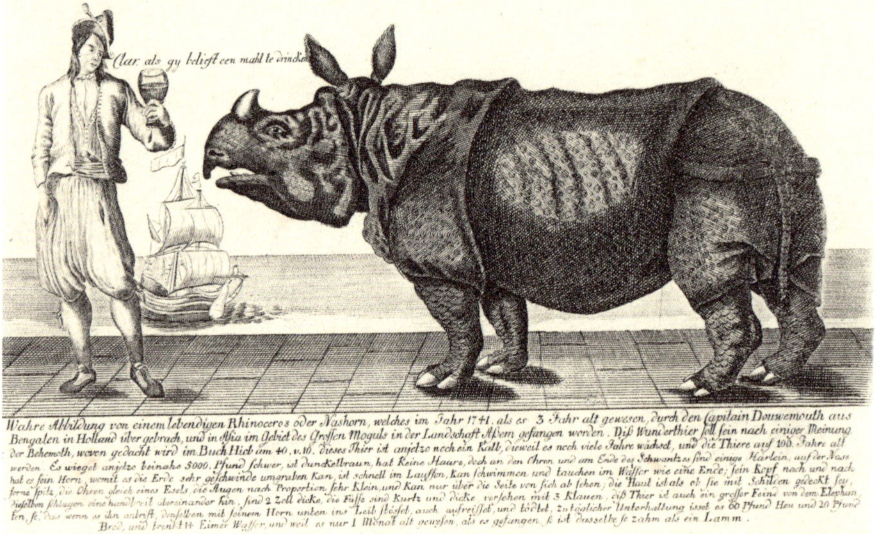

26
Promotional print and souvenir in which the rhinoceros is addressed as Clara and offered a glass of wine, c. 1746

occurred in print: neither in newspapers, advertising posters and other printed matter, nor in scientific papers and descriptions, and hardly ever in drawings. With one exception: a drawing that was made in Würzburg in October 1748. The inscription explains that this rhinoceros was addressed as 'Jungfer Clara' – Miss Clara [fig. 27].[71] Apart from these two instances, there are no other known cases, and although this may not be conclusive, it does seem that the general public never called her by her name during her travels. Most visitors would not have regarded her as an individual. It is much more likely that only Mout and his associates called her by her name and she may well have answered to it. After all they were with her all day, spoke to her constantly, and had to ensure that she stayed or became calm. Year in, year out.

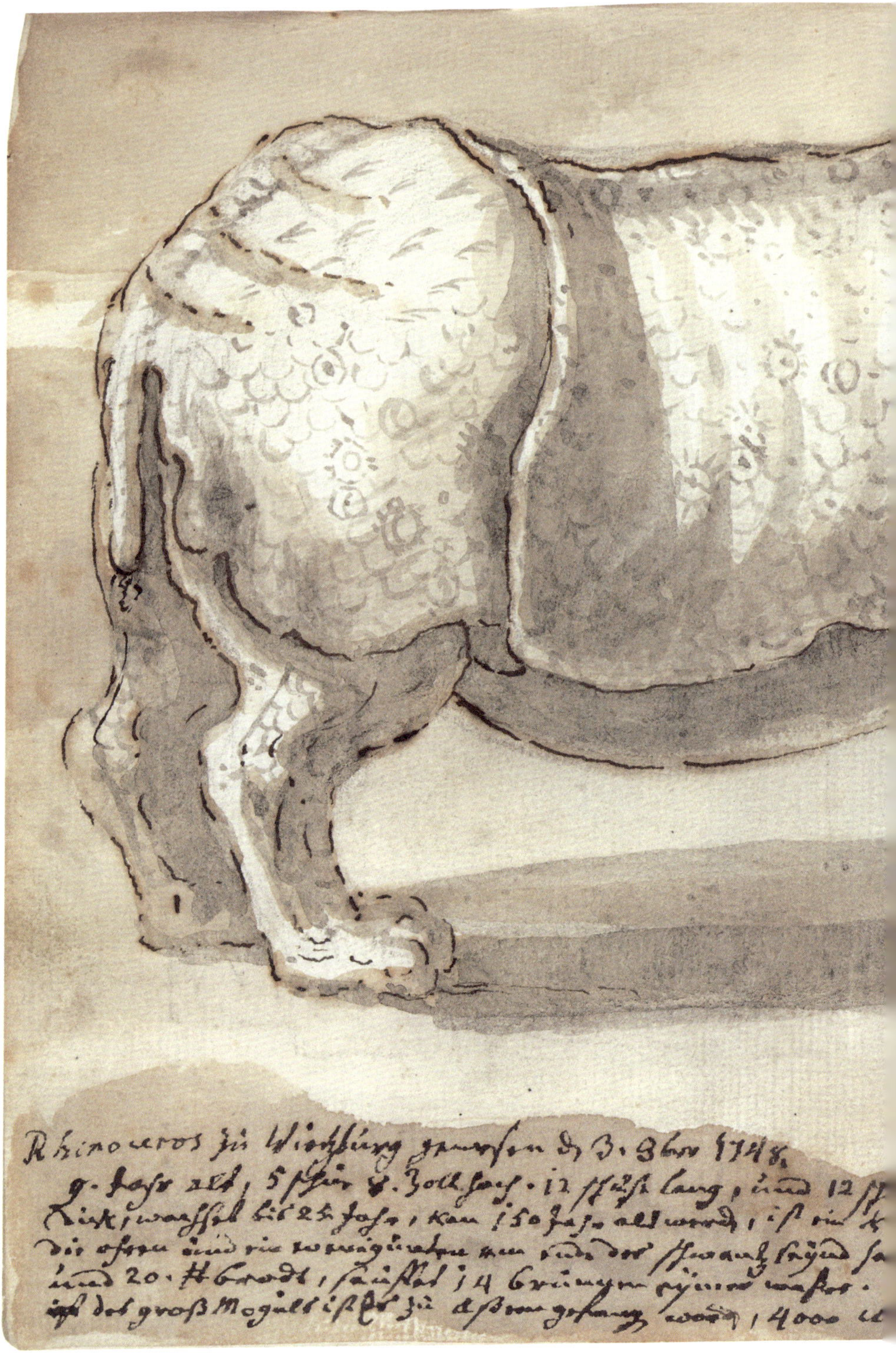
Rhinoceros zu Würtzburg gewesen d. 3. 9bre 1748.
9. Jahr alt, 5 Schu 8. Zoll hoch. 12 Schuh lang, und 12 …

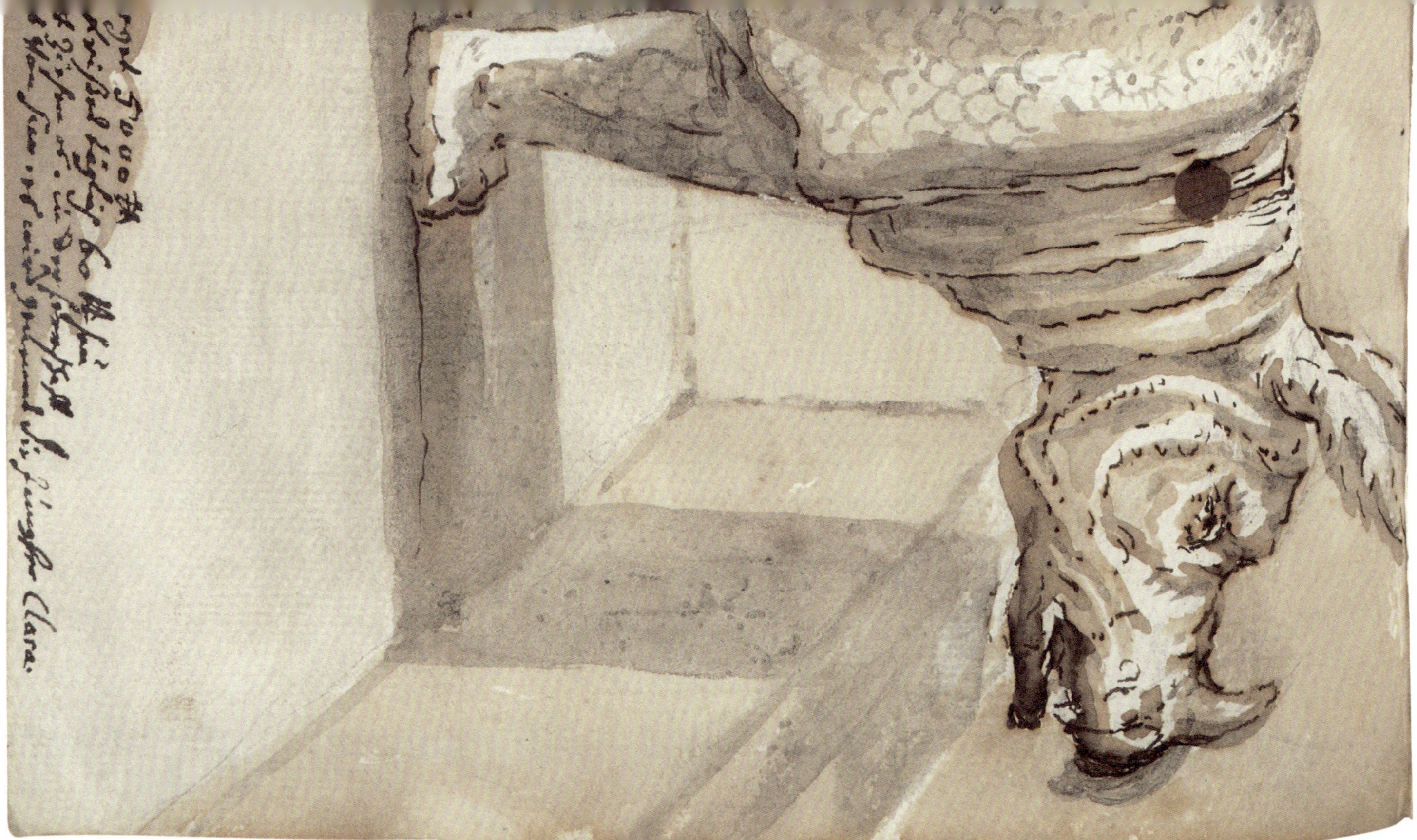

27

Clara in Würzburg, with an inscription in which she is referred to as 'Miss Clara' ('Jungfer Clara') at the end, Anton Clemens Lünenschloss, 3 October 1748

sensation

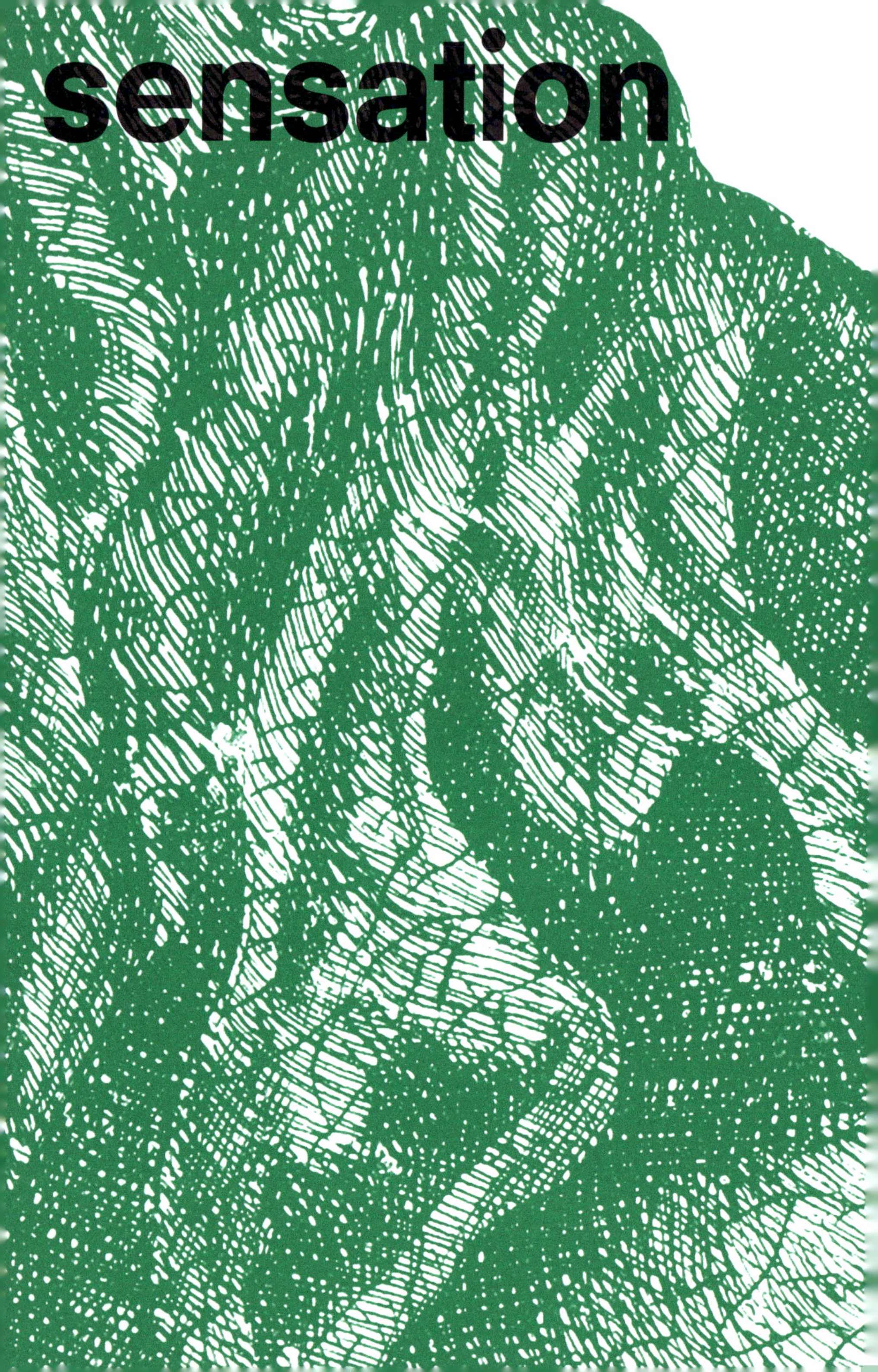

in europe

For six successive years Clara was hauled around Europe during her first grand tour. She criss-crossed virtually every country of the continent: an empire, great kingdoms, small princedoms, city states, republics. She crossed mountain ranges in her wagon: the Alps, the Apennines, the Vosges, the Seven Mountains (*Siebengebirge*). She travelled through the valleys of the Danube, Rhine and Rhône, and crossed countless major and minor rivers. She was hoisted onto a ship and put out to sea again. And everywhere she went, at the end of a day's travelling she found herself in another place: in capital cities and trading centres, in university cities and ports, in small sleepy towns and now and then even in villages [map, pp. 90–91].

And it all began in Hooksiel. For it was this tiny seaport in East Frisia that Mout had chosen as his departure point in the course of 1745. Why? Perhaps because Hooksiel was fairly easy to reach by ship from Amsterdam, although that applied equally to other ports on the North German coast. Perhaps he knew someone from the village who had sailed under him on a VOC ship – young men from this region regularly signed up as sailors in Amsterdam. It may have been that his father, his elder brother Jan or one of his seafaring cousins, all well acquainted with this area, had recommended the port. The fact that the village was the outport of the small town of Jever, some ten kilometres inland, may also have been a contributing factor. Clara was on show in Hooksiel for a few weeks and immediately attracted a large number of visitors, to whom Mout sold his first new prints with her portrait. Anton Clasen, the Jever town clerk, was one of those who had bought a print as a souvenir. Years later he looked back on this special event in his writings and copied the passage from it about a rhinoceros that weighed almost 5,000 pounds. Only the earlier promotional prints referred to Clara's weight in this way; in later advertising the word 'almost' has been omitted. But Clara was a long way away from Hooksiel by then.[72]

From this East Frisian port Mout continued into Germany with Clara in her wagon. First they called on the important court capital of Hanover, and from there in February 1746 travelled on to the annual

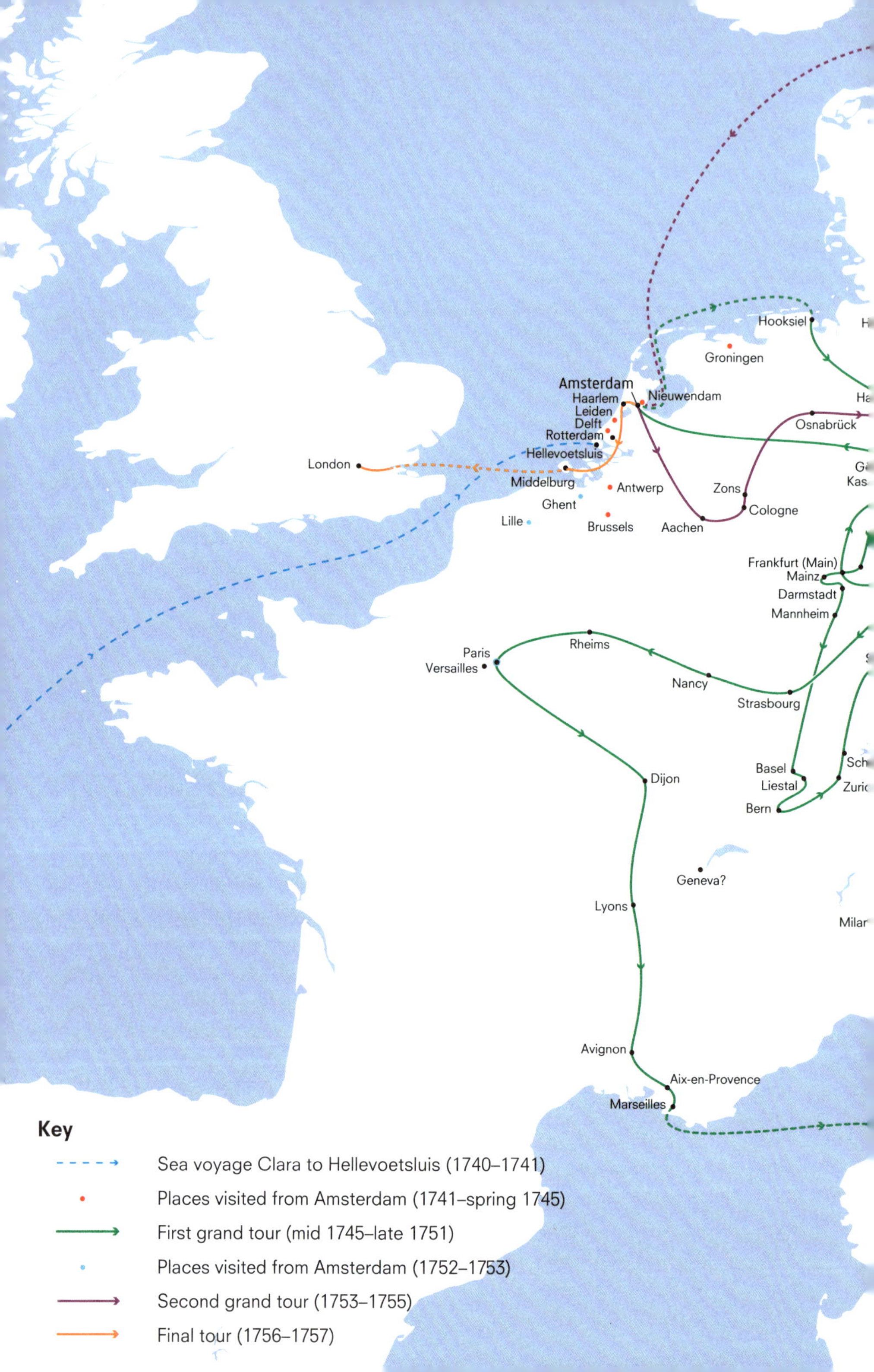
Amsterdam
Nieuwendam
Haarlem
Leiden
Delft
Rotterdam
Hellevoetsluis
London
Middelburg
Antwerp
Ghent
Lille
Brussels
Aachen
Zons
Cologne
Osnabrück
Hooksiel
Groningen
Frankfurt (Main)
Mainz
Darmstadt
Mannheim
Paris
Versailles
Rheims
Nancy
Strasbourg
Basel
Liestal
Bern
Dijon
Geneva?
Lyons
Avignon
Aix-en-Provence
Marseilles
Key
Sea voyage Clara to Hellevoetsluis (1740–1741)
Places visited from Amsterdam (1741–spring 1745)
First grand tour (mid 1745–late 1751)
Places visited from Amsterdam (1752–1753)
Second grand tour (1753–1755)
Final tour (1756–1757)

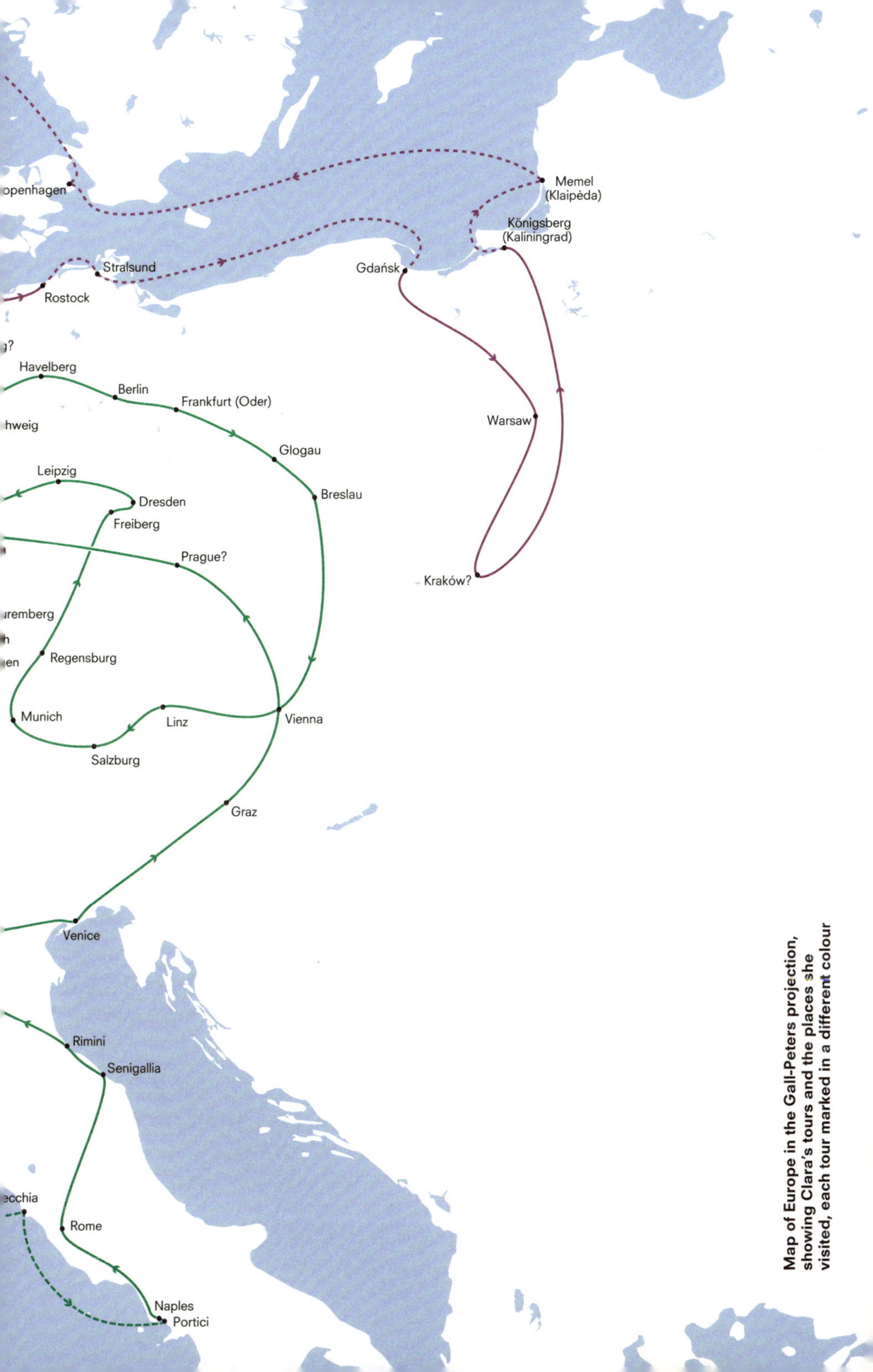

Map of Europe in the Gall-Peters projection, showing Clara's tours and the places she visited, each tour marked in a different colour

winter fair in neighbouring Braunschweig. Fortune smiled on Mout from that moment. For a peace treaty signed in Dresden on 25 December 1745 had put an end to the war that had been waging for years between Prussia, Austria and Saxony, and it was now possible to travel east and on to Berlin, the prosperous capital of the Kingdom of Prussia. Here in April the king himself, Frederick the Great, visited Clara's stable. She was installed in the centre of the city in Spittelmarkt, next to a fish stall, which was handy for the fish oil which was regularly rubbed into her skin to stop her from drying out. The visit earned Mout not only 18 gold ducats (approximately a thousand euros today) but also a pass allowing him to travel freely with Clara all over the Prussian kingdom and to exhibit her for money free of tax or other levies.[73] Above all, the distinguished visitor clearly shows that Clara had instantly become famous. Once this powerful king had honoured her with a visit to her stable, others were eager to follow suit, not just in Berlin, but in every town and city she visited, including Frankfurt an der Oder and Breslau (now Wrocław), the capital of Silesia, which Frederick had won from the Austrian emperor five years before.

A new triumph soon awaited Mout and Clara in Vienna. On 30 October Clara rolled into the city in her wagon drawn by eight horses and escorted by eight cuirassiers. There she was allocated a place in one of the large squares, the Freyung, once more amid the market stalls. A few days later, on 5 November, she was graced with a visit of the highest possible rank: Empress Maria Theresa and her husband Emperor Francis I had come to the city with a large retinue from their palace of Schönbrunn specially to see Clara, thereby following the example of Maria's great rival Frederick the Great in Berlin.

Mout no doubt earned a handsome sum this time, too. Moreover, everything suggests that he was again given a pass enabling him to show his rhinoceros all over the empire unhampered by restrictions and at no extra cost. But he received the most distinguished award on 1 January 1747, when the emperor officially ennobled him. Oddly, in the lengthy citation that specified the grounds for the honour, there is not a single reference to Clara. Instead, Mout's maritime qualities were praised above all else, his greatest achievement being wildly exaggerated as his having twice sailed round the world. Equally puzzling is the coat of arms that Mout had the right to use as a brand-new nobleman: instead of a rhinoceros, it features a dromedary [fig. 28]. Further, it includes a Black man with a bow and arrow (as occasionally depicted in prints of Clara), an American 'savage' and a seascape. Incidentally, there is no evidence that Mout ever used the coat of arms, but he certainly adopted his newly acquired noble surname. From

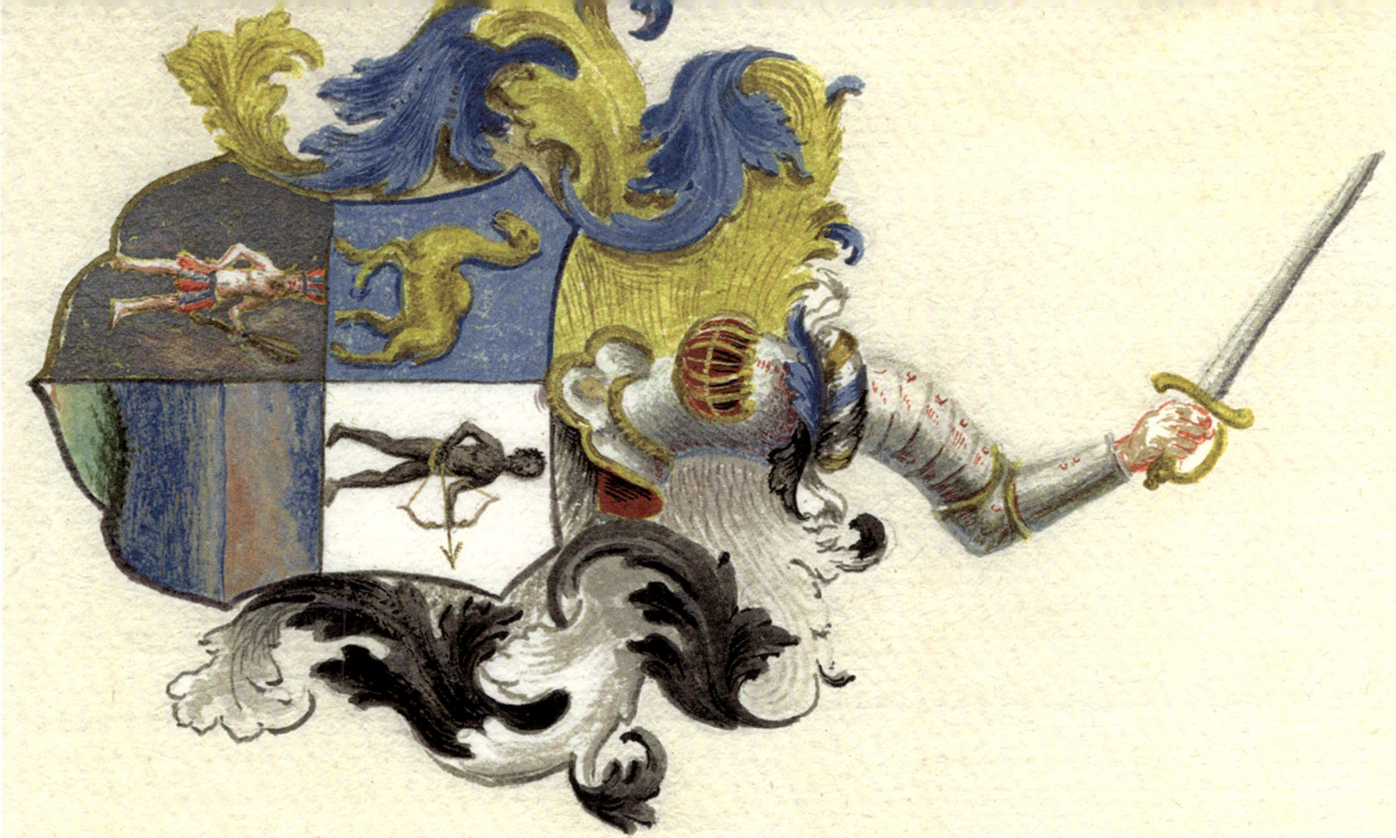

28

Douwe Mout's coat of arms as a member of the Austrian nobility, forming part of his official request for ennoblement, 1747

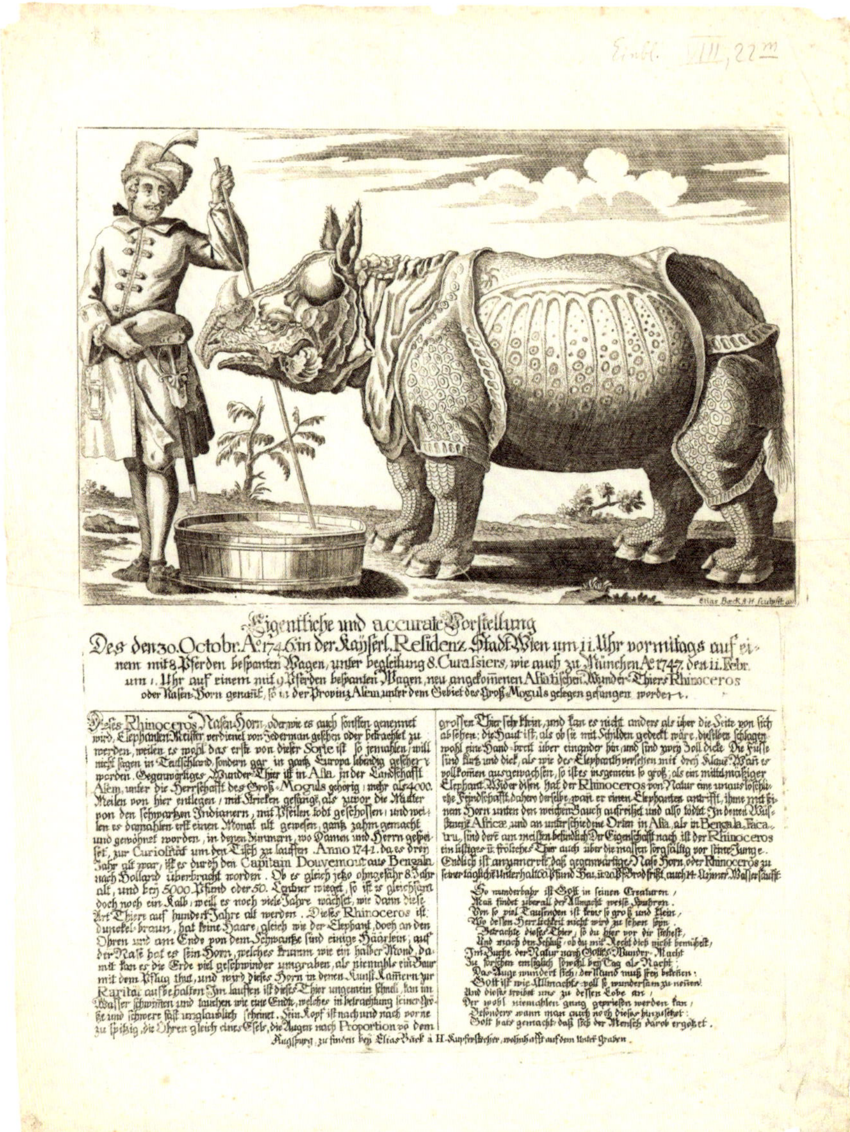

29
Clara on display in Vienna, depicted as a cross between herself and Dürer's rhinoceros, Elias Bäck, 1746

then on, he referred to himself as Mout van der Meer, and not only he, but also his wife, children and their offspring now had the right to use this name. The noble addition 'Van der Meer' alluded to his country estate Wilmkebreek facing Amsterdam, known as 'Het Meertje'. At the same time, for the outside world Mout changed his Frisian Christian name Douwe to the international name David and adopted the title of captain, in reference to his appointment as captain of the *Knappenhof* and the *Goidschalxoord* and to the official grounds for his ennoblement.[74]

By then, Clara was the talk of the town in Vienna. Just how much attention she received during the weeks she stayed there can best be gauged from the prints which various printers and publishers brought out. Visitors could choose between black-and-white or hand-coloured portraits of Clara, although they were not a very good likeness. For one reason or another, the depicted rhinoceros is a curious cross between Clara herself and the well-known Dürer rhinoceros [fig. 29].[75]

It was not until the beginning of January 1747 that Mout left the city with Clara, considerably richer for his many experiences and greatly elevated in status. They arrived in Munich on 11 February 1747 via Salzburg and other towns. For his visit to Munich Mout had had woodcuts specially made that featured the name of the city for the first time. 'Es wird allen Liebhabern in München kund gethan' it reads in bold type at the top: 'All interested parties in Munich are informed' that the rhinoceros can be visited. Like all the existing smaller and larger copper engravings, these prints were on sale as souvenirs, but priced at one Groschen, this simple print, which included a fairly extensive text, was considerably cheaper. Mout was also to have similar affordable prints made for other cities, including Regensburg in March, and Leipzig in April.[76]

Before calling on Leipzig though, Clara was first shown in Dresden, the capital of Saxony. This meant making a detour from Regensburg, but the opportunity to show Clara to the court of the richest and most powerful elector Frederick August II made it worthwhile. After a fortnight in the city, Mout had the rhinoceros specially driven out to the palace to show her to the elector and his household.[77] In Leipzig she formed one of the attractions at the famous and well-attended Easter Fair. People were accustomed to seeing exotic animals and unusual shows here, but the city council thought the visit of the rhinoceros so special that it decided to exempt Mout from the customary stallage.[78] As a special attraction Clara was measured here on 1 May. She turned out to be 5 foot and 7 'thumbs' high, 12 foot long and 12 foot wide, which roughly comes to a height of over 1.70 metres and a length and width of approximately 3.60 metres.[79]

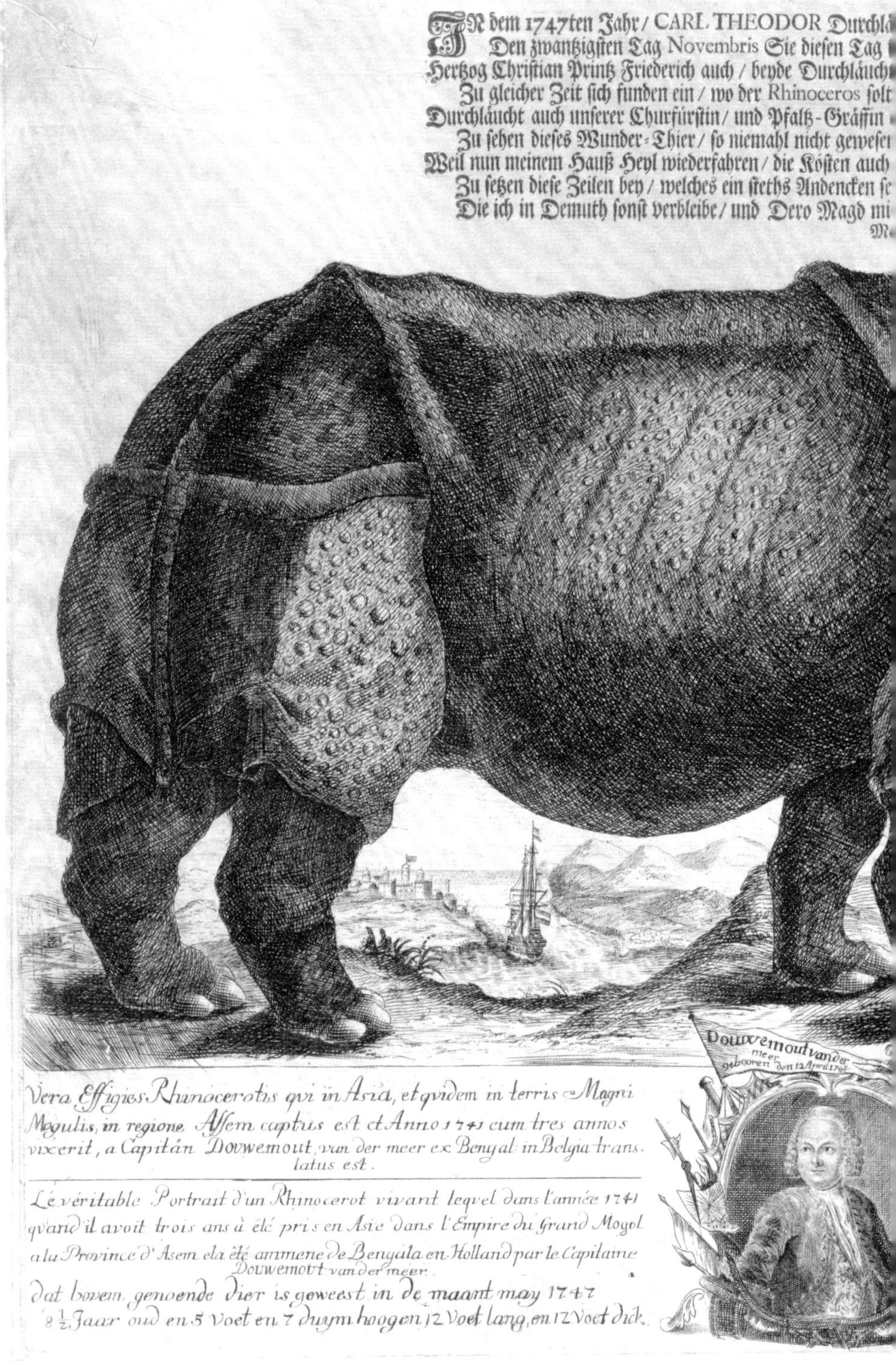
In dem 1747ten Jahr / CARL THEODOR Durchlä
Den zwantzigsten Tag Novembris Sie diesen Tag
Hertzog Christian Printz Friederich auch / beyde Durchläuch
Zu gleicher Zeit sich funden ein / wo der Rhinoceros solt
Durchläucht auch unserer Churfürstin / und Pfaltz-Gräffin
Zu sehen dieses Wunder-Thier / so niemahl nicht geweser
Weil nun meinem Hauß Heyl wiederfahren / die Kösten auch
Zu setzen diese Zeilen bey / welches ein steths Andencken se
Die ich in Demuth sonst verbleibe / und Dero Magd mi
Douwemout van der meer
Vera Effigies Rhinocerotis qui in Asia, et quidem in terris Magni Mogulis, in regione Assem captus est et Anno 1741 cum tres annos vixerit, a Capitan Douwemout van der meer ex Bengal: in Belgia translatus est.
Le véritable Portrait d'un Rhinocerot vivant lequel dans l'année 1741 quand il avoit trois ans à été pris en Asie dans l'Empire du Grand Mogol a la Province d'Asem ela été ammene de Bengala en Holland par le Capitaine Douwemout van der meer.
dat bovem genoemde dier is geweest in de maant may 1747
8 1/2 Jaar oud en 5 Voet en 7 duym hoogen 12 Voet lang, en 12 Voet dick.

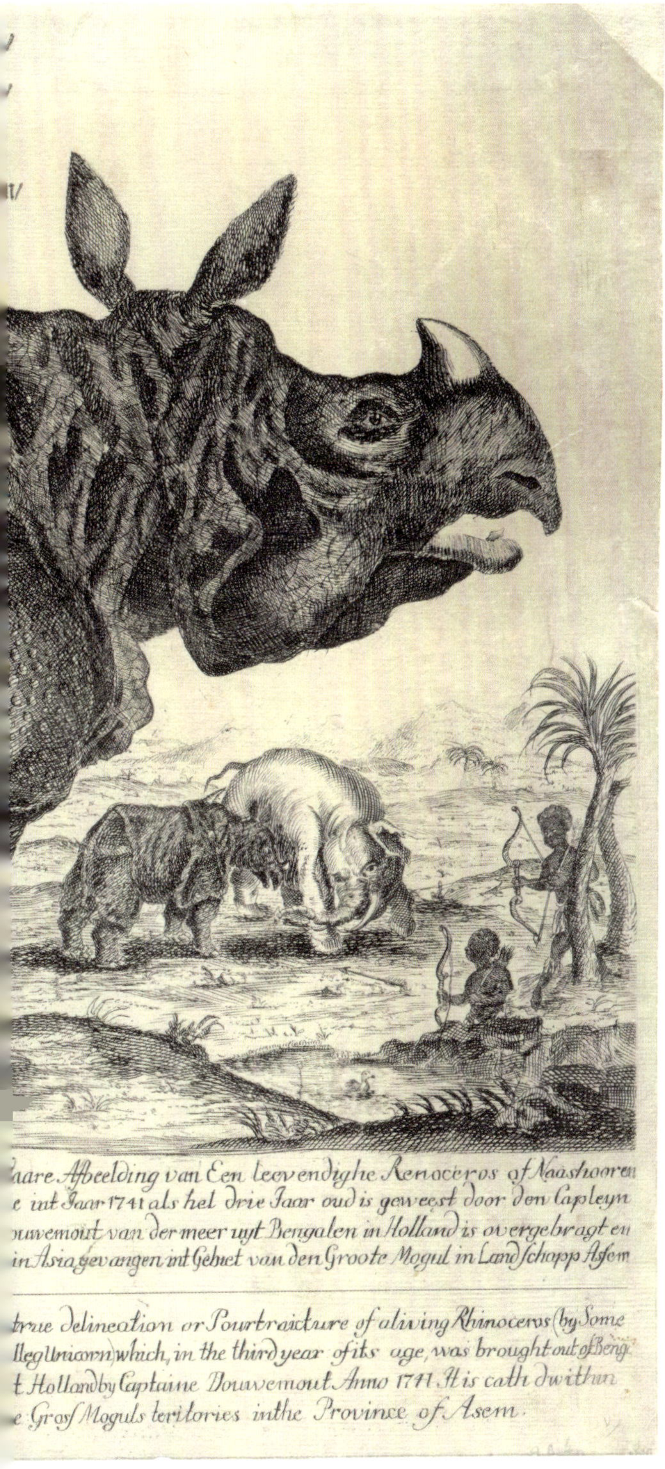

30
A promotional print of Clara to which the poem by innkeeper Maria Endtin commemorating Elector Karl Theodor's visit has been added, Mannheim, 1747

After Leipzig Mout set off for the other major German annual fair, which was held in Frankfurt am Main in September. On the way there Clara was certainly exhibited in Gotha, Kassel – where they were able to enjoy three weeks' rest as guests of the Elector of Hesse – and Hanau, but she would most certainly have been shown in various other towns they passed through. After leaving Frankfurt early in October, the group called on Mainz, Darmstadt and Mannheim where Clara once again received an important visitor, this time Karl Theodor, Elector of the Palatinate, who came especially to see her at the Zum Pfau inn where she was staying. The innkeeper, Maria Barbara Endtin, was so over the moon that she had a poem printed on some of Mout's promotional prints to commemorate the special occasion [fig. 30].[80] This print was a new design that Mout had had made in the course of the year following his ongoing success with Clara. She was the focal point, of course, but Mout had also had a cartouche added in which he too was portrayed along with his noble title, thereby taking advantage of his new status. Moreover, three new scenes were added around the rhinoceros: the fight between the rhinoceros and elephant, for which the well-known Dürer version was used, the hunters who had captured Clara, and the ship on which she had been transported to Europe. Thus, the whole print, which now included short texts in Dutch, French, English and Latin, depicted how Clara had ended up in Europe and who was responsible for her.[81]

The company then drove along the Rhine on to Switzerland. At the beginning of 1748 they first stayed in Basel for a while, and then set off for Bern. On their way there, on 30 January, a remarkable incident occurred, which, although an exception, clearly illustrates the commotion Clara's presence could cause. When she arrived in her wagon at the Zum Schlissel inn for the night in the small town of Liestal, some of the inhabitants did not want to miss the chance of seeing the famous phenomenon with their own eyes. A riot broke out, people became increasingly aggressive, and in the end one of Mout's assistants drew his sabre and stabbed the local smithy as many as three times. Not only was the assistant arrested, but Clara herself was also detained for two days. He was taken off to Basel and Clara would have been locked in a stable on the spot. Fortunately, the situation calmed down. Three weeks later Mout had to pay a hefty fine on behalf of his assistant, but that was the end of it. The residents were found guilty of causing the unrest.[82]

In March Clara was in Zurich, where her popularity found expression in a very different manner. After her departure at the end of the month, the local printer David Redinger brought out two prints

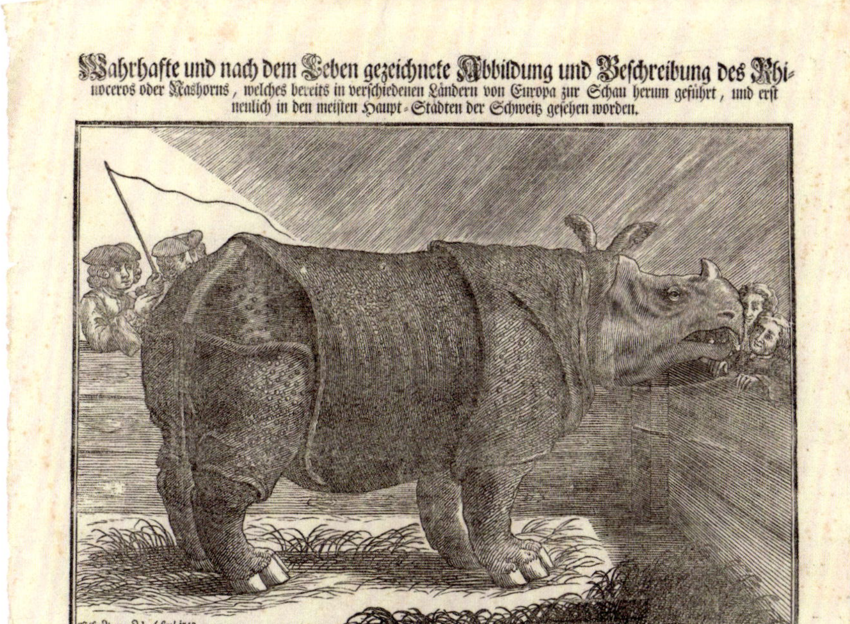

Wahrhafte und nach dem Leben gezeichnete Abbildung und Beschreibung des Rhinoceros oder Nashorns, welches bereits in verschiedenen Ländern von Europa zur Schau herum geführt, und erst neulich in den meisten Haupt-Städten der Schweitz gesehen worden.

Weilen dieses seltsame Thier würdig geachtet wird von Hohen und Niedern in Augenschein genommen, ja auch betastet zu werden, so achtet man billich nicht minder der Mühe werth / den Liebhabern hiemit eine fleissige / nach der Natur und dem Leben gemachte / Zeichnung / wie auch kurze Beschreibung desselben mitzutheilen. Dieses wird einerseits zum Angedenken dienen können denen, welche das Vernügen gehabt, dieses Thier selbs zu sehen, theils denjenigen die Curieusitet um etwas stillen, welche daßelbe zu sehen die Gelegenheit nicht gehabt.

Die Abbildungen, welche wir ausliefern, werden auch den Liebhabern der Natur-Wissenschaften und der Künsten desto angenehmer seyn, weil die meiste übrige in Kupferstichen, Holzschnitten, und so gar auf neuen Medaillen, auch die man hat in Gemählden, wie ungleich, also samtlich nicht allzuwol getroffen und zum theil sehr unfleissig verfertigt sind. Wie dann der Herr und Besitzer dieses Thiers erkennt, daß die Abbildungen, die er ausgibt, an sich selbs schlecht seyen, anbey aber sie für gut genug hält, wann man dieselbe ihm wol bezahlt. Da das Thier auch in allen andern Abbildungen sich nicht anderst als stehend zeiget, hat man nun gut befunden, es stehend und ligend abzubilden; in welcher letztern Gestalt zwahr die Falten, die es in seiner Haut hat, sich nicht so scheinbar zeigen, als wann es stehet und sich strecket. Aus gegenwärtiger Abbildung ist zwahr die Gestalt dieses Wunder-Thiers unschwer abzunehmen, nicht aber die Farb. Deßwegen zum Bericht dienet, daß sie dunkelbraun ist, und etwa einer Krote gleichen mag.

Unter denen Berichten, mit welchen diejenige, welche dieses Thier zu besch[...]en herumführen, daßelbe desto Bewunderungs-würdiger machen wollen, ist die weite Entfehrnung seines ersten Heymaths. Dann wie sie vorgeben, soll es 4000. Meilen weit her seyn. Zumal es in Asia im Gebieth des Grossen Mogols in der Landschaft Assem gefangen, und im Jahr 1741. als es dreyjährig gewesen, durch den Capitain Douwenmouth, oder David Mout van der Meer, aus Bengalen in Holland übergebracht worden. Wann man aber weiß, wie viel Meilen ungefehr der ganze Umkreiß der von uns bewohneten Erd-Kugel ausmacht, so siehet man leicht, daß diese 4000. Meilen von dem weitern Weg zu verstehen, dann den nähern möchte es bey 2500. Meilen minder weit seyn. Eben wie die Reise, welche man mit diesem Thier von Basel über Bern und Zürich gen Schaffhausen gemacht hat, um etwas weiter gewesen, als die nächste Straß, deren sich die Post von Schaffhausen gen Basel bedienet.

Was aber dieses Thier in der That Bewunderungs-würdig macht, ist seine ungeheure Grösse und sein so schweres Gewicht, daß die ungemein starke und wolbesetzte Beine sich doch darunter zu krümmen scheinen. Das hier abgebildete neun jährige ist nur als ein Kalb zu betrachten, zumal diese Thiere auf 100. oder nach anderm Bericht auf 150. Jahre alt werden. Gleichwol soll es bey nahe 5000. Pfund schwer seyn. Nach was für einem Gewicht aber diese Ausrechnung gemacht sey, ist nicht eigentlich zu bestimmen. Seine Höhe soll im Monat May 1747. 5. Schuh 7. Zoll gewesen seyn, die Länge 12. Schuhe. Die Dicke auch 12. Schuhe.

Von dem Horn, welches dieses Thier auf seiner Nase hat, heißt es Nashorn. Daßelbe dienet ihm, wie den Schweinen, mit denen es viel Gleichheit hat, der Rüssel, die Erde sehr geschwind umzugraben, und in den Sümpfen und Morästen, in denen es sich gern aufhält, seine Nahrung zu suchen. Es braucht aber auch dieses Horn zu seiner Verthädigung mit einer ungemeinen Stärke. Wann es mit dem Elephant, mit dem es in grosser Feindschaft stehet, in einen Kampf komt, so sucht es nur denselben unten am Bauch, wo er am weichsten ist, beyzukommen, und wann es diesen Vortheil gewunnen, so ist es ihm ein leichtes, des Elephanten Leib aufzureissen, und ihn also um das Leben zu bringen.

Der Kopf des Nashorns ist sehr groß, doch nach und nach zugespitzt; die Ohren sind gleich eines Esels; die Augen sind nach seiner grossen Gestalt sehr klein und schläferig; es kan mit denselben nur van der Seite nidsich sehen. Es liebet den Rauch-Tabac mit sonderlicher Begird. Die Stimm ist gebrochen, wie eines Hirschen. Die Zunge weich, die untere Lippe wie eines Ochsens, die obere wie eines Pferds; es bedienet sich dieser nach Heu, Gras und anderer Speise zu langen, und kan sie über sechs Zoll ausstrecken und zuspitzen, und, was es damit ergreift, vest halten.

Das seltsamste an dem Nashorn ist seine Panzer-gleiche und undurchdringliche Haut, welche zwey Zoll dick ist, und deßwegen ihm zu einer fast unüberwindlichen Schutzwehr gegen alle seine Feinde dienet. Sie ist über und über mit einer harten Rinde bedecket, welche räudigen Rüfen zu vergleichen, die oben auf dem Rucken nur klein, gegen dem Wanst aber und auf den hintern Backen, auch über die Füsse ziemlich groß sind. Da nun die Haut, wie sie oben beschrieben, ganz unbeugsam ist, also daß wann sie, wie die Haut anderer Thieren, ganz über das Nashorn ausgedähnet wäre, es keine nöhtige Bewegungen machen könte, hat der weise Schöpfer die Einrichtung gemacht, daß sie verschiedene einer Hand breit über einander gehende Falten hat, zwischen denen die Haut so glatt und lind wie Seide ist; da dann je nach dem das Nashorn eine Bewegung zu machen hat, ein Theil der schildförmigen Haut sich leicht über den andern hinschiebet.

Das geringste an diesem Thier ist der Schwanz, der weder lang noch dick ist; Er hat am Ende etliche wenige schwarze und starke aber kurze Häärlein, da sonst das Thier keine Haare hat.

Es ist leicht zu erachten, daß ein so grosses Thier zu seinem Unterhalt viel bedörfe; wie man dann sagt, es brauche täglich 60. Pfund Heu und 20. Pfund Brod; auch trinke es täglich 14. Eymer Wasser; (welches aber nicht von 60. Maß haltenden Eymern zu verstehen ist.)

Ob nun das Nashorn der Behemoth sey, deßen bey Job am XL. Capitel gedacht wird, wollen wir weder bejahen noch verneinen, sondern den Leser aus Entgegenhaltung der daselbs sich befindenden und unserer gegenwertigen Beschreibung und Abbildung selbs schliessen laßen.

Wer eine weitläuffigere und gründliche Beschreibung des Nashorns verlangt, den wollen wir gewiesen haben auf die gelehrte Oration Doctor Caroli Augusti von Bergen, welche er den 16. October 1746. von eben diesem hier gesehenen Rhinoceros gehalten, getruckt zu Frankfurt an der Oder. Deßgleichen auf die natürliche Historie des Nashorns, welche von Doctor Parsons an Martin Folkers Rittern und Präsidenten der Königl. Engl. Societet abgefaßet, und aus dem Englischen in das Deutsche übersezet worden von Doctor Georg Leonhart Huth. Nürnberg 1747.

Zürich, zu finden bey David Redinger.

31

Clara in Zurich, showing her standing inside an enclosure, with (presumably) Douwe Mout on the left, holding a whip, David Redinger, 1748

featuring her [figs. 31, 32]. He did this, he said, because the images that Mout sold did not do justice to the rhinoceros's appearance. His own prints did indeed give a different impression of Clara, though mainly because she is portrayed lying down instead of standing. More importantly, however, the two prints show how Clara was exhibited: inside an enclosure with the public close to her on the other side of the pen. Close enough for one visitor to feel under the folds of her skin. Mout or one of his assistants can be seen holding a whip; for there had to be supervision at all times. Especially interesting is the fact that Redinger even manages to fit Clara's wagon into one of the prints.[83]

The group returned to Germany via Schaffhausen and headed for Stuttgart, where Clara was weighed on 6 May, as is later mentioned on a number of prints. She now proved to weigh a hefty 5,000 pounds. Here, besides selling prints, Mout also sold medals as souvenirs, which he had done for the first time in Switzerland. In Leipzig they were produced by the local medallist Veit Schrempf [fig. 33]. On the front Clara stands under a beaming sun; on the back is a close-set text similar to that which Mout had used in earlier prints.[84] These were quickly snapped up. Once again, he had found a novel and successful way of making money out of his rhinoceros. He then had similar medals struck in silver, bronze and tin in other cities he visited, each time produced by a local silversmith. In Ansbach, Nuremberg and Strasbourg, as in Stuttgart, they featured the name of the city, but with a view to the future, Mout also ordered medals without the name of a city and with the text in German, French or Italian which he could sell everywhere [figs. 34–36].[85]

It was probably near Strasbourg towards the end of the year that Mout crossed the Rhine. For three full years he had exhibited Clara in practically every part of Germany, with excursions to Austria and Switzerland. The tour had been a great success. Everywhere the wonder beast Clara had 'caused a great stir', as they put it.[86] But now the time had come to present Clara in other parts of Europe. Once again, a recently signed peace treaty provided the opportunity for this, for on 18 October 1748 it had put an end to the so-called War of the Austrian Succession, which by that time had involved virtually every European power in one way or another. Prussia and Austria had laid down their arms three years before, and now France and England were doing the same. What is more, France had agreed to withdraw from the Southern Netherlands. Peace and tranquillity had returned to Europe and perhaps it was this that gave Mout the final push to leave Strasbourg for Paris via Nancy and Rheims at the close of 1748.

Mout arrived in Paris with Clara in mid-January 1749, in good time to show her at the celebrated and ever-popular annual fair and *kermis*, the Foire Saint-Germain, which was due to begin in early February. While waiting for it to open, he had enough time to go out to Versailles where Louis XIV had had an enormous royal palace built over fifty years before. This was now the residence of his successor and great-grandson Louis XV. In Brussels early in the summer of 1743, a rumour had been circulating that the king was thinking of adding the rhinoceros to his menagerie in the palace gardens, but either that was mere gossip or else something had led him to change his mind. Mout now made a fresh attempt and offered Clara to him again for no less than 100,000 écu, an exorbitant amount. No wonder Louis XV did not take him up on his offer. Nonetheless, 'the whole court' had turned out to see Clara and Mout was granted royal permission to show Clara to the public for money – presumably his prime objective all along.[87]

Mout swiftly brought Clara back to Paris for the Foire where for eight weeks, from 8 in the morning until 8 at night, people were able to marvel at her [fig. 37]. Traditionally the fair had always featured special attractions, and of course Clara fitted the bill perfectly. But Parisians found Clara more than special and there was a real clamour to see her. 'The whole of Paris ran out in droves to see this phenomenon,' a Parisian recalled. And a fellow citizen reported: '... there are few people who are not curious ..., and the Dutch captain must be making a lot of money.'[88] For fashionable Parisians the arrival of the rhinoceros was an extravagant and welcome novelty and distraction. They saw her primarily as a new form of amusement, an enjoyable pastime, and a good excuse to make jokes and act the fool. Typical of this is a long drawn-out 'prose poem' by Jean-Baptiste Guiard de Servigné published in 1750. Although it is entitled *Le Rhinocéros*, after having been transported from Amsterdam to Paris, notably through the air, the animal plays no further part in the story, which was intended as a satire.

Upper-class ladies and gentlemen cared nothing for the rhinoceros as such. Clara was above all exotic and different and therefore something that had to be seen. A hype. To quote a contemporary: '... the craze of our *François* and our *Françoïses* for this ugly animal was so great that, to immortalize its memory, the ladies named a new kind of coiffure after it which they had dreamed up in their imagination – an eternal breeding ground for these kinds of things – and they were immediately copied by our fashionistas who have named a new type of harness that they fasten to their carriages after this Monster.'[89] Ten years later the famous writer and philosopher Voltaire breathed a sigh of relief when he heard that creations of this sort had at last

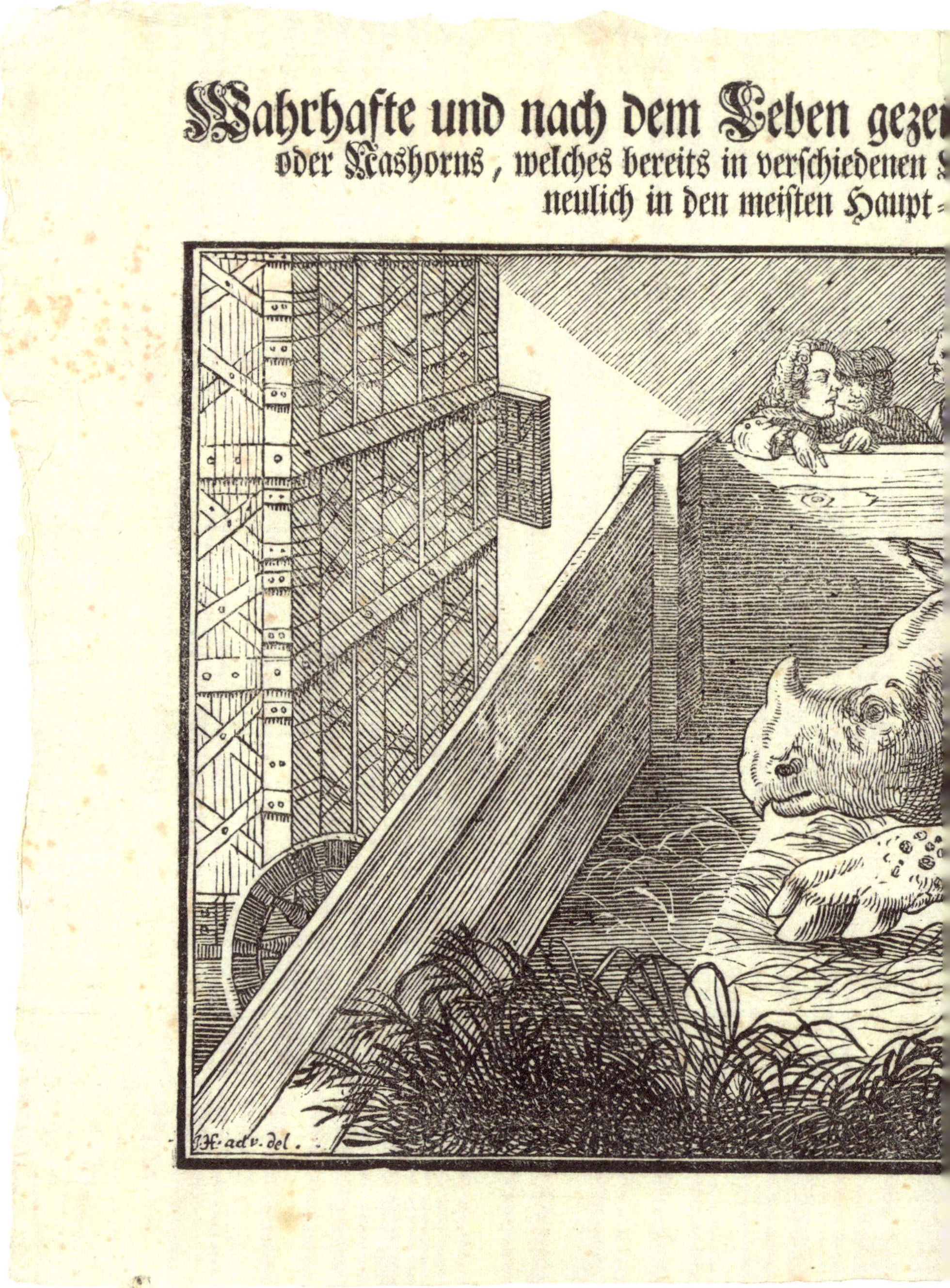

32

Clara lying in her pen in Zurich, with the wagon in which she was transported on the left, David Redinger, 1748

Abbildung des liegenden Rhinoceros
on Europa zur Schau herum geführt, und erst
der Schweitz gesehen worden.

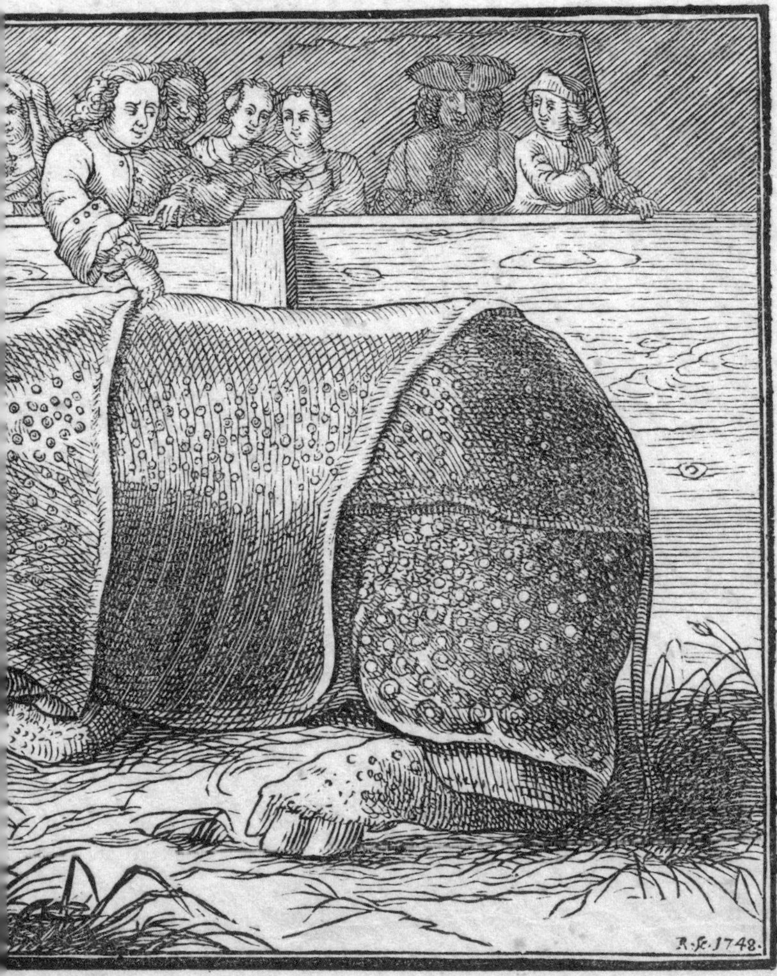

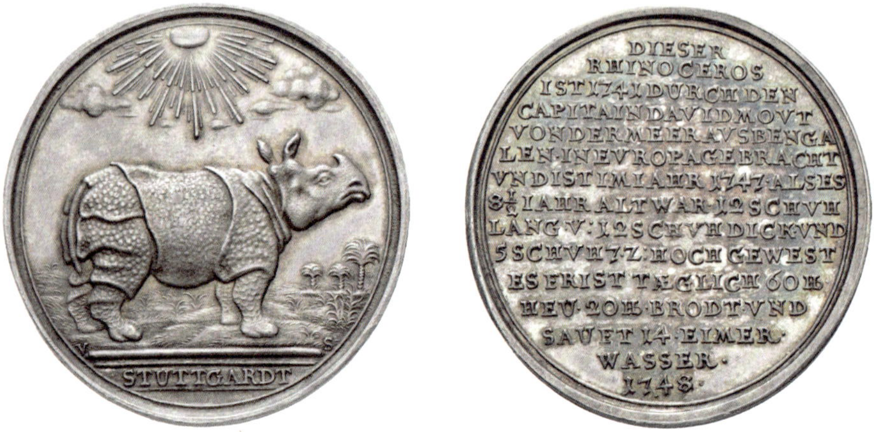

33
Obverse and reverse of a silver medal, commemorating Clara's presentation in Stuttgart, with the text in German, Veit Schrempf, 1748

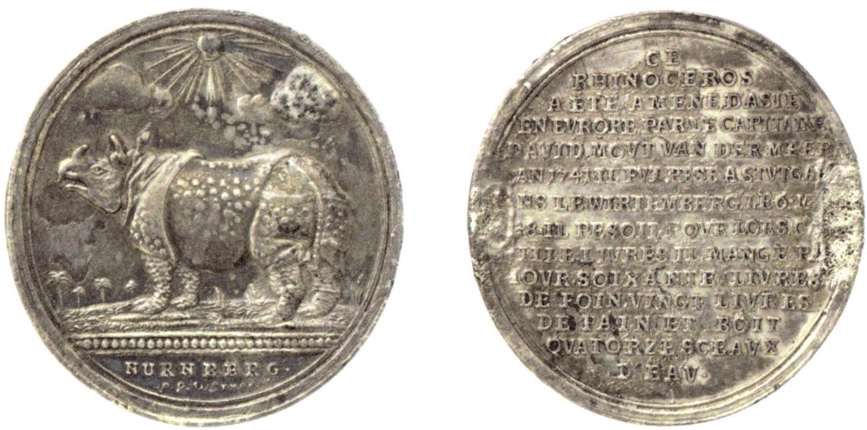

34
Obverse and reverse of a silver medal, commemorating Clara's presentation in Nuremberg, with the text in French, Peter Paul Werner, 1748

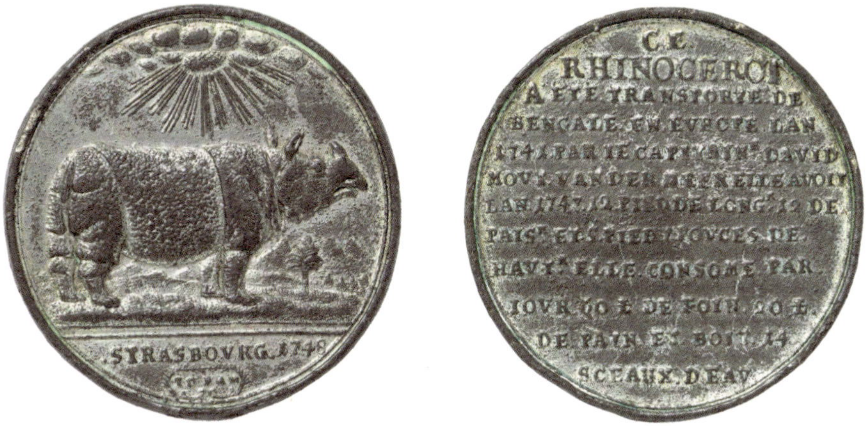

35
Obverse and reverse of a tin medal, commemorating Clara's presentation in Strasbourg, with the text in French, Jean Daniel Kamm, 1748

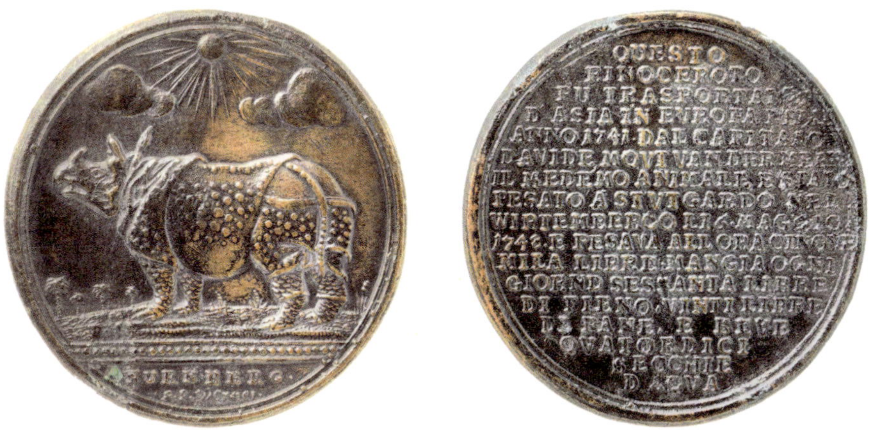

36
Obverse and reverse of a bronze medal commemorating Clara's presentation in Nuremberg, with the text in Italian, Peter Paul Werner, 1748

RHINOCEROT.

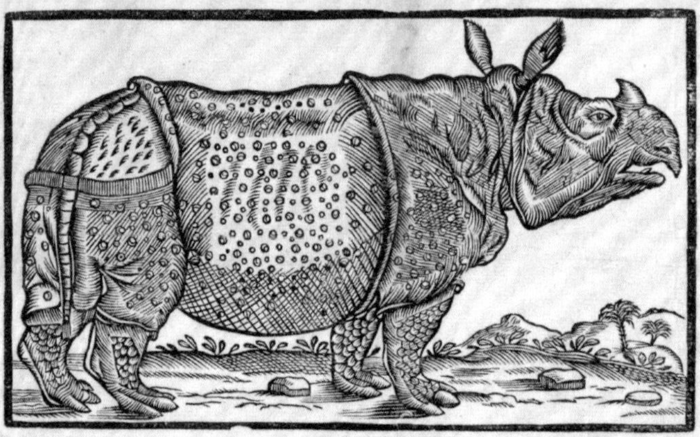

DE PAR LE ROY,

ET MONSIEUR

LE LIEUTENANT GENERAL DE POLICE.

MESSIEURS ET DAMES,

VOUS êtes avertis qu'il eſt arrivé depuis peu dans cette Ville un Animal nommé RHINOCEROT, Animal qu'on a crû apocriphe juſqu'à préſent. Ce Monſtre fut pris en Aſie, dans la Province d'Aſſem, qui appartient au Grand Mogol, en 1741, par un Capitaine Marinier, lequel Capitaine le fit tranſporter de Bengalen par mer en Hollande. Il n'avoit que trois ans quand il fut pris ; ſa taille étoit alors de 5 pieds 7 pouces de hauteur, 12 pieds de longueur, & 12 de groſſeur ; il eſt devenu depuis ce tems-là beaucoup plus grand & plus gros. Ce monſtre eſt de couleur muſc : il n'a point de poil comme l'Eléphant, ſinon aux extrêmités des oreilles, & au bout de la queuë où on en voit tant ſoit peu : il a une corne placée ſur le nez, laquelle corne lui ſert à ſe défendre contre ſon ennemi antipathique qui eſt l'Eléphant ; il court avec une légereté étonnante ; il ſçait nâger, & il aime à ſe plonger dans l'eau comme un Canard ; ſa tête ſe rend un peu pointue au-devant ; ſes oreilles reſſemblent à celles d'un Aſne ; ſes yeux ſont exceſſivement petits pour ſa taille qui eſt énorme ; il ſemble que ſa peau ſoît couverte de coquilles ; elles ſe battent l'une contre l'autre quand l'Animal ſe remue : elles ſont épaiſſes de 2 pouces, ſes pieds ſont quarrés & fort gros ; il a tros griffes. Cet Animal, comme il eſt dit ci deſſus, eſt l'ennemi juré de l'Eléphant : quand ils ſe rencontrent, il eſt infaillible qu'ils ne ſe battent ; le Rhinocerot ſe met deſſous le ventre de l'Eléphant, & lui enfonce ſa corne dans le ventre, juſqu'à ce que l'Eléphant ſuccombant à la douleur, ſe laiſſe tomber, & écraſe ſon ennemi par le propre poids de ſon corps. Pour ſa nourriture, il mange 60 livres de foin, & 20 livres de pain par jour : il boit 14 ſceaux d'eau, & de la bierre : il a été péſé à Stouquarts, dans le Pays de Virtemberg, le 6 May 1748. il péſoit 5000 liv. Il n'eſt point farouche, il eſt tout au contraire très-apprivoiſé, doux, ſi on peut ſe ſervir de ce terme, comme une tendre Colombe, parce qu'il n'avoit qu'un mois quand quelques Indiens l'attraperent avec des cordes ; ils tuérent ſa mere à coups de flèches. A deux ans ce Rhinocerot couroit dans les Appartemens, comme pourroit faire un chien ; il alloit autour des tables des Seigneurs où on le menoit pour le faire voir, & ſe laiſſoit careſſer par tout le monde. Il faut mener ce Monſtre en chariot, & que le chariot ſoit couvert ; il faut quelquefois (c'eſt-à-dire, quand les chemins ſont mauvais) mettre juſqu'à 20 chevaux pour le tirer : il ſort de ſa cabane ſans aucune difficulté. Cet Animal a été vû dans toutes les Cours d'Allemagne, où il a fait l'admiration de tous les Souverains des Cours étrangeres.

Quand un ou deux Rhinocerots ſe trouvent dans un troupeau de Bêtes ſauvages, qui preſſées de la ſoif s'aſſemblent à quelques fleuves, les Rhinocerots commencent à boire les premiers, ſans que les autres Bêtes ſauvages oſent en approcher. La Corne de ce Monſtre eſt fort eſtimée des Indiens qui s'en ſervent contre toutes ſortes de venin, contre l'apoplexie & autres maladies : ſes dents, ſes griffes, ſa chair & ſon ſang, ainſi que ſa fiente & ſon eau, tout eſt ſalutaire pour le corps humain : Nous en avons l'expérience, parce que beaucoup de perſonnes s'en ſont trouvé très-bien. Les ſuſdites choſes ſe prennent de ceux qui le panſent, pour une ſorte de récompenſe.

Au bas de la rue de Tournon, Cul-de-Sac de l'Opera Comique, Rue des Quatre-Vents.

On montrera cet Animal depuis dix heures du matin juſqu'à huit heures du ſoir.

Les premieres Places ſont de 3 liv. les ſecondes de 36 ſols, & les troiſiémes de 12 ſols.

Permis d'imprimer & afficher. A Paris le 19 Janvier 1749, BERRYER.

37 **Print advertising Clara's presentation in Paris, Berryer, 1749**

been banned in the theatre: 'How glad I was when I heard that the theatre was purged of white-powdered people with coiffures 'au rhinocéros' and 'à l'oiseau royal'!'[90]

When the Foire de Saint Germain was over, Clara remained in the French capital for a while, during which time the entrance fees were greatly reduced. It was not until the end of April that Clara left Paris, with yet another pass, for on 11 April the king had given Mout a document which entitled him to show Clara for money 'in every town and place in the kingdom'.[91] France lay wide open to them and this made it a lot easier for Mout to carry out his next plan: to travel to Italy via Dijon, Lyons, Geneva, Avignon, Aix-en-Provence and Marseilles, as already announced in February in an Amsterdam newspaper.[92] Only this time Mout did not go along himself. He returned home – at least for a while.

After touring for some four years, in the spring of 1749 Mout arrived back in Amsterdam. Apparently, it was necessary to put his affairs in order, also in preparation for his next step. On 31 July 1749 he applied to the States of Holland for an exemption from a number of taxes levied in connection with the Wilmkebreek polder. Since he had purchased 'Het Meertje' five years before, he had had to pay 7,000 guilders in costs to keep the polder dry and maintain the dykes around it, which was one-and-a-half times the purchase price. Besides land tax he wanted an exemption from so-called horn money (*hoorngeld*), a duty levied on horned cattle grazing the land – although Clara may also have been included in this category.[93] Five weeks later, on 8 September, when he was 'on the point of leaving to make a journey outside the country', he had two related notarial documents drawn up. The first was a power of attorney in which Mout appointed Quirijn van Niel as his agent to represent him in financial and legal matters during his absence, the other the will of his wife and himself. In this they named each other as mutual heirs, arranged custody of the children and appointed Quirijn van Niel and Gerrit Harting, who had exhibited Clara in Delft in 1742, as the executors of their estate.[94] Clara is also mentioned in the will. 'As far as the cattle, rhinoceros and household effects are concerned, it is left to the wisdom of the guardians to sell or keep these, as they judge to be of the greatest benefit to the minors.' This meant that while the rhinoceros was away in France, Mout remained her owner. Taken together, the two documents seem to imply that Elisabeth was now to accompany her husband, presumably along with their three sons. The fact that Elisabeth gave birth to a daughter some two years later, who must have been conceived during their travels, confirms this.[95]

In the meantime, Clara was on her way to Marseilles, no doubt entrusted to men whom Mout had worked with earlier on the tour. Various sources report that she caused some trouble on the way, although the reliability of these sources is questionable. One story has it that, lovesick, she became so restless that in Lyons she bit five or six people to death and then died herself. This was plainly not true, and that she was lovesick is also highly questionable, although Clara's hormones would certainly have acted up now and then as she was still fairly young. Her life was in any case far from over, as was apparent when she arrived alive and well in Marseilles in November according to plan. Here she was exhibited at the Cours Belsunce, not far from the harbour. Several European newspapers from this port subsequently reported that on her departure she had capsized the boat that was carrying her to the ship due to take her to Italy. She herself had managed to swim ashore, but her keeper and several passengers had drowned, on top of which the money she had earned on the way over the past few months had sunk to the bottom of the sea and disappeared. There is no way of knowing what is true of this story, but one thing is certain: it was not Mout who lost his life in the accident.[96]

The notarial documents Mount had drawn up in Amsterdam reveal that he had plans to exhibit Clara fairly extensively again. No doubt he already had a travel destination in mind as well. It is unclear at what point he picked Clara up; he may have done so in Marseilles or else somewhere in Italy. The first destination was Naples. There, after a stop in Civitavecchia, Clara was brought ashore early in December. She was immediately driven to the palace of the King of the Two Sicilies in Portici, some ten kilometres outside the city 'to show herself to the Court'.[97] King Charles must have heard about Clara and, given this detour, must have 'commissioned' the visit from Mout. She was housed in the palace menagerie where an elephant, lions, panthers and other animals were kept, but her stay was short-lived.

Mout already knew where he wanted to present her next: in Rome. It was 1750, which was reputedly a Holy Year, a special ecclesiastical event which took place every twenty-five years to commemorate the birth of Christ and the origins of Christianity. Such a celebration drew masses of pilgrims to this centre of the Catholic faith. In addition to numerous religious ceremonies, there were all sorts of worldly attractions to see, including that year a rhinoceros. After a brief stay in Naples, the troupe set off for Rome early in February with the wagon, this time drawn by four oxen. There Clara was on display from mid-March until well into June in a large wooden hut by the Baths of Diocletian.

From the scant information that has come down to us about this long stay, one notable fact stands out: shortly before she was due to leave the city Clara lost her horn.[98] Although this never happens of its own accord in nature, it regularly occurs in captivity. The limited space to which Clara was constantly confined, the monotony of her existence, the inability to release her energy, all this and other factors may have contributed to her habit of rubbing her horn against the wooden planks of her wagon, her hut and her enclosure. Clara's loss of her horn must have been a shocking and unforeseen experience for Mout and his assistants. After all, it was her most striking feature, the very thing that people associated her with. Is a rhinoceros without a horn still a rhinoceros? The good news was that the horn was not lost nor was it broken, so that Mout was able to show the horn to the public as a special attraction in the years to come. And it must have been a consoling thought, and have appealed to visitors, that a new horn was slowly growing.

That summer the group journeyed from Rome over the Apennines to the eastern coast of Italy. There Clara spent a whole month in Senigallia, a port under the jurisdiction of the Papal State where in July an annual fair was held that attracted merchants and fairgoers from all the countries around the Adriatic Sea.[99] Drawn by twelve oxen, Clara was next transported northwards along the coast to Rimini and from there over the long, straight Via Emilia to Milan. Clara would almost certainly have been shown to excited residents in most of the towns she passed through, but accounts are known only of Bologna, Parma and the neighbouring Colorno (where the Ducal court viewed her) and Fidenza. This time, too, Mout had brought along medals and prints to sell, probably the same material that he had previously been peddling in Germany and France.[100] In Milan, which then fell under Austrian authority, Mout and Clara arrived – whether or not by coincidence – just in time to enliven the festivities surrounding the inauguration of the new imperial governor, Giovanni Luca Pallavicini. Here from 6 October she could be marvelled at in the Piazza Mercanti.[101]

Venice was the next destination, and in particular the always well-attended Carnival that took place in January and February. Excellent takings were as good as guaranteed. Like most attractions, Clara had a spot in the vicinity of the vast St Mark's Square, in her case a stable in front of the Zecca, the mint, opposite the Doge's Palace. She can be seen here in two almost identical paintings by the celebrated society painter Pietro Longhi [fig. 38]. Behind the enclosure of vertical wooden planks is a kind of stand. The hornless Clara is portrayed munching hay while her dung lies in a heap behind her. She looks noticeably small in comparison with the spectators – too small. The painted text on the pinned-up note in one of these paintings reveals that the painting was commissioned by the twenty-three-year-old Venetian patrician Giovanni Grimani. Naturally, he too figures in the painting, along with his wife and his partly masked family – a Venice tradition, especially during the Carnival. The second painting was commissioned from the painter by another prominent Venetian, Girolamo Mocenigo.[102] Longhi's son Alessandro made a print that depicts the same scene in a slightly different manner, including a rather inept representation of Clara, in which Africa is moreover erroneously named as her country of origin [fig. 39]. In both the paintings and the print a young lad holds up not only a whip but also Clara's horn as if it were a trophy.

The two eminent Venetian families depicted in these paintings were doubtless given VIP treatment. But, as everywhere else, ordinary Venetians were also welcomed. The exhibition tent was generally packed to capacity. The crowd laughed at the strange animal and threw her oranges and bread. Once, on 20 January 1751, it was so crowded that Clara grew restless and began to shake and snort. Suddenly, her growing anxiety made her hurl herself against the enclosure, as if she were trying to escape. A panic broke out, people fled and many were injured. A young boy was even fatally trampled underfoot. It meant the end of Clara's show: the authorities decided that Mout and his rhinoceros had to leave town early.[103]

Prior to his visit to Venice, Mount had showed Clara in Verona. After his premature departure from Venice, it was only logical that he should return to the Veneto mainland and show her there. It was here that a third painting was made, in the style of Longhi, although he was not the artist [fig. 40]. It gives a good insight into the daily routine. Clara stands in an enclosure, four planks high, inside a tall, wooden building. Behind her lies a pile of hay and bread; kneeling next to her, viewed from behind, an assistant – a woman, a boy? – pours water into a tub. The man at the ringside on the extreme right is probably Mout himself in his red coat, whip in hand, eyes firmly fixed on Clara. A wigged gentleman examines the rhinoceros closely through his lorgnette, while an elegant lady looks out at us instead of at Clara. Higher up behind her stand those who paid the lower entrance fee. In the background not only is Clara's wagon in view but her horn can be seen on the shelf. The new one seems to have grown a little.

It is no longer possible to ascertain how long Mout and Clara stayed in the Venice region. We only know that they crossed the Alps and returned to Vienna, arriving on 29 May. As could be read in various newspapers, Mout planned to travel on from here to Frankfurt via

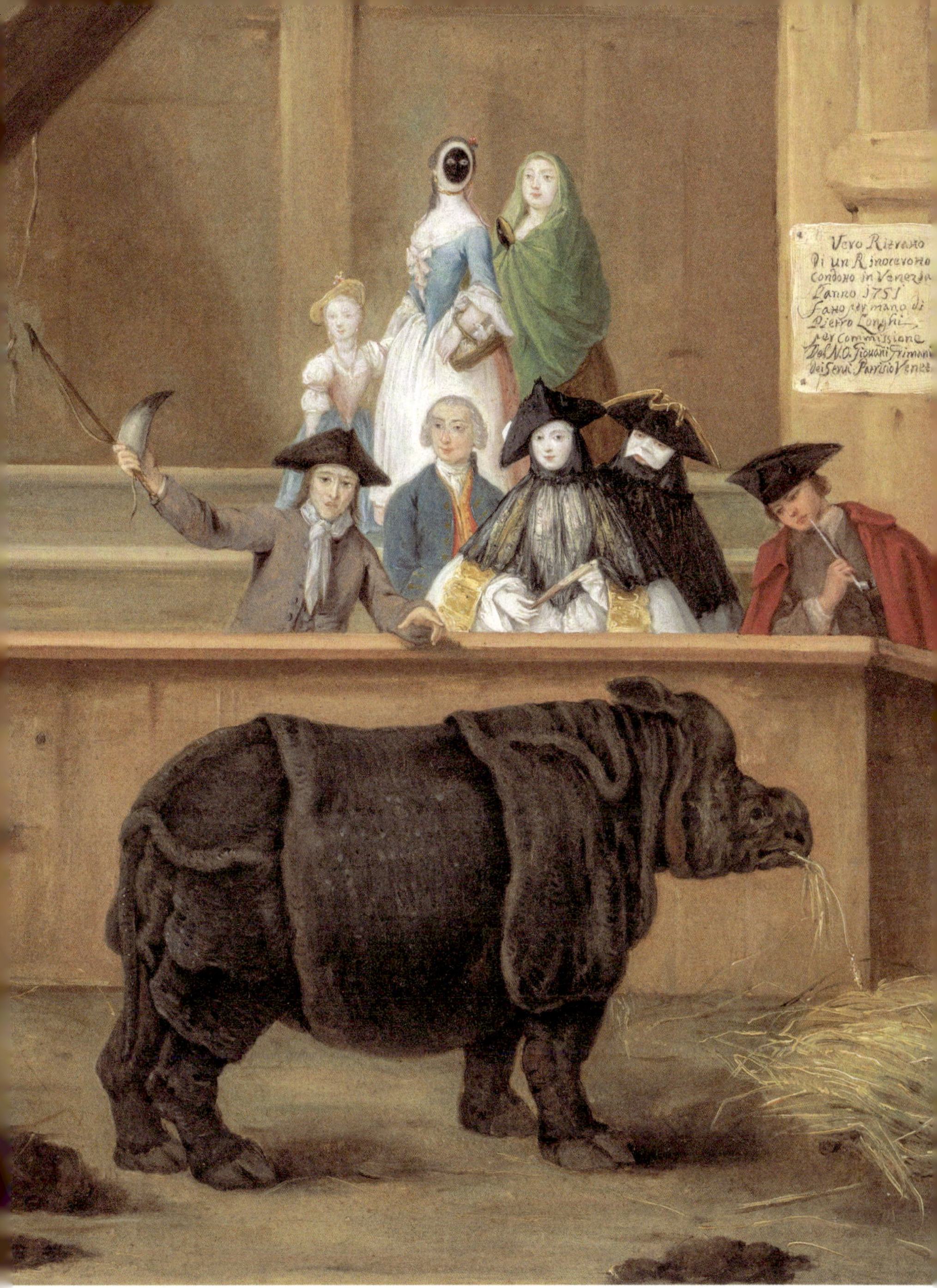

38

Clara on display in Venice, eating hay in front of her audience, Pietro Longhi, 1751

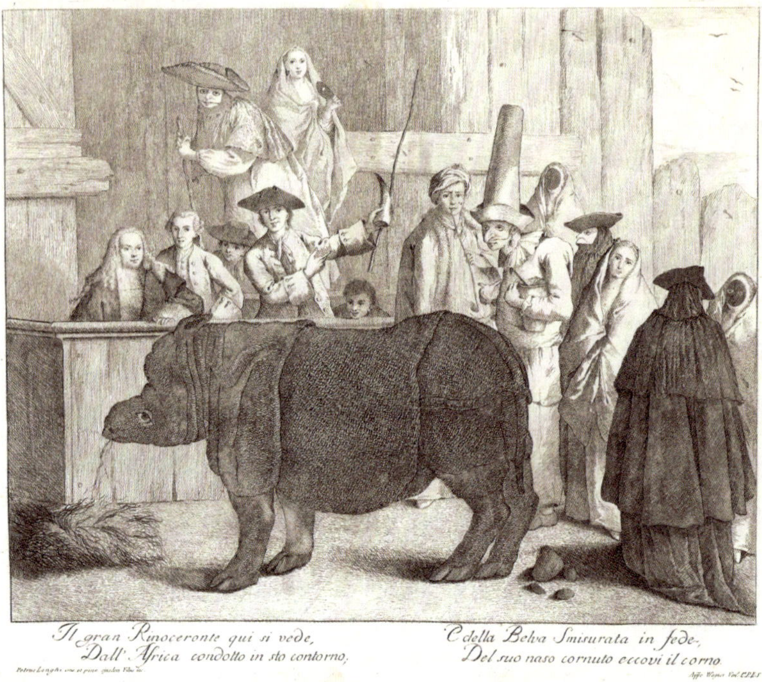

39
Clara in Venice, with Africa mistakenly given as her region of origin, Alessandro Longhi, 1751

Prague to attend the annual fair again in September. From there he intended to journey to England with Clara via the Netherlands before the winter set in.[104] But there is strikingly little information on the realization of these plans. In fact, all that is known is that Clara was shown in Meiningen and Göttingen. Further, there is evidence that a daughter of Douwe Mout and Elisabeth Snel was christened in Leiden on 5 December 1751 and that she was named after her mother. It would seem that everyone was back in the Netherlands then and that the idea of crossing the Channel to England was abandoned. Perhaps this was because the female rhinoceros which had landed in Britain in 1737 and had since been touring English and Scottish cities while Clara was similarly being carted round Europe, was currently being shown there again. A fair amount is known about her stay in London, while there is no trace of Clara there at that time.[105]

The most likely explanation is then that Clara was reinstalled in the Wilmkebreek polder at the end of 1751. After being on the road for some six years she was back in her pasture again. For a while nobody was looking at her, laughing at her or touching her; at last she could rest.

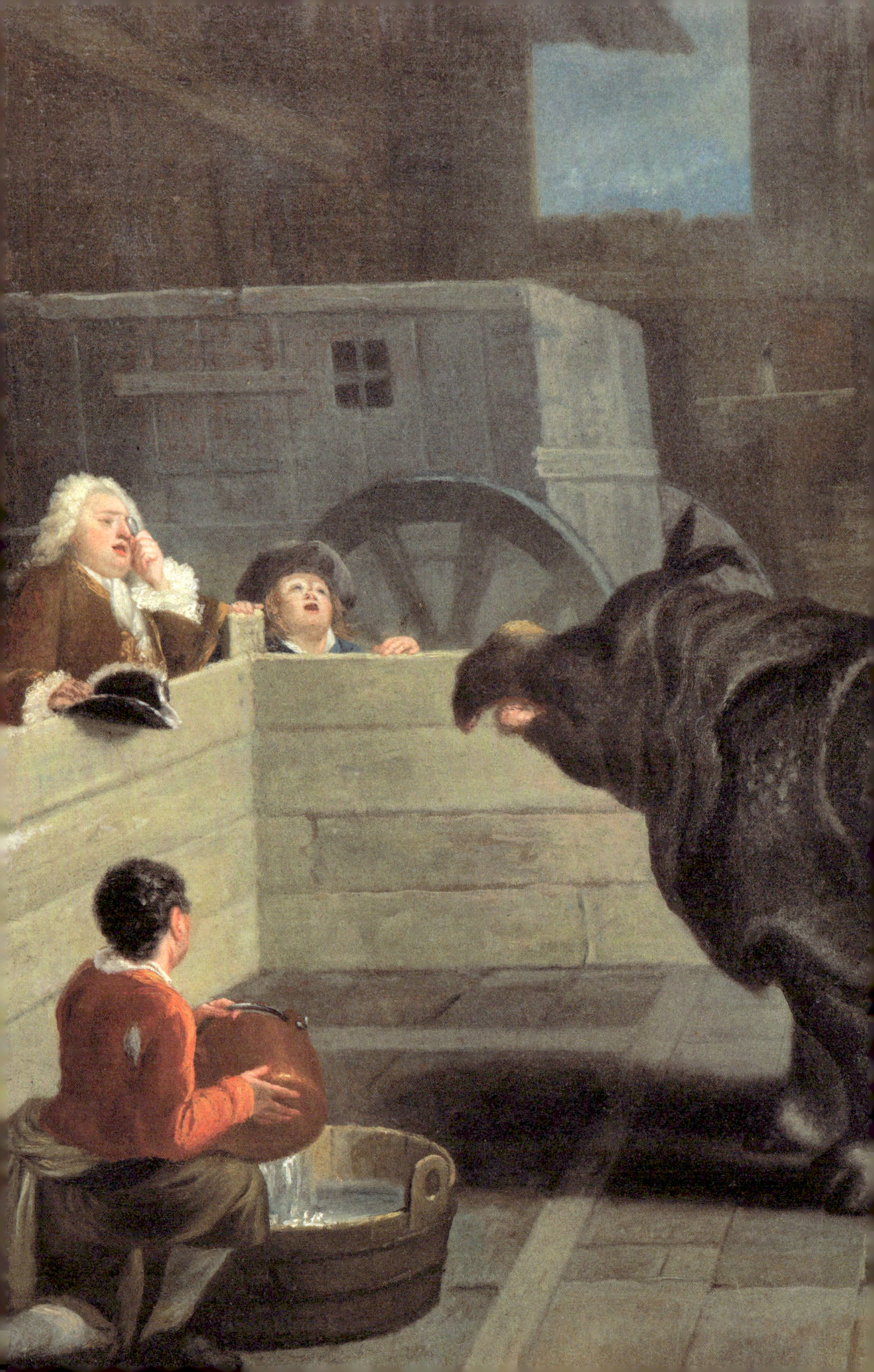

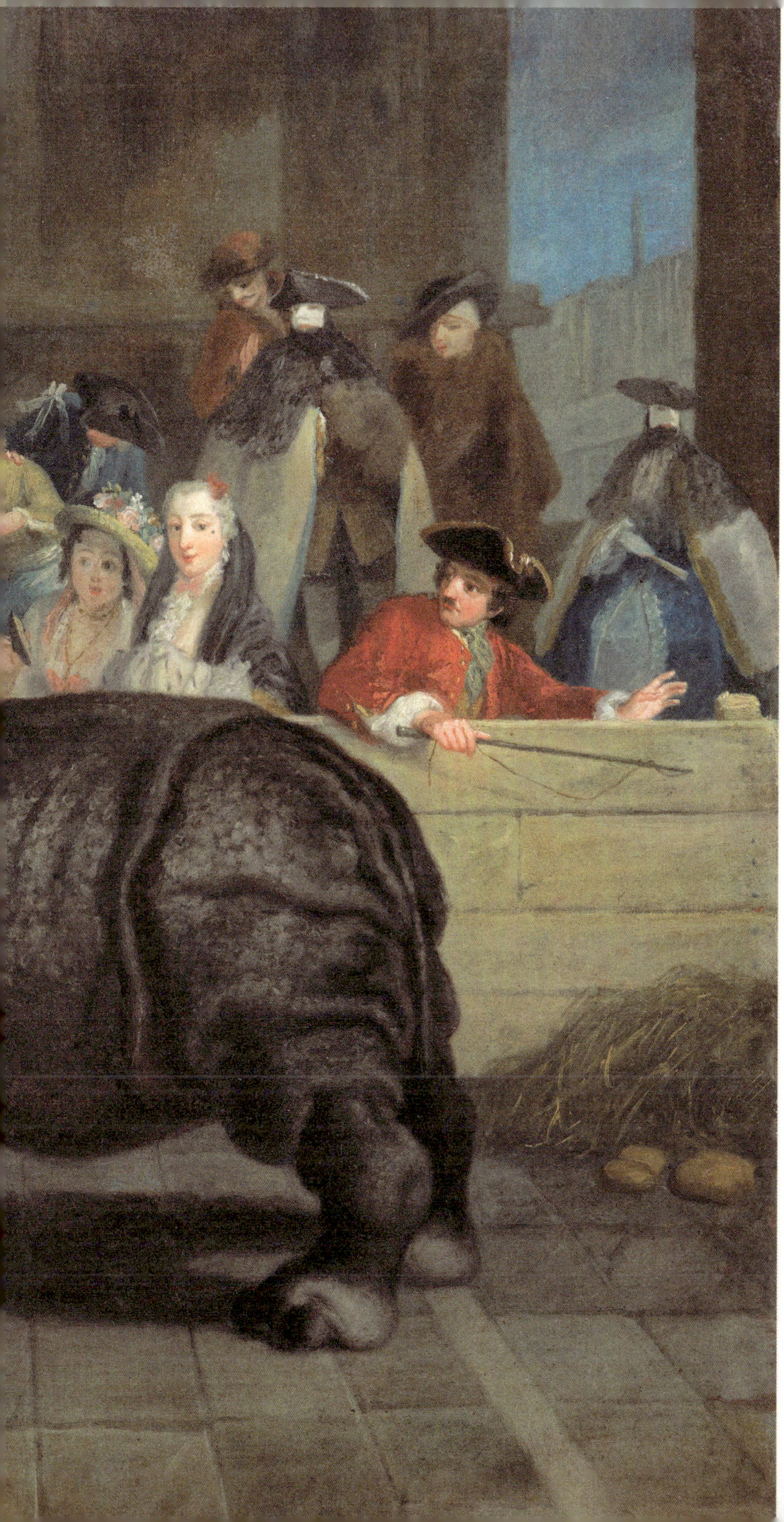

Clara in or around Venice, with her wagon in the background, Venetian School, c. 1751

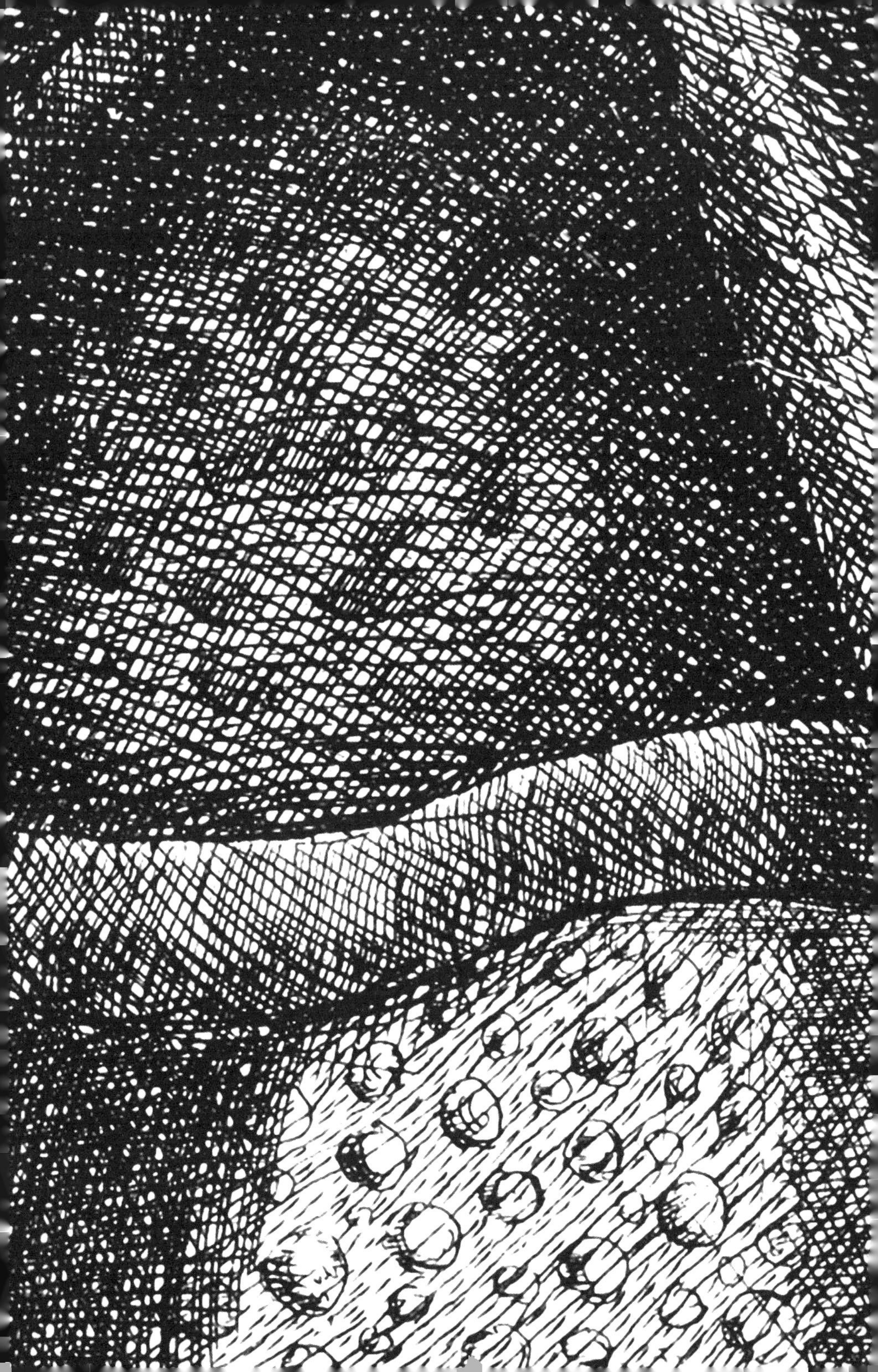

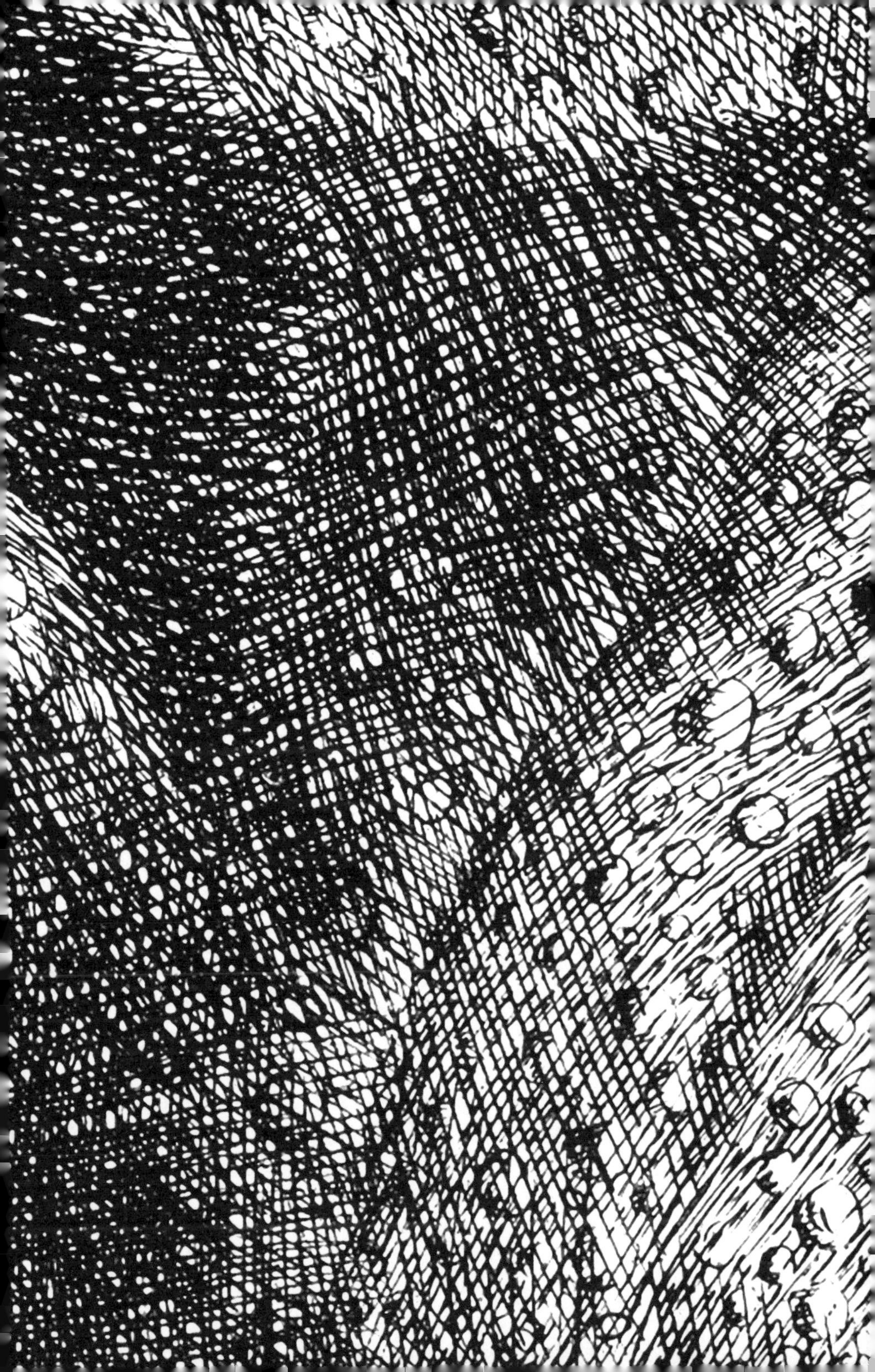

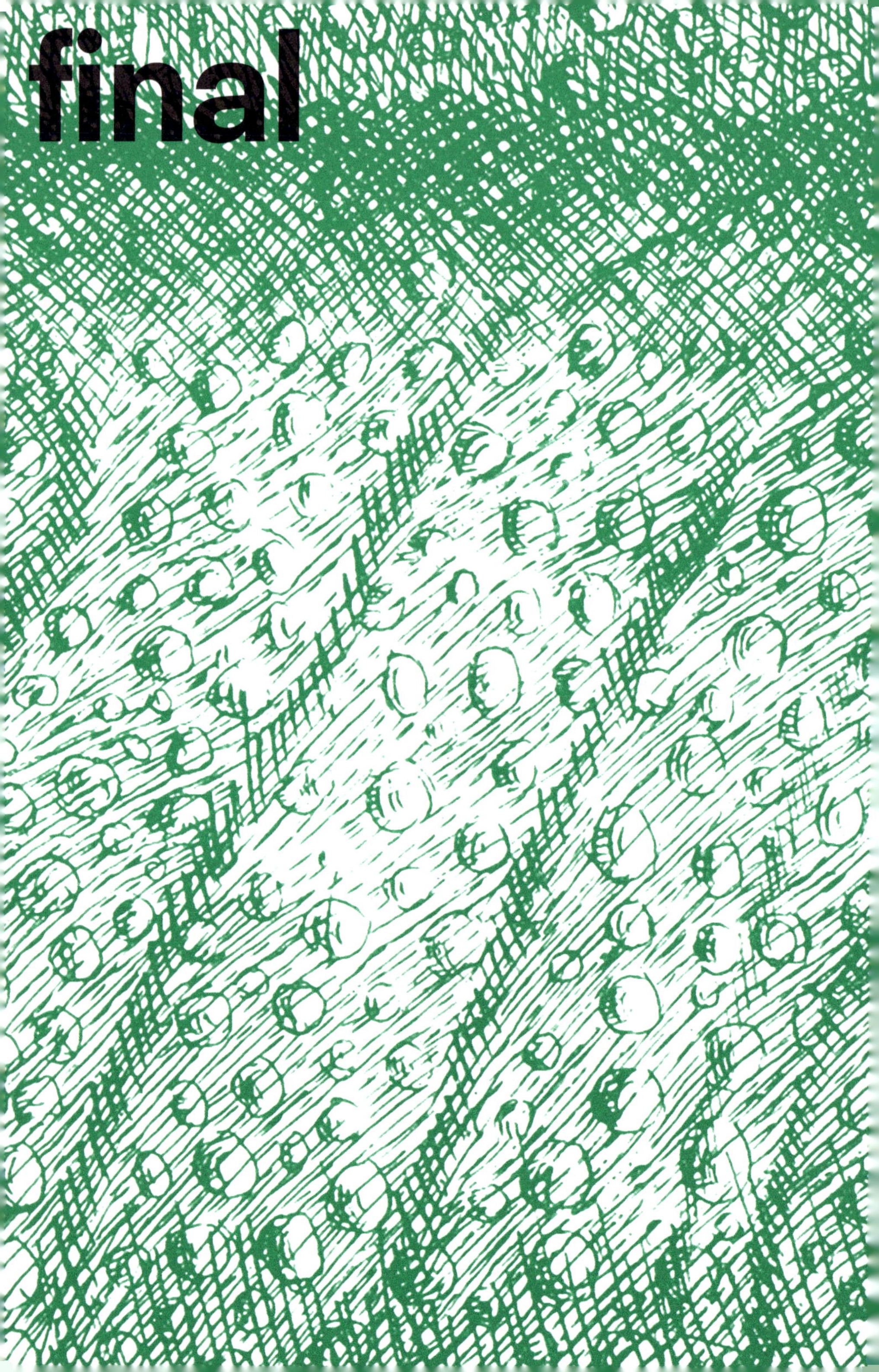
final

years

Clara cannot have stayed in her pasture on the north bank of the IJ for very long. In March 1752 she was on display in the Southern Netherlands in the city of Ghent, and from there travelled straight on to Lille, and a year later to the Foire Saint-Germain in Paris for the second time. By then she was fifteen years old and weighed 6,000 pounds. As usual, many people came to see her, including Casanova. But she does not seem to have been the talk of the town the way she was four years before, as there are few other notices of her.[106]

This trip, and possibly others, were probably undertaken from Amsterdam, as in her early European years, but in the course of 1753 Mout decided to set off with Clara on a longer journey again [map, pp. 90–91]. There were still plenty of places where no-one had ever set eyes on a live rhinoceros. In October 1753 she was displayed in Aachen and then Cologne. From there the party travelled northwards deeper into Germany. In the spring of 1754, she was exhibited in Osnabrück, Hanover and possibly also in Lüneburg and again in Hamburg, and in May she arrived in the trading city of Rostock on the Baltic Sea, where a large annual fair was held around Whitsuntide.

In addition to exhibiting her and selling prints and medals with her portrait, Mout now tried to make money out of his rhinoceros in another way. During Clara's first grand European tour, he had sold healing remedies. Some of his posters subtly claimed that Clara 'gave off' something that had the power to cure sufferers of epilepsy. Every part of her from her teeth and flesh to her dung and urine, which every rhinoceros produced in large quantities, could be used for this, but he specifically mentioned the horn of her hooves as an effective medicine. Those who were interested could buy such a remedy from his associates.[107]

This time, though, he seems to have opted for a different strategy. In an advertisement in a Rostock-based newspaper he announced that he was selling a so-called 'Sal fixum', a salt powder that could cure all sorts of illnesses. One dose of what amounted to 2.5 grammes of this 'rhinoceros salt' was on offer for one ducat. It was not exactly cheap, but it was extremely effective and could remedy everything.

Mout quoted physicians, in particular J.P. de Treytorrent who practised in Lüneburg and who called the powder 'an incomparable medicine' and had assured him that one to three doses were enough to cleanse the entire blood system. The number of illnesses he listed that could be treated with this remedy was virtually endless and moreover the effect would be noticeable within a matter of hours without causing fatigue or loss of appetite. In short, it was a wonder drug, derived from a wonder beast and more specifically from her urine, as is apparent from other publications.[108] Mout himself must have been convinced of the efficacy of this powder, otherwise he would not have sent a sample to the Royal Prussian Academy of Sciences in Berlin in June of that year. There, academy member and chemist Andreas Sigismund Marggraf was commissioned to examine the extract. He made mincemeat of it. In his view, the components that he had distilled from it – alum, vitriol and copper – meant it could not possibly have been compounded from urine and he concluded that as a medicine it could not be effective at all.[109]

After several weeks in Rostock Clara was hoisted onto a ship that was to sail further along the Baltic coast. The first stop was Stralsund, where another annual fair was in full flow, and the second was the Polish cosmopolitan port of Danzig. For the remainder of the trip Mout had at his disposal a pass permitting him to show Clara in the Polish kingdom cost-free as well as the one for Prussia that he had been given in 1746. That autumn Clara was shown in Warsaw, where a special visit was paid to the court. After this, she returned to the Baltic Sea where she stopped off at the Prussian cities of Königsberg and Memel (now the Russian Kaliningrad and the Lithuanian Klaipėda, respectively).[110]

At this point in the trip, Mout wanted to cross the Baltic Sea to present Clara in Stockholm and other Swedish cities, virgin territory for rhinoceroses. But the Swedish king refused his request. An ordinance issued in 1739 banned foreign artists who performed for money from entering the country, and no exception was made for the rhinoceros.[111] With no choice but to leave straight away, he decided to go on to Denmark, where the king did offer him the opportunity to exhibit Clara. From 5 June to 26 July 1755, she could be seen in Copenhagen, just outside one of the city gates.[112] It turned out to be the final stop in her second long tour. By the end of August Clara was back in Amsterdam, where she could be viewed at the Bergenvaarderskamer, an inn outside the city on the River Amstel. She was now 'much larger and heavier than in the year this same animal had been transported from this country to Germany and Italy,' ten years earlier.[113]

The following year Clara called on several other cities, as far as is known all in the Netherlands: in February and March 1756 she was in Groningen, in June and July she was on show at the *kermis* in Haarlem, and in August she was in Middelburg for the second time. Clara was now eighteen years old. And she looked old; at least the drawing that Cornelis van Noorde made of her at the *kermis* in Haarlem gives that impression [fig. 41]. Many of Mout's promotional prints claimed that a rhinoceros could live to be a hundred or a hundred and fifty, a claim totally unsupported by any evidence, while in fact a rhinoceros lives for an average of forty years. In the wild that is. Clara was far younger than this, but we now know that rhinoceroses never reach that age in captivity.

Besides getting on in age she was tired. And no wonder; for fifteen years she had been carted here, there and everywhere in her wooden wagon. She had hardly ever been able to walk, run or swim around freely, let alone behave naturally. All that time she had been completely dependent on the people around her, for her food and drink and for her general wellbeing. In her tent she had constantly had to put up with crowds of rowdy people, pushing and shoving and wanting to touch her. At the same time, at fifty-one, Mout was not getting any younger himself. For him, too, the continuous travel and long spells away from home had taken their toll. This appears to be the reason why in the course of 1756 he decided to dispense with Clara.

He possibly set off with her for London that autumn from Middelburg. In any case, towards the end of the year she could be admired in Lambeth, a popular entertainment area on the south bank of the River Thames. Here she was exhibited in a tent next to the Horse and Groom inn, where visitors could be driven straight in, in their carriages. The royal family came to see her, as did many noblemen and members of the court, according to a print designed to attract still more visitors. Her presentation seems to have been a success, but the woodcut of the animal that was used for the advertisement looks worn: the edge is damaged here and there, a sign not only of frequent use but that Mout was slowly cutting back on new investments.[114]

The other female rhinoceros, which had landed in Britain in 1737, was no longer alive. She had died on her way to another new showground early in 1754, aged about twenty. Clara had the kingdom to herself and a new tour, this time of Great Britain, was now among the possibilities. Mout was no longer to accompany Clara, however. Everything suggests that he managed to sell her in London. In any case he was back in Amsterdam at the end of March 1758, while Clara was still in London. In the meantime, Wilmkebreek had been rented out

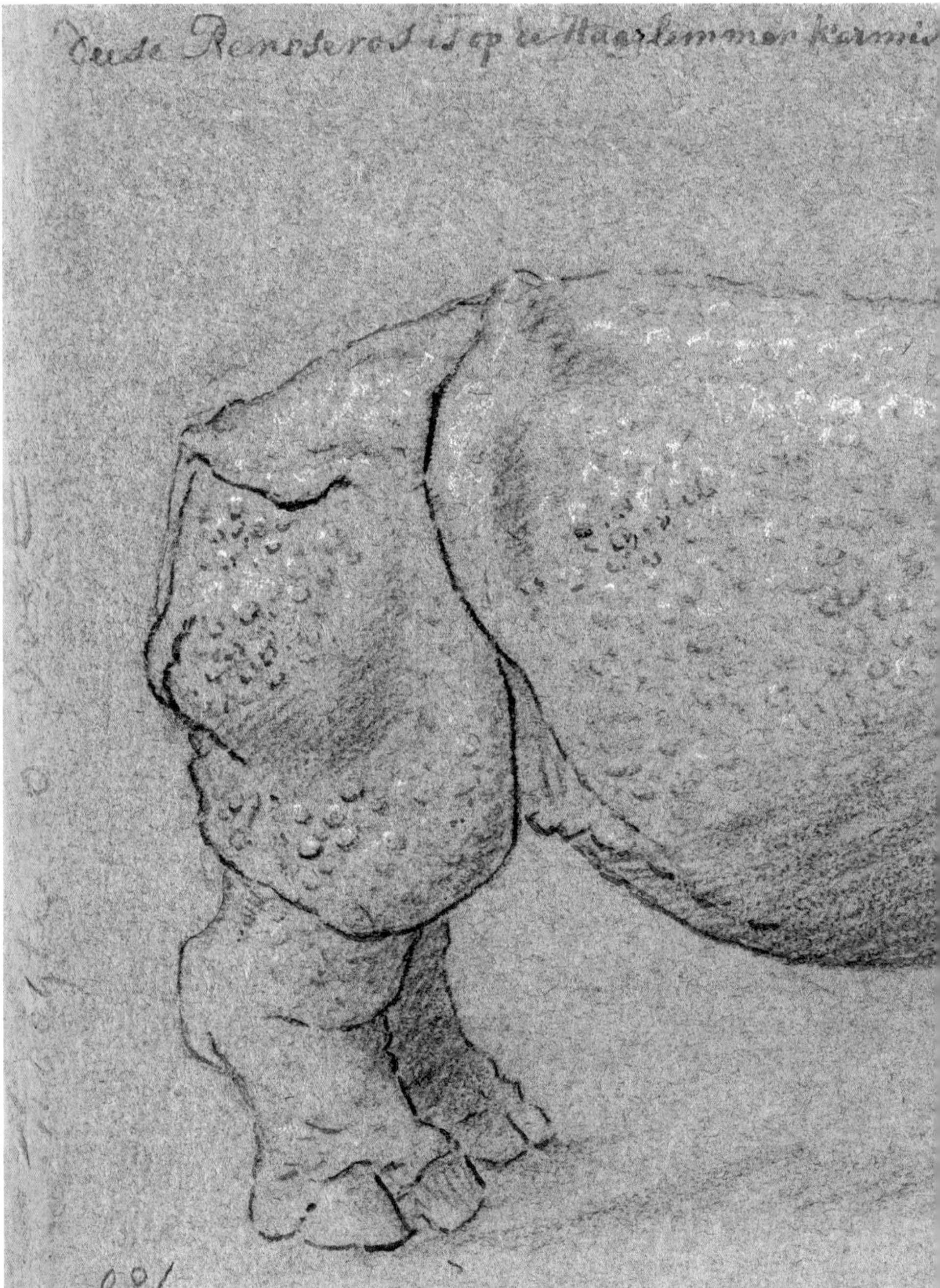

41
Clara during the *kermis* in Haarlem,
Cornelis van Noorde, 1756

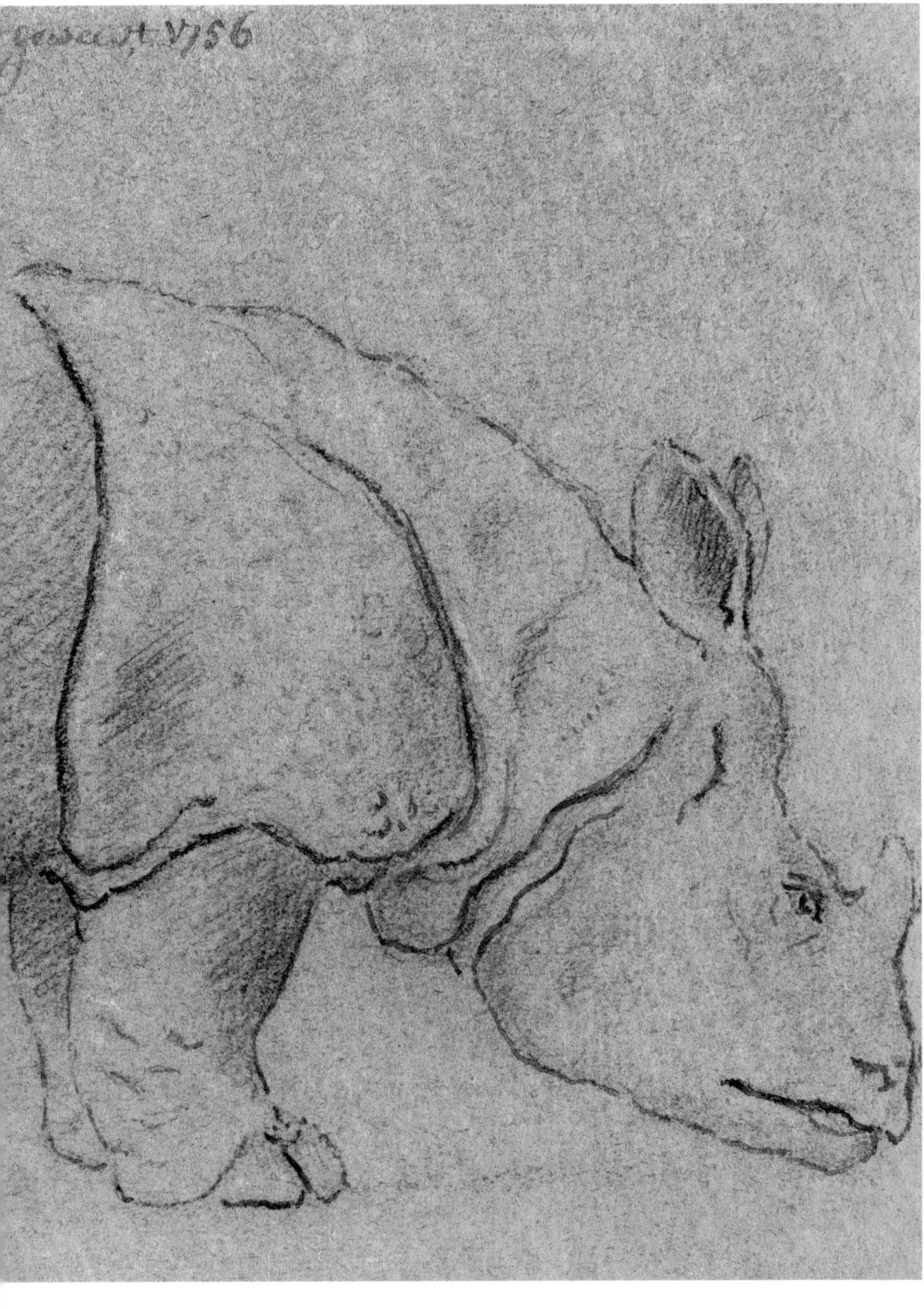

by his wife Elisabeth on Mout's behalf since 1 May 1757, and on 1 April 1758 he sold his estate at public auction. It meant farewell to the pasture he had purchased for Clara in 1744, to the land to which he owed his Austrian noble title, to the house he and his family had considered their home for over a decade. He received 1,800 guilders for it, a good deal less than he had paid nearly fourteen years before.[115]

Two weeks after the auction Clara passed away, after having been in England for some eighteen months. 'Deceased in London on 14 April 1758 at the age of 21', two almost identical prints reported, one produced in Nuremberg, the other in Frankfurt.[116] No other notices are known. We do not know how she died, nor the cause of her death, nor do we have any knowledge of what happened to her enormous corpse. All we know is that Clara was no longer alive.

Little can be traced about Mout's life without Clara in the years that followed. There is no indication that he returned to sea. Douwe and Elisabeth went back to live in Amsterdam. Their last addresses were in Nieuwendijk, not a particularly prosperous part of the city, but not poor either. We do not know whether sufficient money was left over after his many travels with Clara or whether he could still earn a little money on the side by selling rhinoceros cures. He certainly had enough time to work on a plan which he submitted, neatly printed, to the directors of the Dutch West India Company in 1761. But his proposal to restore the company to 'a good and flourishing state' by establishing settlements in distant Patagonia and New Zealand was dismissed without further discussion as 'impracticable'.[117]

After Clara's death, the couple saw two of their sons enter the employ of the VOC. First the nearly twenty-one-year-old Nicolaas sailed to Asia as a steward's mate in 1760, followed, two years later by their eldest son Jan as a steward, thereby treading in their father's footsteps. But fate did not smile on them as kindly. Neither of them returned from their second voyage and both died far away in Asia: first Nicolaas in 1765, then Jan in 1771.[118]

Their second son Jacob chose a very different path from an early age. In October 1751 he left to study law in Leiden and four years later was working as a lawyer. In 1766 Jacob, who consistently used the surname Mout van der Meer, moved to Geertruidenberg where the States General had appointed him Inspector of Import and Export Rights, a good job involving considerable responsibility and autonomy. He passed away in Amsterdam early in March 1778 at the age of forty-three, evidently leaving no wife or children.[119]

Elisabeth, Douwe and Elisabeth's youngest child, was the only sibling who lived close to her parents in their old age. She married

Pieter Pieterse in 1774 and together they had five children. But Douwe never knew them.[120] Early in August 1775, shortly before his eldest child was born, Douwe died at the age of seventy. He is more likely to have left debts than a fortune, otherwise his children Jacob and Elisabeth would not have had to formally renounce their right to their inheritance according to the 1749 will so soon. They were prepared to bear the expenses of the funeral 'solely out of piety', but that was all. Two and a half years later their mother Elisabeth also died, aged sixty-three. Like her husband she was buried at the Noorderkerk cemetery.[121] There is nothing to suggest that they had kept anything that reminded them of Clara and their travels in Europe. And yet this rhinoceros would not be forgotten. On the contrary, she had made such a big impact that others preserved her legacy.

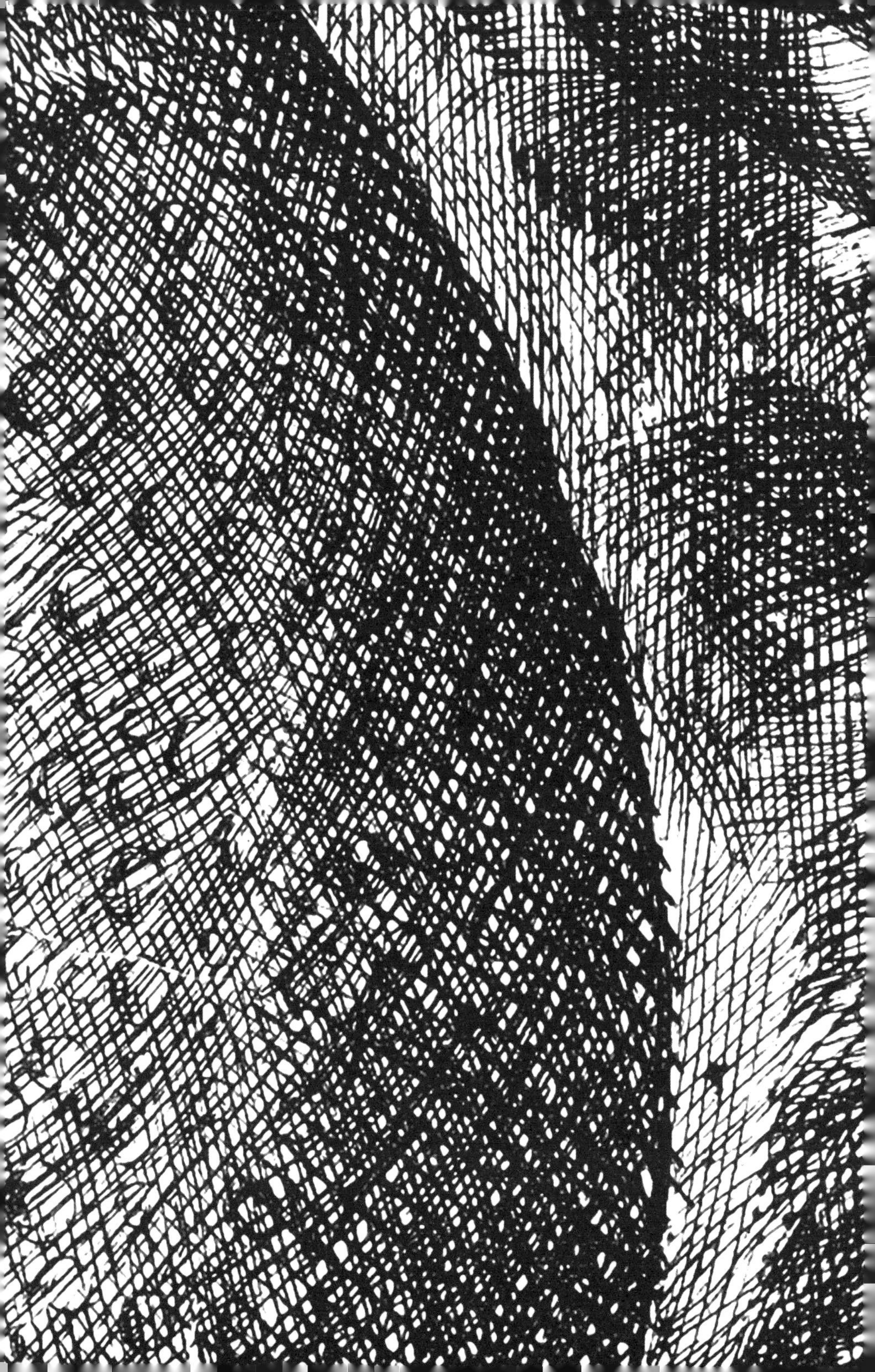

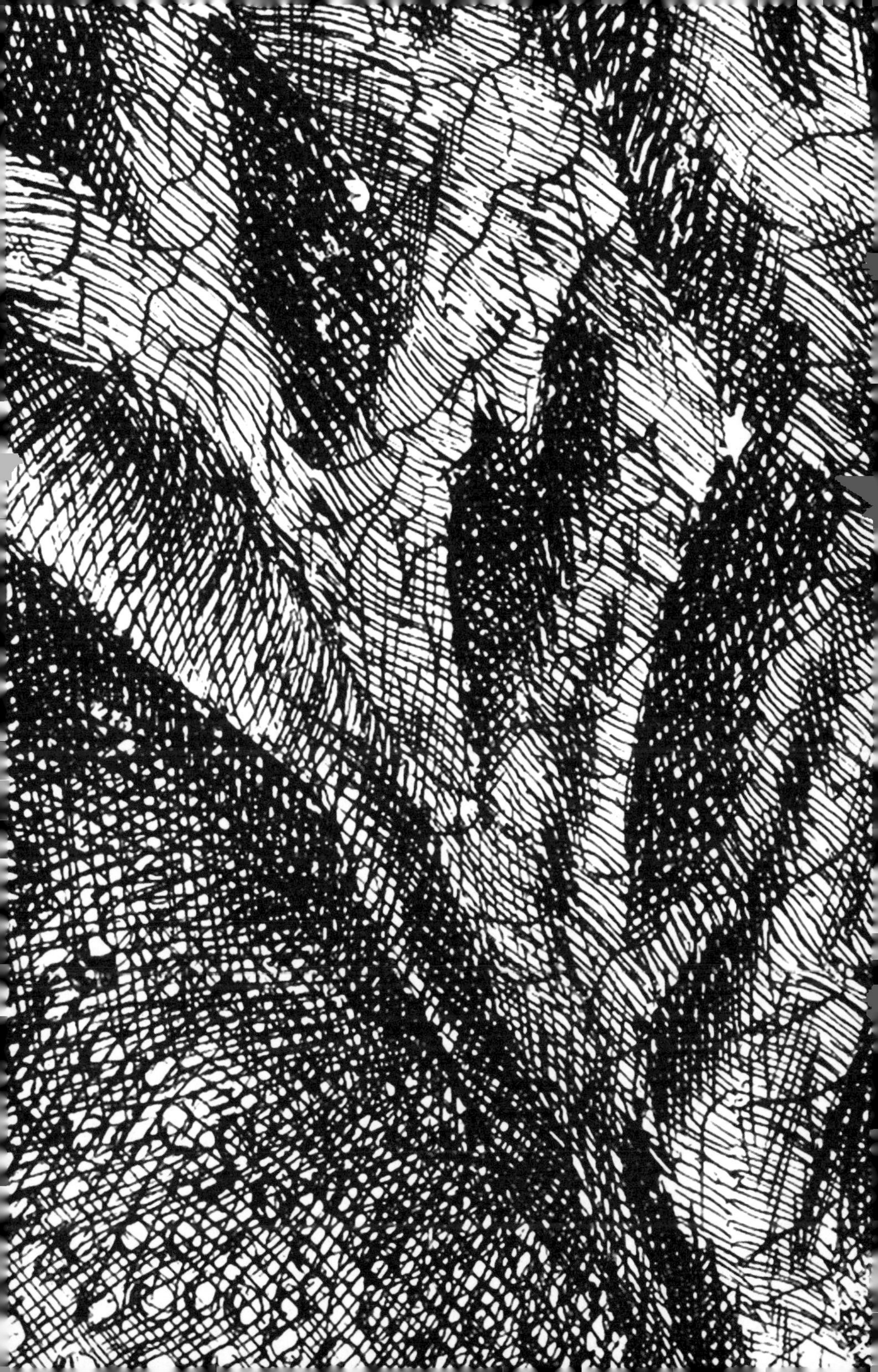

images of

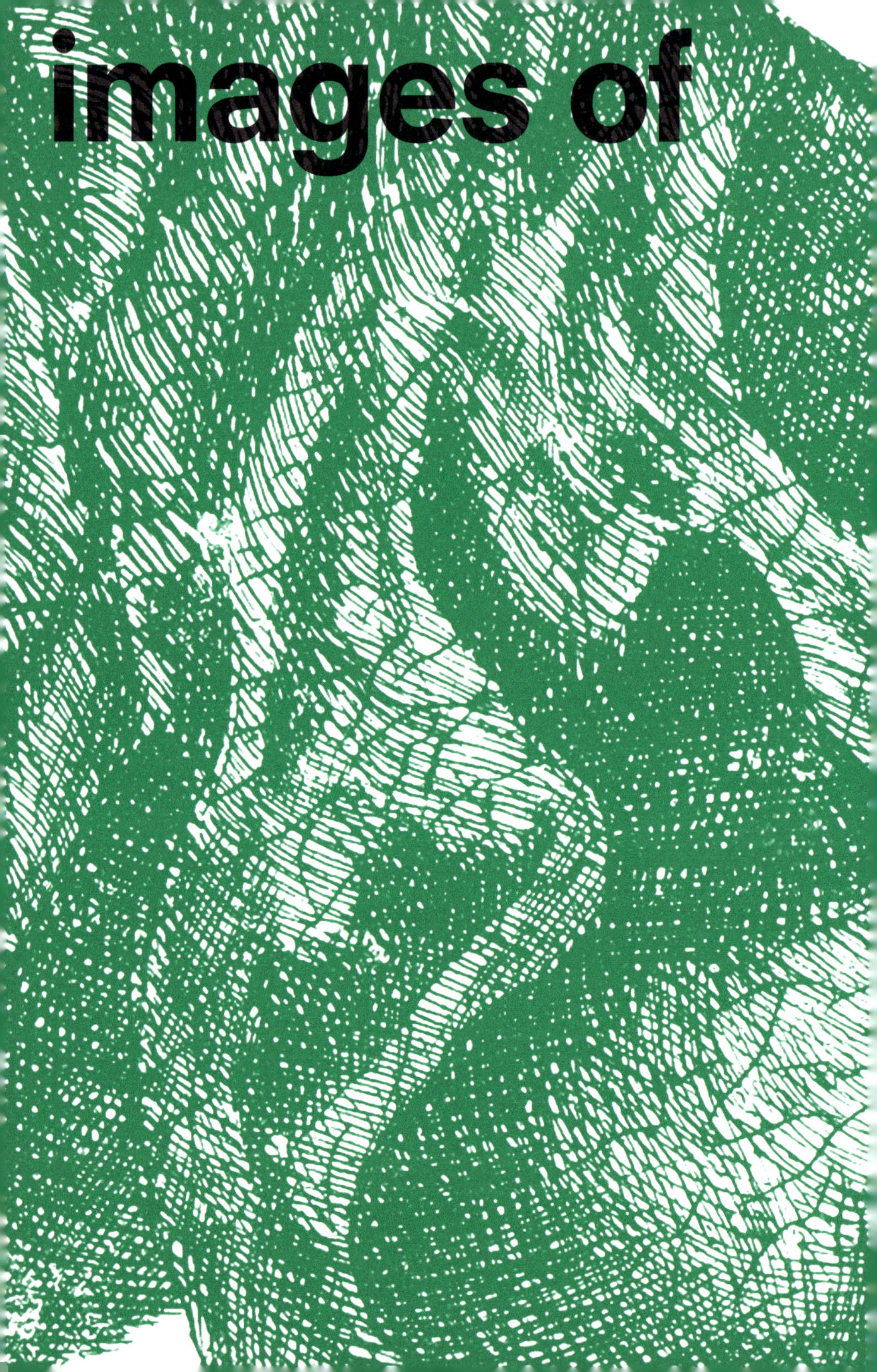

clara

In every city where Clara was exhibited, she had made a deep, often indelible, impression, if only because of her appearance. For many people the confrontation with this extraordinary phenomenon was an utterly unforgettable experience, one of those events you remember for the rest of your life, according to the Walloon physician Guillaume-Lambert Godart in a book on the human soul, published in 1755. For just as you remember being struck by a person of exceptional beauty, you never forget what it was like to stand before a rhinoceros.[122] Nonetheless, to be quite sure of preserving that memory, many people bought a print or a medal on which the animal was portrayed. Also, those who had not been able to see her in real life could get some idea of her through such portraits, even though this did not compare with a live encounter.

Like Dürer's rhinoceros, Clara was portrayed from the side in a static pose on these prints and medals. Apparently, the heaviness and enormity of the animal could best be conveyed from this angle. Although Dürer's representation remained popular for a long time to come, there was a growing awareness of what a rhinoceros looked like in reality. As a result, during her lifetime, Clara gradually ousted the prevailing image of the rhinoceros. Dürer's engraving became outdated, Clara became the new standard.

In addition, various artists had seized the opportunity to record the rhinoceros themselves. While each did so in their own way, they all depicted Clara, just as Camper and Wandelaar had done in Leiden in 1742, as a living and lively creature, an animal of flesh and blood. One of them was Johann Elias Ridinger, who was a specialist in painting animals and hunting scenes and was active in Augsburg. When Clara stayed in this important trading city for four weeks in June 1748, he had sketched her from every angle, capturing her as an individual. Sometimes she lies at complete rest, at other times she turns or lifts her head or looks at her observer [figs. 42–45, 47]. Occasionally he added a detail – a leg, her open mouth – as if he were trying to understand her while drawing. He made a print from one of these sketches [fig. 42] later that year which was widely distributed. A resident of Augsburg

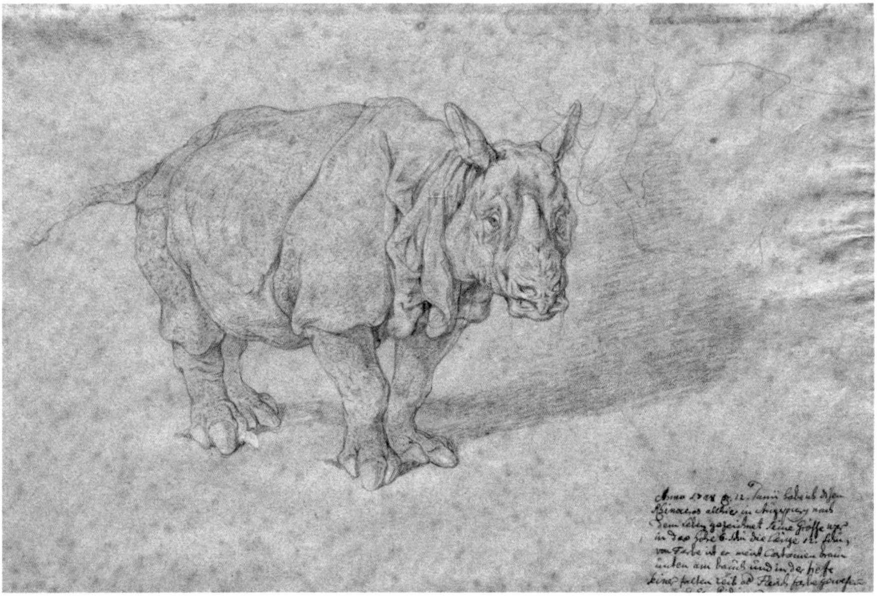

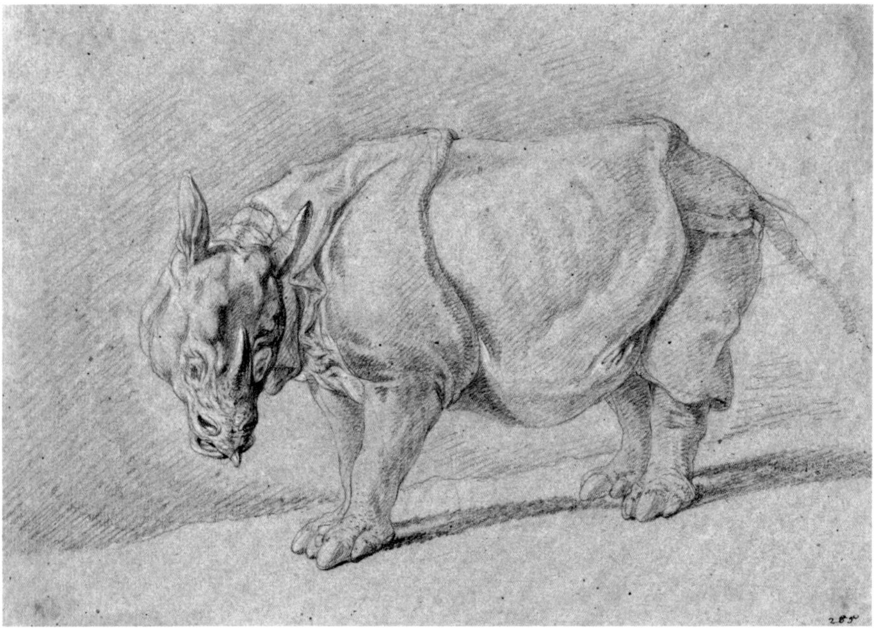

42–45

Portraits of Clara in Augsburg, Johann Elias Ridinger, 1748. A note indicates that Ridinger made his sketches on 12 June of that year

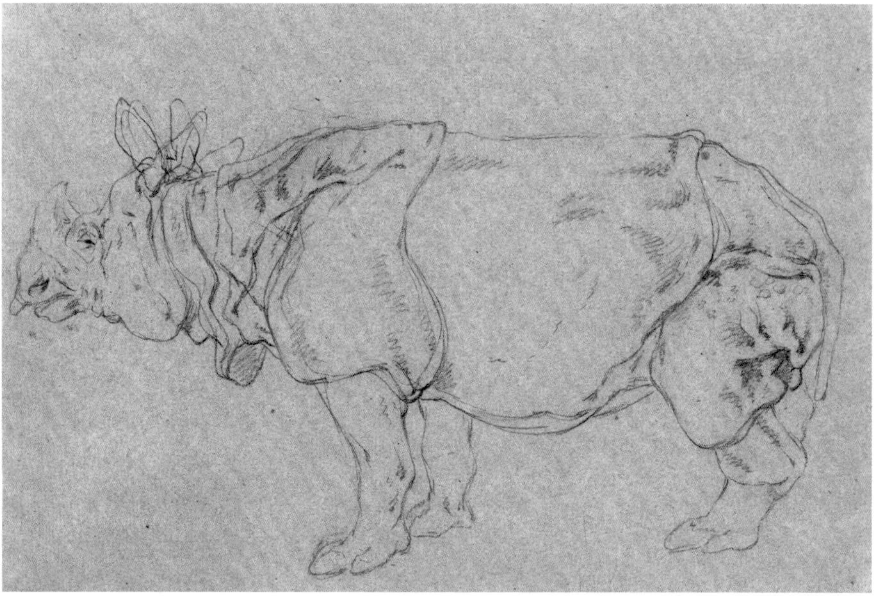

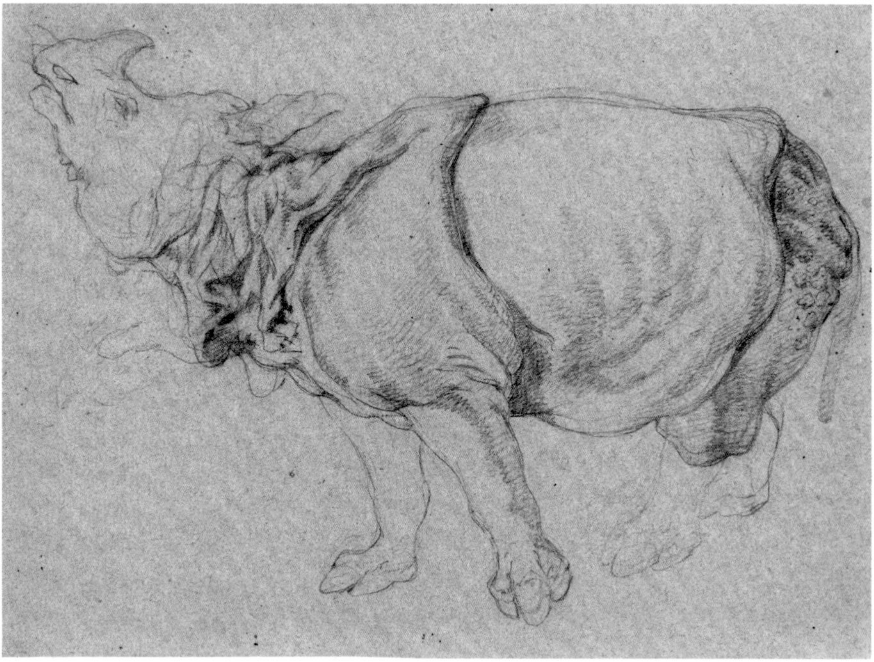

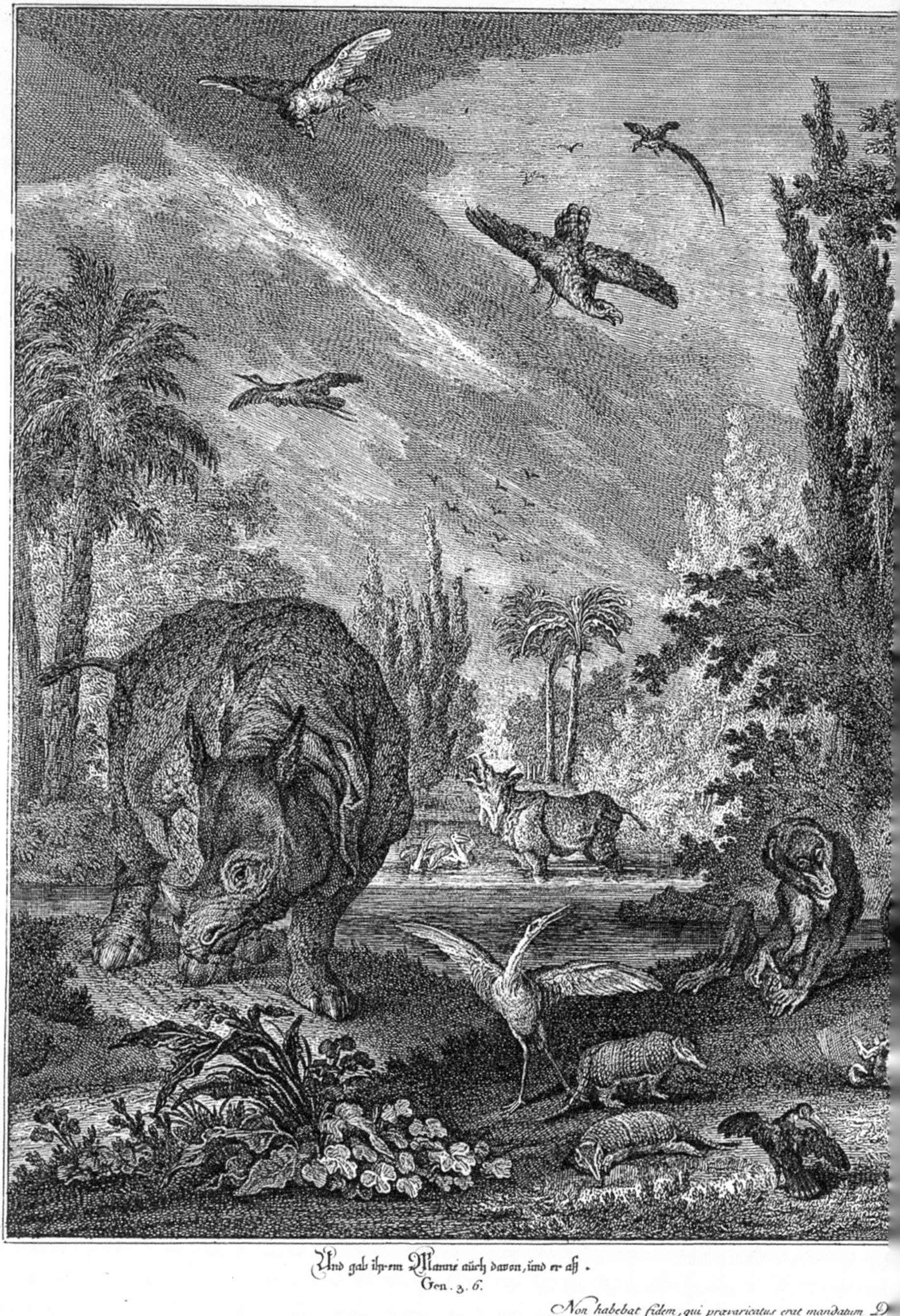

Und gab ihrem Manne auch davon, und er aß.
Gen. 3. 6.

Non habebat fidem, qui prævaricatus erat mandatum D
S. Ambros.

J. El. Ridinger inv. fec. et excud. Aug. Vind.

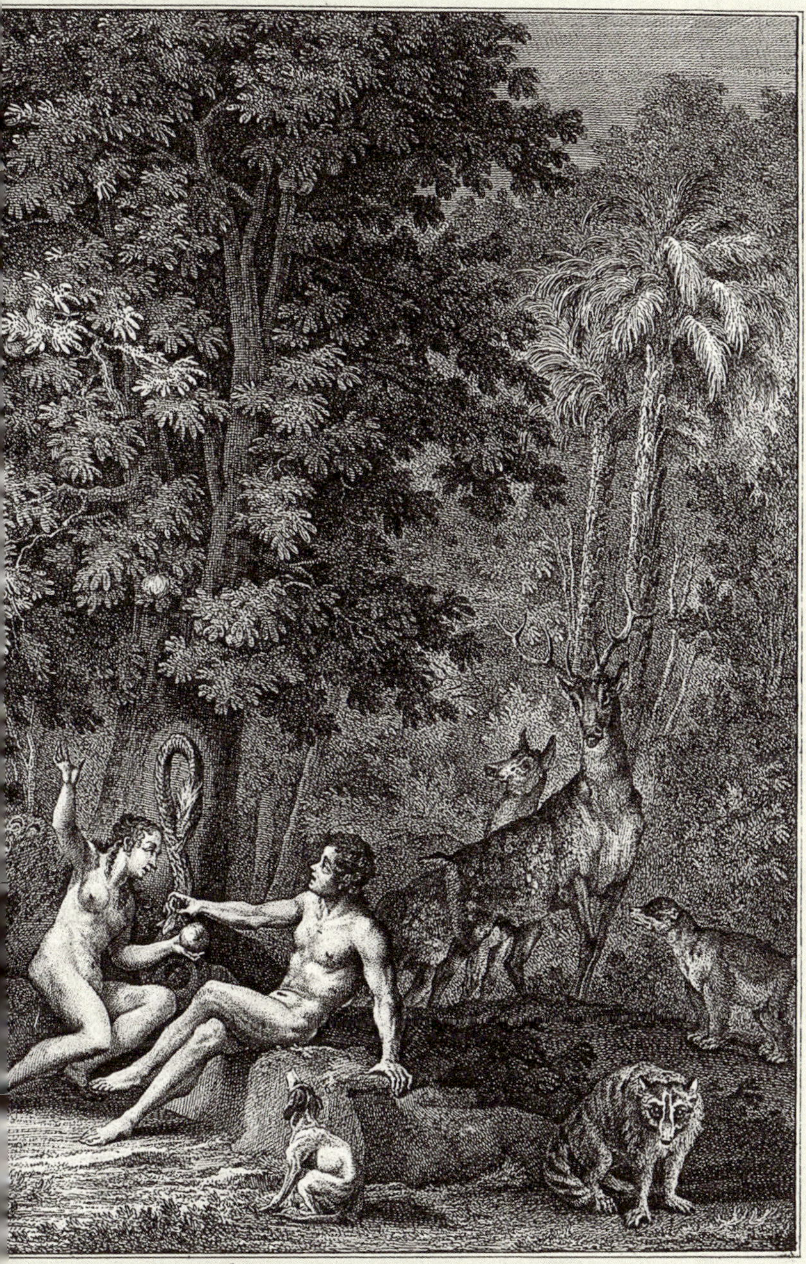

Elle a donné au mari qui en mangeoit.
Gen. 3. 6.

...iā qui de interdicto sibi gustaverat ligno .

46
Adam and Eve with two rhinoceroses (both Clara), Johann Elias Ridinger, 1748 or shortly after

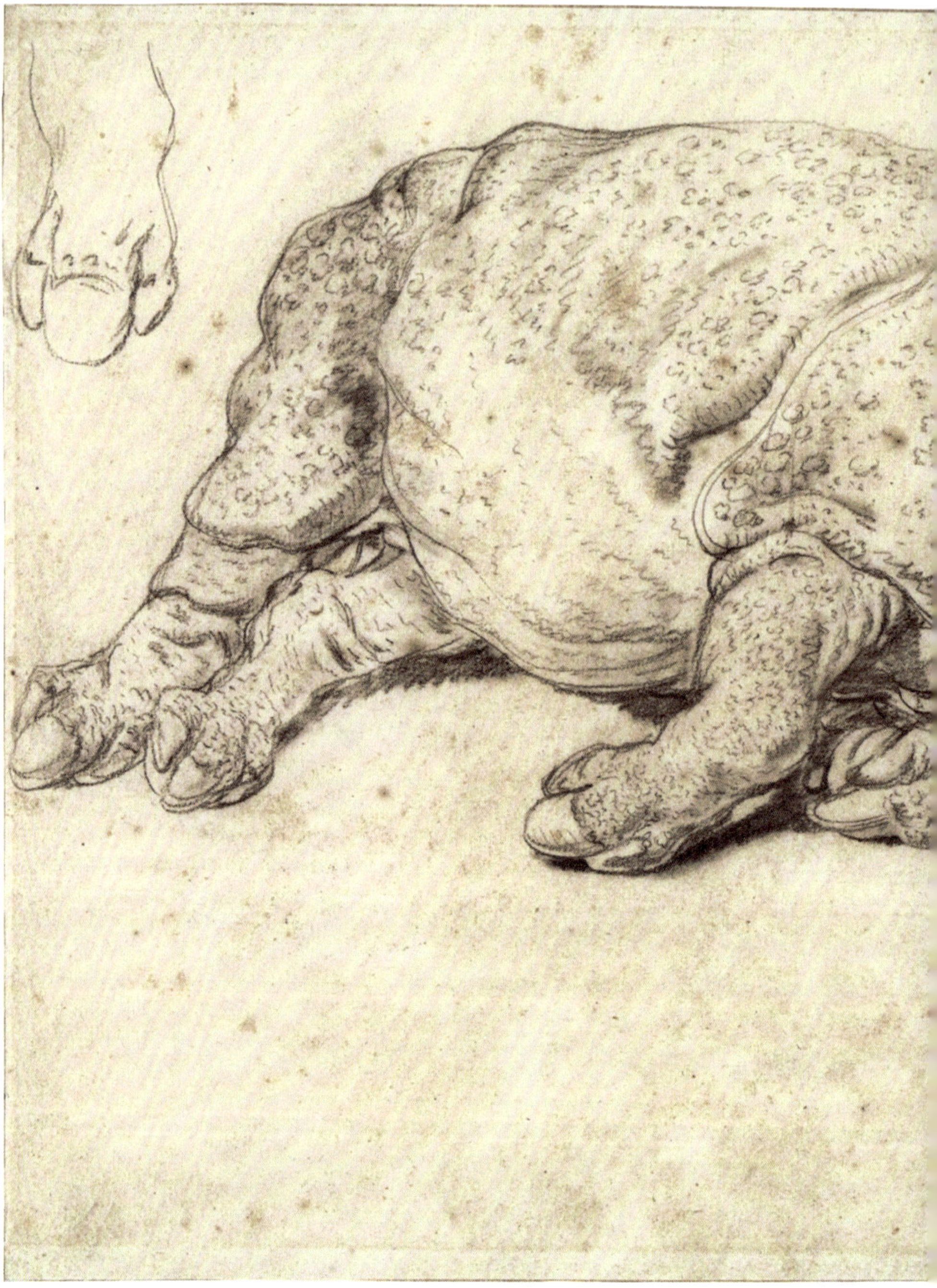

47

Portrait of Clara in Augsburg,
Johann Elias Ridinger, 1748

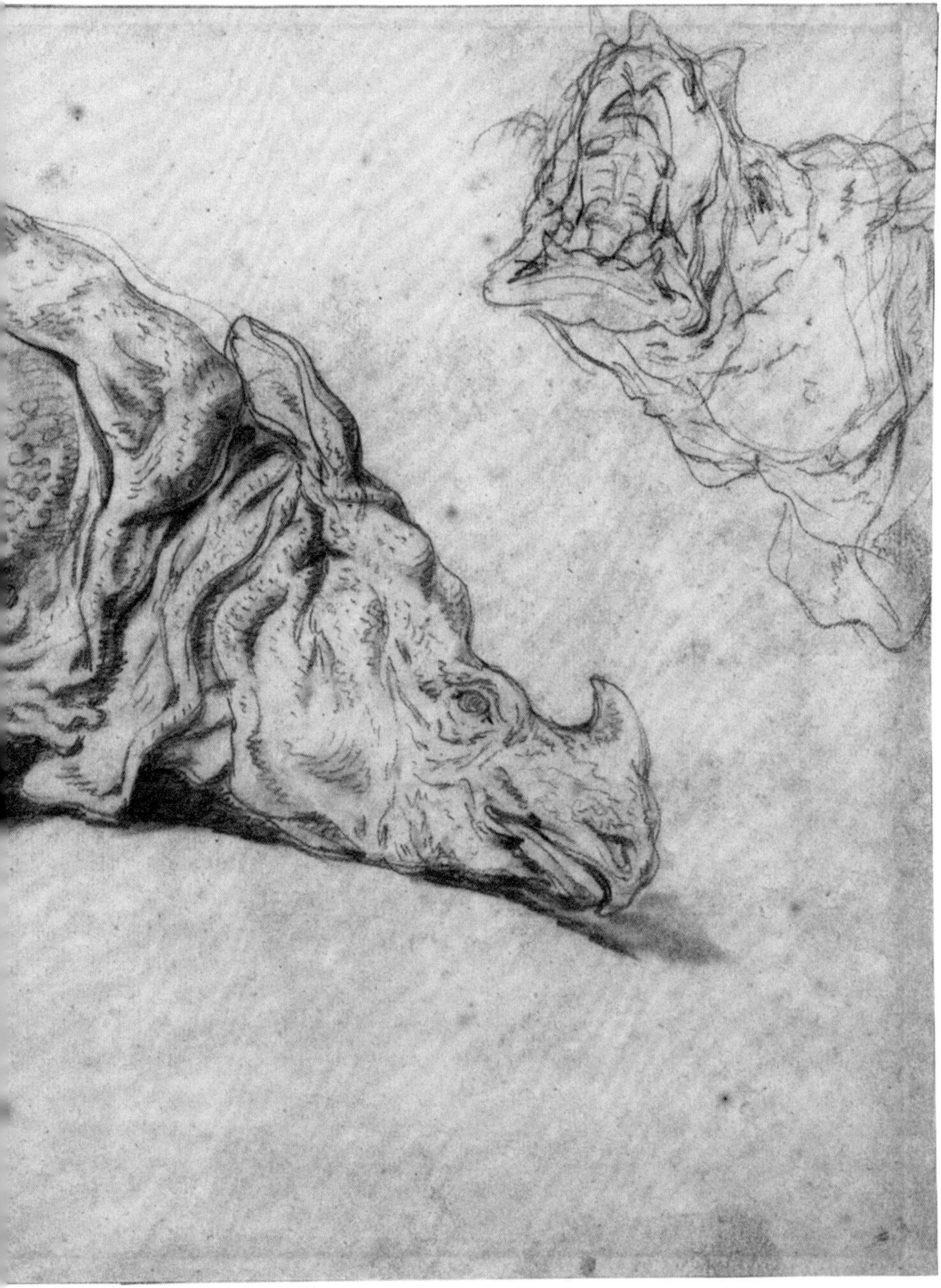

even wrote to a learned friend about it: 'Our animal painter Ridinger is now working on the rhinoceros, which he has drawn from life, for all the previous well-known portraits are incorrect.'[123] It was indeed a portrait full of movement. The somewhat stiff character that Clara displayed in many other prints is completely absent here. Moreover, he used two of these sketches in a print of Adam and Eve in Paradise [fig. 46], and another one in a spectacular rendering of the fight between an elephant and a rhinoceros. Here too Ridinger depicted Clara in action. But above all his sketches are pure and direct; they show Clara as she really looked and behaved.

In Verona and Venice another – now unknown – artist became fascinated with Clara when she was exhibited there early in 1751. He made at least sixteen sketches in black chalk on blue paper which are featured in an album compiled at a later date [figs. 48–51].[124] He recorded her from almost every angle: her rear, her head (with and without a horn), her flank, her legs. Sometimes he captured her with a single fine line, sometimes he sketched her roughly, sometimes he worked his drawings up in considerable detail. Some sheets contain several details, others merely one small aspect of the rhinoceros. Now and then he drew parts of her among sketches of drapery, heads, children or landscapes. Unlike Ridinger he never drew her in her entirety from head to tail; he drew only details. These are real studies, which show that the artist wanted to capture Clara's character. But what motivated him to do so is a mystery. It is quite possible that the artist was the twenty-seven-year-old Francesco Lorenzi, an industrious pupil of the renowned Venetian painter Giambattista Tiepolo. Lorenzi is certainly the author of two other sketches of Clara, which are strongly akin to these.[125] Whatever the case, the artist was well acquainted with the graceful style of Tiepolo, who together with his painter sons realized an enormous virtuoso ceiling painting in the palace in Würzburg from the end of 1750. All sorts of animals figure in this: camels, an ostrich, an elephant, but unfortunately not the rhinoceros – Clara. Nor does a rhinoceros feature in any of the numerous other paintings and mural and ceiling paintings by Tiepolo, his sons, assistants or other artists working in his style. Lorenzi saw Clara and recorded her, but the sketches were never worked up. And the great master himself had evidently missed her.

Fortunately, about two years before, the experienced painter sixty-three-year-old Jean-Baptiste Oudry had had a chance to portray Clara in grand style in Paris. Throughout his long career the artist had specialized in painting animals and large hunting scenes. In the late 1730s he was commissioned to create a series of portraits of animals from the royal menagerie in Versailles. The king had never bought the characterful portraits, many in large format, and Oudry still had them in his possession.[126] The artist must have seen Clara's stay in Paris in 1749 as an opportunity to add the rhinoceros to the series. He decided to paint a life-size portrait of her, a radical decision resulting in a canvas measuring over 3 metres high and approximately 4.5 metres wide. In this he portrayed Clara in the traditional manner from the side, standing still in a hilly though otherwise undefined landscape [fig. 52]. This allowed him to offset her colouring, her size and various other details of her enormous body. The painting is also a real portrait, and although Oudry may have made her horn larger and shinier than it was in reality, it is impossible to get any closer to Clara physically, mainly due to the size of the work. Although the rhinoceros's field of vision is extremely limited, Oudry even conveys the impression that Clara is looking straight at you, the viewer. She stares and is stared at, and of course the same applies vice versa. Even though she is motionless, standing before this enormous painting, you can well imagine the impact and the feelings it aroused in spectators in Paris and elsewhere when they were first confronted with this massive, awesome creature.

Not surprisingly, the painting attracted attention. In December 1749 an anonymous poem was published in the *Mercure de France* which sang the praises of the painting. Besides pointing out the good likeness, the poet remarked that the expression in her eye was so cruel that it made the animal appear insensitive, an impression incidentally that not everyone would have shared.[127] In September 1750 the painting hung in the annual Salon du Louvre, where, true to tradition, numerous painters showed their recent work. By then Oudry had already succeeded in selling the piece along with a number of paintings of the animals from the royal menagerie. For years a fervent collector of Oudry's work, Christian Ludwig II, Duke of Mecklenburg-Schwerin, had purchased it for 800 livres on the recommendation of his son and later successor Friedrich. It was the most expensive though the most desirable of the fifteen paintings the painter had offered the duke. When the Salon was over, the canvas was rolled up and shipped to Schwerin in North Germany, where it has remained ever since.[128]

In addition to being captured two-dimensionally in paint, print or pencil, during her lifetime Clara was also immortalized three-dimensionally in clay and metal, although not full size. In the decorative arts, her live image instantly replaced Dürer's model. The porcelain factory in Meissen had produced several more large rhinoceroses based on Dürer's portrait in 1731, but a few years after Clara's visit to Dresden in 1747, it brought out a figurine of Clara herself, albeit a much smaller image measuring 16.5 centimetres in length [fig. 53].

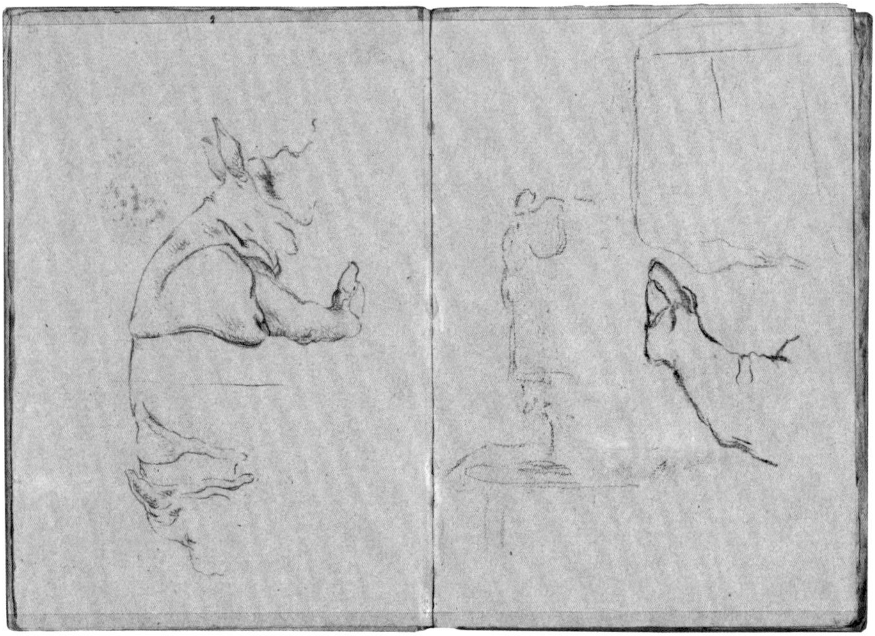

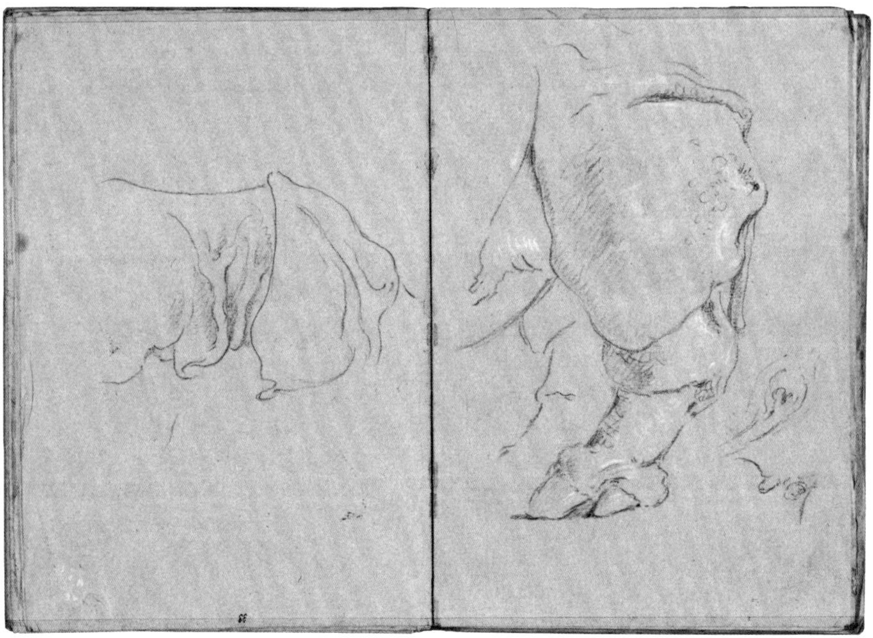

48–51

Sketches of details of Clara by an anonymous artist (Francesco Lorenzi?), 1751

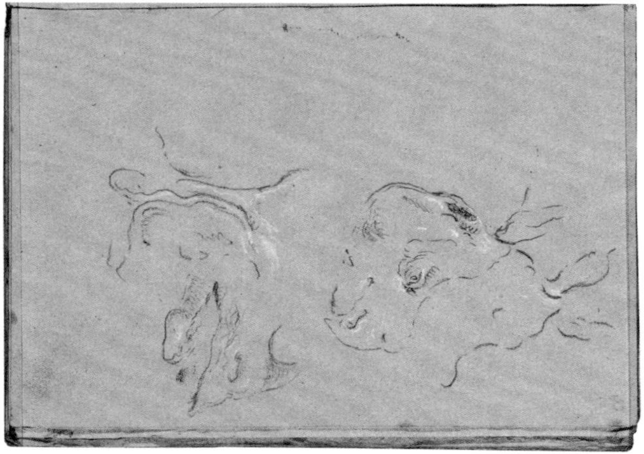
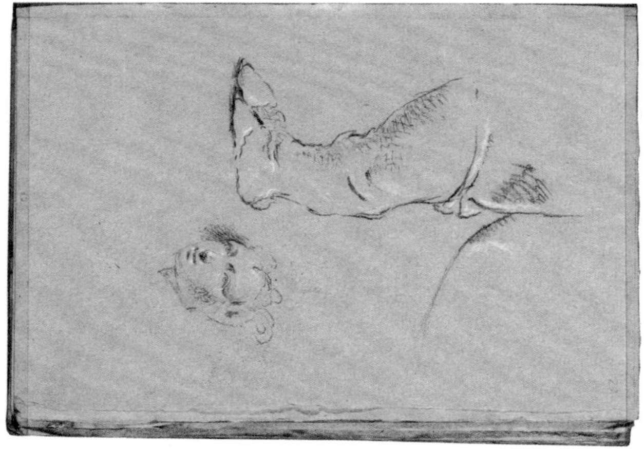

52 [pp. 138–139]
Life-size portrait of Clara in a hilly landscape, Jean-Baptiste Oudry, 1749

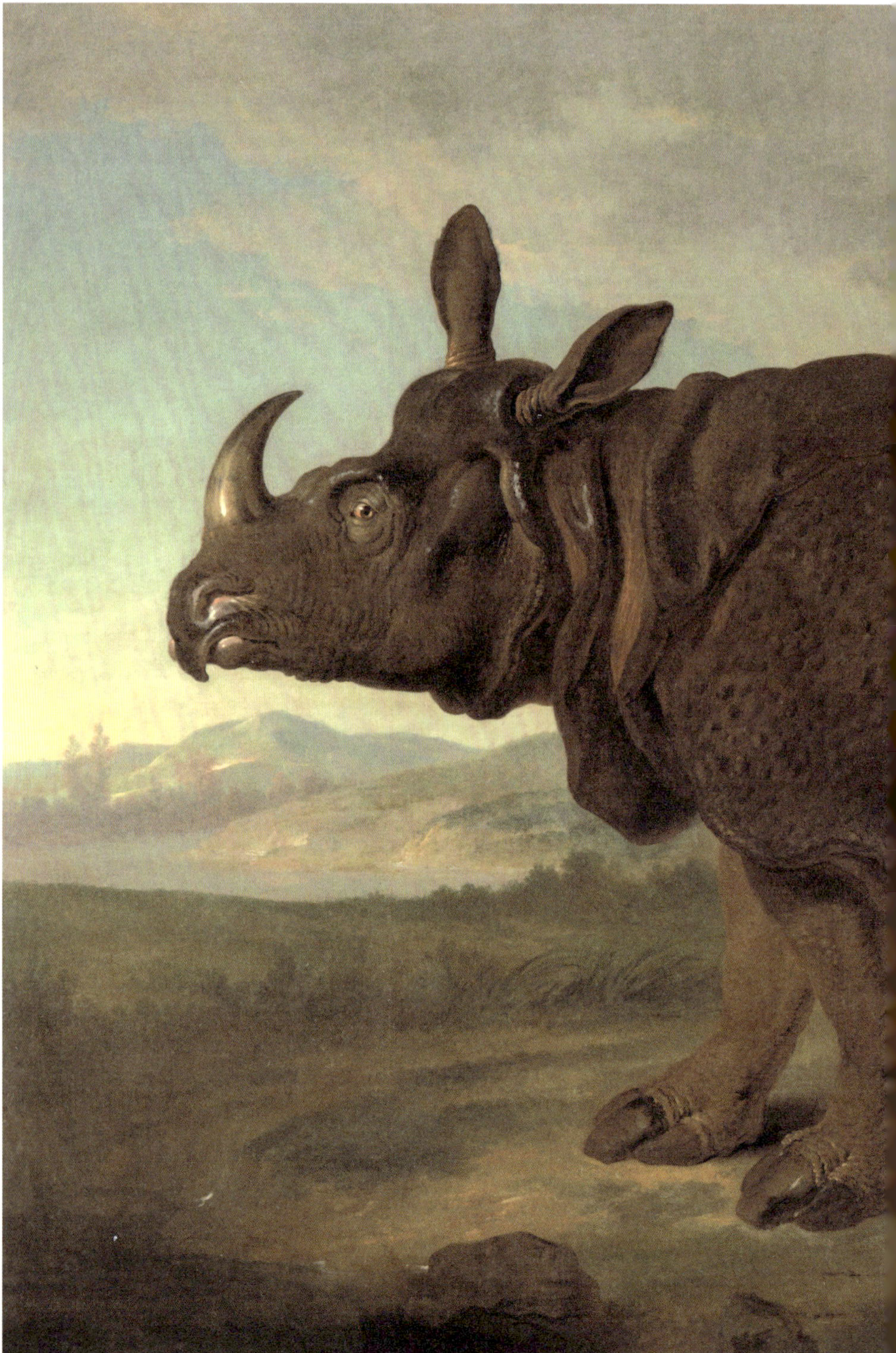

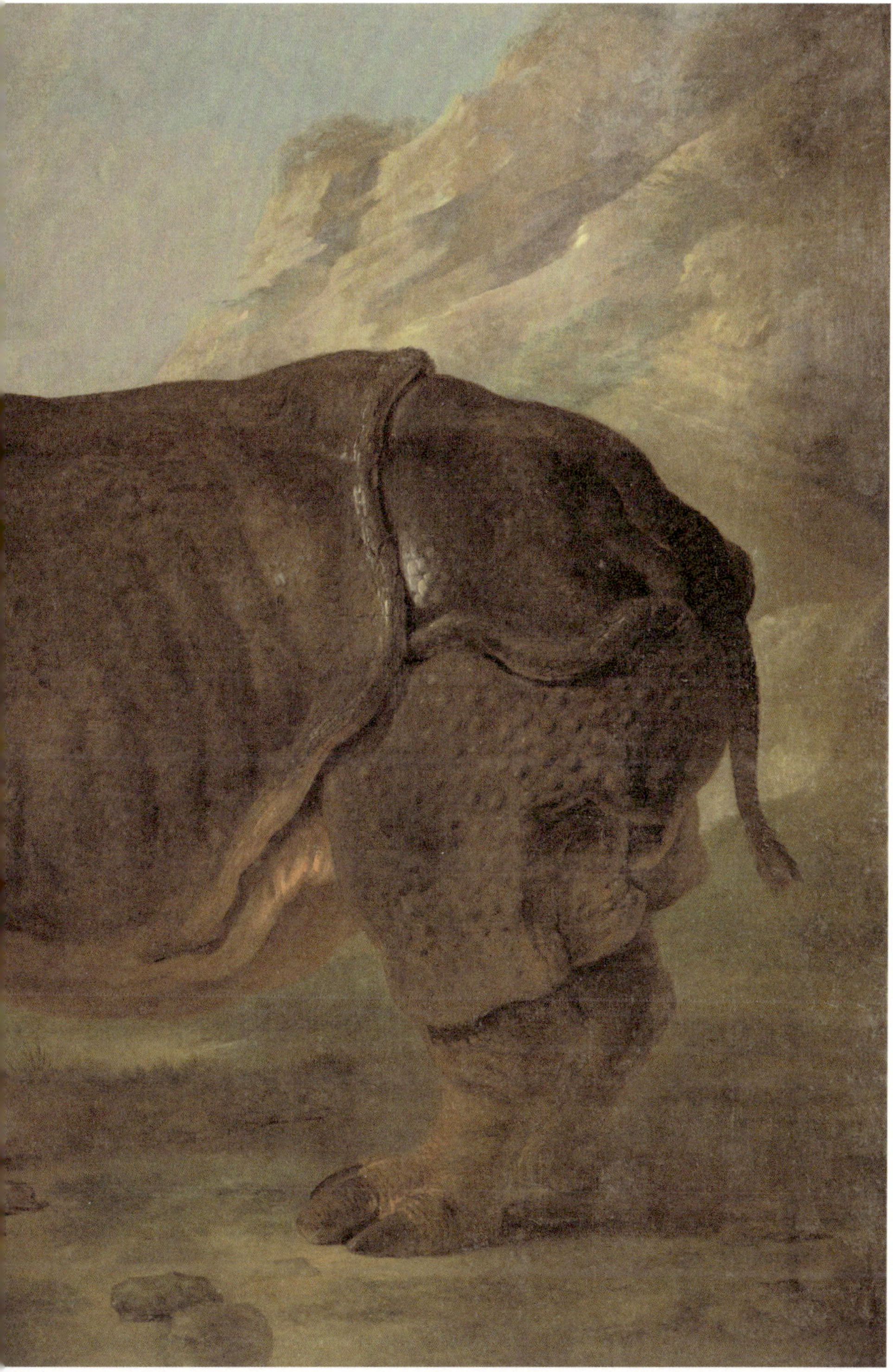

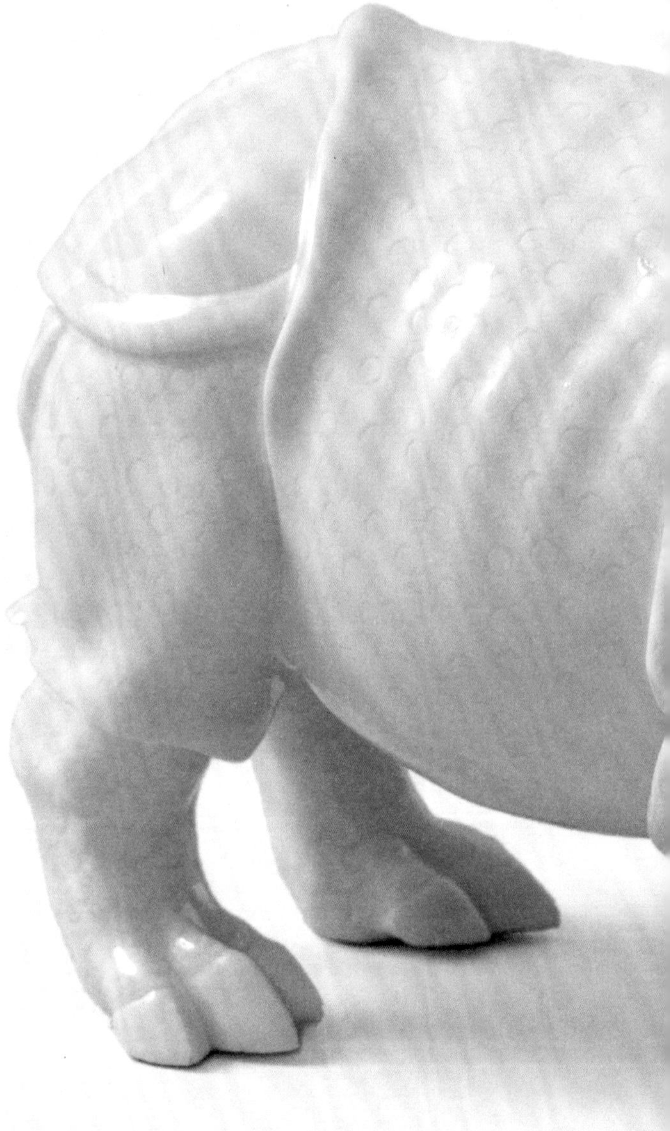

53
Clara in Meissen porcelain,
Johann Joachim Kaendler, 1755

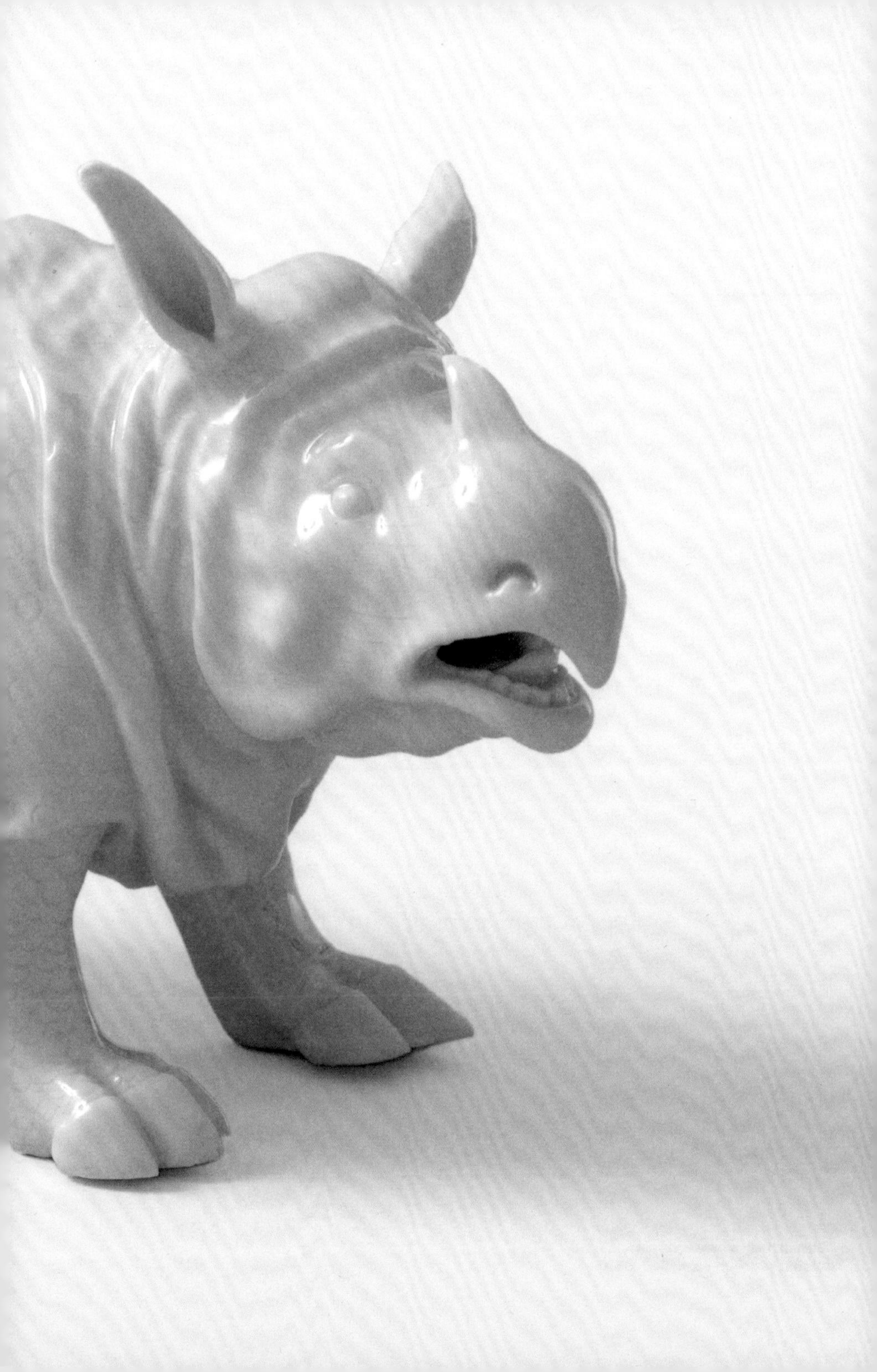

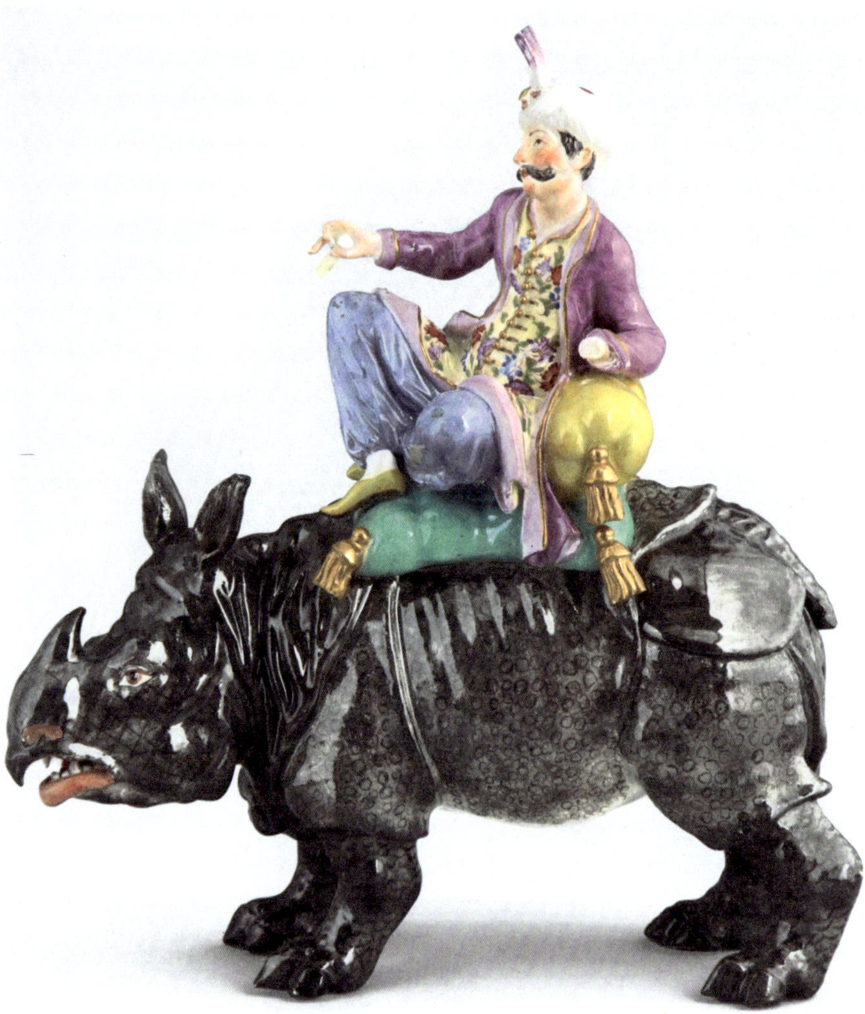

54
Clara with a Turkish man on her back,
Königliche Porzellan-Manufaktur Meissen,
c. 1755

Modeller Johann Joachim Kaendler must have studied and drawn her personally, for his versions undeniably deviate from the then well-known prints. For instance, her head is relatively large in comparison with her body, her upper lip is strongly pronounced and the folds in her skin are accentuated. Kaendler produced several variants. The figurine of Clara was on sale – white or coloured – either on its own or as a prominent component of an exotic scene. In the latter she was given a Turkish rider on her back, or else she was placed alongside a Chinese man and a palm tree, even though both settings had nothing to do with her real origins [figs. 54, 55].[129] A new cliché was born, while at the same time Clara ousted the prevailing image and served as the actual model for the rhinoceros here.

A similar development took place in the workshop of the Parisian bronze-caster and clock-maker Jean-Joseph de Saint-Germain. He produced costly table clocks for a wealthy clientele. His timepieces were often borne by an animal: an elephant, horse, camel or bull, and occasionally a rhinoceros. Before, in the 1740s, he modelled the latter as a matter of course on the Dürer portrait but after Clara was exhibited in Paris in 1749, he made at least two new rhinoceros models which undoubtedly depict Clara. One bears a strong resemblance to Kaendler's Meissen statue, the other shows her with her head up, her ears pricked and her mouth open – as if she was making a sound and could hear something [fig. 56]. This last figurine must have been his own handcrafted design, for it is quite unlike any of the representations known to date. Stand-alone pieces are not known. These small figures cast in bronze were exclusively intended as components for his richly ornamented and gilded clocks that were mounted on a musical box which doubled as a base. Saint-Germain did not make the actual clock movement or music mechanism himself; other specialists were responsible for these, the most important being François Viger. The most prestigious buyers of these highly exclusive objects included the French court and high-ranking persons linked with the royal house. A granddaughter of King Louis XV, Maria Luisa of Parma, even had herself portrayed with such a rhinoceros clock in 1765 when she was sixteen, on the occasion of her marriage to her cousin Carlos, the Crown Prince of Spain, a marriage that was to make her the Spanish queen in 1788 [fig. 57].[130]

Interestingly, there continued to be a demand for special images of Clara for some time after her death, notably from European royal courts. This was partly due to the efforts of the sculptor Pieter Anton Verschaffelt. Born in Ghent in 1710, after having trained in Paris, he settled in Rome, where he may have seen Clara in 1750. Two years later he entered the service of Karl Theodor, Elector of the Palatinate,

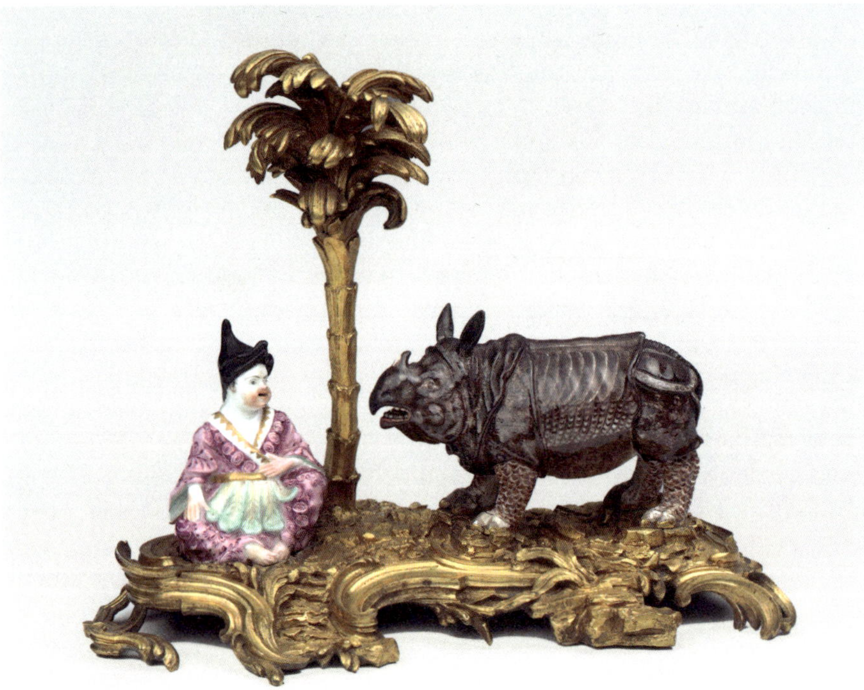

55
Clara with a Chinese figure and palm tree, Königliche Porzellan-Manufaktur Meissen, c. 1755

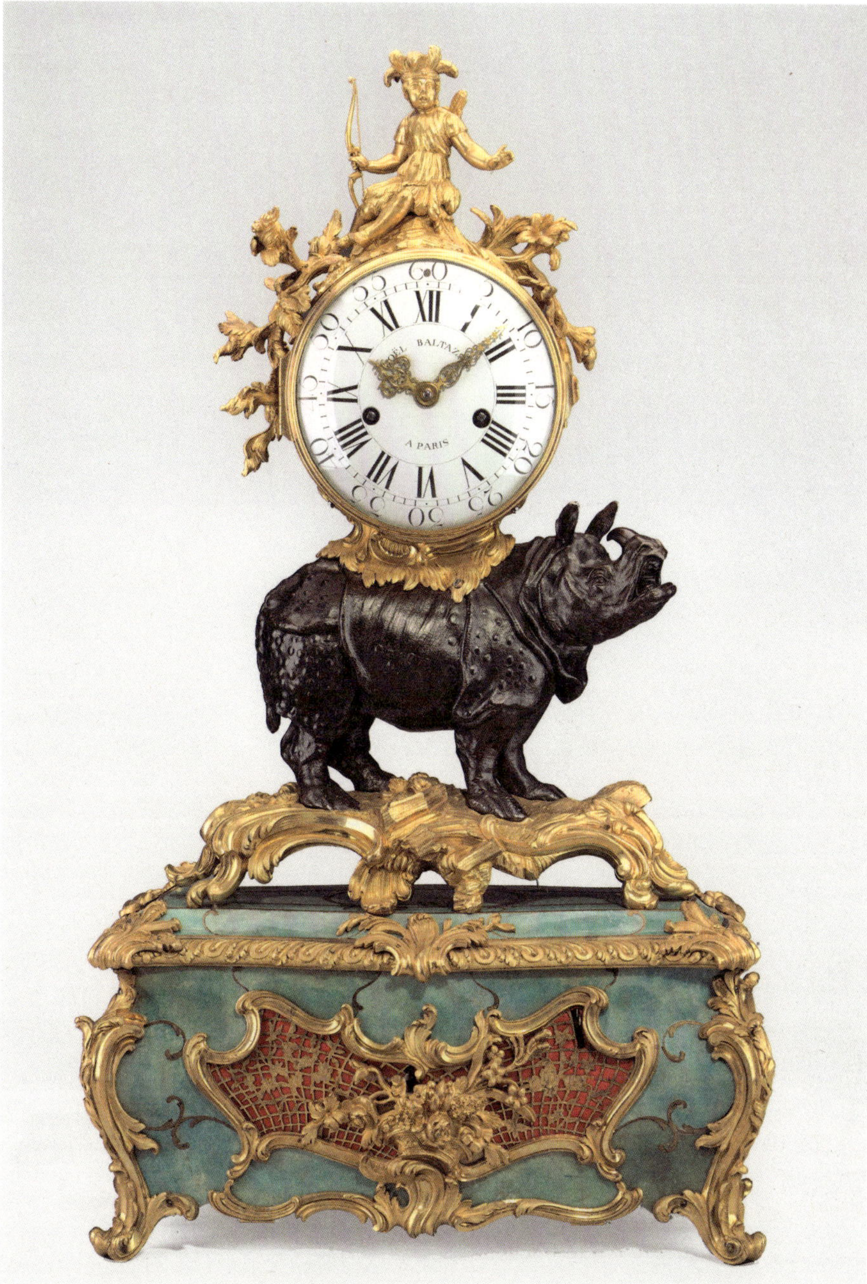

56
Clara standing on a musical box used as a mount for a clock, Jean-Joseph de Saint-Germain and François Viger, 1755/1756

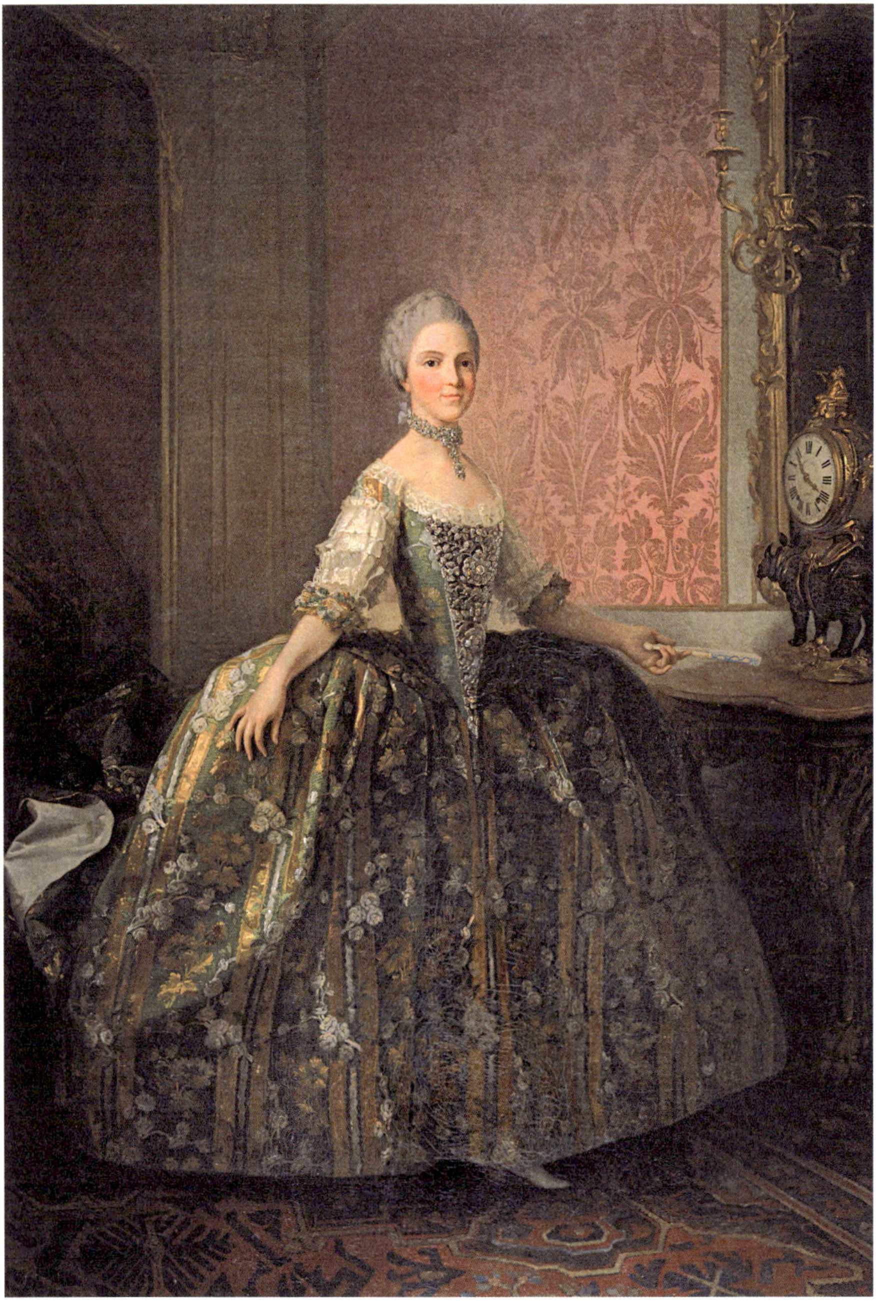

57
Portrait of Maria Luisa of Parma, with a rhinoceros clock on the mantelpiece, Laurent Pecheux, 1765

whose residence was in Mannheim and who had come to see Clara at the Zum Pfau inn of Maria Barbara Endtin in 1747.[131] In his early years here, Verschaffelt had certainly had an opportunity to see Clara – possibly for a second time – when she was travelling through Germany. Whatever the case, he must have seen her somewhere and had the time to study her closely and sketch her on paper or in clay. For his estate included a life-like marble statuette of a rhinoceros over a metre long which he had apparently always kept for himself [fig. 58].[132] The build and weight of the animal is much more convincingly rendered by Verschaffelt than Kaendler had previously done in Meissen porcelain or Saint-Germain in bronze. The proportions of the head, body and legs are much truer to life and the same goes for all the other details: the folds, the hooves, the tail, the skin and, last but not least, the horn. Here we see Clara as she really looked – although she was not white of course.

As court sculptor Verschaffelt was also closely involved with the porcelain factory in Frankenthal, which Elector Karl Theodor had bought in 1762 and which was a direct competitor of the Meissen factory in Saxony. A 1777 price list shows that a separate rhinoceros as well as a clock with a rhinoceros base were among the collection.[133] They are hefty pieces measuring 42 centimetres in length, larger that the Claras from Meissen and Paris. The resemblance to the marble statue is patently obvious; this must have been Verschaffelt's work. Karl Theodor himself kept such a clock in his bedroom in his palace in Mannheim, which he had brought with him when he left for Munich in 1777 as the new Elector of Bavaria. In common with earlier specimens in Meissen porcelain, the rhinoceros is given an exotic touch, in this instance by covering her with a saddle cloth decorated with a totally stereotypical head of an African man. A statuette without a clock but with such a cloth could also be found in the palace in Karlsruhe where Princess Caroline Louise von Baden, born Von Hessen-Darmstadt, had lived since 1751 [fig. 59].[134] She too had seen Clara in the flesh, as we gather from a letter written to her by a confidant in 1753 in which he had described the stir that the popular philosopher Voltaire had caused during a visit to Strasbourg as 'much the same as before [with] the rhinoceros'.[135]

Verschaffelt's Clara was realized in several media. Apart from in porcelain, she was also cast in bronze, probably in the same period. In addition, one of his students, Augustin Portois, likewise from Ghent, sculpted several marble rhinoceroses which, while smaller, are otherwise comparable with Verschaffelt's versions. Thanks to all these different forms in which Clara was portrayed she remained the new archetype of the rhinoceros long after her death.

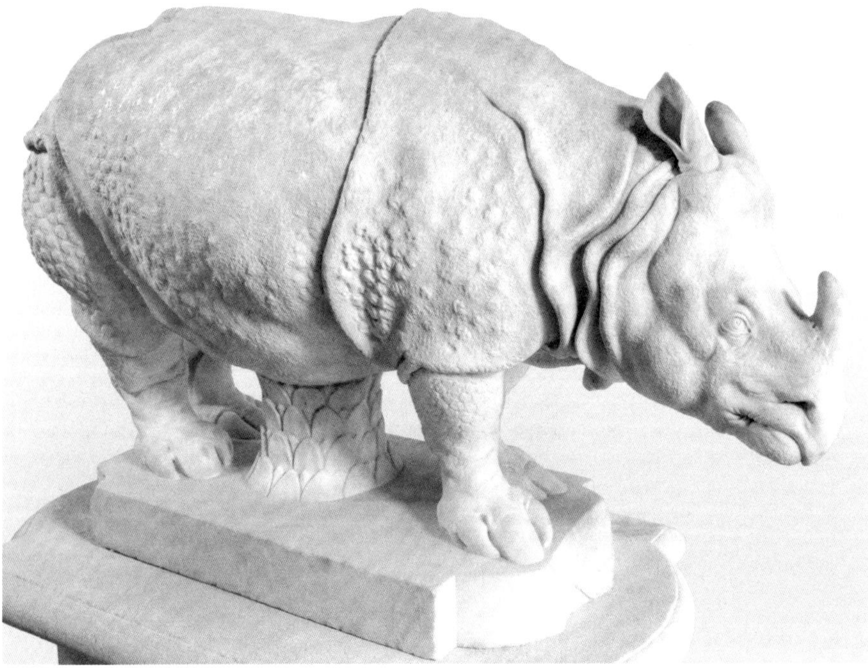

58
Clara in marble, attributed to Pieter Anton Verschaffelt, 1765–1770

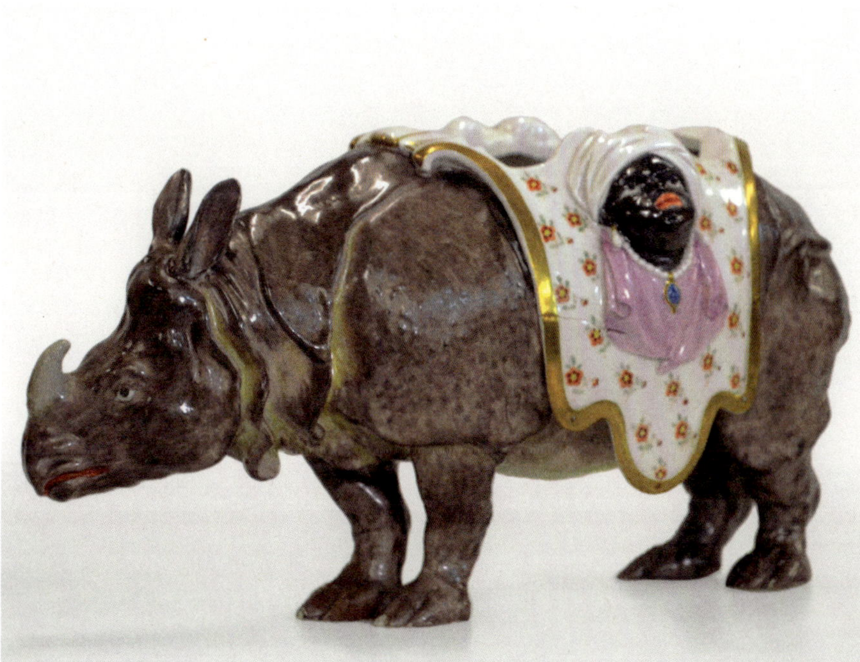

59
Clara with saddle cloth,
Porzellanmanufaktur Frankenthal, 1765–1770

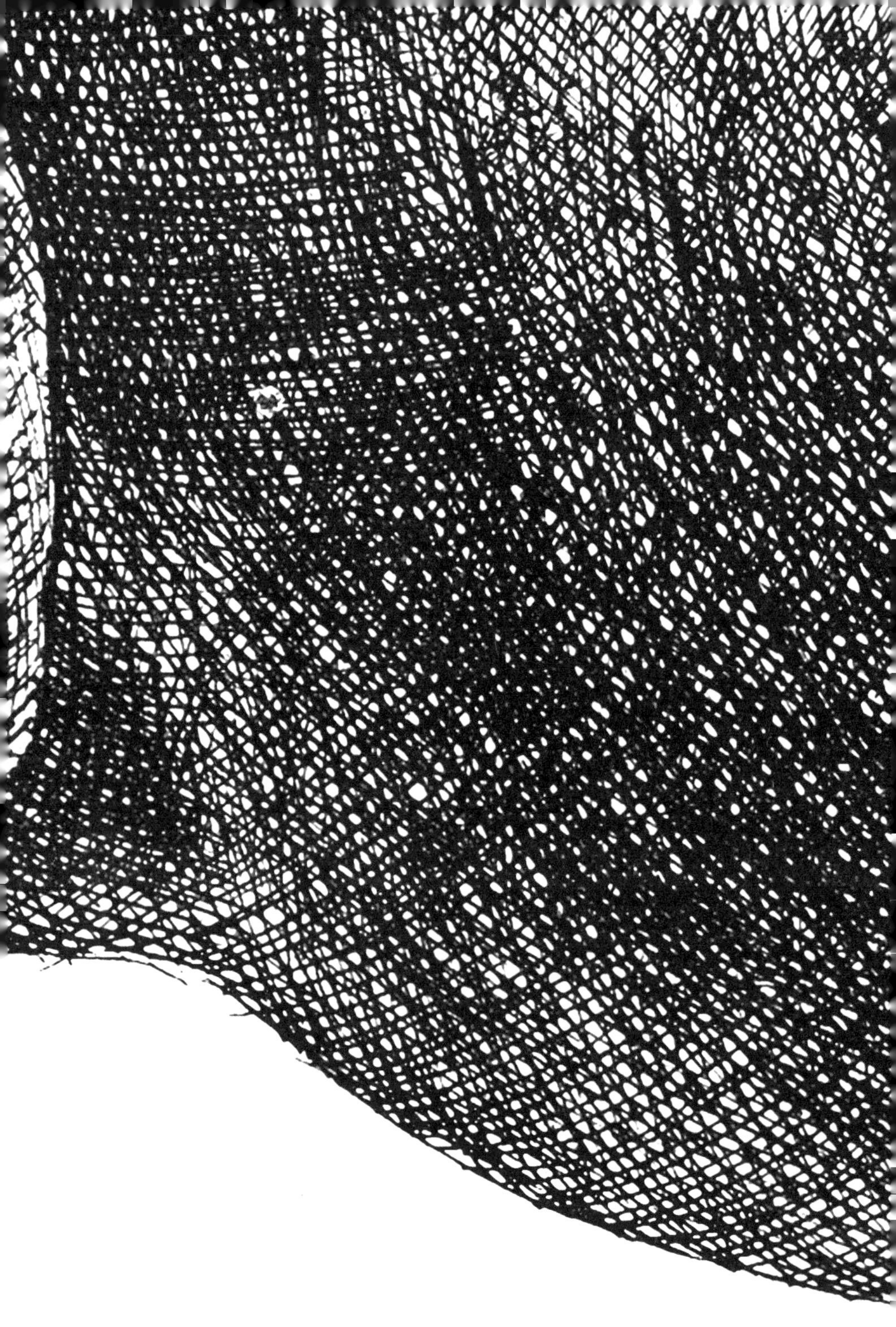

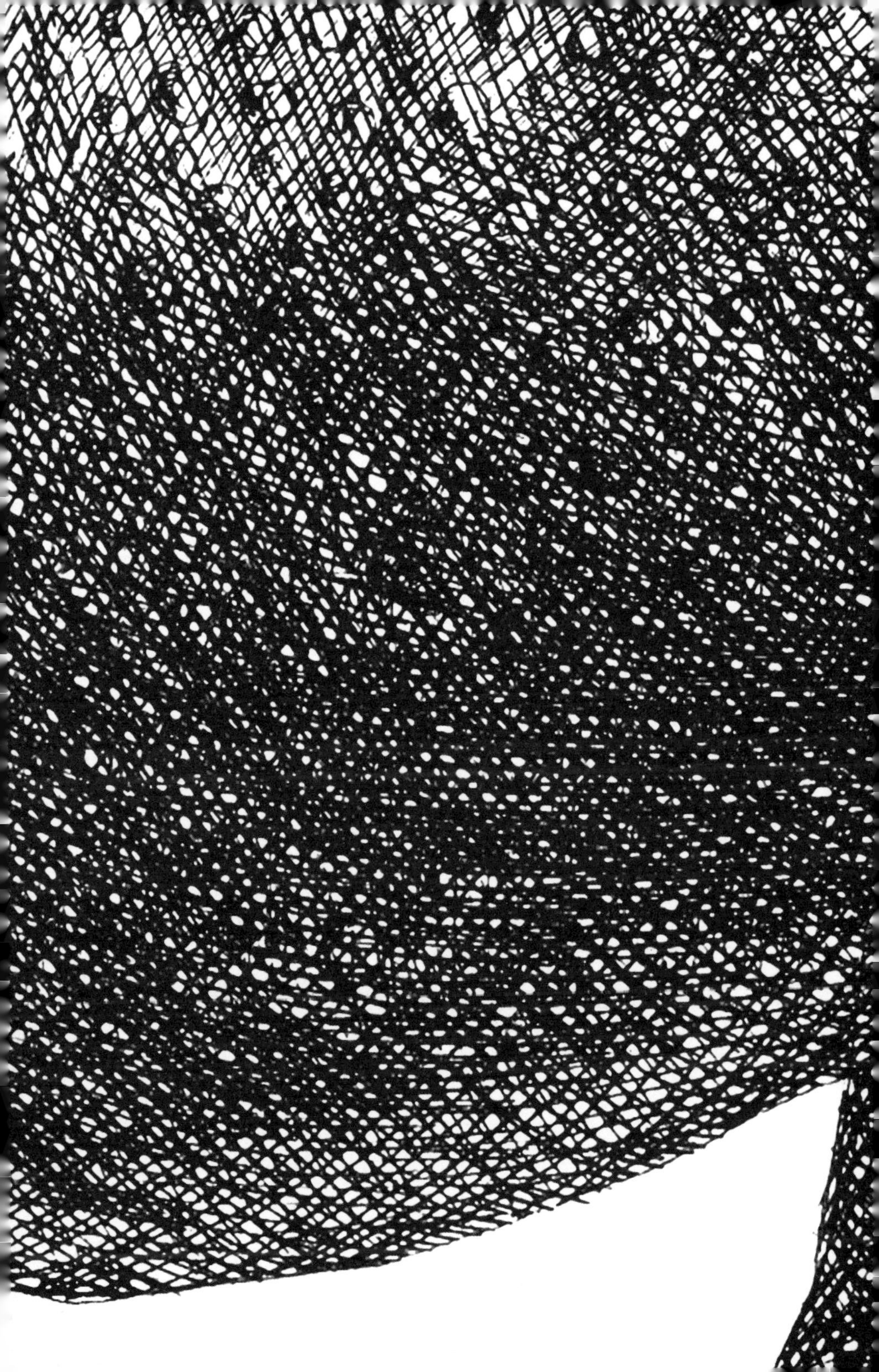

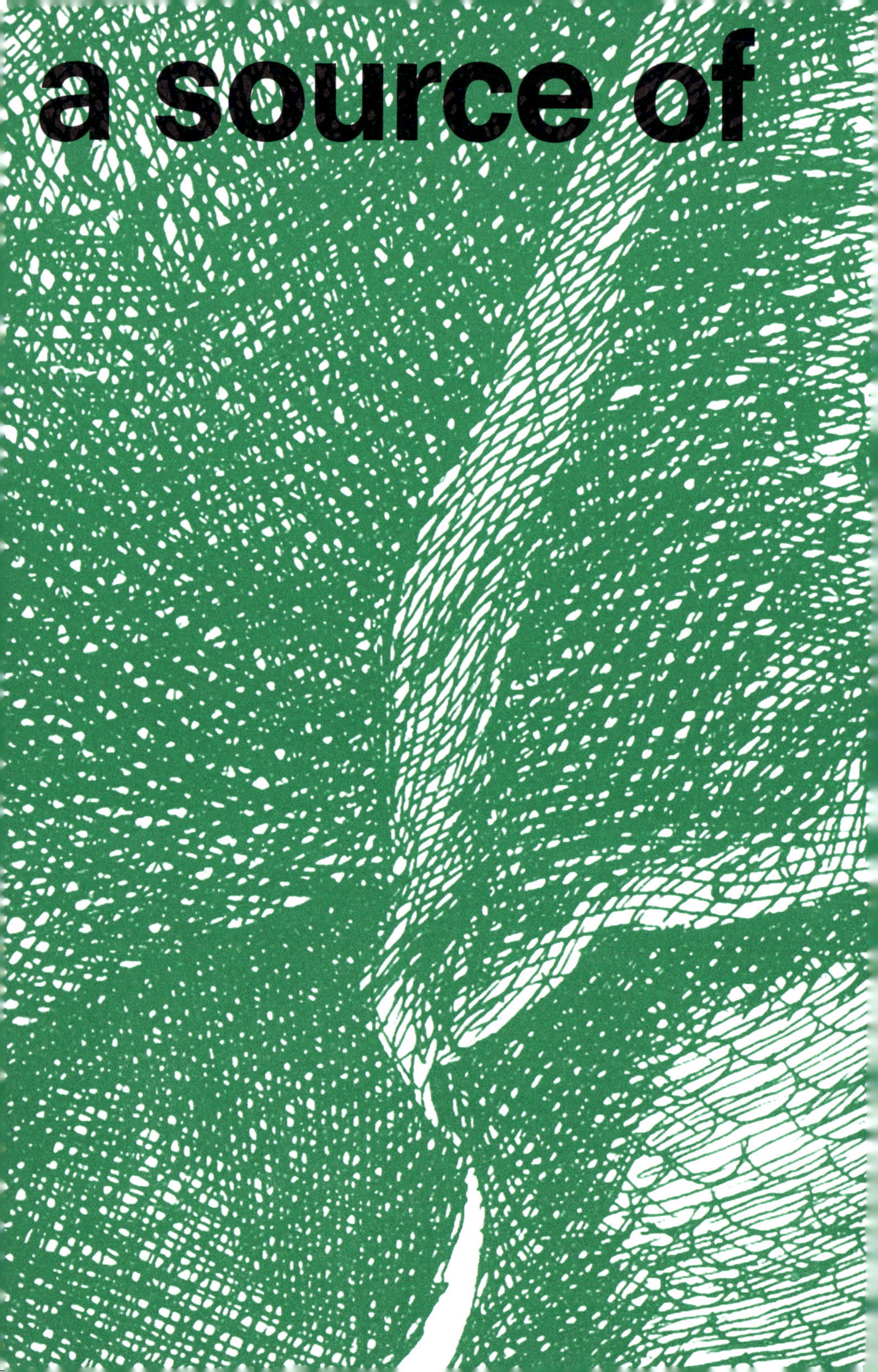
a source of

information

Everywhere Clara went during her long tours she aroused an outburst of enthusiasm which often bordered on hysteria. The commotion she caused was almost proverbial. Princess Wilhelmina of Bayreuth described herself in 1754 as 'a creature as extraordinary as the rhinoceros' because when journeying through France everywhere crowds of people had turned out to see her simply because she was the sister of the Prussian King Frederick the Great.[136] And as late as 1776 Jean-Jacques Rousseau, one of the foremost French philosophers, wrote agitatedly in a letter to an admirer who was constantly harassing him that if she wanted to see a rhinoceros, she should go to the fair and certainly not to his house.[137] All this was inextricably bound up with the fact that Clara was the first and only rhinoceros in mainland Europe. In this respect, the other famous French philosopher, Voltaire, was right in his *Questions sur l'Encyclopédie*, published between 1770 and 1774, when he concluded his entry 'Rare': 'A few years ago people marvelled at a rhinoceros. If there were ten thousand rhinoceroses in an area, people would only be running after them to kill them.'[138]

In addition to sensationalism and curiosity, Clara's unicity also aroused genuine interest. In many a city, both during her stay and long after her departure, scholars and interested amateurs occupied themselves with such questions as to which species she belonged to, and whether or not the existing knowledge and image of rhinoceroses tallied with the animal they saw before them. They studied her from head to toe, looked in her mouth, tapped, touched and felt her, observed her behaviour and discussed her.

Clara's stay in Frankfurt an der Oder in August 1746 prompted Karl August von Bergen, Professor of Anatomy and Botany at the local university, to write a letter to the renowned Swedish biologist Carolus Linnaeus. Linnaeus had obviously never seen a rhinoceros, but he had included the animal in his *Systema naturae*, his new classification of the animal and plant world first published in 1735. He had chosen to class the rhinoceros with the 'four-footers', later renamed 'mammals', and then for some unclear reason, because of its teeth, grouped the species with the elephants. Jokingly, Bergen had told him that after seeing Clara some of his colleagues thought it would be better to class the animal as an amphibian because it was so obviously fond of water – an observation that was nowhere to be found in the literature. Naturally, the remark was never intended to question the class in which the rhinoceros had been placed, but it demonstrates how little was then known about these animals. In his response, the Swedish scholar said he would be interested to receive a more extensive description, partly because he had found previous information so implausible. Although Bergen had to admit to Linnaeus that he had studied the rhinoceros insufficiently, he took up the challenge. That same year he published his findings in his *Oratio de rhinocerote* [fig. 60], the first scientific treatise on the rhinoceros to be issued as a separate publication. In this Bergen mainly presented an overview of the fairly extensive old and recent literature on the rhinoceros, and urged that rhinoceroses be seen as a separate species instead of classing them under other animals, whether they be elephants or, as another scientist, had suggested, swine. In the new edition of his *Systema* that Linnaeus brought out in 1748, the rhinoceros was recorded as *Rhinoceros unicornis* (single-horned rhinoceros), that is, as a separate species, though he continued to class it under rodents because of its teeth![139]

Bergen was by no means the only one to approach Clara in a scientific manner. Within a year a comparable work was published in Leipzig under the simple title *Rhinoceros* [fig. 61]. The author Friedrich Gotthilf Freytag spoke more explicitly than Bergen about the actual animal that had stood before him, but a command of Latin was needed to read these concise texts. As a result, the public remained starved of information, including the natural history enthusiasts who had only heard about the rhinoceros that was touring Germany but had not had a chance to see her, according to a publisher in Nuremberg in 1747. This led him to publish a German translation of the letter that James Parsons had written four years earlier to the Royal Society on the male rhinoceros that had been in London.[140]

Clara raised all sorts of questions. For instance, was she really the behemoth described in the Bible, as Mout claimed in his promotional prints? Following Clara's visit to Regensburg, in March 1747 the Lutheran preacher Johann Matthäus Barth published a slim, six-page paper in which he subscribed to this [fig. 62]. What was written in the Book of Job agreed with what he had seen with his own eyes: the animal ate grass, could swim, loved to wallow in the mud, had extremely strong legs, had a 'sword' in the form of a horn which she constantly whetted – all characteristics of the behemoth described in the Bible. A year later his colleague Laurentius Reinhard in turn refuted all these claims. He did so on purely theological grounds; he had no need to see the rhinoceros for this [fig. 63].

For the general public, however, being able to meet a biblical monster continued to be an appealing idea, although some saw in this wonder beast the very proof of God's omnipotence. One of the prints which were put into circulation at the close of 1746 during Clara's visit to Vienna included a poem that underlined this: 'God made it [the rhinoceros], so that man can marvel at it.'[141] Some even claimed that divine providence could be found in the amazing folds of the skin – the presumed reason why rhinoceroses could move so well. It was a view that delighted the heart of the French philosopher Pierre-Louis de Maupertuis, and not only his. He saw God's creation as something quite separate from the organic development of nature and wished to study the latter unencumbered by theology.[142] Where many a person saw the hand of God in everything, leading European philosophers such as he took the deistic view that God played no active role after the creation and that nature had evolved by itself. To their minds there was no form of providence. Some drew even more far-reaching conclusions from this: a rhinoceros may have been a miracle of nature, but God's omnipotence was certainly not reflected in this.

But most scientists examined her objectively whenever they had a chance. There was nothing like studying this very special animal in the flesh and discussing your findings with others. In March 1748 in Zurich members of the newly founded Physicalische Societät, later the Naturforschende Gesellschaft, devoted meetings to her. On 9 March its chairman Johannes Gessner, an eminent botanist as well as a professor of physics, delivered a long and systematically structured lecture in which he described the rhinoceros in meticulous detail.[143] He was guided by his own observations, which concerned factual aspects and not theological or philosophical issues. He had measured her as accurately as he could. He discussed what had previously been written about rhinoceroses and how these animals had been represented until then. He referred extensively to Parsons's treatise for the Royal Society, which was undeniably about the same animal even though his was a male. Gessner concluded, among other things, that there had to be four species of rhinoceroses: one with a single horn from Bengal and environs (Clara and the London rhinoceros), one with a second horn on its back from western India (the animal Dürer had depicted), and two species with two horns on the nose, which mainly lived in Africa (based on the existing literature and skulls present in 'naturalia' cabinets). To supplement the unpublished treatise a fellow member of

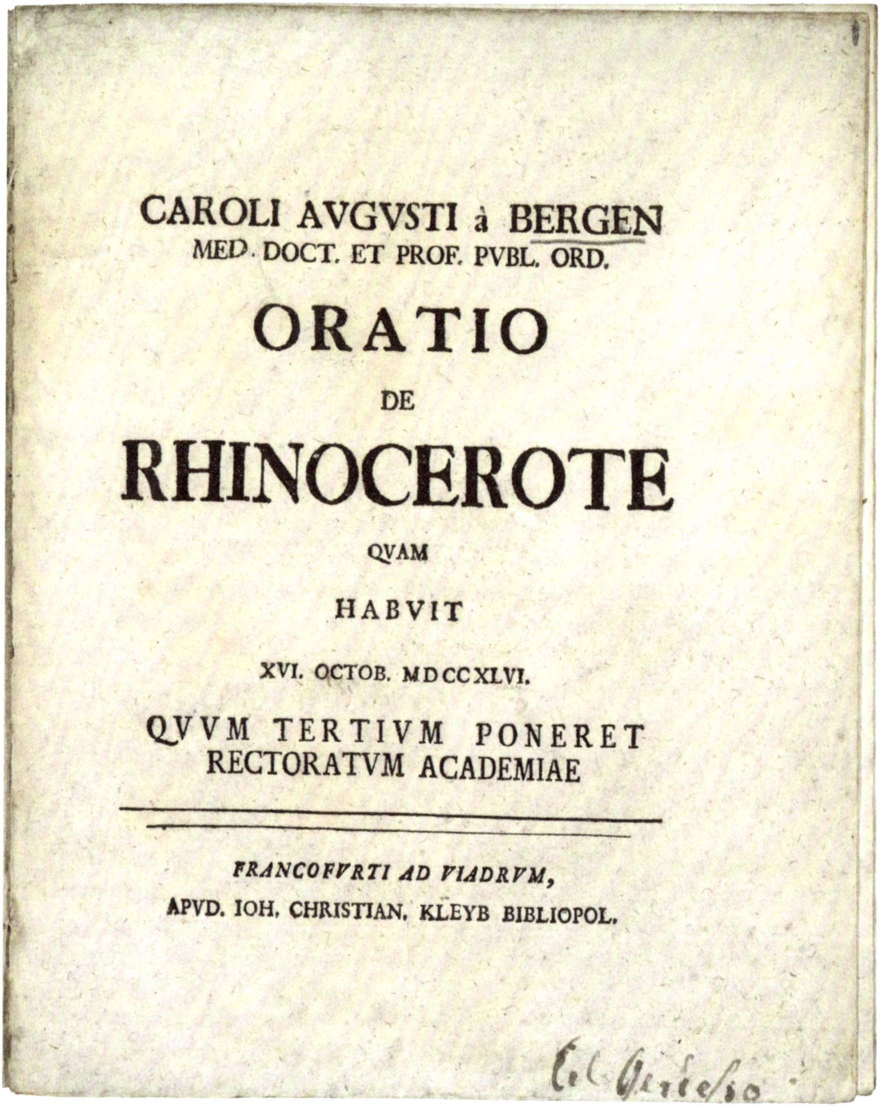

CAROLI AVGVSTI à BERGEN
MED. DOCT. ET PROF. PVBL. ORD.

ORATIO
DE
RHINOCEROTE
QVAM
HABVIT
XVI. OCTOB. MDCCXLVI.
QVVM TERTIVM PONERET
RECTORATVM ACADEMIAE

FRANCOFVRTI AD VIADRVM,
APVD. IOH. CHRISTIAN. KLEYB BIBLIOPOL.

60
Title page of *Oratio de rhinocerote*,
Caroli Augusti à Bergen [Karl August von Bergen],
Frankfurt an der Oder, 1746

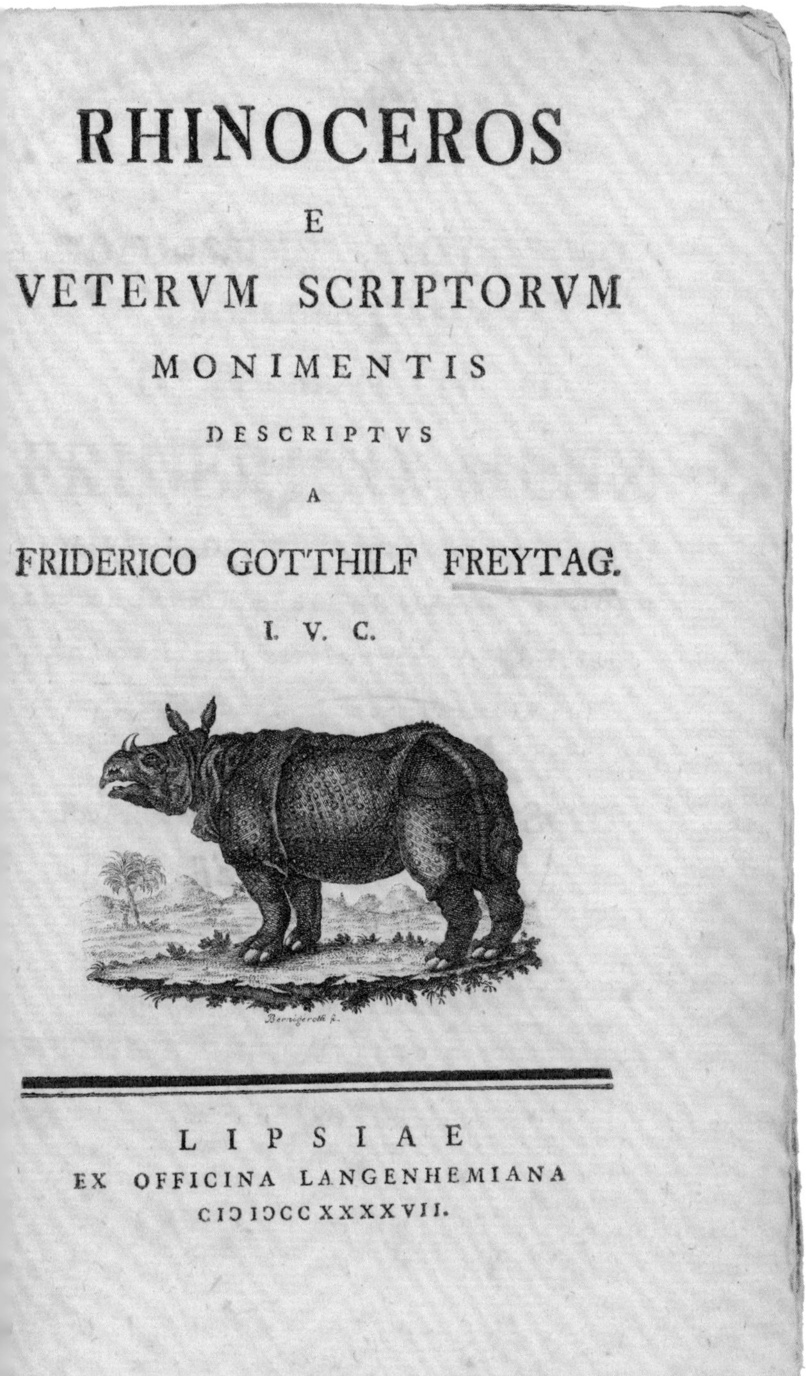

RHINOCEROS
E
VETERVM SCRIPTORVM
MONIMENTIS
DESCRIPTVS
A
FRIDERICO GOTTHILF FREYTAG.
I. V. C.

LIPSIAE
EX OFFICINA LANGENHEMIANA
CIↃIↃCCXXXXVII.

61
Title page of *Rhinoceros e Veterum Scriptorum Monimentis Descriptus*, **Friedrich Gotthilf Freytag, Leipzig 1747**

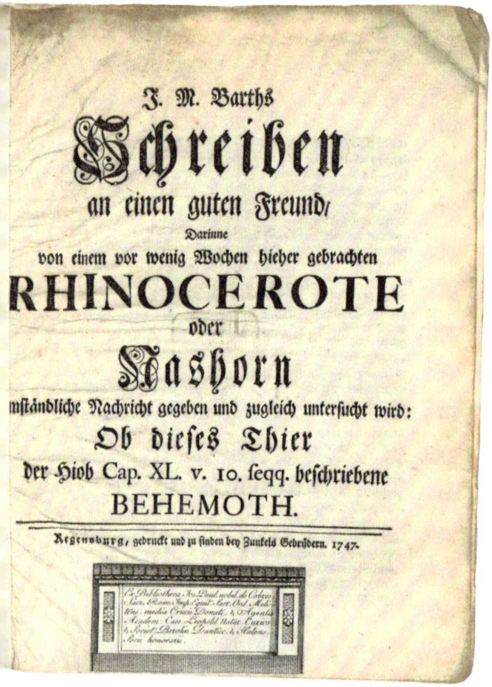
J. M. Barths
Schreiben
an einen guten Freund/
Darinne
von einem vor wenig Wochen hieher gebrachten
RHINOCEROTE
oder
Nashorn
umständliche Nachricht gegeben und zugleich untersucht wird:
Ob dieses Thier
der Hiob Cap. XL. v. 10. seqq. beschriebene
BEHEMOTH.

Regensburg, gedruckt und zu finden bey Zunkels Gebrüdern. 1747.

62
Title page of the booklet in which Johann Matthäus Barth equates the rhinoceros with the behemoth, Regensburg 1747

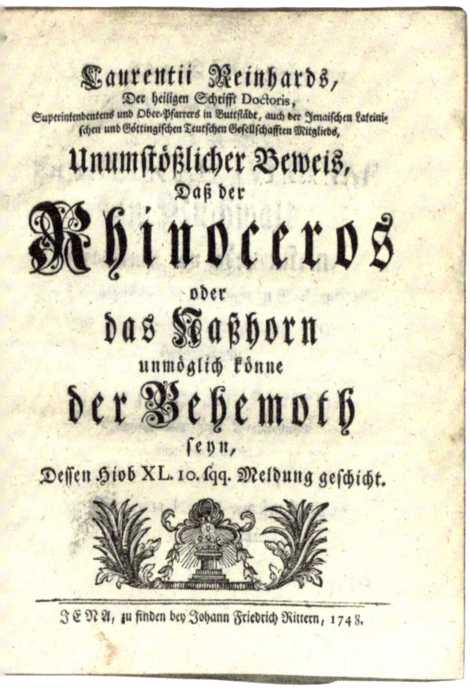
Laurentii Reinhards,
Der heiligen Schrifft Doctoris,
Superintendentens und Ober-Pfarrers in Buttstädt, auch der Jenaischen Lateinischen und Göttingischen Teutschen Gesellschafften Mitglieds,
Unumstößlicher Beweis,
Daß der
Rhinoceros
oder
das Naßhorn
unmöglich könne
der Behemoth
seyn,
Dessen Hiob XL. 10. sqq. Meldung geschicht.

JENA, zu finden bey Johann Friedrich Rittern, 1748.

63
Title page of the booklet in which Laurentius Reinhard denies that the rhinoceros is the behemoth, Jena 1748

the society, artist Johann Felix Corrodi, had drawn a few details of the animal in colour – the wide-open mouth, the head, a leg, the rear – as well as line drawings which he had copied from Parsons's work [fig. 64]. Clara is portrayed lying down in the middle, a simplification of the print by his fellow-citizen David Redinger [see fig. 32].

In the summer of 1754, a similar group of interested citizens discussed Clara in Danzig, and this kind of research probably took place in other cities as well. In Danzig the debate was led by the local zoologist Jacob Theodor Klein, who like Linnaeus and others was busy ordering the animals into a logical system. He had a print made of a picture of Clara in three different positions, with a short explanation in German and Polish, and based on the tripartite hooves concluded that rhinoceroses should be classed as a separate family in the animal kingdom. This view was argued in his *Natürliche Ordnung und vermehrte Historie der vierfüssigen Thiere* that was posthumously published in 1760 with references to Clara's stay in Danzig, and eventually generally accepted. Linnaeus may well have followed his example if he too had had a chance to examine Clara himself, but he was deprived of this opportunity when the Swedish king refused to grant Mout and his rhinoceros access to his kingdom less than a year later. It is doubtful whether Linnaeus, who lived in Stockholm at the time, ever knew he had been so close to a rhinoceros.[144]

Everyone who saw Clara and knew Dürer's print noticed that Clara was different. People tried to find an explanation for this. While Gessner presumed that the print showed a different rhinoceros species, in February 1747 a Nuremberg publisher suspected that this was due to the difference between a male and a female. For this reason, he reproduced both versions in the same print, whereby Clara was based on one of the prints Wandelaar had made in 1742 for Albinus's anatomy atlas [figs. 20, 65]. But most people concluded that Dürer's representation was incorrect. Clara was the proof that a rhinoceros looked very different in reality. Nor did she match up with the various stories that had been circulating for centuries. People even started to doubt Pliny's story that the rhinoceros was the elephant's main enemy. One of those who rejected this and other myths, based on what they themselves saw, was Jean Baptiste Ladvocat, the librarian of the Sorbonne, the university of Paris. After seeing Clara at the Foire Saint-Germain, based on his own observations and rational thinking, he recorded his findings in his *Lettre sur le Rhinoceros*, which was published in 1749 [fig. 66]. The reach and authority of this work remained limited, however, as did that of the previous publications in Germany.

Fig. 6

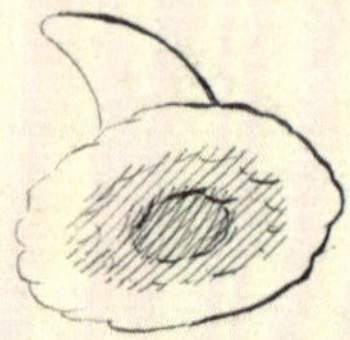

Fig. 2

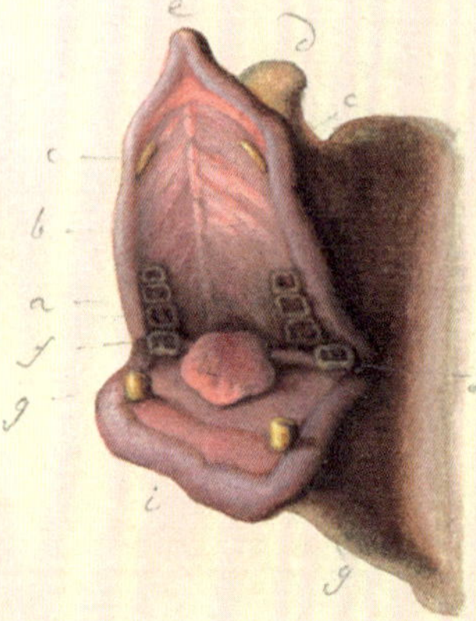

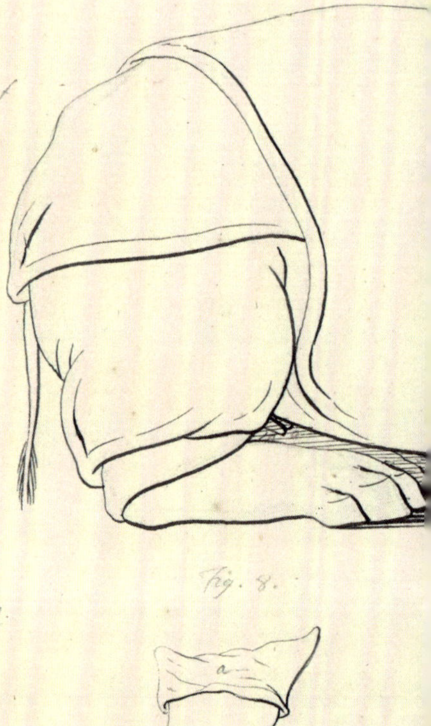

Fig. 3

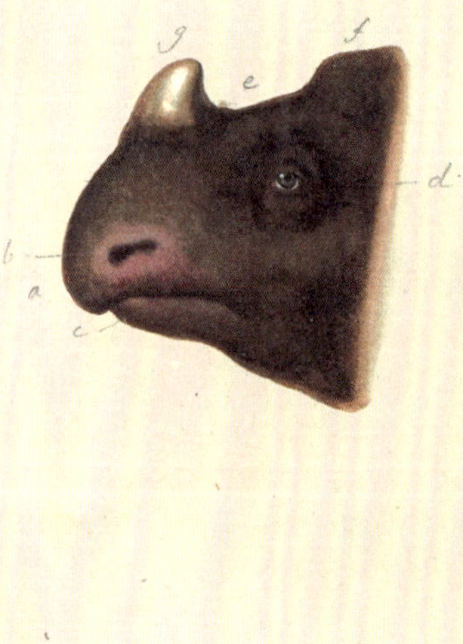

Fig. 8

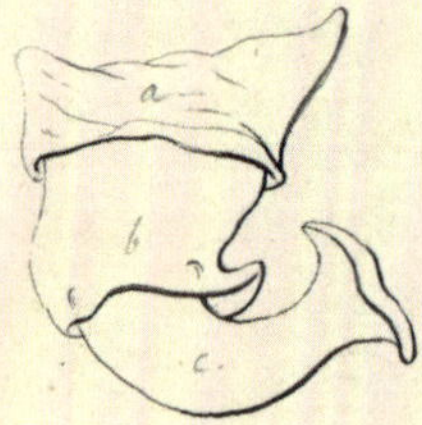

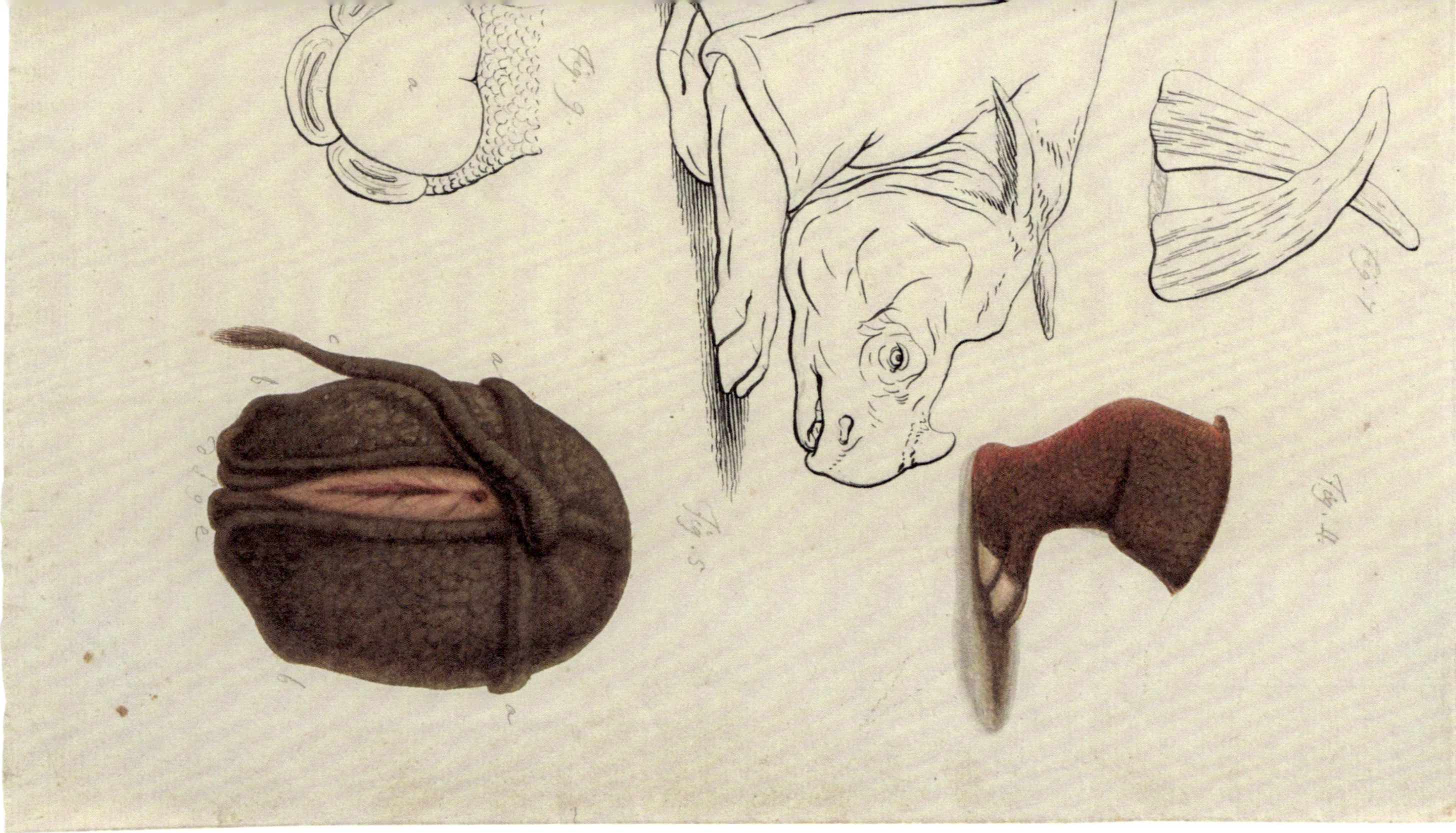

64

Nine sketches of a rhinoceros, the complete animal and four hand-coloured details representing Clara, Johann Felix Corrodi, Zurich, 1748

Yet Clara's stay in Paris would ultimately be of decisive significance for her impact on the understanding of her species. Thanks to two authoritative encyclopaedic works, she would virtually live on forever. The year 1749, the year that Clara was shown in the French capital, saw the appearance of the first volume of an extremely ambitious project which set out to describe the whole of the natural world in a coherent manner. It was the brainchild of Georges-Louis Leclerc, Count of Buffon, who for the past ten years had been director of the Jardin du Roi, the royal botanical gardens on the edge of Paris. With the help of dozens of assistants, Buffon, born in 1707, was to work on this comprehensive overview until his death in 1788. The next year witnessed the issue of the thirty-sixth volume, after which a further eight were to follow until 1804. By then all four-footers, birds, minerals, snakes, fish and whale-like creatures had been described, at least insofar as they were then known.

In 1764 the eleventh volume was issued, one of the volumes on four-footers. In this, immediately after the elephant, Leclerc devoted considerable attention to the rhinoceros, though without creating a new category. Buffon subtly let slip in a note that he had seen Clara himself, without mentioning her name, but significantly he had based his entry mainly on Parsons's publication and various fairly recent travel reports from Asia and Africa. His entry was supplemented, however, by a concrete and detailed description of the animal by Louis-Jean-Marie Daubenton, which was directly based on Clara. The description primarily served to explain the accompanying illustration which depicted Clara [fig. 67]. There can be no doubt about it, for the engraving was directly based on Oudry's large painting, of which drawings also existed. And although this passage was dropped from later editions of the *Histoire naturelle*, as were Daubenton's other animal descriptions, the illustrations were retained in all the ensuing editions. Indeed, four years later, Oudry's painting of Clara was used once again, this time in an entry on rhinoceroses in Denis Diderot and Jean d'Alembert's celebrated and influential *Encyclopédie* [fig. 68]. If a rhinoceros was to be portrayed, from then on it was Clara.

Twelve years after her death, on 11 June 1770, another Indian rhinoceros set foot on European soil, this time a two- to three-year-old male. A few months later he was transported to Versailles, where he remained in the royal menagerie until his death in 1793.[145] Since he could only be viewed here he caused far less of a stir than Clara. Petrus Camper was one of those who saw the animal at Versailles and in 1782, towards the end of his scientific career, he was in a position to compare the two rhinoceroses.[146] He was profoundly struck by their similarities. 'My drawings and painting of the Asiatic Rhinoceros [Clara], more than thirty years ago, clearly show that their eyes are lively and soft: I also found the same thing at Versailles in 1777, again in the live animal,' he wrote.[147] It reinforced his conviction that the Indian rhinoceros was a separate species, characterized by 'a single round horn, and ... distinctive folds and plates over its body' and that another species lived in Africa 'with two, flattened horns, one after the other [and] with no folds or plates'.[148] Camper may never have seen a living African rhinoceros, and based his views on descriptions and skeletal material, especially the head, but it was his personal observations of the two Indian rhinoceroses that had convinced him that there must be two species. And broadly speaking he was right.

Not only did knowledge of rhinoceroses increase in the second half of the eighteenth century, a growing number of living specimens appeared in Europe, first at fairs and festivals, and in the nineteenth century at zoos.[149] More and more became known about them, including about the differences between the rhinoceros species. As a result, Clara became diminishingly important as a source of knowledge. Her fame faded and she gradually fell into oblivion. Only her portrait popped up from time to time. As a rhinoceros, not as Clara.

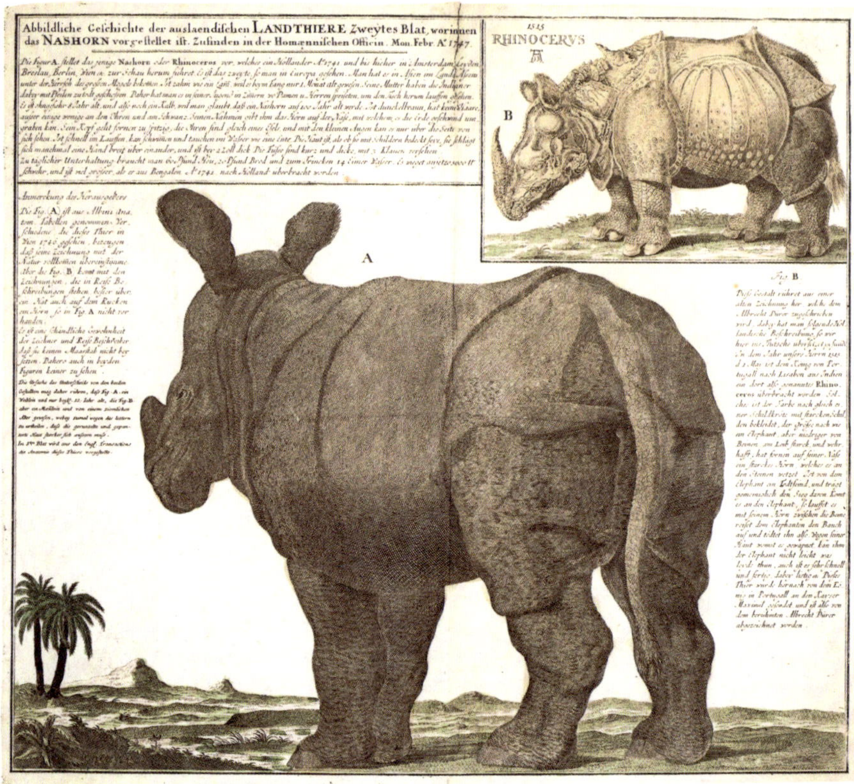

65

A print featuring Clara and Dürer's rhinoceros, said to depict the female and the male rhinoceros, respectively, Homanische Officin, 1747

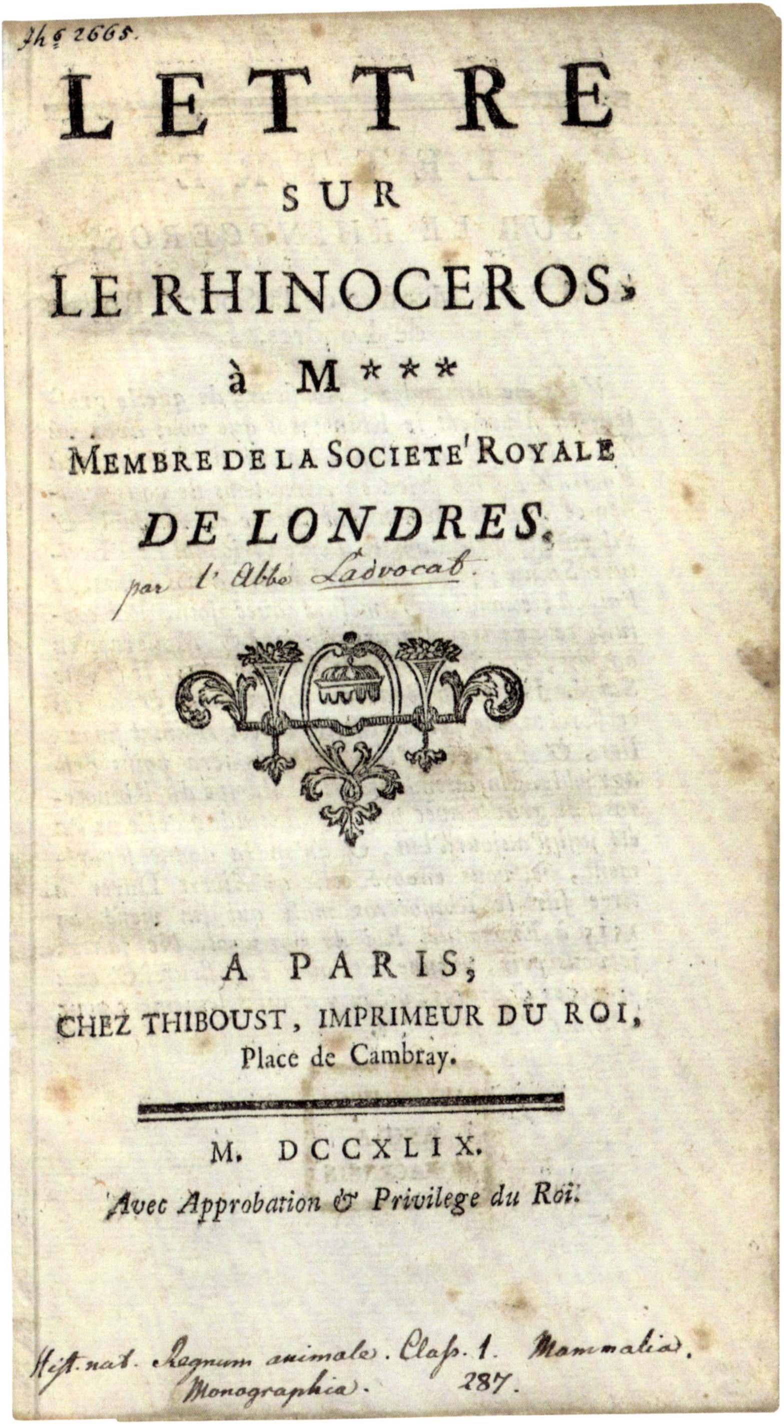
Jh. 2665.

LETTRE
SUR
LE RHINOCEROS,
à M***
MEMBRE DE LA SOCIETE' ROYALE
DE LONDRES.

par l'Abbé Ladvocat.

A PARIS,
CHEZ THIBOUST, IMPRIMEUR DU ROI,
Place de Cambray.

M. DCCXLIX.

Avec Approbation & Privilege du Roi.

Hist. nat. Regnum animale. Class. 1. Mammalia.
Monographica. 287.

Title page of *Lettre sur le Rhinoceros*, Jean Baptiste Ladvocat, Paris 1749

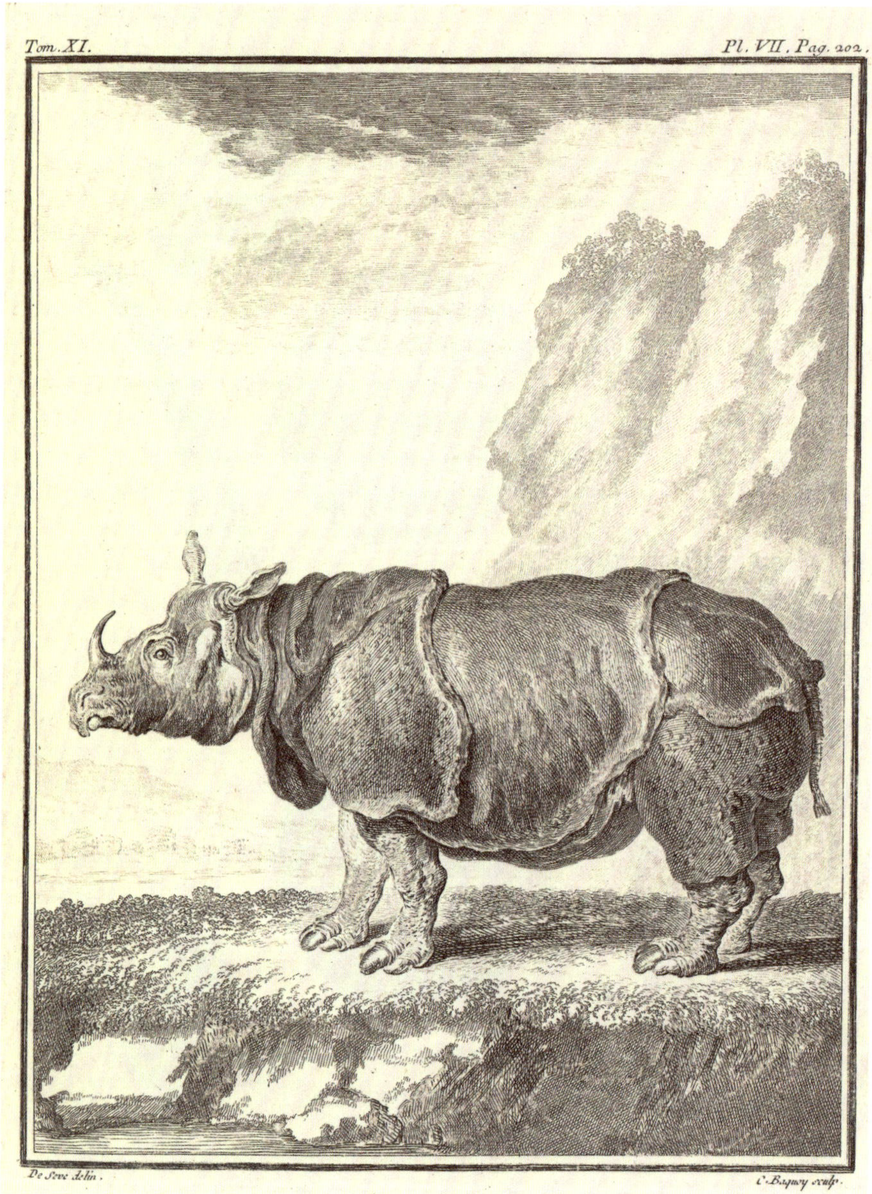

67

Portrait of Clara illustrating the entry on rhinoceroses in volume 11 of the *Histoire naturelle* **by Georges-Louis Leclerc de Buffon, 1764**

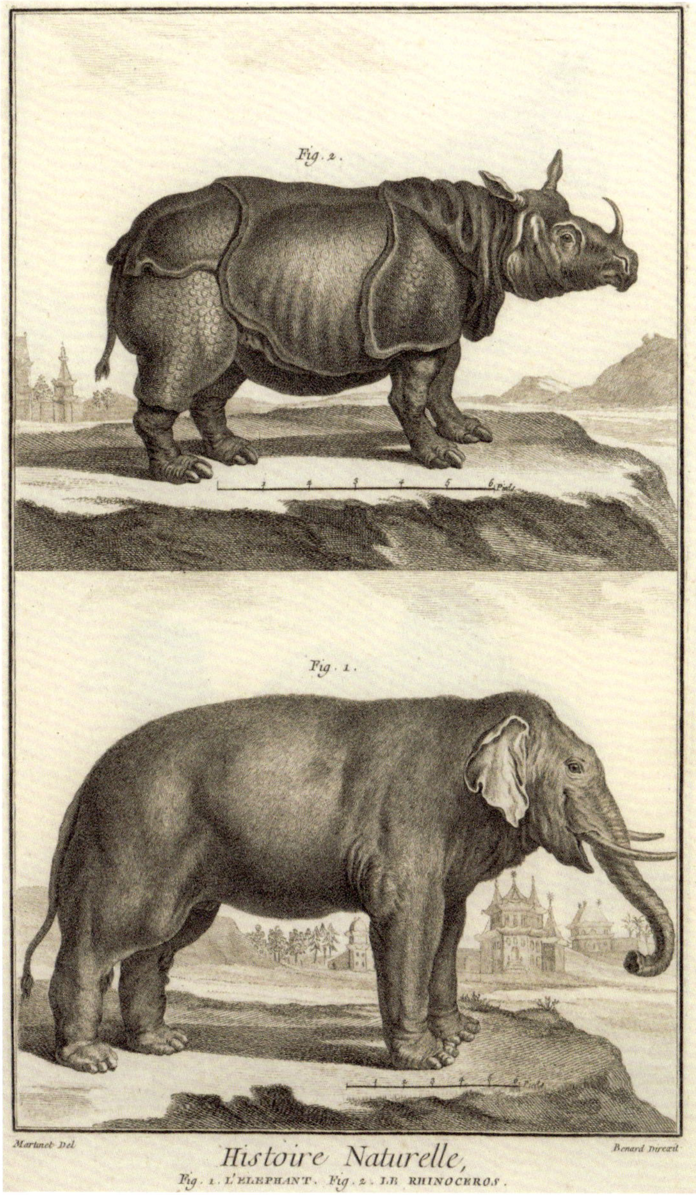

68
Clara and an elephant, illustrating the entry on rhinoceroses in a volume of the *Encyclopédie* by Denis Diderot and Jean d'Alembert, 1768

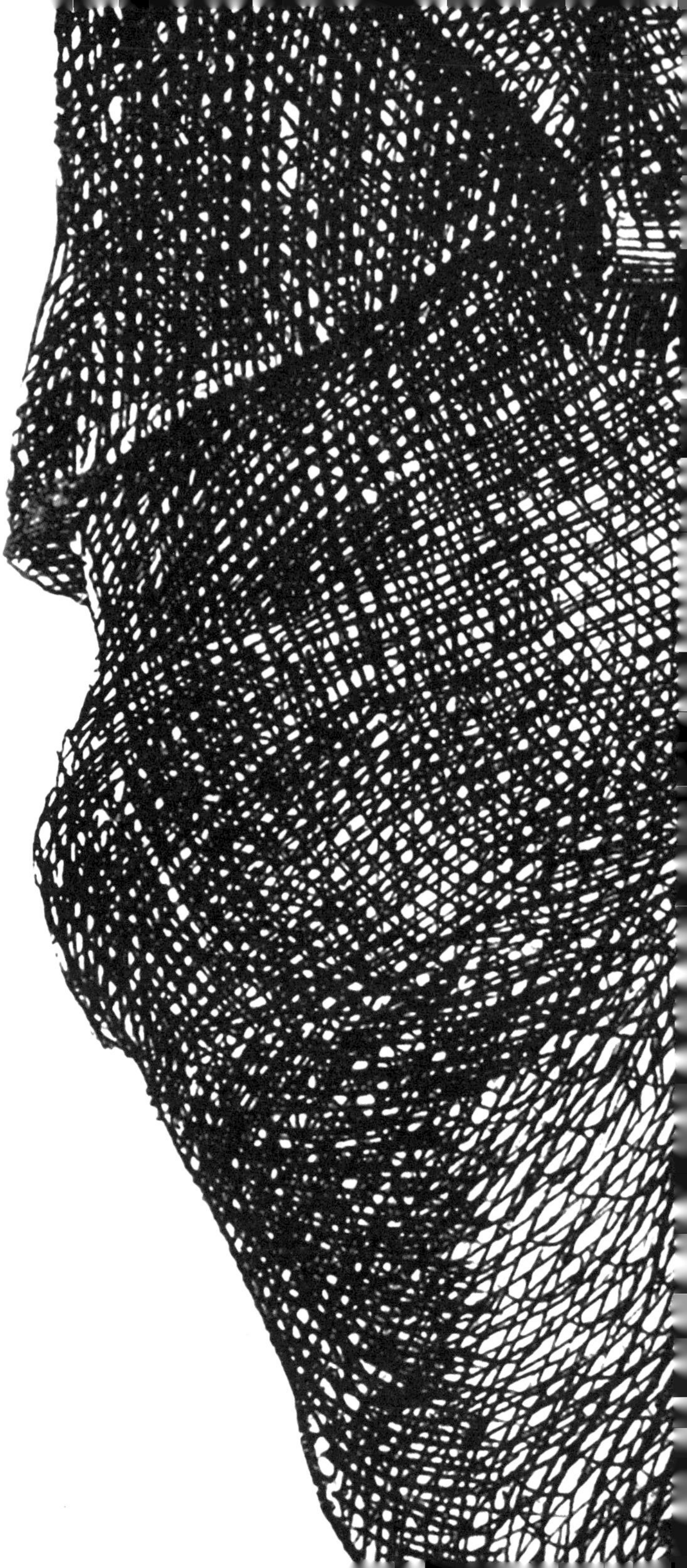

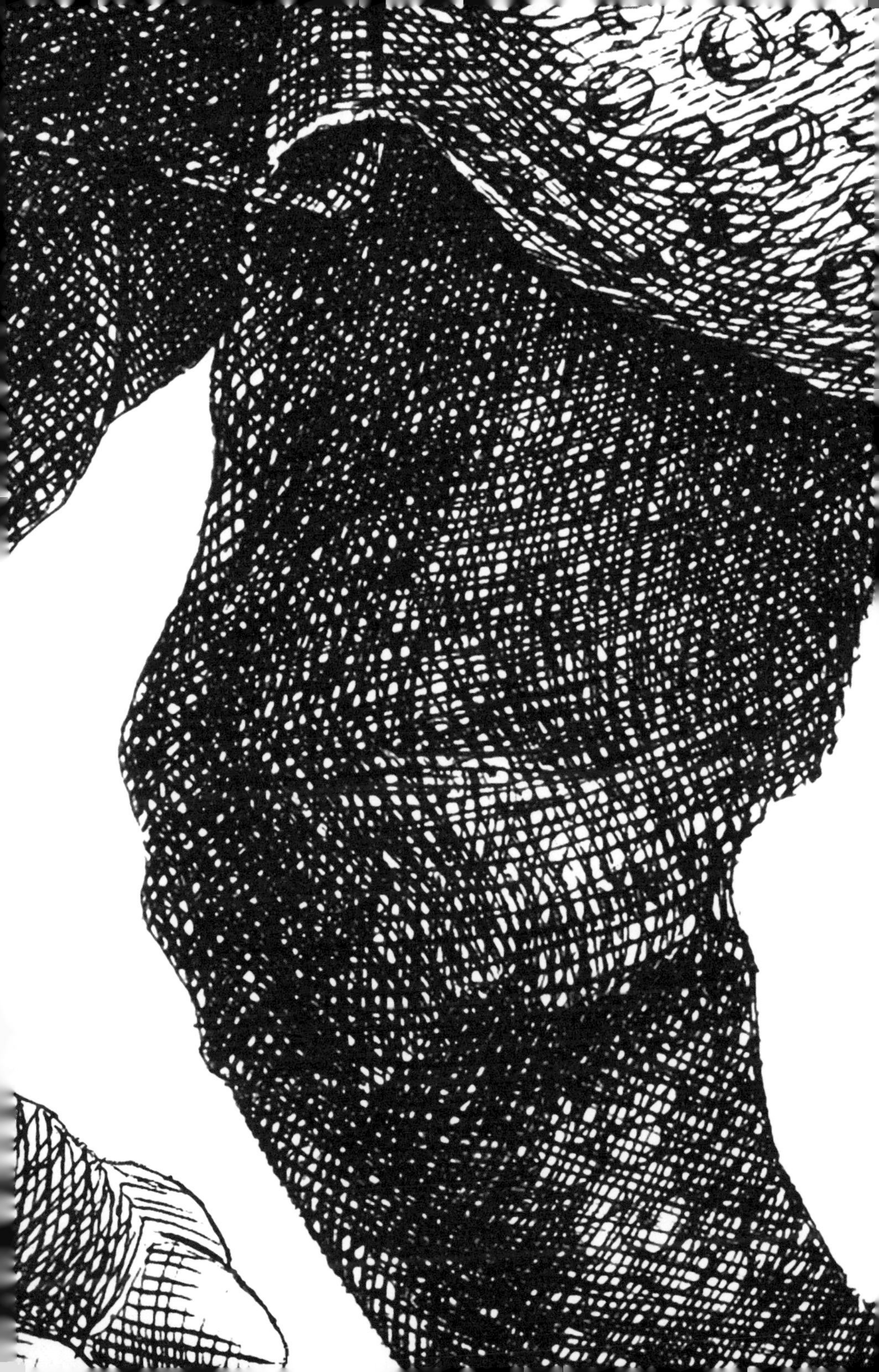

rhinoceros &

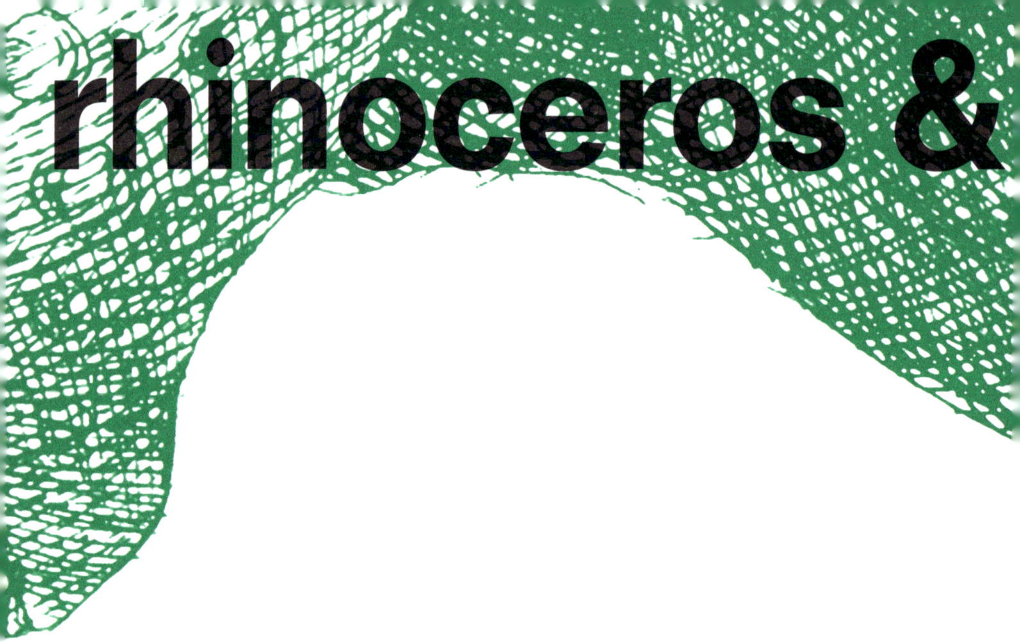

locust

In 1750 Christoph Gottlieb Richter from Nuremberg published the thirtieth volume of his dialogues between 'talking animals'. This time it was a conversation between a rhinoceros and a locust [fig. 69]. The rhinoceros was Clara, the only one of its kind in existence on the European mainland. The locust represented its countless fellow insects which in the autumn of 1749 had plagued large areas of agricultural land in Germany and adjoining countries by eating the crops. The two animals were not chosen without reason; they were both the talk of the day, though for different reasons. 'The former was viewed with pleasure, for it is a natural property of men to amuse themselves with something new ..., the latter caused a general lament; in the former one could admire God's goodness and wisdom... but in the latter we feel God's judgement.'[150] Clearly, Richter was not really interested in these two animals; they were a way of talking about people and their shortcomings, and ridiculing them. Nevertheless, he tells quite a lot about the animals themselves in this small book, which enjoyed at least two reprints.

It opens with a conversation between two men, one of whom argues that animals, contrary to what many think, are perfectly capable of feeling and thinking for themselves, that they have a soul and that they are certainly not machines with purely automatic behaviour. In so doing, he rejected the influential hypothesis of the philosopher René Descartes a century before who went so far as to deny that animals could communicate.[151] 'They can think just as we can and have their own language just as well', the speaker insisted. In that case, his friend wanted to know what the rhinoceros and the locust had to say to each other. They decided to listen in on them, as the title plate shows.

The first thing the rhinoceros says to the locust when they meet is how annoying it is to be groped and gawped at by hordes of people all day long. At the same time though she confesses that she often has to laugh at their arrogance, in particular at their idea that as human beings they are much better than the animal they are looking at. She then continues with the following extraordinary remark: '... were it possible in the future to free myself from the present slavery that now imprisons me, and return to my homeland, in revenge I would exhibit

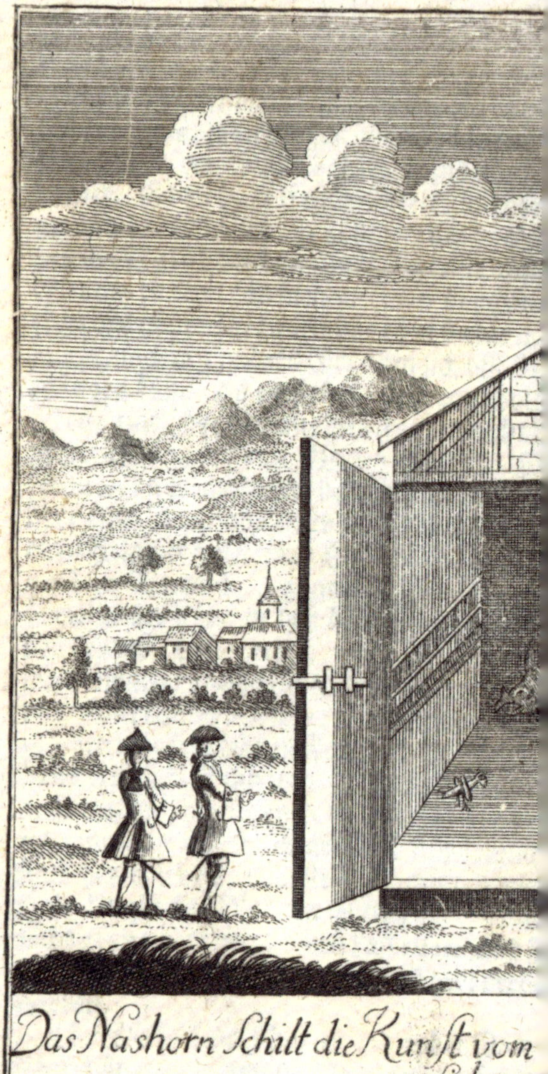

Das Nashorn schilt die Kunst vom
Sich zu
Die Heuschreck lobet sie. Folgt Mens
ner Lehr

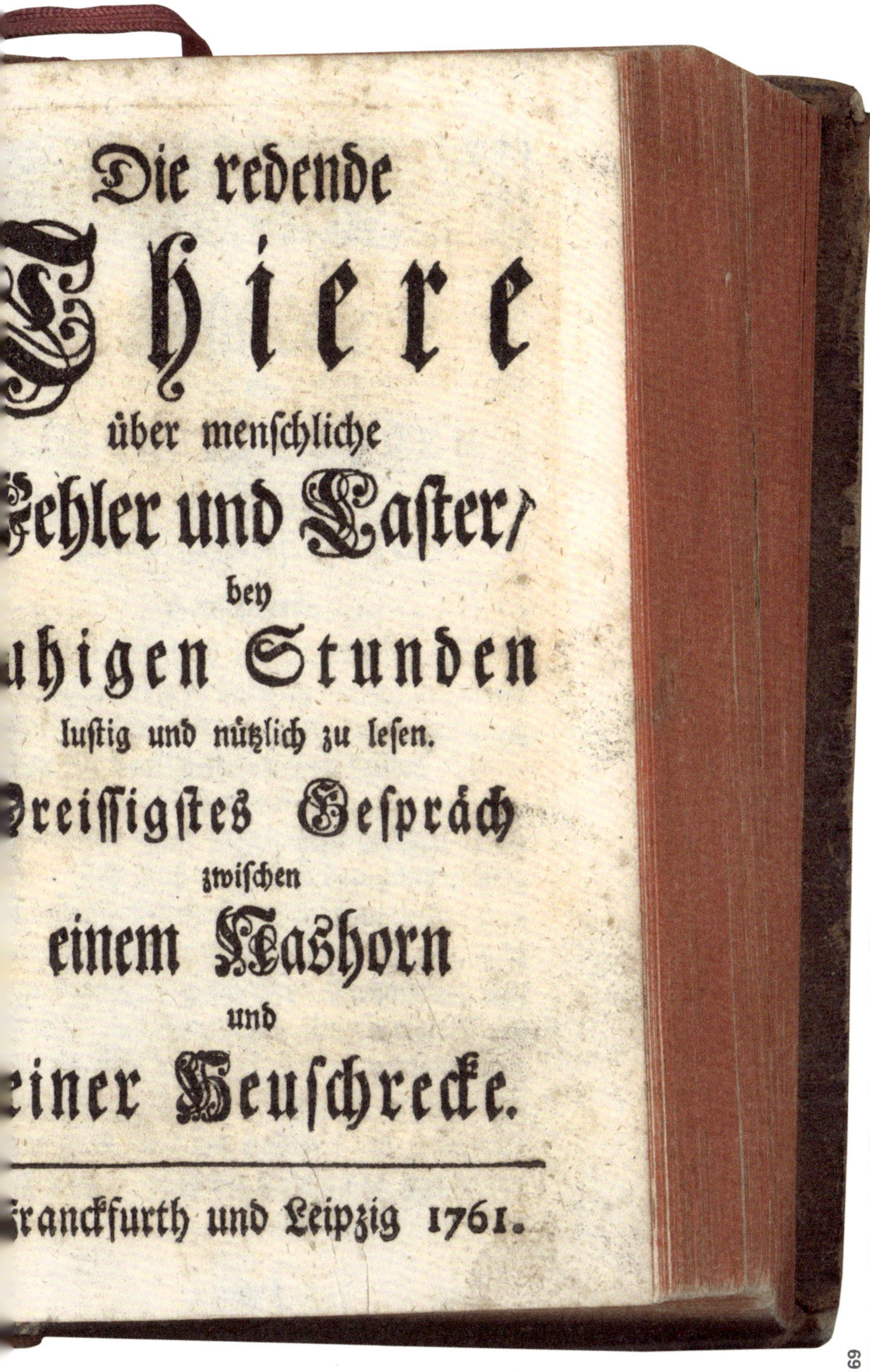

69
Title page of *Die redende Thiere über menschliche Fehler und Laster* ... **Christoph Gottlieb Richter, Frankfurt/ Leipzig 1766 (orig. ed. 1750). Clara and the locust can be seen in the picture on the left**

men to my brethren. I am sure that the genus of rhinoceroses views the miracle animal that man seems to be with more favour than human beings view a rhinoceros.'[152]

In this passage the rhinoceros – Clara – constantly looks back at the people staring at her. She observes and judges them just as they look and talk about her. Thus, the roles are reversed, and a very different light is shed on the rhinoceros's situation. Here the wonder beast is a living creature in captivity, an object that is abused, a victim that has been made dependent on people and that lives in an alien, unnatural environment. At the same time, though, it is about an individual animal with a mind and feelings of its own.

This small book is one of the most remarkable and striking reactions to Clara's presentation in all those European cities. Those reactions can be put down to the fact that no one in those days had ever had a chance to see a live rhinoceros before. This was the reason why Clara was called a wonder beast, became a phenomenon and aroused people's curiosity. In this tale Richter tried to put himself in the rhinoceros's place. Of course, it is impossible to know what Clara really thought. In a sense you could say that she did not know any better, for people were all she was used to. At the same time, it is certain that in her captivity she could never be the rhinoceros she would have been in the wild.

After having been out of the public eye for a long time, in the last quarter of the twentieth century Clara found herself in the limelight again. The Dutch zoologist Kees Rookmaaker and the British ceramic expert T.H. Clarke were the first to publish on her.[153] First and foremost Rookmaaker may be credited with Clara's rediscovery. He began to reconstruct her travels and to unravel her significance and impact on the collective image and understanding of the rhinoceros. Since then, not only has more and more become known about her, among others through the formidable *Zoologische Einblattdrucke und Flugschriften vor 1800* by Ingrid Faust, published in 2003, but she herself has become a celebrity again. A good example is the campaign that the J. Paul Getty Museum in Los Angeles organized in 2007 for an exhibition on Jean-Baptiste Oudry of which the restored portrait of Clara formed the centrepiece. With the slogan 'I saw Clara at the Getty Center', the museum created a hype comparable with the excitement that Clara herself had caused over two hundred and fifty years earlier [fig. 70].

In recent years Clara has become a wonder beast again, like a kind of people's darling: endearing, special and amusing. And, of course her story appeals to many. It is almost miraculous that she was dragged round Europe all those years, was kept alive and well all that time, and was observed and studied by many thousands of people from all levels of society in numerous countries. Simply by being there she has helped the understanding and image of the rhinoceros shift from myth into reality. She was a phenomenon and, given her name, for some an individual. But it is good for us to realize that the history of Clara is first and foremost a European, Western story about an Asiatic, oriental animal, moreover an animal that for the whole of its life, bar the first few weeks, lived in captivity on a continent where rhinoceroses do not belong.

In her 2016 installation *Clara* the Italian artist Rossella Biscotti showed in her way that Clara's life played out against a background of Western expansionism and global trade flows characterized by exploitation, power and inequality. Dutch bricks stamped with Clara's profile stacked on pallets formed the hub of this work [figs. 71, 72]. In Clara's days bricks were brought to Asia from Europe as ballast on VOC ships like the *Knappenhof* and altogether they stand here for Clara's adult weight of 5,000 pounds. The pile of tobacco leaves next to them refers to the unnatural rhinoceros food that Clara consumed, a logo on the wall shows how much money Mout wanted for her and alludes to the commercial exploitation of the animal. In this way Biscotti stays remarkably close to Clara herself, deliberately leaves aside the effect her presence had on people and poses the question how these values that were applied to Clara by the outside world relate to the original animal herself. As in all good art, the answer is left to the viewer.[154]

Nowadays rhinoceroses are no longer unknown to people, and it may well be that human beings are no longer unknown to rhinoceroses. Today the fate of rhinoceroses lies in the hands of humanity far more than in Clara's day. In Asia as well as in Africa their existence is threatened by humankind. But there are people who protect them, by creating reserves and setting up breeding programmes in zoos and allowing these animals the space to be themselves.

Clara was a special rhinoceros, that is for sure. But she was above all an ordinary rhinoceros, a rhinoceros which had the right to live. As, incidentally, do locusts.

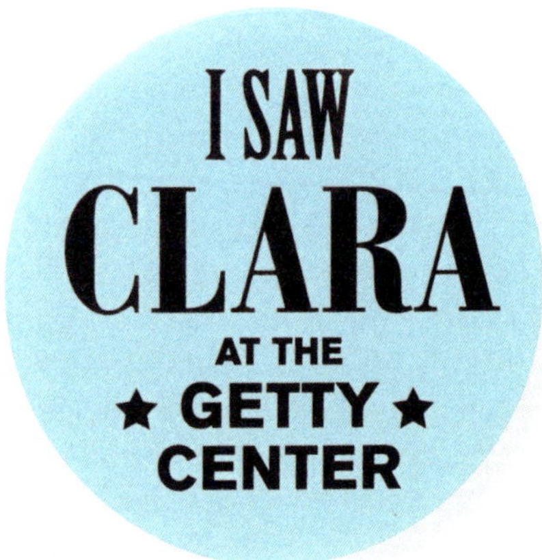

70
Badge from the J. Paul Getty Museum, Los Angeles, produced for the exhibition *Oudry's Painted Menagerie*, **2007**

Detail of fig. 71

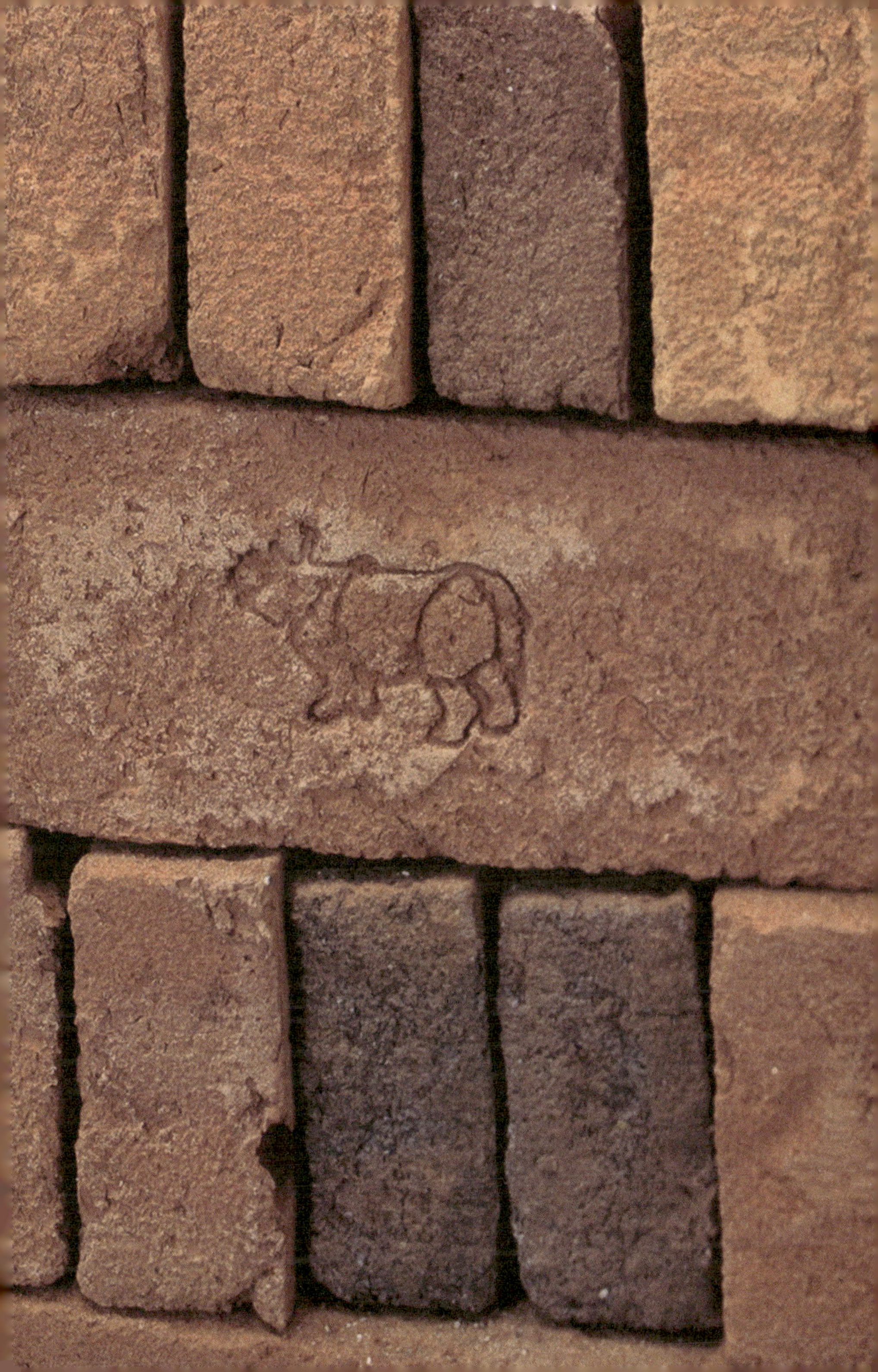

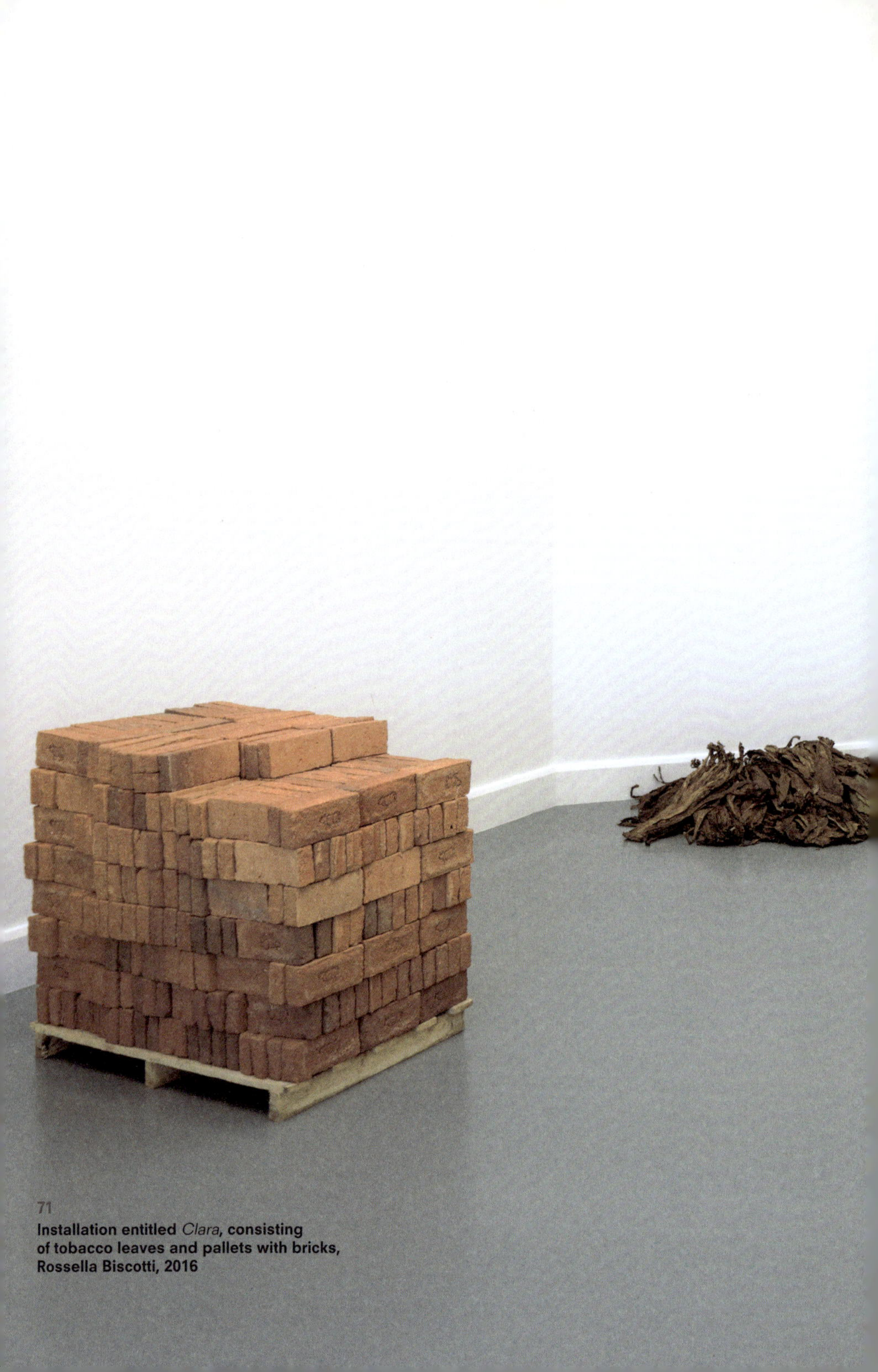

71
Installation entitled *Clara*, consisting of tobacco leaves and pallets with bricks, Rossella Biscotti, 2016

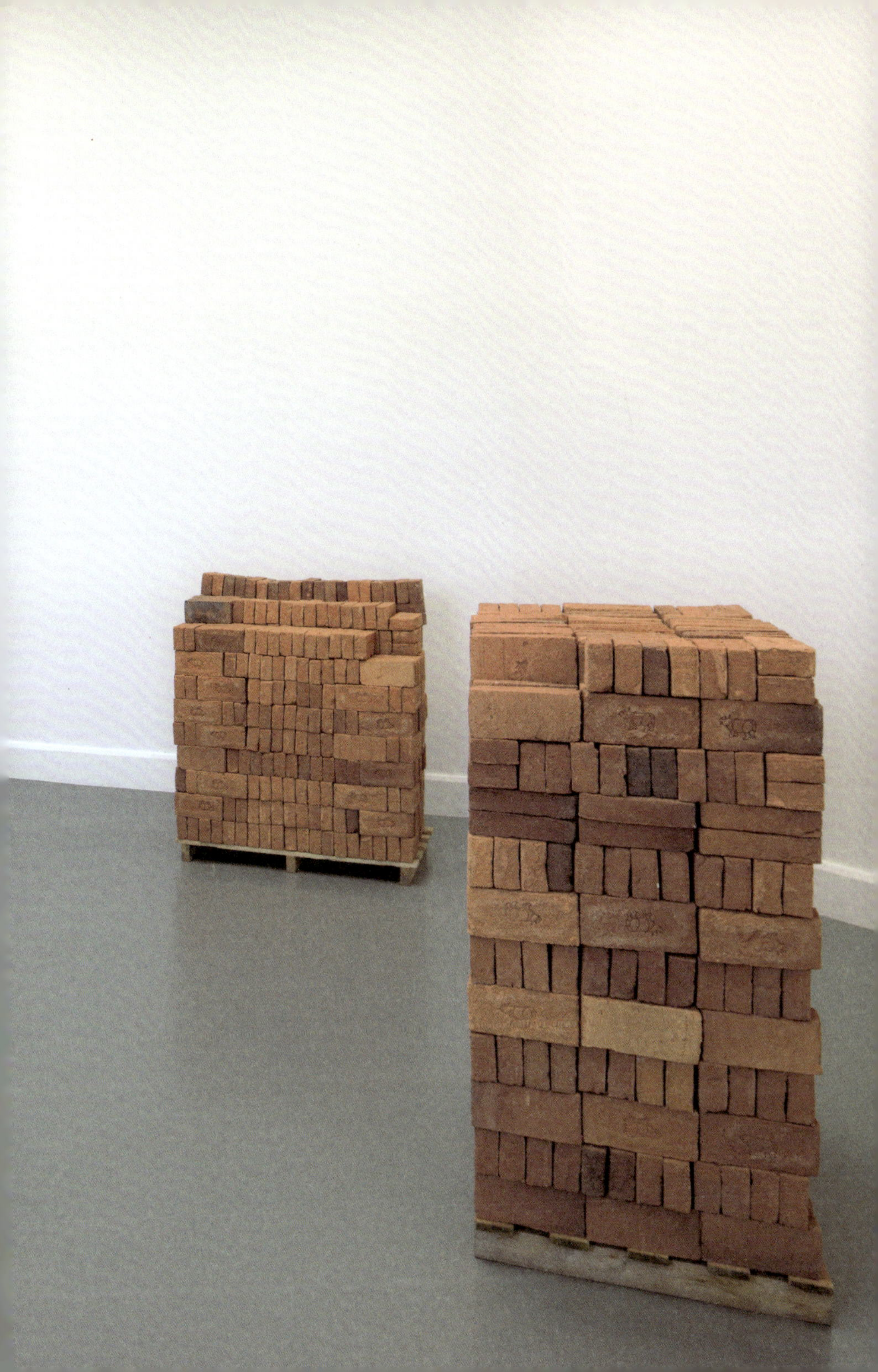

places

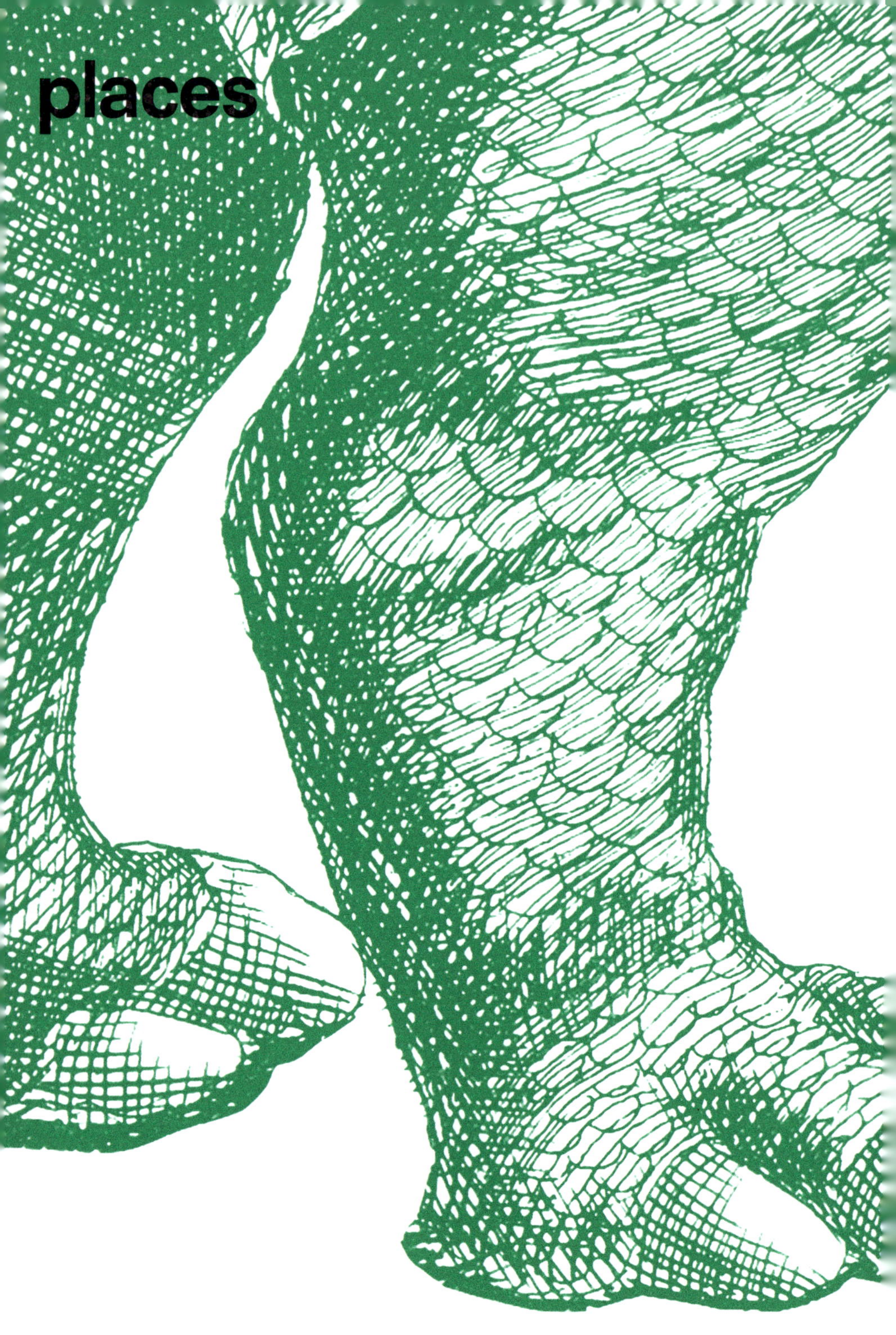

clara visited

I – From Amsterdam (1741–spring 1745)

1741

Late August
Nieuwendam, premises of Matthys Wylacker[155]

September–October
Amsterdam, during the *kermis* in Botermarkt, next to the weighhouse[156]

4 December–early January 1742
Leiden, Stadsherberg at Wittepoort (Haagpoort); Garenmarkt near Raamsteeg[157]

1742

From 12 June
Delft, on a ship during the *kermis*[158]

Late July–early August
Middelburg, Dam by Molstraat ('across Molstraat near the crane')[159]

October
Amsterdam, ship 'lying in the Amstel by the Halvemaen Bridge'[160]

1743

14–18 June
Antwerp, Sint-Pietersvliet (by the River Schelde)[161]

June
Brussels[162]

12–17 October
Amsterdam, Leidseplein[163]

Early November–late February 1744
Hamburg[164]

1745

29 January–late March
Groningen, Grote Markt[165]

II – First grand tour (mid-1745–late 1751)

1745

?
Hooksiel (East Frisia)[166]

Autumn/winter?
Hanover, Ballhoftheater[167]

1746

2 February/March
Braunschweig,
Johann Herman Cordes Haus, Südtstrasse[168]

April
Havelberg[169]
Berlin, Spittelmarkt[170]

July–August
Frankfurt an der Oder[171]

August
Glogów[172]

3 September–3 October
Breslau, Grosse Ring[173]

30 October–early January 1747
Vienna, Freyung[174]

1747

January
Linz[175]

27 January–early February
Salzburg[176]

11–23 February
Munich, premises of 'Frau Thalerin Gastgebin', Weinstrasse[177]

4–16 March
Regensburg[178]

Early April
Freiberg, Wiesemann inn[179]

5–19 April
Dresden, 'Red Deer inn in front of the Pirnaisch Gate'[180]

23 April–early May
Leipzig, Peters-Thor[181]

19 June
Gotha, Reithaus (stables)[182]

25 June–18 July
Kassel, Karlsaue (the castle's orangery)[183]

13 August
Hanau, Gasthaus zur guldnen Ganß[184]

12 September–early October
Frankfurt am Main, Gasthaus Zum Pfau, Friedburger Thor[185]

8–? October
Mainz[186]

November
Darmstadt[187]
Mannheim, Gasthof Zum Pfau[188]

1748

6–30 January
Basel[189]

30 January–21 February
Liestal, Wirdshaus zum Schlissel[190]

February/March
Bern[191]

March
Zurich, Münsterhof ('in a strange hut set up for the purpose')[192]

Late March/early April
Schaffhausen[193]

Early May
Stuttgart[194]

18 May–16 June
Augsburg, Siegelhaus, Weinmarkt (in 'hut')[195]

June/July
Nördlingen, Gasthof zum Fuchs[196]
Ansbach[197]

22 July–20 August
Nuremberg, Island of Schütt[198]

From 3 October
Würzburg, Marktplatz[199]

October/November
Strasbourg[200]

Late November
Nancy[201]

?–30 December
Rheims[202]

1749

19 January–late April
Paris, rue de Tournon, Cul-de-Sac de l'Opéra Comique, rue de Quatre-Vents (Foire Saint-Germain)[203]

27 January–3 February
Versailles, Cheval Rouge, rue de l'Orangerie[204]

12–c. 23 May
Dijon, Faubourg Saint-Nicolas[205]

From late May
Lyons[206]

?
Geneva[207]
Avignon[208]
Aix-en-Provence[209]

October–late November
Marseilles, Cours Belsunce[210]

Late November
Civitavecchia[211]

2–? December
Portici, royal menagerie[212]

Late December or early January/February 1750
Naples[213]

1750

14 March–June
Rome, Baths of Diocletian[214]

July
Senigallia, Osteria della Campana[215]

August
Rimini[216]

24 August–7 September
Bologna, Strada de Pignatarri, former Osteria della Rosa, by the Church of San Petronio[217]

September
Parma
Colorno, near Parma, ducal palace[218]
Fidenza (then Borgo Sandovino)[219]

Early October
Milan, Piazza Mercanti[220]

Late December/early January 1751
Verona, Amphitheatre[221]

1751

January
Venice, St Mark's Square, Zecca[222]

March/April
Graz[223]

29 May–5 June
Vienna, Freyung[224]

?
Prague?[225]
Meiningen[226]

September
Frankfurt am Main[227]

October
Göttingen[228]

Return to Amsterdam

III – From Amsterdam (1752–1753)

1752

23–? March
Ghent, Hemelryck[229]

March/April
Rijssel (Lille)[230]

1753

February/March
Paris, Foire Saint-Germain[231]

IV – Second grand tour (1753–1755)

1753

October
Aachen[232]

25 October–? October/November
Cologne[233]

November
Zons[234]

1754

20–? March
Osnabrück[235]

5 April
Hanover, Marktstrasse, Englische Krone[236]

April/May
Lüneburg?[237]

May
Hamburg?[238]

May/June
Rostock, Ballhaus[239]

22 June–? July
Stralsund, Lange Brücke[240]

July
Danzig, Kettrausche Thor[241]

November
Warsaw[242]

?
Kraków?[243]

1755

January?
Königsberg[244]

April
Memel[245]

5 June–26 July
Copenhagen, Norreport, premises of Poul Nygaard[246]

Late August
Amsterdam, Bergenvaarderskamer, outside the Utrechtse Poort[247]

V – Final tour (1756–1757)

1756

February/March
Groningen, Botermarkt[248]

June/July
Haarlem, *kermis*[249]

Early August
Middelburg, Markt[250]

September–?
London, The Horse and Groom, Lambeth Market[251]

1758

14 April
Dies in London[252]

notes

1 Lach 1970, pp. 159–161; Rookmaaker 1998, pp. 27–29; see also Frenz 2017, pp. 25–27.

2 Clarke 1986; Bedini 1998, pp. 111–132.

3 Schoch et al. 2001–2004, vol. 2, no. 241; Clarke 1986, pp. 19–23; Faust 2003, cat. no. 678.1; Walter 1989, passim; britishmuseum.org/collection/object/P_SL-5218-161 (drawing) and britishmuseum.org/collection/object/P_1895-0122-714 (print).

4 Walter 1989; Clarke 1986, pp. 23–27; Faust 2003, cat. nos. 686 (Penni), 688 (Burgkmair).

5 Faust 2003, cat. no. 687; Schoch et al. 2001–2004, vol. 2.

6 Faust 2003, cat. nos. 698.1–2, 690.1–3.

7 See for extensive information: Lach 1970, pp. 166–172; Clarke 1986, passim; exh. cat. London 2002; see also Leitch 2017, passim.

8 Pietsch 2006, cat. nos. 177, 178; Wittwer 2004, pp. 64–70.

9 Clarke 1986, pp. 28–34; Haag 2015, pp. 132–135; Faust 2003, cat. no. 691 (Galle).

10 Winters 2017, p. 157; Rookmaaker 1976, p. 88 and note 6.

11 Houtzager 1979.

12 Blancken 1698, no. 7 (entrance); several other rhinoceros parts were in the large cabinet A (nos. 9 and 21).

13 Clarke 1986, pp. 37–41; Faust 2003, cat. nos. 692–694; the only copies known to Faust are held by the Hunterian Library in Glasgow.

14 See Clarke 1986, pp. 41–46, on the male, and Grigson 2015, passim, on both rhinoceroses.

15 Hanson 2010, pp. 548–551.

16 See, for example, Faust 2003, cat. no. 706 (text on print 'Braunschweig 1746'); some sources say that she was 8 days old when she was captured, see for example Faust 2003, cat. no. 704 (print 'Hamburg 1744').

17 See, for example, the poster used in Middelburg in August 1742, pasted in Pieter Boddaert, *Aantekeningen van allerhande nature* (The Hague, National Library of the Netherlands (KB)), KW 135 K 37), under Heerebout 2014, passim.

18 Rookmaaker 1980; Rookmaaker 1983a; Rookmaaker et al. 2017; Divyabhanusinh et al. 2018.

19 There are five rhinoceros species in total: three in Asia (the Indian, the Sumatran and the Javan rhinoceros) and two in Africa (the so-called white and black rhinoceros). The Indian and Javan rhinoceroses have one horn, the others have two horns.

20 Divyabhanusinh et al. 2018, pp. 64–79.

21 Ibid., pp. 79, 95.

22 Ladvocat 1749, p. 18: '… une de ces flèches avoit fendu une oreille à celui'.

23 Lequin 1982, p. 104; Jacobs 2000, p. 83; Gommans 2018, pp. 73–80; Holtrop 2021, pp. 149–156. General: Roy 1968; Prakash 2004.

24 Lequin 1982, p. 120; this could not be found in note 194 of the given source. See also Jacobs 2000, pp. 73–104.

25 See for extensive information: Jacobs 2000, pp. 73–104. For the slave trade see Holtrop 2021.

26 See for extensive information: Jörg et al. 2014; Kühne-van Diggelen 1995; Feith 1914. In 1745 Sichterman returned to Groningen where he lived in an enormous, new urban palace amid his large collection of opulent and exotic Asian treasures until his death in 1764.

27 Freytag 1747, pp. 1, 8; Faust 2003, cat. no. 706 (print 'Braunschweig 1746'): 'Es hat dieses Thier, wie es gar jung gewesen, 2 Jahr in denen Zimmern um den Tisch gelauffen, zur Curiosität, wo Damen und Herren gespeiset.'

28 The Hague, National Archives (NA), 1.04.02, inv. no. 2489, fols. 242v–243v. The Maas Chamber was one of the five Dutch branches that made up the VOC.

29 Jan Mout: see, for example, Amsterdam City Archives (ACA), Notariële archieven 5075, inv. no. 5290A, akte 50163 (22 August 1701), inv. no. 6793, akte 506165 (10 June 1711), inv. no. 6860A, akte 555620 (3 January 1714); ACA, Averijgrossen 5061, inv. no. 2807 (27 February 1703), 2814 (10 July 1709); The Hague, NA, Indexes, Sontregisters, 12 June 1722, 8 D 1722. On Douwe Minnes, the father of Trijntje, see https://texelsegenealogie.blogspot.com/p/zeebrieven.html#douweminnes (consulted 3 May 2022; search term: Douwe Minnes); for grandfather Pieter Mout: Leeuwarden, Tresoar, archive no. 28, inv. no. 745, akte 1213: Lidmatenregister, 28 August 1692 (see allefriezen.nl). Marriage: ACA, DTB 531 (21 November 1699). Their six children were all baptized much later at the same time in 1716 in the Oude Kerk in Amsterdam: ACA, DTB 17 (31 January 1716).

30 First voyage: NA, 1.04.02, inv. no. 5857, fol. 8. Second voyage: ACA, Notariële archieven 5075, inv. no. 8525, akte 527757

(23 April 1736); ibid. inv. no. 11687, akte 330647 (20 March 1739); Dutch-Asiatic Shipping, nos. 3033.3, 6999.3 (resources.huygens.knaw.nl/das). Third voyage: NA, 1.04.02, inv. no. 6098, fol. 4; ibid., inv. no. 2489, fol. 397v; ibid., inv. no. 2489, fol. 242v.

31 Faust 2003, cat. no. 735: Sichterman gave her to Mout 'Wegen verursachten grossen Schade verschenkte' ('on account of great damage caused').

32 Copy letter Sichterman to Directors Delft and Rotterdam Chambers, 22 November 1740: NA, 1.04.02, inv. no. 2489, fols. 266r–v; value: ibid., inv. no. 2504, fol. 786v.

33 NA, 1.11.06.11, inv. no. 1694, fols. 466–467, dossiers 250, 251, 274, 282, 351.

34 NA, 1.04.02, inv. no. 6098, fol. 4.

35 ACA, 5072, inv. no. 2178–943.

36 ACA, 5075, inv. no. 9158, akte 170381 (27 October 1741).

37 NA, 1.04.02, inv. no. 2489, fol. 263v.

38 ACA, DTB 573 (Notice of marriage 23 May 1732); Elisabeth Snel was 18 years old at the time of her marriage; Jan was baptized on 15 March 1733, Jacob on 17 November 1734 and Nicolaas on 31 July 1739 (ACA, DTB 21, 51, 23).

39 His father lived in Hekelveld at the time of his marriage in 1699, Douwe himself lived in Wieringenstraat in 1725 shortly before his first trip to Asia, and in Herenmarkt at the time of his marriage in 1732; ten years later he lived on the corner of Brouwersgracht and Korte Prinsengracht (see indexes ACA, under Mout). Captains and seamen traditionally lived in this district: Bruijn 2008, p. 83.

40 *Amsterdamse Courant*, 22 August 1741 (quotation), 24 and 26 August 1741; *Leydse Courant*, 21, 23 and 25 August 1741; *Oprechte Haerlemse Courant*, 26 and 29 August 1741; Rookmaaker 1978a. A *stiver* was a 5-cent piece.

41 *Amsterdamse Courant*, 21 and 22 September 1741; *Oprechte Haerlemse Courant*, 21 September 1741; *Leydse Courant*, 22 September 1741. For the calculation: www.iisg.amsterdam/nl/onderzoek/projecte/hpw (consulted February 2022).

42 Pieters 2002; Sierman 1990.

43 ACA, library 3551, Dagboek Jacob Bicker Raye, p. 39 (28 September 1741).

44 Broberg 2006. Celsius's diary is held by the Kungliga Biblioteket, Stockholm, inv. no. M 231. A second drawing was made by H. van Rooijen and was once part of the D.C. Meijer Collection but has been missing since 1910: Rookmaaker 1978a, p. 17.

45 *Leydse Courant*, 4 December 1741, 1 January 1742.

46 Camper 1782, p. 176, see also pp. 147, 161–162.

47 Ibid., p. 139.

48 Wilson-Pauwels 2009; exh. cat. Leiden 1991.

49 For an overview, compiled with the greatest possible accuracy, of all the towns and cities Clara is known to have visited, along with the sources, see pp. 182–185 in this book.

50 Middelburg: Boddaert, 'Aantekeningen van allerhande nature...', KB, KW 135 K 37, 73/74; Heerebout 2014.

51 Feijoo 1750.

52 *Hamburgische Berichte von gelehrten Sachen*, no. 14 (18 February 1744), pp. 105–112, no. 15 (21 February 1744), pp. 113–114.

53 Harting: Delft, City Archives, Archieven van het stadsbestuur, inv. no. 4255, Register van vergunningen voor activiteiten op de kermissen te Delft en Delfshaven 1722–1808, p. 39; in 1749 Harting was to be appointed one of the three guardians of Mout's children (ACA, 5075, inv. no. 12307, akte 206142), but other than this nothing is known about him. Mout: see resources.huygens.knaw.nl/das, Dutch-Asiatic Shipping, nos. 3245.4 and 7195.4; see also ACA, 5075, inv. no. 8548, akte 553269 (16 April 1742), and ibid., inv. no. 10222, akte 357913 (23 April 1742).

54 Anonymous 2008, passim; Purmerend, Waterlands Archief 0011, Schepenbank te Landsmeer, inv. no. 3439, fol. 12.

55 Faust 2003, cat. nos. 718.4, 718.5 (advertising prints 1747 and 1748), also for the following.

56 In comparison, the rhinoceros's journey by wagon from Lorient to Versailles in 1770 (a distance of c. 480 km) took 16 days, which works out at an average of approximately 30 km a day: Rookmaaker 1983b, p. 308; also Lacroix 1978.

57 Two images are known to depict a wagon: a print made by David Redinger in March 1748 (Faust 2003, cat. no. 725) and a painting from early 1751 by an unknown Venetian artist showing a different wagon.

58 Clarke 1986, p. 48, assumes that there was a keeper, a foreman, a clerk and someone who collected the entrance fee, but these tasks may also have been combined; Ladvocat 1749, p. 18: '... ceux qui montrent le Rhinoceros'; ten men, see http://digital.slub-dresden.de/werkansicht/dif/17457/1 (consulted 4 May 2022); tongue: Ladvocat 1749, p. 6; Casanova: Watzlawick 2001. See figs. 31, 32, 38–40.

59 Groningen: Doornbos 2006; Breslau: *Schlesische Zeitung*, 26 September 1746; Rain: Barth 1747, p. 4v ('mit Lust eine Weile darinne gebadet').

60 Johann Heinrich Redecker, *Historische Collectanea von der Königlichen und Churfürstlichen Residenz-Stadt Hannover ...*,

vol. 2, pp. 1032–1035, Stadtarchiv Hannover I.AA.3, no. 8288 (with thanks to Carola Piepenbring-Thomas).

61 Graz, Steiermärkisches Landesarchiv, Repräsentation und Kammer 1751-III-130, 20 March 1751 (with thanks to Mag. Dr. Gernot Obersteiner); several other permissions: Faust 2003, pp. 56, 57 (Mainz, October 1747 – formal request dated 15 July –; Bern, March 1748; Schaffhausen, March 1748); quarter of the revenue: Groningen 1755, see Doornbos 2006, p. 35.

62 See, for instance, Faust 2003, cat. nos. 718.4, 718.5.

63 Ladvocat 1749, pp. 9–11.

64 Advertisement Middelburg 1742, see Heerebout 2014.

65 *New World Translation of the Holy Scriptures (Study Edition)*, Watch Tower Bible and Tract Society of New York Inc., 2006, Job 40:19, 40:24 and 41:8, www.jw.org/en/library/bible/study-bible/books/job/40/ (consulted 10 June 2022).

66 Faust 2003, cat. no. 718.8.

67 Touching: Servigné 1750, p. 4; enclosure: Barth 1747, p. 2v. See also Richter 1750, p. 64.

68 For an overview, see Faust 2003, cat. nos. 707–715, and Rookmaaker and Monson 2000.

69 Advertisement in *Braunschweigische Anzeigen*, 26 March 1746. Faust 2003, cat. no. 707; Unaware of this advertisement, Faust erroneously claims that this print by Beck and Schmidt formed the basis for all the prints that Mout had made. In Dresden a separate version was brought out by Moritz Bodenehr (Faust 2003, cat. no. 721; Rookmaaker and Monson 2000, no. 10).

70 Faust 2003, cat. no. 710.

71 Neubert 2007, passim.

72 A.B. Clasen, Notizen über Kuriosa: Oldenburg, Niedersächsisches Landesarchiv, Dep 25 JEV, Best. 262-4 Nr. 5254 (with thanks to Pia Mecklenfeld, NLA Oldenburg). At that time the pound was not a metric unit and differed in weight from city to city.

73 See Schattullrechnungen, 11 and 13 May 1746, https://quellen.perspectivia.net/de (consulted 4 May 2022); pass: Geheimes Staatsarchiv Berlin, II. HA GD, Abt. 7, IV Nr. 2446.

74 Vienna, Österreichisches Staatsarchiv, AVA Adel RAA 283.53 Mout, David.

75 Faust 2003, cat. nos. 717.1, 717.2; see also advertisements in *Wienerisches Diarium*, 19 November 1746 and *Wiener Zeitung*, 16 November, 7 and 11 December 1746.

76 Faust 2003, cat. nos. 718.1, 718.2, 718.4, 718.5.

77 Emmerig 1978, p. 21, cited from *Curiosa Saxonica*.

78 Stadtarchiv Leipzig, Standgeldrechnungen, May 1747, on circusbarnoti.de/html/18-1738-1747.html (consulted 4 May 2022); general: Kroker 1890.

79 Faust 2003, cat. no. 713.2.

80 Ibid., cat. no. 723.2.1.

81 Ibid., cat. no. 723.1–5; Rookmaaker and Monson 2000, pp. 328–333.

82 Faust 2003, p. 56, based on a manuscript in the Universitätsbibliothek Basel, VB Mscr. H 43c, pp. 309–311.

83 Faust 2003, cat. nos. 725, 726. His criticism in 725: 'Die Abbildungen, welche wir ausliefern, werden auch den Liebhabern der Natur-Wissenschaften und der Künsten desto angenehmer seyn, weil die meiste übrige in Kupferstichen, Holzschnitten, und so gar auf neuen Medaillen, auch die man hat in Gemählden, wie ungleich, also samtlich nicht allzuwol getroffen und zum theil sehr unfleissig verfertigt sind. Wie dann der Herr und Besitzer dieses Thiers erkennt, dass die Abbildungen, die er ausgibt, an sich selbs slecht seyen, anbey aber sie für gut genug halt, wann man dieselbe ihm wol bezahlt.' ['The illustrations that we supply will also be the more attractive for lovers of the natural sciences and the arts, because most of the others are on copper engravings, woodcuts, and even on new medals, even those that you have in paintings, are so inferior. All in all, they are not well depicted and individually they are very poorly made. Moreover, the master and owner of this animal realizes that the illustrations he publishes are themselves bad, but accepts them as good enough, yet one pays him the same.']

84 Emmerig 1978, cat. no. IV.1.

85 Ibid., pp. 23–25.

86 Reinhard 1748, p. 5.

87 *Gazette de Berne*, 8 February 1749; Barbier 1851, pp. 68, 69.

88 Anonymous 1750: 'Tout *Paris* courut en foule pour voir cette espèce de Phénomene'; Barbier 1857, p. 356 ('Il y peu de gens qui ne le voient par curiosité, et le capitaine hollandais doit gagner beaucoup'). *Les Affiches de Paris*, 10 April 1749.

89 Anonymous 1750: '… la folie de nos *François* & de nos *Françoïses* pour ce vilain Animal a été si grande, que, pour immortaliser sa mémoire, les Dames ont donné … son nom à une nouvelle espece de Coëffures que leur imagination, toujours fertile pour ces sortes de choses, leur a fait inventer, en quoi elles ont été imitées aussi-tôt par nos Petits-Maitres qui ont aussi donné le nom de ce Monstre à une mode nouvelle de harnois qu'ils ont fait faire à leur carosses'.

90 Letter from Voltaire to d'Argental, 18 June 1759, cited in Frantz 2020 ('Que je fus aise quand j'appris que le théâtre était purgé de blanc-poudrés, coiffés au rhinocéros et à l'oiseau royal!'). These were high hair-

styles incorporating a kind of horn or special feathers.

91 Paris, Archives Nationales, Maison du Roi, Minutes ou transcriptions authentiques d'actes émanés des rois Louis XIV et Louis XV, O/1/93 141 ('de faire voir dans touts les villes et lieux du Royaume pour l'argent un Rhinoceros').

92 *Gazette d'Amsterdam*, 25 February 1749.

93 *Resolutien van de Heeren Staten van Holland en Westvriesland over 1751*, vol. 2, pp. 908–910; on 19 September 1751 the States General took a decision which largely rejected his request, ibid., pp. 910–912.

94 SAA, 5075, inv. no. 12307, akte 180680; ibid., akte 206142. For the rest, very little is known about Niel, except that according to other deeds he took on this kind of responsibility more often and was a shoemaker by trade, established in Weteringstraat.

95 Estate Leiden 1004, Baptism Pieterskerk 1741–1769, inv. no. 229 (5 December 1751).

96 Lyons: Rathery 1863, p. 485, diary entry, 30 May 1749. Marseilles: Rathery 1864, p. 77, diary entry, 21 November 1749; *Auszug der neuesten Weltgeschichte auf das Jahr 1749 ...*, Nuremberg 1749, p. 610; *Kiøbenhavnske Danske Post-Tidender*, 5 December 1749. No record of the incident could be found in the police and judicial files of the period; kind communication Benoît Jégouzo, Conservateur du patrimoine, Archives Municipales de Marseille, to Gijs van der Ham, e-mail, 28 December 2021.

97 *Gazette de Berne*, 3 January 1750.

98 Mentioned in a promotional print of which the original no longer survives: Faust 2003, cat. no. 718.9.

99 Badioli 2008, based on *Le Cronache Mastai*.

100 Ricci 1888, p. 692.

101 See www.storiadimilano.it/cron/dal1726al1750.htm (consulted 6 February 2022).

102 London, National Gallery, inv. no. 1101. See Levey 1971, pp. 154–156; in note 10 Levey mentions a further three paintings in the style of Longhi, the whereabouts of which are unknown.

103 See www.conoscerevenezia.it/?p=52563 (consulted 12 October 2021), based on an article by Giovanni Malgarotto in *Il Gazzettino*, 29 May 1926. Inquiries at the Archivio di Stato di Venezia yielded no information from direct sources (e-mails from Monica del Rio to Gijs van der Ham, 25 and 27 October 2021). For this reason, it is uncertain whether this decision was enforced.

104 *Wiener Zeitung*, 29 May 1751; *Opregte Groninger Courant*, 15 June 1751.

105 See Grigson 2015, passim.

106 Ghent, Lille: *Gazet van Gent*, 23 March 1752. Paris: *Annonces, affiches, et avis divers*, 14 February 1753, p. 28; Casanova: Watzlawick 2001, who did not know about Clara's visit in 1753, however, and therefore erroneously assumed that Casanova's mention in his *Mémoires* must refer to 1749. The Dutch medical physician Wouter van Doeveren also visited her in Paris in 1753, see Van Heiningen 2014, p. 95 (diary entry 24 February 1753).

107 See Faust 2003, cat. nos. 718.2, 718.3 and more extensively cat. nos. 718.4–8.

108 *Curieuser Extract derer Neuesten Zeitungen*, Rostock, 10 June 1754 (no. 46); later that year an advertisement appeared in a Paris newspaper: *Annonces, affiches, et avis divers*, 28 November 1754.

109 See https://akademieregistres.bbaw.de/data/protokolle/0350-1754_07_04.xml (consulted 7 September 2021); Marggraf 1758; ibid., *Journal de médicine, chirurgie, et pharmacie, &c*, Paris, vol. IX/9 ? (December 1758), pp. 530–536.

110 Passes, Memel: Stockholm, Riksarkivet, Tullväsende, vol. 11, 'Mout' (letter Mout to the King of Sweden, 6 April 1755); Warsaw: Heikamp 1980, pp. 315–316; Königsberg: Berlin, Geheimes Staatsarchiv Preussischer Kulturbesitz, II. HA GD, Abt. 7, IV Nr. 2446 (Schaustellung eines Rhinozeros durch Kapitän Douse Mout in Königsberg).

111 Stockholm, Riksarkivet, Utrikesexpeditionens protokoll, vol. A 1:51 (with thanks to Örjan Romefors, Senior Archivist Riksarkivet Stockholm Marieberg).

112 Jørgensen 1986; *Stockholms Post Tidningar*, June 1755.

113 *Amsterdamse Courant*, 30 August 1755.

114 Faust 2003, cat. no. 718.10; Grigson 2015, pp. 80–81.

115 Anonymous 2008, p. 15; Purmerend, Waterlands Archief, 0011 Oud-Rechterlijk Archief, Schepenbank te Landsmeer, 3440, fol. 165.

116 'Alt geworden 21 Jahr in London crepirt den 14. April 1758' [na bronvermelding zoals elders?], Faust 2003, cat. nos. 734, 735; Rookmaaker and Monson 2000, nos. 19, 20.

117 NA, 1.05.06 (Verspreide West-Indische Stukken), inv. no. 1005; NA, 1.05.01.02 (WIC 1674–1791), inv. no. 14, fol. 58.

118 Jan: NA, 1.04.02, inv. no. 14787, fol. 17, and inv. no. 6488, fol. 7. Nicolaas: ibid., inv. no. 6393, fol. 12 and inv. no. 6431, fol. 5 (via index VOC: Opvarenden).

119 'Controleur van de Convoijen en Licenten'. *Album studiosorum Academiae Lugduno Batavae 1575–1875*, p. 1035; *Naamwyzer waar in vertoond worden de Naamen en Woonplaatsen van ... de Heeren Regeerders etc der Stad Amstelredam, dezes Jaars 1757. Als meede van eenige Bedienden der zelve ...*,

p. 47; NA, 1.01.02, inv. no. 12290, fol. 141. Deceased: ACA, DTB 1116, fol. 164v–165 (funeral 10 March 1778).

120 Deposition for marriage (*ondertrouw*) to Pieter Pieterse (later Keller, died 1788) 18 November 1774 (ACA, DTB 619); children: Pieter Gerrardus, baptized 20 August 1775 (ACA, DTB 57); Elisabeth Katharina, baptized 29 January 1777 (ACA, DTB 58); Jacob, baptized 23 June 1779 (ACA, DTB 102); Catharina, baptized 7 June 1782 (ACA, DTB 31); Maria Elisabeth, baptized 2 February 1786 (ACA, DTB 127). Elisabeth was widowed in 1788 and from 1793 was registered as 'poor, living at home' and died thus in 1824: ACA, 349 (Huiszittenhuizen), inv. no. 866, p. 666.

121 Distance: ACA, 5075, inv. no. 10191, akte 341579; death Douwe: ACA, DTB 1085 (10 August 1775); death Elisabeth Snel: ACA, STB 1085 (10 February 1778).

122 Godart 1755, pp. 287–288.

123 Letter from Brucker to Johann Christoph Gottsched, 21 December 1748, in Gottsched 2020, p. 36. General: Stubbe 1966.

124 Van der Ham 2005, passim.

125 Clarke 1986, p. 60 and fig. 37 for sketches he definitely made; see for the album, now at the Rijksmuseum: Van der Ham 2005; on Lorenzi in general: Chignola et al. 2005.

126 Morton 2007, in particular, pp. 1–28, 119–123.

127 *Mercure de France*, December 1749, p. 50: 'Là, d'un monstre à qui l'Inde a donné la naissance,/ Tu peins la masse enorme, & cette ressemblance,/ Ces replis de sa peau bizarrement formés,/ Cette corne, l'effroi d'un ennemi terrible,/ Cet oeuil aussi cruel qu'il paroît insensible,/ Font parler ta Peinture à mes regards charmés.' ('There, of a monster to whom India gave birth,/ You paint the enormous mass, and this likeness,/ These folds of its skin strangely formed,/ This horn, the terror of a terrible enemy [elephant, GH],/ This eye as cruel as it seems insensitive,/ Make your Painting speak to my enchanted eyes.')

128 Frank 2007, pp. 37–38, 52–57; Droguet et al. 2003, pp. 85–91, 135–146.

129 Clarke 1976, pp. 10–11; Bostock 2021.

130 See Augarde 1986, passim; Kjellberg 1997, pp. 128–132; Clarke 1986, pp. 131–134; Augarde 2022, cat. no. 70.

131 Roelandts 1939.

132 Avery et al. 2021, pp. 17–20, cat. no. 1 (research and text by Robert Wenley, Barber Institute of Fine Arts, Birmingham). See this also for Verschaffelt's sculptures.

133 Ibid., p. 18.

134 Kind communication Dr Uta Coburger, Konservatorin Region Kurpfalz, Staatliche Schlösser und Gärten Baden-Württemberg, to Gijs van der Ham (e-mail, 27 October 2021).

135 Letter Georg Wilhelm Fleischmann to Karoline Luise von Baden, 7 September 1753, www.Karoline-Luise.la-bw.de (consulted 6 May 2022).

136 Letter Wilhelmine von Brandenburg-Bayreuth to Frederick the Great, Lyons, 31 October 1754, see 'Briefwechsel der Wilhelmine von Bayreuth' on quellen.perspectivia.net, search term: nashorn: 'Ich bin überall ein ebenso aussergewöhnliches Lebewesen, wie das Nashorn'.

137 Maugras 1886, p. 455; Lilti 2017, p. 136.

138 Voltaire 1775, p. 284 (https://voltairefoundation.wordpress.com/2013/10/09/le-dodo-et-le-rhinoceros-voltaire-au-pays-des-merveilles/; consulted 6 May 2022).

139 Letter Bergen to Linnaeus, 9 August 1746; Linnaeus to Bergen, 10 October 1746; Bergen to Linnaeus, 16 March 1747, consulted via www.alvin-portal.org (search term: rhinoceros); Bergen 1746, passim; for Linnaeus, see Rookmaaker 1996–1997, pp. 61–62; rhinoceros as swine: *Göttingische Zeitungen von gelehrten Sachen*, 13 March 1747, pp. 164–165.

140 Freytag 1747, passim; Parsons 1747.

141 Faust 2003, cat. no. 717.1: 'Gott hats gemacht, dass sich der Mensch darob ergötzet'.

142 Maupertuis 1750, pp. 28–29; refuting this: Maleville 1756, p. 68. See Vartanian 1949, in particular, p. 57.

143 Zurich, Staatsarchiv, B IX 243 Abhandlungen der Naturforschenden Gesellschaft, 1746–1754, fols. 1r–9v.

144 Faust 2003, cat. no. 733, also for the print; Heikamp 1980, p. 316.

145 Rookmaaker 1983b; Péquignot 2013.

146 Camper 1782, pp. 145–180.

147 Ibid., p. 161.

148 Ibid., p. 180.

149 For an imposing overview, see Rookmaaker 1998b, passim. See also Van den Berg 2021, pp. 66, 126.

150 Richter 1750, pp. 5–6.

151 Meijer 2019, pp. 18–23.

152 Richter 1750, p. 13: 'Wäre es mir möglich, künftig einmal von der itzige Knechtschaft, die mich gefangen hält, mich los zu reissen und in mein Heimath zurück zu kehren: so wollte ich, um mich zu rächen, auf eben diese Art, als man mir thut, einen Menschen unter meinen Brüdern zur Schau herum führen. Ich bin versichert, dass das Geschlecht der Nashörner, ein solches Wunderthier, als der Mensch ihnen zu seyn scheint, mit

weit mehrern Nutzen betrachten würde, als es die Menschen bey Erblickung eines Nashorns zu thun pflegen.'

153 For the books and articles by this and other authors subsequently mentioned, see the list of consulted works.

154 See also Roy 2021.

155 Rookmaaker 1978a.

156 Ibid.; *Leydsche Courant*, 22 September 1741.

157 *Leydsche Courant*, 4 December 1741, 1 January 1742.

158 Delft, Stadsarchief, Archieven van het stadsbestuur, inv. no. 4255, Register van vergunningen voor activiteiten op de kermissen te Delft en Delfshaven 1722–1808, p. 39.

159 '...over de Mol straadt bij de kraan', Heerebout 2014, passim.

160 '...liggende op den Amstel by de Halvemaensbrug', *Amsterdamse Dingsdaegse Courant*, 2 and 9 October 1742.

161 *Gazette van Antwerpen*, 14 October 1743.

162 Feijoo 1750, pp. 23–28.

163 *Amsterdamse Courant*, 12 October 1743.

164 *Hamburgische Berichte von gelehrten Sachen*, 18 and 21 February 1744; Faust 2003, cat. nos. 704, 705.

165 Doornbos 2006, passim.

166 Niedersächsisches Landesarchiv – Abteilung Oldenburg, NLA OL Dep 25 JEV, Best. 262-4 Nr. 5254, Nachlass und Sammlung des Bürgermeisters A. B. Clasen – Notizen über Kuriosa.

167 Hanover, Stadtarchiv, I.AA.3, Nr. 8288 Johann Heinrich Redecker: Historische Collectanea von der Königlichen und Churfürstlichen Residenz-Stadt Hannover ... am 8. Julii 1723 angefangen, Bd. 2; Faust 2003, cat. no. 709.

168 *Braunschweigischen Anzeigen*, 2 February 1746; Faust 2003, cat. nos. 706, 707.

169 *Neu-Eröffneter Historien-Saal, das ist, kurze, deutliche und unparteyische Beschreibung der Allgemeinen Welt- und Kirchen-Geschichten*, vol. 7 (1744–1749), Basel 1756, p. 660.

170 Rookmaaker 1998, p. 63.

171 Ibid.

172 Ibid.

173 *Schlesische Zeitung*, 3 and 26 September 1746.

174 *Wienerisches Diarium*, 9 and 19 November 1746; *Oprechte Haerlemsche Courant*, 19 November 1746.

175 Faust 2003, cat. no. 717.1.

176 Faust 2003, p. 90.

177 Faust 2003, cat. nos. 717.2, 718.1.

178 Barth 1747; Faust 2003, cat. no. 718.2.

179 *Beschreibung Des Ausländisches Thier welches zu Freyberg in den ersten Tagen des Monats April 1747 in Wiesemannischen Gasthof zum güldnen Stern lebendig von seinen Eigenthums-Herrn vielen Leuten ist gezeiget worden* ['Description of the foreign animal which was shown alive by its owner-master to many people in Freyberg in the first days of the month of April 1747 at the Wiesemann Golden Star inn'].

180 'Rother Hirsch vor dem Pirnaisches Thor', Emmerig 1978, p. 21; Faust 2003, cat. nos. 721.1–2.

181 Rookmaaker 1998, p. 64; Emmerig 1978, p. 21; circusbarnoti.de.

182 Landesarchiv Thüringen – Staatsarchiv Gotha, Fourierbücher im Bestand Oberhofmarschallamt, Nr. 681 c 1747 III: 'Nach der Tafel haben Hochfürstliche Gnädigste Herrschaft den Renocerum in reuthause besehen'. ['After dining, Their Most Gracious Highnesses viewed the Rhinoceros in the stables.'] With thanks to Albrecht Loth, Landesarchiv Thüringen – Staatsarchiv Gotha.

183 Clarke 1986, p. 52 (note 18).

184 Faust 2003, cat. no. 724.

185 Emmerig 1978, p. 21.

186 Faust 2003, p. 56.

187 Ibid.

188 Rookmaaker and Monson 2000, no. 16.

189 Faust 2003, p. 56.

190 Ibid.

191 Emmerig 1978, p. 24 (note 8).

192 '... in einem sonderbaren dazu aufgerichteten Haus', Faust 2003, cat. nos. 725, 726.

193 Ibid., p. 57.

194 Rookmaaker 1998, p. 64.

195 '... in 'Hütte', Emmerig 1978, p. 21.

196 Faust 2003, p. 57.

197 Emmerig 1978, no. 1.

198 Faust 2003, cat. no. 718.7; Emmerig 1978, pp. 21–22.

199 Neubert 2007, passim.

200 Emmerig 1978, no. 3; Clarke 1986, p. 52. The existing medals are dated 1748. Clarke suspects that Clara was here in April, but, given the places she visited in 1748, November/December would be more logical. Online research in *Les registres des déli-*

bérations du Conseil des XXI (Archives de Strasbourg) failed to yield any information.

201 Nicolas Durival, *Journal*, fol. 57v (29 November 1748): 'J'ai vu à Nancy un Rhinocéros femelle, de dix mois' ['In Nancy I saw a ten-month-old female Rhinoceros']. Bibliothèque de Nancy, Ms. 1311 (863). Kind communication from Thierry Franz, Château de Lunéville (e-mail, 20 October 2021).

202 Rookmaaker 1998, p. 65.

203 *Les Affiches de Paris*, 2 February and 10 April 1749; Faust 2003, cat. nos. 718.8, 728.1–2.

204 *Les Affiches de Paris*, 27 January 1749; *Gazette de Berne*, 8 February 1749.

205 Marchant 1884.

206 Rathery 1859–1867, vol. 5 (1863), p. 485.

207 *Gazette d'Amsterdam*, 25 February 1749.

208 Ibid.

209 Ibid.

210 *Auszug der neuesten Weltgeschichte: auf das Jahr 1749 …*, Nuremberg 1749, p. 610.

211 *Oprechte Haerlemsche Courant*, 18 December 1749.

212 *Gazette de Berne*, 14 January 1750.

213 Ibid.

214 *Diario Ordinario*, 14 March 1750.

215 Badioli 2008.

216 Rookmaaker 1998, p. 66.

217 Ricci 1888, p. 692.

218 *Oprechte Haerlemsche Courant*, 15 October 1750.

219 Ibid.

220 Paolo Colussi, 'Cronologia di Milano dal 1726 al 1750'; https://scripofilia.it/it/antichi-stati/9593-1755-nuovo-monte-dei-creditori-di-giustizia-cesareo-real-diploma-29-gennaio-1753-ducato-di-milano.html.

221 Clarke 1986, p. 60.

222 See www.conoscerevenezia.it/?p=52563, based on an article by Giovanni Malgarotto in *Il Gazzettino*, 29 May 1926; Marchesi and Crevatin 2006, pp. 34–35.

223 Graz, Steiermärkisches Landesarchiv, Protokoll der Repräsentation und Kammer 1751-III-130 (20 March 1751).

224 *Wiener Zeitung*, 29 May 1751.

225 *Opregte Groninger Courant*, 15 June 1751.

226 Landesarchiv Thüringen – Staatsarchiv Meiningen, 4-99-004 Archivaliensammlung des HAV/ Akten, Archivalien-Signatur: 36, Auszüge aus dem Kirchenbuch von Witzelroda, gefertigt 1836, Einträge des Pfarrers Christian Daniel Wallich, 1–3: Durchzug eines Nashorns, 1751.

227 *Opregte Groninger Courant*, 15 June 1751.

228 Kleinecke 2016, p. 56.

229 *Gazet van Gent*, 23 March 1752.

230 Ibid.

231 *Annonces, affiches, et avis divers*, 14 February 1753.

232 *Oprechte Haerlemse Courant*, 30 October 1753.

233 Ibid.

234 Schwabach 2005.

235 *Wiener Zeitung*, 13 April 1754.

236 *Hannoverische Anzeigen*, 5 April 1754.

237 Cf. *Curieuser Extract derer Neuesten Zeitungen* (Rostock), 10 June 1754.

238 *Annonces, affiches, et avis divers*, 28 November 1754.

239 *Curieuser Extract derer Neuesten Zeitungen* (Rostock), 10 June 1754.

240 *Stralsunder Relationscourier*, 22 June 1754; *Intelligenzen von Täglichen Vorkommenheiten in Pommern und Rügen*, 2 July 1754.

241 *Intelligenzen von Täglichen Vorkommenheiten in Pommern und Rügen*, 16 August 1754; Faust 2003, cat. no. 733; Heikamp 1980, p. 316.

242 *Kurtz-gefasster historischer Nachrichten zum Behuf der neuern europäischer Begebenheiten …*, October 1754; Heikamp 1980, pp. 315–316.

243 Clarke 1986, p. 63.

244 Berlin, Geheimes Staatsarchiv, II. HA GD, Abt. 7, IV Nr. 2446 Schaustellung eines Rhinozeros durch Kapitän Douse Mout in Königsberg.

245 Stockholm, Riksarkivet, Tullväsende, vol. 11, 'Mout' (Mout to King of Sweden, 6 April 1755).

246 *Kiøbenhavnske Danske Post-Tidender*, 20 June 1755; Jørgensen 1986, passim.

247 *Amsterdamse Courant*, 30 August 1755.

248 Doornbos 2006, p. 35.

249 Rookmaaker 1998, p. 66.

250 Heerebout 2014, pp. 90–94.

251 Grigson 2015, pp. 80–81.

252 Faust 2003, cat. nos. 734, 735.

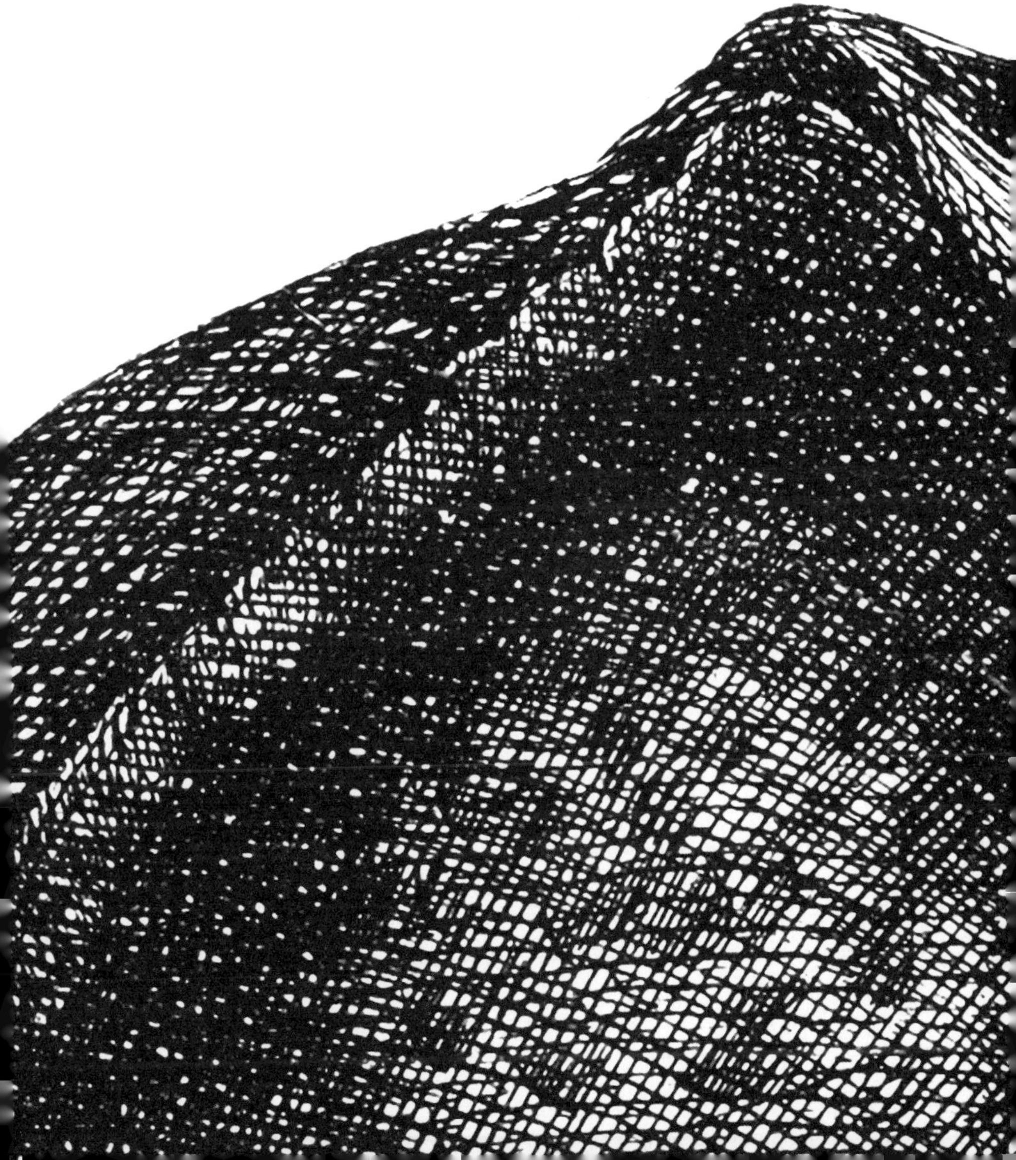

research &

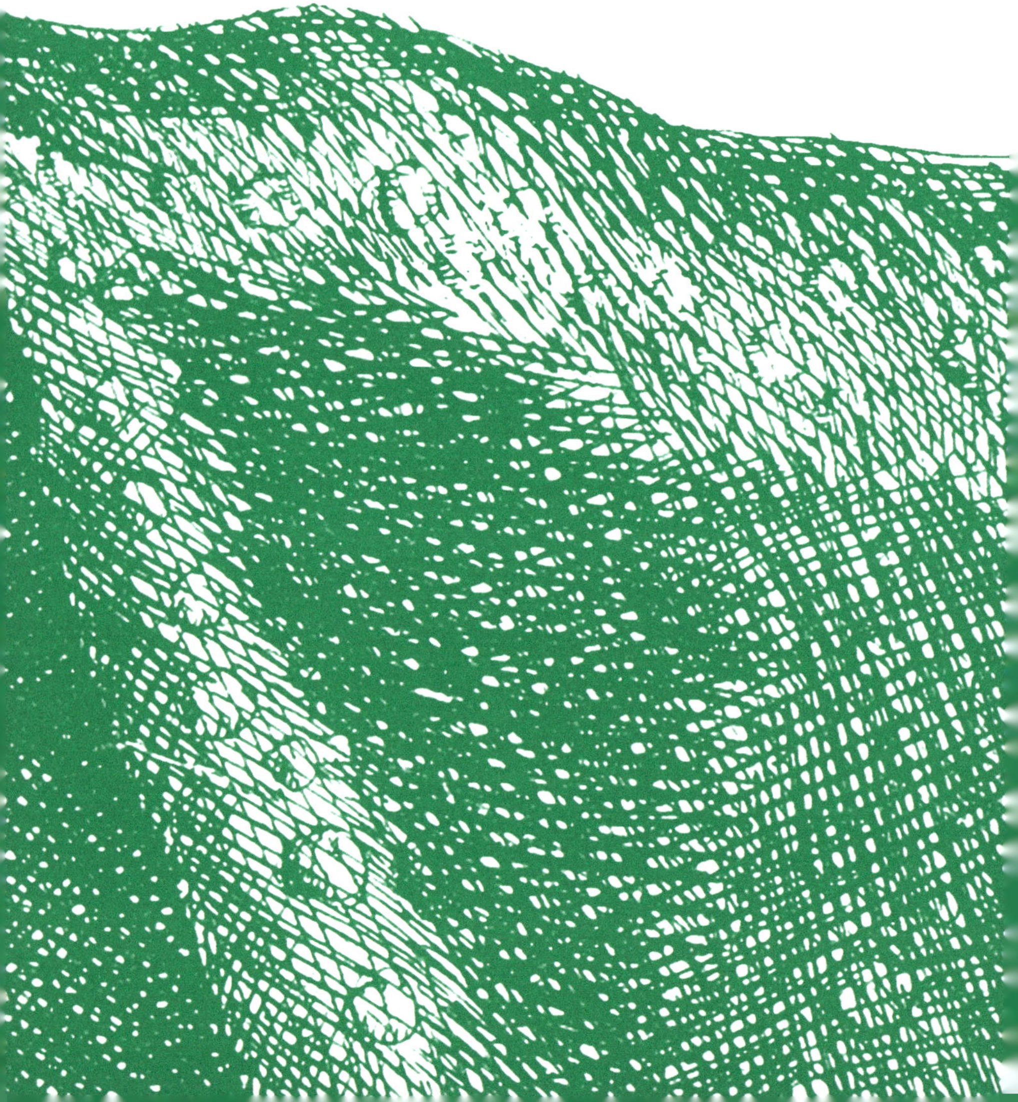

literature

During my research for this book and the exhibition at the Rijksmuseum, I have primarily made use of the many publications on Clara's life and travels that have been issued in recent decades. Various authors have tried to reconstruct her journeys from the information available to them at the time, in particular, T.H. Clarke, Hubert Emmerig, Ingrid Faust, Detlef Heikamp, and last but not least Kees Rookmaaker. Moreover, the latter has not only published a great deal about Clara and the rhinoceros in general, but is also the founder of the website rhinoresourcecenter.com, a treasure trove for anyone seeking information on rhinoceroses. I have found the site incredibly useful.

To get to grips with the subject, I, too, have tried to reconstruct the travels of Clara and Mout as accurately as possible. Inevitably, this often meant tracking down and piecing together snippets of information, tiny details and accidental finds that came to light largely due to the increasing digitization of archives and sources, such as newspapers. In an attempt to fill in the gaps in the journeys of Clara and Mout I also wrote to a number of European archives. I regularly carried out extensive searches via Google and on websites for key words such as rhinoceros, Nashorn and Mout, resulting in several surprising discoveries. Lastly, I conducted additional online research into Mout and his family with the help of digitized records at Amsterdam City Archives and the VOC archive at the National Archives of the Netherlands.

The first book to tell Clara's story in its entirety was Glynis Ridley's *Clara's Grand Tour*, published in 2004. Like many others, it was the first time I had heard about Clara. Unfortunately, this enjoyable book contains major mistakes, for instance about Mout, whom the author knew nothing about, and incorrect assumptions and interpretations are made, in particular relating to parts of Clara's tour. My book is based much more closely on factual information.

No doubt even more information will come to light about Clara and Mout in the coming years as new research is conducted and archives and other sources are further digitized. I am very curious to know what will be found.

Consulted archives

The Hague, National Archives of the Netherlands (NA)
1.04.02, Archief van de Verenigde Oost-Indische Compagnie (VOC):
inv. no. 123: Resoluties Heren [Decisions Lords] XVII, 1741–1742
inv. nos. 2440, 2441, 2455, 2469, 2489, 2504, 2518, 2537, Overgekomen brieven en papieren uit Indië: Bengaalse brievenboeken [Letters and documents brought over from the Indies: Bengali books of letters], 1739–1742
inv. no. 6098, Scheepssoldijboeken: Grootboek en journaal Phoenix [Ships' wage payment records: Ledger and log Phoenix], 1739–1740

1.04.18.02, Archief Boekhouder-Generaal te Batavia [Archive Bookkeeper-General in Batavia], 1699–1801:
inv. no. 10772, Generaal journal [General log], 1740–1741
inv. no. 10829, Negotie grootboek [Trade ledger], 1740–1741

1.11.06.11, Nederlandse bezittingen India, digitale duplicaten [Dutch possessions India, digital duplicates]:
inv. no. 1694, Kantoor Bengalen [Bengal Office], 1740–1743

Indexes
VOC/Opvarenden [VOC/crew members]
VOC/Overgekomen brieven en papieren [Letters and documents brought over from Asia]

Amsterdam City Archives (ACA)
Indexes, searches for Mout, Elisabeth Snel, rhinoceros

Leiden, Erfgoed Leiden
0501A, Stadsbestuur:
inv. no. 119, Gerechtsdagboeken [Court journals], 11 May 1741–27 December 1742
inv. no. 172, Burgemeestersdagboeken [Mayors' journals], 1 October 1739–23 February 1743
inv. no. 200, Notuulboeken burgemeesters [Mayors' minute books], 10 November 1739–10 November 1742
inv. no. 283, Ingekomen requesten [Requests received], 1738–1742
inv. no. 293, Afgeslagen en nader te onderzoeken requesten [Requests denied and subject to further examination], 1741–1750
inv. no. 9945/9948, Ontvangsten/uitgaven [Revenue/expenditure], 1741–1742

0519, Heilig Geest- of Arm Wees- en Kinderhuis [Holy Spirit Orphanage]:
inv. no. 2498, Register van inkomsten uit de verhuur van plaatsen op kermissen en jaarmarkten, [Register of revenue from rental of places at *kermissen* and fairs] 1740–1774
inv. no. 2499, Register van ontvangst van de heffingen op kermis- en toneelvoorstellingen ... [Register of the receipt of levies on *kermis* and theatre performances], 1750–1816

Purmerend, Waterlands Archief
0011, Oud-Rechterlijk Archief, Schepenbank te Landsmeer [Old Judicial Archive, Alderman's Court in Landsmeer]:
inv. nos. 3439, 3440

Archives contacted by e-mail:
Bremen, Staatsarchiv
Brno, City Archives
Erfurt, Stadtarchiv
Freiburg, Stadtarchiv
Gotha, Staatsarchiv
Göttingen, Stadtarchiv
Graz, Landesarchiv
Jena, Stadtarchiv
Klagenfurt, Landesarchiv
Lyons, Archives
Mannheim, Stadtarchiv
Maribor, City Archives
Marseilles, Archives
Olomouc, Stadsarchief
Stralsund, Stadtarchiv
Strasbourg, Archives
Venice, Archivio di Stato
Weimar, Stadtarchiv, Landesarchiv

Specific websites (among others)

Rhinoresourcecenter.com: literature on rhinoceroses
Delpher.nl: Dutch newspapers
Digipress.digitale-sammlungen.de: newspapers and other publications
www.e-newspaperarchives.ch: newspapers
Gallica.bnf.fr: publications

Literature

Anonymous 1750
Anonymous [Charles de Fieux de Mouhy] (ed.), 'No. 9.' (letter 23 April 1750), *La Bigarure* 3 (1750), no. 9, pp. 65–72, in Klaus-Dieter Ertler and Elisabeth Hobisch (eds.), *Die 'Spectators' im internationalen Kontext. Digitale Edition*, Graz 2011–2019, hdl.handle.net/11471/513.20.4640

Anonymous 2008
Anonymous, 'De Wilmckebreek ook wel genaamd "Het meertje"', *De Croosduyker* 12 (2008), no. 23, pp. 13–18

Augarde 1986
Jean-Dominique Augarde, 'Jean-Joseph de Saint-Germain (1719–1791). Bronzearbeiten zwischen Rocaille und Klassizismus', in Hans Ottomeyer and Peter Pröschel (eds.), *Vergoldeten Bronzen. Die Bronzearbeiten des Spätbarock und Klassizismus*, Munich 1986, vol. 2, pp. 521–538

Augarde 2022
Jean-Dominique Augarde, *A Journey Through Clocks: Masterworks of the Parnassia Collection*, Paris/Amsterdam 2022

Avery et al. 2021
Charles Avery et al., *Miss Clara and the Celebrity Beast in Art, 1500–1860*, Birmingham 2021

Badioli 2008
Leonardo Badioli, *Il Rinoceronte*, librisenzacarta.it/2008/02/24/il-rinoceronte-clara, 2008

Barbier 1851/1857
Edmond Jean François Barbier, *Journal historique et anecdotique du règne de Louis XV*, **vol. 3, Paris 1851, vol. 4, 1857**

Barth 1747
Johann Matthäus Barth, *Schreiben an einen guten Freund, Darinne von einem vor wenig Wochen hieher gebrachten Rhinocerote … Nachricht gegeben … wird*, **Regensburg 1747**

Bedini 1998
Silvio A. Bedini, *The Pope's Elephant*, **Nashville 1998**

Van den Berg 2021
Arie van den Berg, *De leeuw van Alpi. Handel en wandel van een beestenman*, **Amsterdam/Antwerp 2021**

Bergen 1746
Caroli Augusti à Bergen [Karl August von Bergen], *Oratio de Rhinocerote*, **Frankfurt an der Oder 1746**

Berger 2009
John Berger, *Why Look at Animals?*, **London 2009**

Van Berkel and Ramakers 2015
Klaas van Berkel and Bart Ramakers (eds.), *Petrus Camper in Context: Science, the Arts, and Society in the Eighteenth-Century Dutch Republic*, **Hilversum 2015**

Blancken 1698
Gerard Blancken, *A catalogue of all the chiefest rarities in the publick theater and anatomie-hall of the University of Leyden which are so set in order that all may easily bee found in their places*, **Leiden 1704**

Bostock 2021
Sophie Bostock, 'Clara in Qatar: A New Life for a Meissen Porcelain Rhinoceros', *Luxury* **8 (2021), no. 1, pp. 59–75**

Broberg 2006
G. Broberg, 'Review of Faust's "Zoologische und Botanische Einblattdrücke"', *Svenska Linnésällskapets Årsskrift* **(2006), pp. 167–171**

Bruijn 2008
Jaap R. Bruijn, *Schippers van de VOC in de achttiende eeuw, aan de wal en op zee*, **Amsterdam 2008**

Camper 1782
Petrus Camper, *Natuurkundige verhandelingen van Petrus Camper over den Orang Outang; en eenige andere aap-soorten. Over den Rhinoceros met den Dubbelen Horen; en over het Rendier*, **Amsterdam 1782**

Chignola et al. 2005
Ismaele Chignola et al. (eds.), *Francesco Lorenzi (1723–1787). Un allievo di Tiepolo tra Verona, Vicenza e Casale Monferrato*, **Caselle di Sommacampagna 2005**

Clarke 1976
T.H. Clarke, 'The Rhinoceros in European Ceramics', *Keramik-Freunde der Schweiz, Mitteilungsblatt* **89 (1976), pp. 3–20**

Clarke 1986
T.H. Clarke, *The Rhinoceros from Dürer to Stubbs, 1515–1799*, **London 1986**

Daniëls 1880
C.E. Daniëls, *Het leven en de verdiensten van Petrus Camper*, **Utrecht 1880**

Dittrich 2007
Lothar Dittrich, 'Der Import von Wildtieren nach Europa – Einführen von der frühen Neuzeit bis zur Mitte des 20. Jahrhunderts', in Dagmar Schratter and Gerhard Heindl (eds.), *Tiere unterwegs: Historisches und Aktuelles über Tiererwerb und Tiertransporte*, **Vienna 2007, pp. 1–64**

Divyabhanusinh et al. 2018
Divyabhanusinh, Asok Kumar Das and Shibani Bose, *The Story of India's Unicorns*, **Mumbai 2018**

Doornbos 2006
Willem G. Doornbos, 'Clara de Rinoceros', *Stad & Lande* **15 (2006), no. 4, pp. 32–35**

Droguet et al. 2003
Vincent Droguet et al. (eds.), *Animaux d'Oudry. Collection des ducs de Mecklembourg-Schwerin*, **Paris 2003**

Emmerig 1978
Hubert Emmerig, 'Das Rhinozeros in Europa 1741–1758 und seine Medaillen', *Money-trend* **10 (1978), no. 5, pp. 20–25, 50, 52**

Faust 2003
Ingrid Faust, *Zoologische Einblattdrucke und Flugschriften vor 1800, Band V: Unpaarhufer: Nashörner, Tapire, Pferdartige. Sammelblätter. Monster*, **Stuttgart 2003**

Feijoo 1750
Benito Jerónimo Feijoo, *Cartas eruditas y curiosas (1742–1760)*, **vol. 3, Madrid 1750**

Feith 1914
J.A. Feith, 'De Bengaalsche Sichterman', *Groningsche Volksalmanak*, **Groningen 1914, pp. 14–74**

Frank 2007
Christoph Frank, 'Pictorial Relations: New Evidence on Jean-Baptiste Oudry and the Court of Mecklenburg-Schwerin', in Morton 2007, pp. 31–57

Frantz 2020
Pierre Frantz, *Le Moment Voltaire*, **2020, https://cfrp.mitpress.mit.edu/pub/moment-voltaire**

Frenz 2017
Lothar Frenz, *Nashörner: Ein Portrait*, **Berlin 2017**

Freytag 1747
Friderico Gotthilf Freytag, *Rhinoceros e Veterum Scriptorum Monimentis Descriptus*, **Leipzig 1747**

Godart 1755
Guillaume-Lambert Godart, *La Physique de l'Âme Humaine*, **Berlin 1755**

Gommans 2018
Jos Gommans, *De verborgen wereld. Nederland en India vanaf 1550*, **Amsterdam/Nijmegen 2018**

Gottsched 2020
Johann Christoph Gottsched, *Briefwechsel, Band 14: November 1748–September 1749*, **Berlin/Boston 2020**

Grigson 2015
Caroline Grigson, 'New Information on Indian Rhinoceroses (*Rhinoceros unicornis***) in Britain in the Mid-Eighteenth Century',** *Archives of Natural History* **42 (2015), no. 1, pp. 76–84**

Haag 2015
Sabine Haag (ed.), *Echt tierisch! Die Menagerie des Fürsten*, **Vienna 2015**

Van der Ham 2005
Gijs van der Ham, 'Clara in beeld', *Bulletin van het Rijksmuseum* **53 (2005), no. 2, pp. 192–203**

Hanson 2010
Craig Ashley Hanson, 'Representing the Rhinoceros: The Royal Society between Art and Science in the Eighteenth Century', *Journal for Eighteenth-Century Studies* **33 (2010), no. 4, pp. 545–566**

Heerebout 2014
G.R. Heerebout, 'Een neushoorn in Middelburg', *Zeeland* **23 (2014), no. 3, pp. 91–94**

Heikamp 1980
Detlef Heikamp, 'Seltene Nashörner in Martin Sperlichs Nashorngalerie und anderswo', in ibid. (ed.), *Schlösser, Gärten, Berlin: Festschrift für Martin Sperlich zum 60. Geburtstag*, **Tübingen 1980, pp. 301–325**

Van Heiningen 2014
T.W. van Heiningen (ed.), *Wouter van Doeveren and Petrus Camper in Paris: Travel Diaries, Kept in the Years 1752–1753, 1777 and 1787 and Related Correspondence*, **The Hague 2014**

Holtrop 2021
Maria Holtrop, 'Van Bengalen', in Eveline Sint Nicolaas et al., *Slavery*, **Amsterdam 2021, pp. 147–175**

Houtzager 1979
H.L. Houtzager, 'Dieren in Delft', *Gewina* **2 (1979), no. 2, pp. 52–61**

Huisman 2002
Tim Huisman, *Een theater voor de anatomie. Het Leidse theatrum anatomicum 1594–1821*, **Leiden 2002**

Jacobs 2000
Elisabeth Maria Jacobs, *Koopman in Azië. De handel van de Verenigde Oost-Indische Compagnie tijdens de 18de eeuw*, **Zutphen 2000**

Jörg et al. 2014
Christiaan J.A. Jörg, Egge Knol and Denis A. Campbell, *Jan Albert Sichterman, 1692–1764. Een imponerende Groninger liefhebber van kunst*, **Groningen 2014**

Jørgensen 1986
Bent Jørgensen, 'A Visit by Douwe Mout's Rhinoceros to Copenhagen', *Zoologische Garten* **56 (1986), no. 6, pp. 385–386**

Kalof 2007
Linda Kalof, *Looking at Animals in Human History*, **London 2007**

Kjellberg 1997
Pierre Kjellberg, *Encyclopédie de la pendule française du Moyen Age au XXe siècle*, **Paris 1997**

Kleinecke 2016
Dagmar Kleinecke (ed.), *Pfarrchronik der Kirchengemeinde Obernjesa-Dramfeld. Ein Rechnungsbuch mit chronikalischen Notizen 1737 bis 1807*, **Göttingen 2016**

Kroker 1890
Ernst Kroker, 'Schaustellungen auf den Leipziger Messen', *Mitteilungen der Deutschen Gesellschaft zur Erforschung Vaterländischer Sprache und Altertümer in Leipzig*, **Leipzig 1890, pp. 97–137, slub-dresden.de**

Kühne-van Diggelen 1995
Wiet Kühne-van Diggelen, *Jan Albert Sichterman. VOC-dienaar en 'koning' van Groningen*, **Groningen 1995**

Lach 1970
Donald F. Lach, *Asia in the Making of Europe, Volume 2: A Century of Wonder*, **Chicago/London 1970**

Lacroix 1978
Jean-Bernard Lacroix, 'L'approvisionnement des ménageries et les transports d'animaux sauvages per la Compagnie des Indes au XVIIIe siècle', *Revue française d'histoire d'outre-mer* **65 (1978), no. 239, pp. 153–179**

Ladvocat 1749
Jean Baptiste Ladvocat, *Lettre sur le Rhinoceros*, **Paris 1749**

Exh. cat. Leiden 1991
De volmaakte mens. De anatomische atlas van Albinus en Wandelaar, **Leiden (Museum Boerhaave) 1991**

Leitch 2017
Stephanie Leitch, 'Dürer's *Rhinoceros* **Underway: The Epistemology of the Copy in the Early Modern Print', in Debra Taylor Cashion et al. (eds.),** *The Primacy of the Image in Northern European Art, 1400–1700. Essays in Honor of Larry Silver*, **Leiden/Boston 2017, pp. 241–254**

Lequin 1982
Frank Lequin, *Het personeel van de Verenigde Oost-Indische Compagnie in Azië in de achttiende eeuw, meer in het bijzonder in de vestiging Bengalen*, **Leiden 1982**

Levey 1971
Michael Levey, *The Seventeenth and Eighteenth Century Italian Schools. National Gallery Catalogues*, **London 1971**

Lilti 2017
Antoine Lilti, *The Invention of Celebrity: 1750–1850*, **Cambridge 2017**

Exh. cat. London 2002
Giulia Bartrum, *Albrecht Dürer and His Legacy: The Graphic Work of a Renaissance Artist*, **London (British Museum) 2002**

Maleville 1756
Guillaume Maleville, *La religion naturelle et la révélée …*, **vol. 2, Paris 1756**

Marchant 1884
Louis Marchant, 'Un rhinocéros en France au dix-huitième siècle', *Magasin Pittoresque* **52 (1884), p. 152**

Marchesi and Crevatin 2006
Ilaria Marchesi and Franco Crevatin, *Gli Annali di Pietro Gradenigo*, **Trieste 2006**

Marggraf 1758
M. Marggraf, 'Examen Chymique du Sel, auquel on a voulu donner le nom de véritable sel alcali fixe de *rhinocéros*', **in** *Histoire de l'Academie Royale des Sciences et Belles Lettres, Année MDCCLVI*, **Berlin 1758, pp. 145–148**

Maugras 1886
G. Maugras, *Voltaire et J.-J. Rousseau*, **Paris 1886**

Maupertuis 1750
Maupertuis, *Essai de Cosmologie*, **1750**

Meijer 2019
Eva Meijer, *When Animals Speak: Towards an Interspecies Democracy*, **New York 2019**

Morton 2007
Mary Morton (ed.), *Oudry's Painted Menagerie: Portraits of Exotic Animals in Eighteenth-Century Europe*, **Los Angeles 2007**

Neubert 2007
M. Neubert, 'Jungfer Clara – Das Holländische Rhinozeros, portraitiert vom Hofmaler Anton Clemens Lünenschloß, auf dem Marktplatz zu Würzburg', in A. Mettenleiter (ed.), *Tempora mutantur et nos? Festschrift Walter M. Brod*, **Pfaffenhofen 2007, pp. 328–331**

Van Nimwegen 2002
Olaf van Nimwegen, *De Republiek der Verenigde Nederlanden als grote mogendheid. Buitenlandse politiek en oorlogvoering in de eerste helft van de achttiende eeuw en in het bijzonder tijdens de Oostenrijkse Successieoorlog (1740–1748)*, **Amsterdam 2002**

Parsons 1747
[James] Parsons, *Die natürliche Historie des Nashorns* **(trans. Georg Leonhart Huth), Nuremberg 1747**

Péquignot 2013
A. Péquignot, 'The Rhinoceros (fl. 1770–1793) of King Louis XV and its Horns', *Archives of Natural History* **40 (2013), no. 2, pp. 213–227**

Pieters 2002
Florence Pieters, 'Menagerieën op de kermis: oorsprong van circus en dierentuin', in Johanna Jacobs (ed.), *Kennis, kunstjes en kunnen. Kermis: de wondere wereld van glans en glitter*, **Amsterdam 2002, pp. 59–74**

Pietsch 2006
Ulrich Pietsch, *Die figürliche Meissner Porzellanplastik von Gottlieb Kirchner und Johann Joachim Kändler*, **Munich 2006**

Prakash 2004
Om Prakash, *Bullion for Goods: European and Indian Merchants in the Indian Ocean Trade, 1500–1800*, **New Delhi 2004**

Rathery 1863/1864
E.J.B. Rathery (ed.), *Journal et Mémoires du Marquis d'Argenson*, **vol. 5, Paris 1863, vol. 6, 1864**

Reesink 2021
Maarten Reesink, *Dier en mens. De band tussen ons en andere dieren*, **Amsterdam 2021**

Reinhard 1748
L. Reinhard, *Unumstösslicher Beweis, dass der Rhinoceros oder das Nasshorn unmöglich könne der Behemoth seyn*, **Jena 1748**

Ricci 1888
Corrado Ricci, *I Teatri di Bologna nei Seicoli XVII e XVIII*, **Bologna 1888**

Richter 1750
Christoph Gottlieb Richter, *Die redende Thiere über menschliche Fehler und Laster, Bey Ruhigen Stunden Lustig und nützlich zu lesen. Dreissigstes Gespräch, zwischen einem Nashorn und einer Heuschrecke*, **Frankfurt/Leipzig 1750**

Ridley 2004
Glynis Ridley, *Clara's Grand Tour: Travels with a Rhinoceros in Eighteenth-Century Europe*, **London 2004**

Roelandts 1939
Oscar Roelandts, *Beeldhouwer Pieter-Antoon Verschaffelt, 1710–1793*, **Brussels 1939**

Rookmaaker 1976
L.C. Rookmaaker, 'An Early Engraving of the Black Rhinoceros (*Diceros bicornis* **[L.]) Made by Jan Wandelaar',** *Biological Journal of the Linnean Society* **8 (1976), no. 1, pp. 87–90**

Rookmaaker 1978a
Kees Rookmaaker, 'De neushoorn van 1741', *Ons Amsterdam* **30 (1978), no. 1, pp. 16–17**

Rookmaaker 1978b
L.C. Rookmaaker, 'Two Collections of Rhinoceros Plates Compiled by James Douglas and James Parsons in the Eighteenth Century', *Journal of the Society for the Bibliography of Natural History* **9 (1978), no. 1, pp. 17–38**

Rookmaaker 1980
L.C. Rookmaaker, 'The Distribution of the Rhinoceros in Eastern India, Bangladesh, China, and the Indo-Chinese Region', *Zoologische Anzeiger* **205 (1980), nos. 3–4, pp. 253–268**

Rookmaaker 1983a
L.C. Rookmaaker, 'The Former Distribution of the Indian Rhinoceros (*Rhinoceros unicornis***) in India and Pakistan',** *Journal of the Bombay Natural History Society* **80 (1983), no. 3, pp. 555–563**

Rookmaaker 1983b
L.C. Rookmaaker, 'Histoire du rhinocéros de Versailles (1770–1793)', *Revue d'Histoire des Sciences* **36 (1983), nos. 3–4, pp. 307–318**

Rookmaaker 1996–1997
L.C. Rookmaaker, 'The Sources of Linnaeus on the Rhinoceros', *Svenska Linnésällskapets Årsskrift* **(1996–1997), pp. 61–80**

Rookmaaker 1998
L.C. Rookmaaker, *The Rhinoceros in Captivity. A List of 2439 Rhinoceroses kept from Roman times to 1994*, **The Hague 1998**

Rookmaaker et al. 2017
L.C. Rookmaaker et al., *The Greater One-Horned Rhino: Past, Present and Future*, **Gland 2017**

Rookmaaker and Monson 2000
Kees Rookmaaker and Jim Monson, 'Woodcuts and Engravings Illustrating the Journey of *Clara*, **the Most Popular Rhinoceros of the Eighteenth Century',** *Der zoologische Garten* **N.F. 70 (2000), no. 5, pp. 313–335**

Roscam Abbing 2016
Michiel Roscam Abbing, *Rembrandt's Elephant: The Story of Hansken*, **Amsterdam 2006**

Roy 1968
Atul Chandra Roy, *History of Bengal: Mughal Period (1526–1765 AD)*, **Calcutta 1968**

Roy 2021
Tania Roy, *Rossella Biscotti. Clara and Other Specimens*, **Salzburg 2021**

Schoch et al. 2001–2004
Rainer Schoch, Matthias Mende and Anna Scherbaum, *Albrecht Dürer. Das druckgraphische Werk*, **3 vols., Munich 2001–2004**

Schuller tot Peursum-Meijer and Koops 1989
J. Schuller tot Peursum-Meijer and W.R.H. Koops (eds.), *Petrus Camper (1722–1789): onderzoeker van nature*, **Groningen 1989**

Schwabach 2005
Thomas Schwabach, *Die Schwieren-Chronik aus Zons. Bemerkenswertes aus einer niederrheinischen Kleinstadt und ihrer Umgebung 1733–1823*, **Neuss 2005**

Senior 2007
Matthew Senior (ed.), *A Cultural History of Animals in the Age of Enlightenment*, **Oxford/New York 2007**

Servigné 1750
Jean-Baptiste Guiard de Servigné, *Le Rhinoceros, poème en prose*, **Paris 1750**

Sierman 1990
Barbara Sierman, '"Ten profyte van het gemeen": kermis in de achttiende eeuw', *Literatuur* **7 (1990), pp. 134–140**

Stubbe 1966
Wolf Stubbe, *Johann Elias Ridinger*, **Hamburg/Berlin 1966**

Vartanian 1949
Aram Vartanian, 'From Deist to Atheist: Diderot's Philosophical Orientation 1746–1749', *Diderot Studies* **1 (1949), pp. 46–63**

Verheij 1992
Irene Verheij, *Op reis met Clara. De geschiedenis van een bezienswaardige neushoorn*, **Rotterdam 1992**

Visser 1985
Robert Paul Willem Visser, *The Zoological Work of Petrus Camper (1722–1789)*, **Amsterdam 1985**

Voltaire 1775
Voltaire, 'Questions sur l'Encyclopédie, VI', in *Œuvres complètes de Voltaire*, **Geneva 1775, vol. 30**

Walter 1989
Hermann Walter, 'Contributi sulla recezione umanistica della zoologia antica. Nuovi documenti per la genesi del "1515 Rhinocervs" di Albrecht Dürer', *Res Publica Litterarum* **12 (1989), pp. 267–277**

Watzlawick 2001
Helmut Watzlawick, 'À la rencontre de "Demoiselle Clara"', *L'Intermédiaire des Casanovistes* **18 (2001), pp. 42–44**

Wilson-Pauwels 2009
Linda Wilson-Pauwels, 'Jan Wandelaar, Bernard Siegfried Albinus and an Indian Rhinoceros Named Clara Set High Standards as the Process of Anatomical Illustration Entered a New Phase of Precision Artistic Beauty, and Marketing in the 18th Century', *Journal of Biocommunication* **35 (2009), no. 1, pp. E10–E17**

Winters 2017
Ria Winters, *Exotische dieren in historisch Amsterdam*, **Amsterdam 2017**

Wittwer 2004
Samuel Wittwer, *Die Galerie der Meissener Tiere. Die Menagerie August des Starken für das Japanische Palais in Dresden*, **Munich 2004**

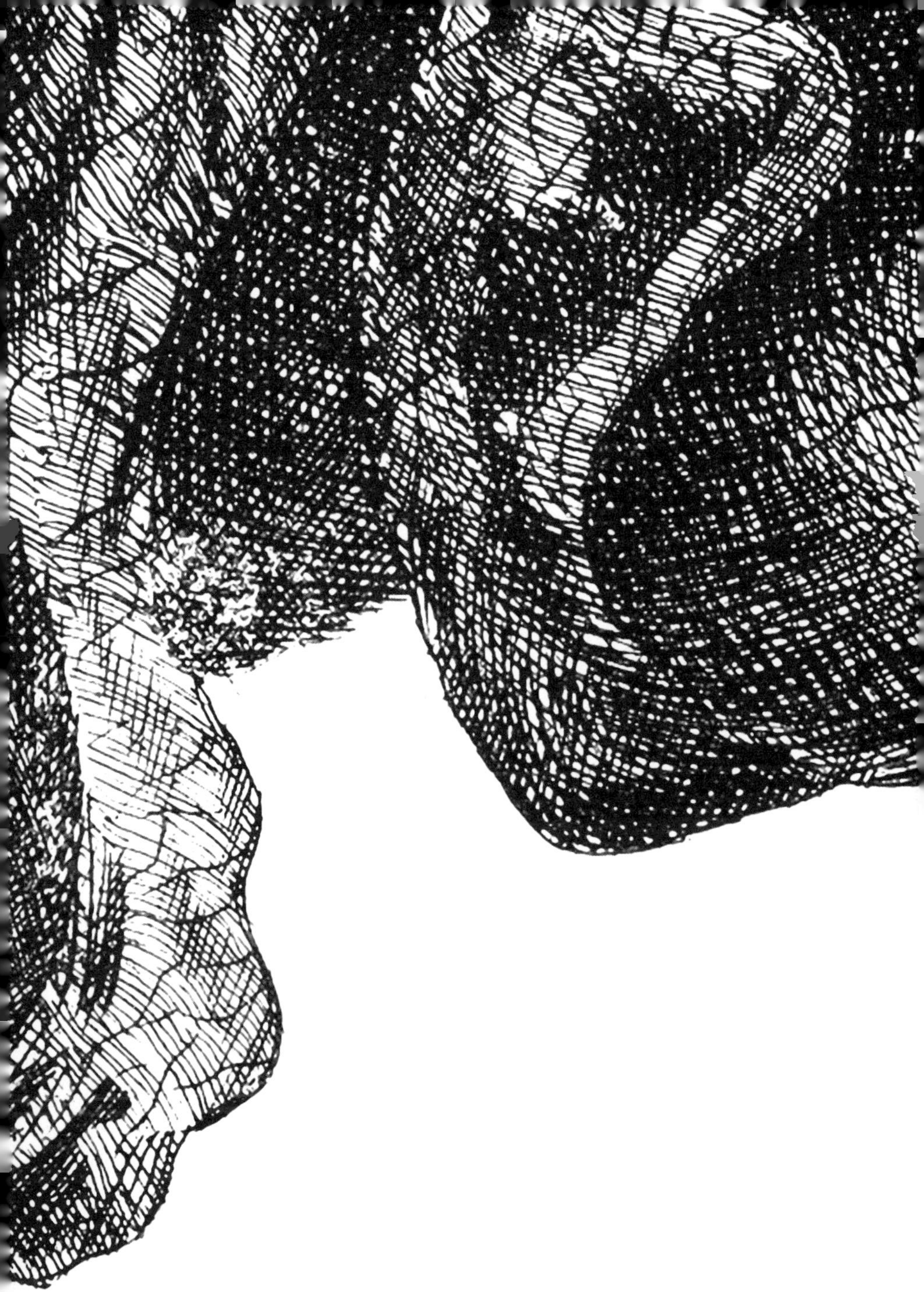

exhibited works

supplemented by supporting illustrations in this book (marked with *)

a true rhinoceros?

1

Albrecht Dürer, *Rhinocerus*, **1515**
Woodcut, 253 × 313 mm (sheet)
Braunschweig, Herzog Anton Ulrich-Museum, inv. no. ADürer V 3.210H

2

Hans Mayer(?), *Lidded Goblet Made from Rhinoceros Horn*, **c. 1650**
Rhinoceros horn, silver, h. 41.3, diam. 11.7 cm
Stuttgart, Landesmuseum Württemberg, inv. no. KK braun-blau 44
Photo: Hendrik Zwietasch

3

Anselmus de Boodt after Albrecht Dürer, *Indian Rhinoceros*, **1596–1610**
Brush in watercolour and body colour in colours heightened with white body colour, sketch in pencil, handwriting in pen in brown, 175 × 290 mm (sheet)
Amsterdam, Rijksmuseum, inv. no. RP-T-BR-2017-1-2-11; on loan from a private collection

4

Conrad Gessner, *Von dem Rhinocer*, **hand-coloured woodcut in** *Thierbuch*, **Zurich 1563**
Private collection

5

Roelant Savery, *Orpheus Charming the Animals with his Music*, **1627**
Oil on panel, 62 × 131.5 cm
The Hague, Mauritshuis, inv. no. 157

6

Johann Gottlieb Kirchner, *Rhinoceros*, **1731**
Meissen porcelain, unpainted (white), 67.9 × 106.5 × 48.4 cm
Dresden, Staatliche Kunstsammlungen, Porzellansammlung, inv. no. PE 56
Photo: Adrian Sauer

7*

Cornelis de Man, *Anatomy Lesson of Cornelis 's-Gravesande*, **1681**
Oil on canvas, 173 × 212 cm
Delft, Museum Prinsenhof, inv. no. PDS 276; gift of Reinier de Graaf Groep

8

Pieter van den Berge after Francis Barlow, *Elephant and Rhinoceros*, **1686–1696**
Mezzotint and engraving, 231 × 322 mm
Amsterdam, Rijksmuseum, inv. no. RP-P-1906-2905

diplomatic gift

9

Attributed to Bishandas, *The Great Mughal Zahiruddin Muhammad Babur during a Rhinoceros Hunt*, **c. 1590**
Miniature from the *Baburnama*, **345 × 230 mm (sheet)**
Zurich, Museum Rietberg, inv. no. RVI 1800; gift of Eberhard and Barbara Fischer
Photo: Rainier Wolfsberger

10*

Philip van Dijk, *Portrait of Jan Albert Sichterman and his Sons Jan Albert and Gerrit Jan*, **1745**
Oil on canvas, 148.5 × 117 cm
Groningen, Groninger Museum, inv. no. 1992-212; purchased with the support of Commissie van Spijsuitdeling, J.B. Scholtenfonds, Vereniging Rembrandt, and made possible with the assistance of the Prins Bernhard Fonds
Photo: John Stoel

11

Hendrik van Schuylenburgh, *The Trading Post of the Dutch East India Company in Hooghly, Bengal*, **1665**
Oil on canvas, 203 × 316 cm
Amsterdam, Rijksmuseum, inv. no. SK-A-4282

12

Anonymous, *Plate with the Coat of Arms of the Sichterman Family*, **c. 1730–1735**
Porcelain, glaze, enamel, gold, diam. 28 cm
Amsterdam, Rijksmuseum, inv. no. AK-NM-13380; J.G.A.N. de Vries Bequest, The Hague

shipped to the netherlands

13

The official loading list of the *Knappenhof*, **compiled by the VOC on the ship's departure from Hooghly, November 1740**
Manuscript, 340 × 260 × 100 mm (closed)
The Hague, National Archives of the Netherlands, 1.04.02, inv. no. 2489, fols. 266r–v

for every person to see

14*

Magnus Celsius, *Two Sketches of Clara's Head Made at the 'Kermis' in Amsterdam*, **1741**
Stockholm, National Library of Sweden, inv. no. M 231

15

Petrus Camper, *Two Sketches of Clara's Head*, **1742(?)**
Black and white chalk on blue-grey paper, 217 × 164 mm
Allard Pierson, University of Amsterdam, Collection Petrus Camper, Port. A X

16*
Petrus Camper, *Clara as a Young Rhinoceros,* **1742(?)**
Black and white chalk on blue-grey paper, 217 × 164 mm
Allard Pierson, University of Amsterdam, Collection Petrus Camper, Port. A

17
Petrus Camper, *Clara alongside the Measuring Stick,* **1742(?)**
Black and white chalk on blue-grey paper, 199 × 282 mm
Allard Pierson, University of Amsterdam, Collection Petrus Camper, Port. A X

18
Petrus Camper, *Clara in Relief,* **1742(?)**
Gilded clay in frame, 19 × 24 cm
Leiden, Naturalis Biodiversity Center, inv. no. 174-1

19
Jan Wandelaar, *Muscle Man with Browsing Rhinoceros, Both Viewed from the Front,* **1742**
Engraving for Bernard Albinus, *Tabulae sceleti musculorum corporis humani,* **Leiden 1747, pl. IV, 568 × 404 mm (edge of plate)**
Rotterdam, Onno van Seggelen Fine Arts

20
Jan Wandelaar, *Muscle Man with Rhinoceros, Both Viewed from the Rear,* **1742**
Engraving for Bernard Albinus, *Tabulae sceleti musculorum corporis humani,* **Leiden 1747, pl. VIII, 566 × 403 mm (edge of plate)**
Rotterdam, Onno van Seggelen Fine Arts

21
'Advertissement' for Clara's Exhibition in Middelburg, **1742**
In Pieter Boddaert, *Aantekeningen van allerhande nature,* **woodcut pasted in album, printed and handwritten text, 198 × 320 mm (open)**
The Hague, KB – National Library of the Netherlands, KW 135 K 37

22
Register recording that Gerrit Harting was given permission to exhibit Clara on a ship during the *kermis* **in Delft**
Delft, City Archives, Archieven van het stadsbestuur, inv. no. 4255, Register van vergunningen voor activiteiten op de kermissen te Delft en Delfshaven 1722–1808, p. 39

carted from town to town

23*
Johannes Condet, *Map of Amstelland* **(detail), in or after 1749**
Engraving with pencil in grey and pen in black, 578 × 758 mm
Amsterdam, Rijksmuseum, inv. no. RP-P-AO-8-72-1

24
Anonymous, *Clara's Standard Promotional Poster,* **c. 1745–1746**
Etching and engraving, 191 × 290 mm
Amsterdam, Rijksmuseum, inv. no. RP-P-1910-2144

25
A.A. Beck and J.G. Schmidt, *Clara in Braunschweig (Le véritable portrait d'un Rhinocerot vivant ...),* **1746**
Engraving, 541 × 643 mm
Wolffenbüttel, Herzog August Bibliothek, Graph. A3: 74

26
Anonymous, *Promotional Poster and Souvenir in which Clara is Addressed by Name and Offered a Glass of Wine,* **c. 1746**
Kraków, Biblioteka Jagiellónska, in Libri picturatie A 38, Miscellanea Cleyeri, fol. 24

27
Anton Clemens Lünenschloss, *'Jungfer Clara' in Würzburg,* **3 October 1748**
Pen in brown ink, 260 × 195 mm
Würzburg, Martin von Wagner Museum, Skizzenbuch S 11 (WS 139)

sensation in europe

28*
Douwe Mout's Coat of Arms as a member of the Austrian Nobility ('Reichsadel'), 1747
Vienna, Österreichisches Staatsarchiv, Wappen aus Reichsadelsakt Mout 1747, fol. 13

29
Elias Bäck, *Clara in Vienna (Eigentliche und accurate Vorstellung des ... Asiatischen Wunder-Thiers Rhinoceros ...),* **1746**
Engraving, 440 × 340 mm
Munich, Bayerische Staatsbibliothek, Einbl. VIII, 22 m

30
Anonymous, *Clara in Mannheim (Waare afbeelding van een leevendighe Renoceros ...),* **1747**
Engraving, 449 × 558 mm
Amsterdam, Rijksmuseum, inv. no. RP-P-OB-75.362

31
David Redinger, *Clara in Zurich (Wahrhafte ... Abbildung ... des Rhinoceros),* **1748**
Woodcut, 484 × 394 mm (sheet)
Zurich, Zentralbibliothek, Graphische Sammlung, Einblattdrucke, Varia Tiere, II, 3
Photo: Zentralbibliothek Zürich, Department of Prints and Drawings/Photo Archive

32
David Redinger, *Clara in Zurich, Lying Down (Wahrhafte ... Abbildung ... des liegenden Rhinoceros),* **1748**
Woodcut, 251 × 386 mm (sheet)
Zurich, Zentralbibliothek, Graphische Sammlung, Einblattdrucke, Varia Tiere, I, 5
Photo: Zentralbibliothek Zürich, Department of Prints and Drawings/Photo Archive

33
Veit Schrempf, *Clara in Stuttgart,* **1748**
Silver, diam. 3.9 cm
Stuttgart, Landesmuseum Württemberg, inv. no. MK 17883
Photo: Hendrick Zwietasch

34
Peter Paul Werner, *Clara in Nuremberg*, **1748**
Silver, diam. 4 cm
Amsterdam, private collection

35
Jean Daniel Kamm, *Clara in Strasbourg*, **1748**
Tin, diam. 4 cm
Amsterdam, private collection

36*
Peter Paul Werner, *Clara in Nuremberg*, **1748**
Bronze, diam. 4 cm
Amsterdam, private collection

37
Berryer, *Clara in Paris (Rhinocerot)*, **1749**
Woodcut, 415 × 260 mm
Munich, Bayerische Staatsbibliothek, Res/Slg.Faust 171

38
Pietro Longhi, *The Rhinoceros*, **1751**
Oil on canvas, 62 × 50 cm
Venice, Fondazione Musei Civici di Venezia – Ca' Rezzonico, Museo del Settecento Veneziano, inv. no. Cl. I n. 1312
Photo: Matteo De Fina © Photo Archive – Fondazione Musei Civici di Venezia

39
Alessandro Longhi after Pietro Longhi after Joseph Wagner, *The Rhinoceros Clara in Venice*, **1751**
Etching, 470 × 400 mm
Amsterdam, Rijksmuseum, inv. no. RP-P-2021-70; purchased with the support of the F.G. Waller-Fonds

40
Venetian School, *The Rhinoceros (Il Rinoceronte)*, **c. 1751**
Oil on canvas, 55.5 × 72.1 cm
Vicenza, Gallerie d'Italia, Palazzo Leoni Montanari, Intesa Sanpaolo Collection, inv. no. A.A.-00088A-C/BI
Photo: Archivio Patrimonio Artístico Intesa Sanpaolo/photo Valter Maino, Vicenza

final years

41
Cornelis van Noorde, *Clara in Haarlem*, **1756**
Chalk on paper, 155 × 510 mm (open album)
Haarlem, Noord-Hollands Archief, inv. no. 1100_53999001
Photo: Beeldcollectie van de Gemeente Haarlem

images of clara

42
Johann Elias Ridinger, *Clara, Looking at the Viewer*, **1748**
Chalk on paper, 286 × 438 mm
Washington, National Gallery of Art, inv. no. 2007.111.29; Wolfgang Ratjen Collection, Patrons' Permanent Fund, 2007

43
Johann Elias Ridinger, *Clara, with Head Turned*, **1748**
Chalk on paper, 251 × 364 mm
Private collection
Photo: René Gerritsen

44
Johann Elias Ridinger, *Clara in Augsburg*, **1748**
Chalk on paper, 257 × 369 mm
Private collection
Photo: René Gerritsen

45
Johann Elias Ridinger, *Clara, with Head Raised*, **1748**
Chalk on paper, 240 × 320 mm
Private collection
Photo: René Gerritsen

46*
Johann Elias Ridinger, *Eve Presents Adam with the Apple*, **1748 or shortly thereafter**
Etching and engraving, 395 × 546 mm
London, Wellcome Collection, Wellcome Library, 20727i

47
Johann Elias Ridinger, *Clara in Augsburg*, **1748**
Chalk on paper, 263 × 427 mm
London, The Courtauld (Samuel Courtauld Trust), inv. no. D.1952.RW.2164
Photo: Bridgeman Images © The Courtauld

48–51
Anonymous Venetian artist, *Sketches of Clara*, **1751**
Black and white chalk on paper, 315 × 450 mm (open)
Amsterdam, Rijksmuseum, inv. no. RP-T-1953-359a; purchased with the support of the J.W. Edwin Vom Rath Fonds/ Rijksmuseum Fonds

52
Jean-Baptiste Oudry, *Rhinoceros*, **1749**
Oil on canvas, 306 × 453 cm
Staatliches Museum Schwerin, inv. no. G 1928
Photo: bpk | Staatliche Schlösser, Gärten und Kunstsammlungen Mecklenburg-Vorpommern

53
Johann Joachim Kaendler, *Indian Rhinoceros*, **1755**
Porcelain, 10.1 × 16.5 × 6.9 cm
Dresden, Staatliche Kunstsammlungen, Porzellansammlung, inv. no. PE 7311
Photo: Adrian Sauer

54
Königliche Porzellan-Manufaktur Meissen, *Rhinoceros with Turkish Man on its Back*, **c. 1755**
Porcelain, 27.8 × 25.5 × 11 cm
Kassel, Museumslandschaft Hessen Kassel, Sammlung Angewandte Kunst, inv. no. SM 4.1.854

55
Königliche Porzellan-Manufaktur Meissen, *Rhinoceros with Chinese Figure and Palm Tree*, **c. 1755**
Porcelain, gilded bronze, 26.5 × 34.5 × 21 cm
Frankfurt am Main, Museum Angewandte Kunst, inv. no. 12335

56
Jean-Joseph de Saint-Germain and François Viger, *Clock Carried by a Rhinoceros*, **1755/1756**
Bronze, green horn, 86 × 51 × 24 cm
Private collection
Photo: René Gerritsen

57

Laurent Pecheux,
Portrait of Maria Luisa of Parma, **1765**
Oil on canvas, 224 × 150 cm
Florence, Le gallerie degli Uffizi, Palazzo Pitti, Galleria Palatina, OdA Pitti n. 1391
Photo: Gabinetto Fotografico delle Gallerie degli Uffizi

58

Attributed to Pieter Anton Verschaffelt,
Indian Rhinoceros, **1765–1770**
Marble, 64 × 106 × 38 cm
Waddesdon (Rothschild Family)
Photo: Waddesdon Image Library, Mike Fear

59

Porzellanmanufaktur Frankenthal,
Rhinoceros, **1765–1770**
Porcelain, 11 × 38 × 17 cm
Mannheim, Barockschloss, inv. no. G 7523; on loan from the Staatliche Schlösser und Gärten Baden-Württemberg

a source of information

60

Caroli Augusti à Bergen [Karl August von Bergen], *Oratio de rhinocerote*, **Frankfurt an der Oder 1746**
Allard Pierson, University of Amsterdam, OTM: O 64-27

61

Friderico [Friedrich] Gotthilf Freytag,
Rhinoceros e Veterum Scriptorum Monimentis Descriptus, **Leipzig 1747**
Amsterdam, private collection

62

Johann Matthäus Barth, *Schreiben an einen guten Freund, Darinne von einem vor wenig Wochen hieher gebrachten Rhinocerote … Nachricht gegeben … wird*, **Regensburg 1747**
Munich, Bayerische Staatsbibliothek, 4 Zool. 21

63

Laurentius Reinhard, *Unumstösslicher Beweis, dass der Rhinoceros … unmöglich könne der Behemoth seyn …*, **Jena 1748**
Munich, Bayerische Staatsbibliothek, 4 Diss. 685; 2e ex: 4 Exeg. 981,11

64

Johann Felix Corrodi,
Rhinoceros, Depicted Nine Times, **1748**
Watercolour and pencil on paper, 266 × 373 mm
Zurich, Kunsthaus, Collection of Prints and Drawings, inv. no. Z 1921/0030; donated by Naturforschende Gesellschaft Zürich, 1921

65

Homanische Officin, *Abbildliche Geschichte der auslaendischen Landthiere … worinnen das Nashorn vorgestellet ist*, **1747**
Engraving, hand-coloured, 42 × 55 cm
Nuremberg, Germanisches Nationalmuseum, inv. no. HB4965

66

Jean Baptiste Ladvocat,
Lettre sur le Rhinoceros, **Paris 1749**
Munich, Bayerische Staatsbibliothek, Zool. 322

67

Georges-Louis Leclerc de Buffon, *Histoire naturelle, générale et particulière*, **Paris 1764, vol. 11, pl. VII**
The Hague, KB – National Library of the Netherlands, KW 3157 C 11

68

Denis Diderot and Jean d'Alembert,
Encyclopédie, ou Dictionnaire raisonné des sciences, des arts et des métiers, Recueil des planches, **Paris 1768, vol. 5, pl. 1**
Allard Pierson, University of Amsterdam, OTM: KF 62-2262-2296

rhinoceros & locust

69

Christoph Gottlieb Richter, *Die redende Thiere über menschliche Fehler und Laster, Bey Ruhigen Stunden Lustig und nützlich zu lesen. Dreissigstes Gespräch, zwischen einem Nashorn und einer Heuschrecke*, **Frankfurt/Leipzig 1766 (original ed. 1750)**
Amsterdam, Rijksmuseum Research Library, 2021/5011c

70

Badge occasioned by the exhibition
Oudry's Painted Menagerie
Los Angeles, J. Paul Getty Museum, 2007
Amsterdam, private collection

71

Rossella Biscotti, *Clara*, **2016, during installation of the work at the Van Abbemuseum, Eindhoven**
Bricks on pallets, tobacco leaves, vinyl wall lettering
Collection of the artist
Photo: Collectie Van Abbemuseum, Eindhoven/ Peter Cox

index

This book was published on the occasion of the exhibition *Clara the Rhinoceros* at the Rijksmuseum in Amsterdam, 30 September 2022–15 January 2023

The exhibition and this publication have been made possible in part thanks to generous contributions from a private donor and Stichting Every Act Matters Foundation through the Rijksmuseum Fonds

author
Gijs van der Ham,
Senior Curator of History at the Rijksmuseum from 2001 to 2021

dutch text editing
Marieke de Jong, Rijksmuseum

project management
Barbera van Kooij, Rijksmuseum

translation dutch–english
Karen Gamester

english text editing
Kate Bell

image research
Ellen Slob, Rijksmuseum

index
Miekie Donner

photography
Image Department of the Rijksmuseum and other institutions and individuals as indicated in the list of exhibited works (pp. 202–205)

cartography
CartoNext, Utrecht

design
Irma Boom Office
(Irma Boom, Frederik Pesch)

lithography
BFC (Bert van der Horst)

printing and binding
Wilco Art Books, Amersfoort

publisher
Rijksmuseum
Postbus 74888
1070 DN Amsterdam
The Netherlands
publicaties@rijksmuseum.nl
rijksmuseum.nl

distribution
nai010 publishers
Korte Hoogstraat 31
3011 AX Rotterdam
The Netherlands
sales@nai010.com
nai010.com

Distribution North, Central and South America
ARTBOOK/DAP
dap@dapinc.com
www.artbook.com

ISBN 978 94 6208 747 7
NUR 646, 680

Ministry of Education, Culture and Science

FOUNDER
PHILIPS

MAIN SPONSORS
VRIENDENLOTERIJ ING kpn